Research Series on the Chinese Dream and China's Development Path

Drawing on a large body of empirical studies done over the last two decades, this Series provides its readers with in-depth analyses of the past and present and forecasts for the future course of China's development. It contains the latest research results made by members of the Chinese Academy of Social Sciences. This series is an invaluable companion to every researcher who is trying to gain a deeper understanding of the development model, path and experience unique to China. Thanks to the adoption of Socialism with Chinese characteristics, and the implementation of comprehensive reform and opening-up, China has made tremendous achievements in areas such as political reform, economic development, and social construction, and is making great strides towards the realization of the Chinese dream of national rejuvenation. In addition to presenting a detailed account of many of these achievements, the authors also discuss what lessons other countries can learn from China's experience.

More information about this series at https://link.springer.com/bookseries/13571

Peilin Li · M. K. Gorshkov
Editors

Life Expectations of the People

A Comparative Sociological Analysis of China and Russia

SSAP

Springer

Editors
Peilin Li
Chinese Academy of Social Sciences
Beijing, China

M. K. Gorshkov
Institute of Sociology of FCTAS RAS
Beijing, China

ISSN 2363-6866 ISSN 2363-6874 (electronic)
Research Series on the Chinese Dream and China's Development Path
ISBN 978-981-16-2504-6 ISBN 978-981-16-2505-3 (eBook)
https://doi.org/10.1007/978-981-16-2505-3

Jointly published with Social Sciences Academic Press
The print edition is not for sale in China (Mainland). Customers from China (Mainland) please order the print book from: Social Sciences Academic Press.
ISBN of the Co-Publisher's edition: 978-7-5097-2286-2

Translation from the Chinese Simplified language edition: *Life Expectations of the People* by Peilin Li, and M.K. Gorshkov, © Social Sciences Academic Press 2020. Published by Social Sciences Academic Press. All Rights Reserved.

This Springer imprint is published by the registered company Springer Nature Singapore Pte Ltd.
The registered company address is: 152 Beach Road, #21-01/04 Gateway East, Singapore 189721, Singapore

Series Preface

Since China's reform and opening began in 1978, the country has come a long way on the path of Socialism with Chinese characteristics, under the leadership of the Communist Party of China. Over 30 years of reform, efforts and sustained spectacular economic growth have turned China into the world's second largest economy and wrought many profound changes in the Chinese society. These historically significant developments have been garnering increasing attention from scholars, governments, and the general public alike around the world since the 1990s, when the newest wave of China studies began to gather steam. Some of the hottest topics have included the so-called China miracle, Chinese phenomenon, Chinese experience, Chinese path, and the Chinese model. Homegrown researchers have soon followed suit. Already hugely productive, this vibrant field is putting out a large number of books each year, with Social Sciences Academic Press alone having published hundreds of titles on a wide range of subjects.

Because most of these books have been written and published in Chinese, however, readership has been limited outside China—even among many who study China—for whom English is still the lingua franca. This language barrier has been an impediment to efforts by academia, business communities, and policy-makers in other countries to form a thorough understanding of contemporary China, of what is distinct about China's past and present may mean not only for her future but also for the future of the world. The need to remove such an impediment is both real and urgent, and the *Research Series on the Chinese Dream and China's Development Path* is my answer to the call.

This series features some of the most notable achievements from the last 20 years by scholars in China in a variety of research topics related to reform and opening. They include both theoretical explorations and empirical studies and cover economy, society, politics, law, culture, and ecology, the six areas in which reform and opening policies have had the deepest impact and farthest-reaching consequences for the country. Authors for the series have also tried to articulate their visions of the "Chinese Dream" and how the country can realize it in these fields and beyond.

All of the editors and authors for the *Research Series on the Chinese Dream and China's Development Path* are both longtime students of reform and opening and recognized authorities in their respective academic fields. Their credentials and expertise lend credibility to these books, each of which having been subject to a rigorous peer review process for inclusion in the series. As part of the Reform and Development Program under the State Administration of Press, Publication, Radio, Film, and Television of the People's Republic of China, the series is published by Springer, a Germany-based academic publisher of international repute, and distributed overseas. I am confident that it will help fill a lacuna in studies of China in the era of reform and opening.

Shouguang Xie

The original version of the book was revised: Affiliations of chapter authors have been updated. The correction to the book is available at https://doi.org/10.1007/978-981-16-2505-3_19

Contents

Editors and Contributors

About the Editors

Peilin Li is an academic member of the Chinese Academy of Social Sciences (CASS). He now serves as vice-president of CASS. Prior to his current position, he was the director of the Institute of Sociology at CASS and served as the president of Chinese Sociological Association. He earned his Ph.D. at the University of Paris (Pantheon-Sorbonne) in 1987. He has published and edited many articles, books, and essay collections, in Chinese, English, and French, on social stratification and mobility (particularly on Chinese domestic migrant workers) and economic sociology (particularly on Chinese State-Owned Enterprises). He has also hosted several large projects, including the "Chinese general social survey," one of largest and earliest national sociological surveys conducted since 2006.

M. K. Gorshkov is the director of the Russian Academy of Sciences Institute of Sociology. He is one of the most prominent modern Russian sociologists, renowned for his investigations in social philosophy, the sociology of mass consciousness and public opinion, methodology and methods of sociological research, sociology of youth, sociology of identity, sociology of social inequalities, sociology of Russian everyday life, etc. He earned his Full Doctorate degree in Philosophical Sciences in 1989 and was elected Academician (Full Member) of the Russian Academy of Sciences in 2011.

Contributors

Yan Cui, Ph.D. is an assistant professor at the CASS Institute of Sociology and specializes in social development research and social research methods. Major publications include *Research on the Motivation of Citizens' Environmental Organization Participation* and *the General Public's Urban Attributes During the Process of Urbanization.*

L. M. Drobizheva is a doctor of History and the professor and head of the Center for Interethnic Relations Studies at the Russian Academy of Sciences Institute of Sociology. She is also a professor at the National Research University Higher School of Economics and a member of the Russian President's Council on International Relations. Her main areas of research include the theory and methodology of ethnic sociology, inter-ethnic relations, ethnic identity, policy and social practice in a multicultural society. She is one of the most heavily cited Russian scholars. Selected publications include: *Social Inequality of Ethnic Groups: Image and Reality* (2002); *The Social Problems of Interethnic Relations in Post-Soviet Russia* (2003); and *Ethnicity in the Socio-Political Space of the Russian Federation: The Experience of 20 Years* (2013).

Lei Fan, Ph.D. is an associate professor at the CASS Institute of Sociology and specializes in social development research and social research methods. Major publications include *The Division of Labor in the Current Chinese Labor Market During the Process of Urbanization* and *The Political Attitude of the Post-80s Generation.*

I. A. Khaliy is the head of the department for research on social and cultural development in Russian regions at the Russian Academy of Sciences Institute of Sociology. She holds a doctorate in Sociology and has more than 170 scientific publications, including several individual and collective monographs such as: *Modern Social Movements: Innovative Potential of Russian Transformations in traditional Social Milieu*; *Self-portrait of a Local Community*; and *Institutionalization of Environmental Policy*. Now, she is a leader of three scientific research projects: "The ratio of traditions and innovations in the minds and livelihoods of local communities," "The role of civil society structures in the development of social processes of modern Russia," and "Regional and local management: feedback of state power bodies and communities."

P. M. Kozyreva Doctor of Sociology, is the first deputy director at the Russian Academy of Sciences Institute of Sociology. She also serves as a director of the Center for Longitudinal Studies at the National Research University Higher School of Economics. She has conducted research on social stratification and related topics throughout her career. She is also a specialist on survey research methods. She directs one of the largest longitudinal surveys in Russia—"The Russia Longitudinal Monitoring Survey of HSE" (RLMS-HSE), which has been conducted since 1994. Selected publications include: *Ethnicity and Trust: Evidence from Russia, American Political Science Review*, 2005 (in co-authorship with D. Bahry, M. Kosolapov and R. Wilson); *Trust and Its Recourses in Modern Russian Society*, monograph, 2011; "Interpersonal Trust in the Context of Social Capital Formation," *Sotsiologicheskie issledovaniia*, 2009, No. 1; "The Social Adaptation of the Russian Population in Post-Soviet Period," *Sociological Research*, 2012, Vol. 51, No. 5, September–October; *Recourses and Practices of Socio-Economic Adaptation of the Russian Population*, monograph, 2013 (in co-authorship with A. Smirnov and A. Nizamova); *Consumption and Lifestyles in Russia*, in *Handbook on Social Stratification in the*

BRIC Countries: Change and Perspective, Editors: Peilin Li (Chinese Academy of Social Sciences, China), M. K. Gorshkov (Russian Academy of Sciences, Russia), Celi Scalon (Brazilian Sociological Society, Brazil), K. L. Sharma (Jaipur National University, India), World Scientific Publishing Co. Pte. Ltd. 2013 (in co-authorship with A. Smirnov and A. Nizamova); "Economic Change in Russia: Twenty Years of the Russian Longitudinal Monitoring Survey," *Economics of Transition*, 2015, Vol. 23, No. 2, pp. 293–298 (in co-authorship with Klara Sabirianova Peter).

Yu. V. Latov is a leading researcher at the Academy of Management of the Interior Ministry of Russia and a leading researcher at the Russian Academy of Sciences Institute of Sociology. He is also a professor at the Plekhanov Russian University of Economics. He is a sociologist (Ph.D. in Sociology—2008) with a background in economics (Ph.D. in Economics—1993). His research and consulting practice concentrates on the shadow economy, comparative studies, sociology of education, civil society, and prevention of extremism. He is the author of over 350 articles and chapters in scientific monographs. He is a co-author of the monograph *Continuing Education as a Stimulus for Human Development and a Factor in Socio-Economic Inequality* (2014) and a author of the monograph *Economy Outside of the Law* (2001).

N. V. Latova is a senior researcher at the Russian Academy of Sciences Institute of Sociology. She holds a Ph.D. in Sociology from the Institute of Sociology (2011) and is the author of more than 80 articles and chapters in scientific monographs. She also annually participates in scientific grants. Her professional interests include comparative studies, the sociology of education, economic sociology, and migration problems such as "brain drain." She is co-author of the monograph, *Continuing Education as a Stimulus for Human Development and a Factor in Socio-Economic Inequality* (2014).

Yu. P. Lezhnina is an assistant professor at the National Research University Higher School of Economics (HSE) and a senior researcher at the Russian Academy of Sciences Institute of Sociology. She holds a Ph.D. in Sociology from the Higher School of Economics (2010). Her main areas of interest include social policy, aging, socio-demographic modernization, and socio-cultural dynamics. She is the author of over 40 articles and chapters in scientific monographs. Her recent publications in English include: "The Family in Value Orientations," published in *Russian Education and Society* (2011); "Socio-demographic Factors Determining the Risk of Poverty and Low-Income Poverty," *Sociological Research* (2011); and "Socio-Demographic Characteristics of Poverty," *Sociological Studies*, 2014, Issue 1.

Chunling Li is a research fellow at the Chinese Academy of Social Sciences (CASS) Institute of Sociology and the director of the Department of Youth Studies and Social Problems at the Institute. She is also a professor in the CASS Department of Sociology. Her primary research interests are social stratification, sociology of education and youth studies. Her published books include: *Attitudes, Experiences and Social Transformation: A Sociological Study of "Post-1980" Youth*; *Rising*

Middle Classes in China; *Gender Stratification and the Labor Market*; *Formation of the Middle Class in Comparative Perspective: Process, Influence, and Socioeconomic Consequences*; *Theories of Social Stratification; Cleavage or Fragmentation: A Empirical Analysis of Social Stratification in Contemporary China*; *Social Mobility in Urban China*; *Youth and Social Change: A Comparative Study Between China and Russia.*

Wei Li is a research associate at the CASS Institute of Sociology and the director of the Department of Social Development. His main research field is sociology of development, social research methods, and social surveys.

S. V. Mareeva is a senior researcher at the Russian Academy of Sciences Institute of Sociology and an assistant professor at the National Research University Higher School of Economics. She holds a Ph.D. in Sociology from the Institute of Sociology (2009). Her main areas of interest include social stratification, middle-class dynamics, socio-cultural modernization, and cultural dynamics. She is the author of over 50 articles and chapters in scientific monographs. She is a co-author of the monograph on the *Russian Middle Class* (2009). Her recent publications in English include the chapter "Understanding Health" in the monograph *Health and Health Care in the New Russia* (London, 2009); the chapter "The Middle Class in Russian Society: Homogeneity or Heterogeneity?" in the *Handbook on Social Stratification in the BRIC Countries: Change and Perspective*, Editors: Peilin Li (Chinese Academy of Social Sciences, China), M. K. Gorshkov (Russian Academy of Sciences, Russia), Celi Scalon (Brazilian Sociological Society, Brazil), K. L. Sharma (Jaipur National University, India), World Scientific Publishing Co. Pte. Ltd. (2013); "Values and Opinions of the Middle Class of the Desired Vector of Development of the Country," *Sociological Studies*, 2015, Issue 1.

A. E. Nizamova is currently a senior researcher at the Russian Academy of Sciences Institute of Sociology. She is also a deputy director of the Center for Longitudinal Studies at the National Research University Higher School of Economics. She graduated from the economic faculty of Moscow State University, Department of Political Economy and did her post-graduate studies at the Russian Academy of Sciences Institute of Sociology, where she received her Ph.D. Candidacy in Sociology in 2011. Her main research focus lies in the area of population material well-being in Russia, households' economic inequality and social adaptation. Her latest publications include: "The Peculiarities of Adaptation of Specialists to the Realities of a Transforming Society," *Sociological Studies*, 2011, Issue 1; "The Evaluation of Professionals' Adaptation to the Conditions of a Transforming Society," *Bulletin of the Russian Peoples' Friendship University*, Series: Sociology, 2012, Issue 1); "Consumption and Lifestyles in Russia," in the *Handbook on Social Stratification in the BRIC Countries: Change and Perspective*, Editors: Peilin Li (Chinese Academy of Social Sciences, China), M. K. Gorshkov (Russian Academy of Sciences, Russia), Celi Scalon (Brazilian Sociological Society, Brazil), K. L. Sharma (Jaipur National

University, India), World Scientific Publishing Co. Pte. Ltd. 2013 (in co-authorship with P. Kozyreva and A. Smirnov).

A. I. Smirnov Doctor of Sociology, is a senior researcher at the Russian Academy of Sciences Institute of Sociology in Moscow. His major interests include political sociology, social factors of Russian society consolidation (including institutional changes in the army, family, etc.), and dynamics of socio-economic conditions of the Russian population. His publications are wide ranging, and include: "Factors Forming Trust in the Russian Army," *Sociological Studies*, 2009, Issue 2; "Labyrinths of Democracy in Russia," Institute of Sociology, Russian Academy of Sciences, 2007, (in co-authorship with Kozyreva P.); "Consumption and Lifestyles in Russia," in the *Handbook on Social Stratification in the BRIC Countries: Change and Perspective*, Editors: Peilin Li (Chinese Academy of Social Sciences, China), M. K. Gorshkov (Russian Academy of Sciences, Russia), Celi Scalon (Brazilian Sociological Society, Brazil), K. L. Sharma (Jaipur National University, India), World Scientific Publishing Co. Pte. Ltd. 2013 (in co-authorship with P, Kozyreva and A. Nizamova).

N. E. Tikhonova Doctor of Sociology, is a professor at the National Research University Higher School of Economics and a chief researcher at the Russian Academy of Sciences Institute of Sociology. She is a recognized specialist in cultural dynamics, social stratification, and social policy. She is the author of about 400 scientific works, three individual monographs, and four co-authored monographs, including three monographs published in Great Britain between 2000 and 2009. Her main publications in English include: *Work and Welfare in the New Russia* (London, 2000, in co-authorship); *Poverty and Social Exclusion in the New Russia* (London, 2004, in co-authorship) *Health and Health Care in the New Russia* (London, 2008, in co-authorship). Her publications in Russian include: *Middle Class: Theory and Reality* (2009, in co-authorship), and *The Social Structure of Russia: Theory and Reality* (2014).

I. O. Tyurina is a leading researcher at the Russian Academy of Sciences Institute of Sociology. She specializes in the fields of economic sociology, the modern Russian labor market, employment and unemployment across different population groups, external labor migration, foreign-born labor force participation in the labor market of post-reform Russia, Internet as a mediator of communicative space and Russian youth. In 1999, she earned a Ph.D. in Sociology with a specialization in sociology of management. She was awarded the title of Associate Professor in 2006 and is actively engaged in education. She is a member of the International Sociological Association and the European Sociological Association. She is the author of more than 40 articles, essays, and reviews, published in Russian and English, on the post-reform labor market, external and internal labor migration, the communicative space of the Internet, and the information society in Russia.

Junxiu Wang is a research fellow at the CASS Institute of Sociology and the director of the Department of Social Psychology at the Institute. His research interests focus on the social mentality of the Chinese people, risk perception and risk society, social space and autosociety. His recent publications include: *The Theory of Social Mentality: A Macro Social Psychology* (Wang, 2015); *Research on Social Mentality in Contemporary China* (Yang and Wang, 2013); *Annual Report on the Auto Society in China* (2011) (Wang, 2011); *Annual Report on Auto Society in China* (2012–2013) (Wang, 2013); *Annual Report on Social Mentality in China* (2011) (Wang and Yang, 2011); *Annual Report on Social Mentality in China* (2012–2013) (Wang and Yang, 2013); *Annual report on Social Mentality in China* (2014) (Wang and Yang, 2014).

Yiyin Yang is a research fellow at the CASS Institute of Sociology. She received her Ph.D. in Sociology (social psychology) from the Graduate School of Chinese Academy of Social Sciences (1998). As the Head of the Center for Social Psychology Studies of the Institute of Sociology, she also served as president of the Chinese Association of Social Psychology (2010–2014). Her current research focuses on cultural social psychology that mediates the Chinese concept of self and "we-ness." She is also interested in the dynamic of social change from the perspective of social mentality, such as values, psychological modernity, cultural identity, and citizenship in Chinese contemporary society. She has published and translated papers and books in these fields and has hosted several large projects.

Yi Zhang is a research fellow at the CASS Institute of Sociology and deputy director of the Institute of Sociology. He is the chief-editor of *Youth Study*, and the Executive Chief Editor of *The Journal of Chinese Sociology*. He is also the vice-president of the Chinese Social Psychology Society, vice-secretary-general of the Chinese Association of Sociology, and vice-president of the Beijing Association of Sociology. In recent years, his research has been focused on the fields of class structure, population sociology, family sociology, and so on. He published works include the following: *Familialized State-Owned Enterprises*; *The Political Attitude of the Middle Class in Present China; Research on Class Conflict Consciousness in Chinese Cities*; *The Attainment of Chinese Social Status: Class Inheritance and Intergenerational Mobility*; *The Attainment of Social Class Status and Education as Affected by Family Background*; and *The Floating Population and Family Risks of Migrant Workers.*

Di Zhu is an Associate Professor at the Chinese Academy of Social Sciences. She got her Ph.D. and M.Sc. degrees from the University of Manchester, and B.A. degree from Fudan University. Her research interests include the sociology of consumption and social stratification. Her main publications include: *Taste and Material Aspiration: Consumption Patterns of the Middle Class in Contemporary China* (book) in 2013, and *Endeavor to Shape the Olive-Pattern of Distribution Structure—Based on Analysis of the China Social Survey 2006–2013* (2015).

List of Figures

List of Tables

Chapter 1
Introduction 1: The Origin, Meaning and Analytical Framework of the Chinese Dream

Peilin Li

The Sino-Russia Social Comparative Study Program is a long-term cooperative program between the Institute of Sociology at the Chinese Academy of Social Sciences and the Institute of Sociology at the Russian Academy of Sciences. Now in its seventh year, the Program was originally established in 2009 by Professor M.K. Gorshkov, Director of the Institute of Sociology at the Russian Academy of Sciences, and myself, Director of the Institute of Sociology at the Chinese Academy of Social Sciences. The comparative study of the "Chinese Dream" and the "Russian Dream" is the third phase of the program. The first and second phases involved the study of Sino-Russian social stratification and Sino-Russian youth, respectively. The first-phase Sino-Russian social stratification study was included in a larger-scale comparative study of the BRIC countries, which resulted in the publication of the 800-page *Handbook on Social Stratification in the BRIC Countries* written in English, *Changes and Comparison of Social Stratification in the BRIC Countries* in Chinese and *Sino-Russia Social Stratification Study* in Russian. The outcome of the second phase, the Sino-Russian youth study, resulted in the book titled *Youth and Social Change: A Sino-Russia Comparative Study,* written in Chinese and Russian. The comparative study of the Chinese Dream and the Russian Dream was first proposed by Professor M.K. Gorshkov when he visited the Chinese Academy of Social Sciences in 2011 to explore themes for the third phase of the cooperative study. When he suggested comparing dreams between our two countries, I was very surprised. The word "dream" has only recently become an analytical concept in humanities and social sciences in China. Moreover, Chinese sociology, which focuses on empirical studies, does not even touch upon this field of research. Even in Western humanities

P. Li (✉)
Chinese Academy of Social Sciences, Beijing, China
e-mail: lipl@cass.org.cn

P. Li and M. K. Gorshkov (eds.), *Life Expectations of the People*,
Research Series on the Chinese Dream and China's Development Path,
https://doi.org/10.1007/978-981-16-2505-3_1

and social sciences, dreams are rarely an object of study, other than the book *The Interpretation of Dreams* written by the master of psychoanalysis, Sigmund Freud. Furthermore, the word "dream" is often associated with fantasy in traditional Chinese culture, such as in the famous "Butterfly Dream",[1] "Golden Millet Dream",[2] "Nanke Dream"[3] and "Dream of the Red Mansion."[4] Professor M.K. Gorshkov explained his idea of comparative research on dreams to me in detail, as well as the reasons Russian sociology attaches such importance to the study of dreams. He also informed me that they were conducting a national sample survey on Russian dreams. I still thought that it was a very philosophical topic, but agreed to consider it seriously.

On November 29, 2012, Xi Jinping, the General Secretary of the Central Committee of the Communist Party of China (CPC), led the new central collective leadership in a visit to an exhibition at the National Museum of China called "The Road to Rejuvenation." In a speech he noted that "everyone has personal ideals and pursuits as well as dreams. All people are now talking about the Chinese Dream. I think that the realization of China's great rejuvenation is the grandest dream of the Chinese nation in modern times. It is a coalescence of the hopes of the Chinese people over many generations, demonstrates the overall interests of the Chinese nation and its people, and reflects an aspiration shared by all Chinese people." Ever since, the idea of the "Chinese Dream" has grown in significance and has now become a powerful

---

[1] The "Butterfly Dream" is from the writing of Chuang Tzu, an ancient Chinese philosopher. According to *Chuang-Tzu: Qiwulun* (Equality of Things), the author dreams he is a butterfly, and returns to human form again when he wakes up. He is unable to tell whether he was the one who turned into a butterfly or whether it was a butterfly that turned into him. The point of this story is that the universe is relative, without differences between him and other things, "things and I form a single being".

[2] The "Golden Millet Dream" originated from the book *Pillow Story* written by Shen Jiji, a historian and novelist from the Tang Dynasty (AD 618–907) of China. According to the book, when Lu Sheng came across a Taoist named Lv Weng at an inn in Handan, he sighed at his poverty. Lv Weng then took a celadon pillow out of his bag and let Lu Sheng sleep on the pillow while the inn owner was cooking. Lu Sheng fell asleep and enjoyed wealth and prosperity in his dreams. When he woke up, the millet was still cooking. He asked with wonder, "Was it a dream!?" Lv Weng said with a smile, "Everything is actually like this!" Afterwards, "pipe dream" became a Chinese idiom, signifying that wealth and prosperity can vanish like a bubble.

[3] The "Nanke Dream" sprang from the book *The Biography of the Nanke Governor*, written by Li Gongzuo during the Tang Dynasty of China. According to the book, Chun Yufen was reading in his study, which had a window facing south. Outside the window, there was an old Chinese scholar tree with two nests of ants. When he was tired of reading, he often watched the ants crawling around. One day, he unwittingly fell asleep as he was reading and dreamed that he went to Huai'an State to act as the governor of Nanke prefecture. He had a princess as his wife, and enjoyed great wealth and glory, but was sent back after the defeat of his expedition. He woke up to find that there was an ant hole in the tree in front of his window, namely the capital of Huai'an State in his dream, and Nanke prefecture was the other ant nest under a limb on the south side of the Chinese scholar tree. The Chinese idiom "Nanke Dream" refers to illusiveness as well as inconstant gains and losses of wealth.

[4] *Dream of the Red Mansion* represents the pinnacle of Chinese classical novels. Set against the backdrop of a family's rise and fall, with love and marriage as the main storyline, the novel demonstrates the dreamlike aspect of life and the inconstancy of human relationships through the tragic fate of its rebels.

expression of China's development goals and philosophy. Within this context, it was decided that the third phase of the cooperative study would focus on "Comparative Research on the Chinese Dream and the Russian Dream."

1.1 Historical Origins of the Chinese Dream

China's civilization goes back more than 5000 years. With diligence and wisdom, the Chinese nation was the leading civilization in the ancient world. However, China fell behind when history entered modern times. After the Opium War of 1840, a series of Western powers engaged in aggressive wars against China. The corrupt and weak feudal emperors were forced to sign numerous unequal and humiliating treaties, ceding sovereign control of large territorial areas to foreign aggressors. The culmination of these unequal treaties was reached when the *Boxer Protocol* was signed.

In the 50 plus years between the Opium War of 1840 and the Sino-Japanese War of 1894, China paid a total of thirty-nine million and twenty thousand taels (a tael is equal to 37.3 g) of silver in war reparations. The first war reparation of the Qing Dynasty came during the First Opium War, in which China paid a total of seventeen million five hundred twenty thousand taels of silver in war reparations. In August 1842, the comprehensive failure of the Qing government's military resistance resulted in the signing of the first unequal treaty in modern Chinese history—the *Treaty of Nanking*. The treaty stipulated that China should pay Britain six million silver dollars (Spanish Carolus dollar) in opium costs, three million silver dollars as total fees owed to British businessmen, and twelve million silver dollars for military expenditures, totaling twenty-one million silver dollars. In addition, the Qing government ceded Hong Kong and five other trading ports to the British, as well as the consular jurisdiction shared by Englishmen in China.

During the Taiping Rebellion in China, which occurred between the years of 1851 and 1864, Britain and France successively passed the grossly unfair "Treaty of Tianjin" and the "Beijing Treaty." These treaties forced the Qing Government to pay 16 million taels of silver in compensation for the Second Opium War.

The Sino-Japanese War of 1894 in the Yellow Sea resulted in the obliteration of the Beiyang Navy. Li Hongzhang, as representative of the Qing government, signed the humiliating "Treaty of Shimonoseki" with Japan, which forced China to pay a huge indemnity of two hundred million taels of silver. According to historical data, the Qing government's annual income was only seventy to eighty million taels at that time.

In September 1901, the Qing government signed the "Boxer Protocol" with the imperialist powers, which not only resulted in the invasion and oppression of China by those powers, but also made the Qing Dynasty a semi-colony politically. According to the treaty, China would pay compensation of nearly four hundred fifty million taels of silver to the eight countries. Because the Qing government was unable to make these payments, the compensation became a loan to be paid off over thirty-nine years, with an annual interest rate of 4%. By 1940, the total reached nine hundred and eighty-two million taels of silver, including principal and interest. Adding the twenty million taels of silver in local compensation required from the provinces, the Boxer Indemnity totaled more than one billion taels of silver.

The impact of these indemnities on China's modern history is extremely significant. China's modern history is full of tragedy, with China paying a heavy price for its inferior military force and political corruption, resulting in economic collapse and diplomatic humiliation. It is from this historical context that the salvation and rejuvenation of China became the dream of countless Chinese people in modern times. These lofty thinkers, in the face of struggle and hardship, sought to build a powerful country through political reforms and learning from the West. China experienced several reform movements, including the Westernization Movement, the Hundred Days' Reform, the Revolution of 1911 and the May Fourth Movement. However, each of these reforms failed in the end, and the Chinese nation did not reach a fundamental turning point until the birth of the Communist Party of China and the founding of the People's Republic of China. This is the historical soil that precipitated the nation's collective memory that fostered the Chinese Dream.

1.2 Meaning of the Chinese Dream

After the founding of the People's Republic of China in 1949, the economy rapidly developed and there was a dream to quickly catch up with developed countries like the UK and the US. However, the implementation of unrealistic strategies led to serious setbacks in China's economic and social development. The catastrophe of the Cultural Revolution caused substantial harm to China's economic development. In 1978, China started its reform and opening, and started down the correct path of "socialism with Chinese characteristics" and economic development as the centerpiece of government policy. From 1980 to 2010, China's average annual GDP growth reached approximately 10%. People's living standards greatly improved, laying a solid foundation for China to realize its dream.

Against the backdrop of China's historical experiences and lessons, China attaches great importance to the planning and designing of realistic long-term roadmaps. In 1979—the beginning of China's reform and opening—Deng Xiaoping decided to postpone the target timeframe for China's modernization from the "end of 20th century" to the "mid-21st century." Likewise, he and readjusted the strategic goal to achieve a "well-off level" for the average living standard to the "end of 20th century." In June 1984, when Deng Xiaoping met with the Japanese delegation for the second meeting of the Sino-Japan Non-Governmental Committee, he said: "We proposed four modernizations with the lowest goal to achieve a well-off society by the end of the century. I talked about it for the first time in December 1979 when Masayoshi Ohira, former Prime Minister of Japan, visited China. The so-called 'well-off' level refers to a per capita GNP of $800 US by the end of the century, which is low for your country but is ambitious for us."[5] The 12th and 13th Congresses of the Communist Party of China in 1982 and 1987 elevated Deng Xiaoping's strategic assumption to a long-term goal of the entire party and the whole nation, resulting in the famous "three steps" strategy for China to realize modernization. First, the GNP of 1990 would double that of 1980 and any food and clothing issues for Chinese people would be resolved. Second, the GNP at the end of twentieth century would triple that of 1980 to improve people's ability to live at a "well-off" level. Third, a per capita GNP of $4000 US would be achieved in the mid-twenty-first century, a figure close to that of moderately developed countries, and would result in more affluence and basic modernization.[6] Of course, China's actual development has seen a faster pace. China's per capita GDP reached approximately $7000 US in 2013, based on the exchange rate of that year.

By 2000, after 20 years of effort, the original goal of a well-off society (Xiaokang society), mainly measured by the tripling of the GNP in 1980, had been generally achieved. There has been controversy over what targets to establish for the years 2000–2050, a period of half a century, in order to make modernization a reality. It is widely believed that although China has generally reached the "well-off society level with a per capita GDP of more than $800 US, development across the country remains unbalanced, uncoordinated and incomplete.

In 2002, the report of the 16th Congress of the CPC clearly stated that the first 20 years of the new century is an important strategic opportunity for China, and established the developmental objective of "building a well-off society in an all-round way." "In the first 20 years of this century, we shall concentrate resources on comprehensively building a higher level of a well-off society, which will benefit over one billion people, and result in a further developed economy, improved democracy, advanced science and education, enriched culture, a more harmonious society and further upgraded life for people."[7]

---

[5] Deng Xiaoping, "Building Socialism with Chinese Characteristics" from *The Selected Significant Documents of CPC and the State Since the Third Plenary Session of the 11th Central Committee of CPC*, compiled by the Department of Educational Administration of CPC Central Party School. CPC Central Party School Press, 2008, pp. 163–164.

[6] Hu Yaobang, "Creating Comprehensively New Situations of Socialist Modernization" (The report of the 12th Congress of CPC) from *The Selected Significant Documents of CPC and the State Since the Third Plenary Session of the 11th Central Committee of CPC*, compiled by the Department of Educational Administration of CPC Central Party School. CPC Central Party School Press, 2008, pp. 126–127.

Zhao Ziyang, "Taking Great Strides Along the Road to Socialism with Chinese Characteristics" (The report of the 13th Congress of CPC) from *The Selected Significant Documents of CPC and State since the Third Plenary Session of the 11th Central Committee of CPC*, compiled by the Department of Educational Administration of CPC Central Party School. CPC Central Party School Press, 2008, p. 196.

[7] Jiang Zemin, "Building a Well-off Society in An All-round Way and Creating a New Situation of Socialism with Chinese Characteristics" (The report of the 16th Congress of CPC) from *The Selected Significant Documents of CPC and the State Since the Third Plenary Session of the 11th Central Committee of CPC*, compiled by the Department of Educational Administration of CPC Central Party School. CPC Central Party School Press, 2008.

The 2012 report of the 18th Congress of the CPC proposed two overall goals for building a well-off society in an all-round way. By 2020, "we shall make great progress in the transformation of our mode of economic development, and the GDP and the per capita income of urban and rural residents shall be double that of 2010 on the basis of significant improvements in balanced, coordinated and sustainable development."[8]

The Chinese Dream, the great rejuvenation of Chinese nation, is the goal of China's long-term development. It is not just an imaginary ideal, but is backed by a concrete roadmap and timetable. The medium and long-term periodical objectives of the Chinese Dream are now summarized as the "200-year goal," in which China achieves a comprehensive well-off society by the time the CPC is 100 years old in 2021, and develops into a prosperous, democratic and harmonious socialist country by the year 2049, the middle of this century, 100 years after the founding of People's Republic of China.[9] The latter goal was also envisaged by Deng Xiaoping in 1979.

1.3 Analytical Framework of the Chinese Dream

The realization of the Chinese Dream, the great rejuvenation of the Chinese nation, has become the new goal of China. The most significant characteristic of the Chinese Dream is the unity of the country, the nation and individuals as a community under a shared destiny in order to achieve the goals of a powerful country, national rejuvenation and the people's happiness. In this sense, the Chinese Dream represents the state's dream, the nation's dream and also the Chinese people's dream.

The comparative sociological study of the Chinese Dream and the Russian Dream focuses on the achievement of concrete results according to an indexed set of metrics, so the dream is grounded and integrated into real life. This requires an analytical framework of study.

A key measure of the progressiveness of a social system and its applicability to national conditions is whether it can quickly and continuously improve people's living standards, which is not only reflected in the material aspects of life. People are increasingly aware of a social system with improvements in their living standards.

The overall layout of socialism with Chinese characteristics covers five areas, namely the economic, political, cultural, social and ecological sectors. The division relates to both development and people's lives. Based on our findings of people's expectations for their future lives, we designed the following analytical framework. With respect to economics, the Chinese Dream means moving towards a more affluent society with more social contentment in life and work. In terms of political aspects,

[8] Hu Jintao, "Unswervingly Advancing Along the Road of Socialism with Chinese Characteristics, and Striving to Build a Well-off Society in All Respects" (The report of the 18th Congress of CPC) from *The Selected Significant Documents Since the 18th Congress of CPC*, compiled by CCCPC Party Literature Office. Central Party Literature Press, 2014, p. 13.

[9] Xi (2014, pp. 35–36).

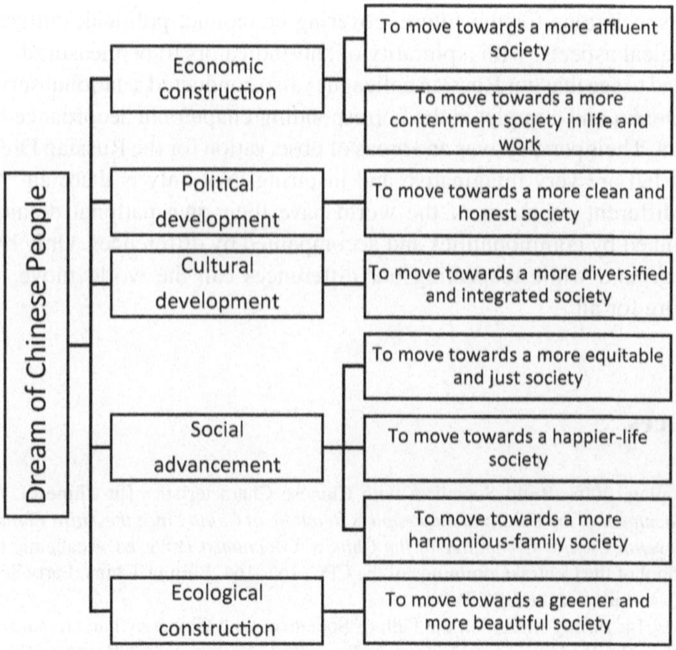

Fig. 1.1 Analytical framework of the Chinese Dream

the Chinese Dream refers to a more clean and honest society. The cultural aspect refers to achieving a more diversified and integrated society. The social aspect of the Chinese Dream refers to a more equitable and just society, a happier-life, and more harmonious families. In ecological aspects, the Chinese Dream refers to a greener and more beautiful society (as shown in Fig. 1.1). The eight sectors contained in these five aspects are the themes of the eight chapters in this book. The primary data for description and analysis comes from the fourth "China Social Survey (CSS2013)" conducted by the Institute of Sociology of the Chinese Academy of Social Sciences (CASS).

From June to October 2013, the CASS Institute of Sociology launched the fourth "China Social Survey (CSS2013)". The sampling survey covered 604 villages (residential committees) in 151 counties (including cities and districts) in 32 provinces (including autonomous regions and municipalities directly under the central government) of Mainland China. Door-to-door interviews were conducted with 7388 urban and rural residents from the age of 18–69 and above. The survey was carried out four times, in 2006, 2008, 2011 and 2013.The first three surveys generated the publications "The Harmony and Stability of Contemporary China," "The Livelihood of Contemporary China" and "Urbanization and its Social Impact in Contemporary China," which reflect the themes of the three surveys. The theme of the 2013 survey was "The Chinese Dream and Quality of Life". The survey design was focused on the Chinese Dream as a comprehensive evaluation of the country's situation and the public's expectations for the future, covering economic, political, cultural, social, and ecological aspects, with a plurality of sub-indicators to be measured.

I am glad to see that our Russian colleagues also conducted a national survey on the Russian Dream and completed the corresponding chapters in accordance with their survey data. Their perspectives and areas of observation for the Russian Dream differ from ours but are very imaginative and inspiring. Not only is there an "American Dream," different countries of the world have their own national dreams, which are interlinked by commonalities and accompanied by differences. Only by seeking common ground while respecting our differences can the world move towards a better future for all.

References

Deng, Xiaoping. 2008. Build Socialism with Chinese Characteristics [in Chinese]. In *Selected Major Document of the CPC and the People's Republic of China Since the Third Plenary Session of the Eleventh Central Committee of the Chinese Communist Party*, ed. Academic Division of Party School of the Central Committee of the CPC, 163–164. Beijing, China: Party School of the Central Committee of the CPC Press.

Hu, Jintao. 2014. Firmly March on the Path of Socialism with Chinese Characteristics and Strive to Complete the Building of a Moderately Prosperous Society in All Respects (Report to the Eighteenth National Congress of the Communist Party of China) [in Chinese]. In *Selection Major Documents Since the Eighteenth National Congress of the Communist Party of China*, ed. Central Committee of the CPC Literature Office, 13. China, Beijing: The Central Literature Press.

Hu, Yaobang. 2008. Create a New Situation in All Fields of Socialist Modernization (Report to the Twelfth National Congress of the Communist Party of China) [in Chinese]. In *Selected Major Document of the CPC and the People's Republic of China since the Third Plenary Session of the Eleventh Central Committee of the Chinese Communist Party*, ed. Academic Division of Party School of the Central Committee of the CPC, 126–127. Beijing, China: Party School of the Central Committee of the CPC Press.

Jiang, Zemin. 2008. Build a Well-Off Society in an All-Round Way and Create a New Situation in Building Socialism with Chinese Characteristics (Report to the Sixteenth National Congress of the Communist Party of China) [in Chinese]. In *Selected Major Document of the CPC and the People's Republic of China Since the Third Plenary Session of the Eleventh Central Committee of the Chinese Communist Party*, ed. Academic Division of Party School of the Central Committee of the CPC. Beijing, China: Party School of the Central Committee of the CPC Press.

Xi, Jinping. 2014. The Greatest Dream of the Chinese Nation in Modern History Is the Great Rejuvenation of the Chinese Nation [in Chinese]. In *Xi Jinping: The Governance of China*, 35–36. Beijing, China: Foreign Languages Press.

Zhao, Ziyang. 2008. Advance along the Road of Socialism with Chinese Characteristics (Report to the Thirteenth National Congress of the Communist Party of China) [in Chinese]. In *Selected Major Document of the CPC and the People's Republic of China Since the Third Plenary Session of the Eleventh Central Committee of the Chinese Communist Party*, ed. Academic Division of Party School of the Central Committee of the CPC, 196. Beijing, China: Party School of the Central Committee of the CPC Press.

Chapter 2
Introduction 2 Understanding of the "Ideal Society" in China and Russian

M. K. Gorshkov

From a layperson's point of view, a dream is usually an ardent wish that brings people instant happiness the moment it comes true. A sociologist, however, goes further than that, interpreting a dream as a mental creation of a concept of the desired future, a source of motivation, and an incentive. Here we can remember K. G. Paustovsky, who wrote: "If we take away the human ability to dream, we take away one of the most powerful drivers engendering culture, art, science and the desire to struggle for a wonderful future". With this understanding of the dream, its study using sociological methods becomes not only important but also necessary. Only relevant analysis makes it possible to determine the image of the desired future that the population of a certain country is trying to achieve or to determine the desired model of society that exists in the ideas of its citizens and serves as a basis for them to form their expectations from the state.

Cross-country comparisons in this field are of special interest. They make it possible not only to determine the specific nature of a population's dreams and their basic elements in different countries but also determine the cultural and civilizational peculiarities of these countries, reflected in the dreams that are typical of its citizens. That is why the sociological institutes of two Academies of Sciences—Russian and Chinese—made the decision to conduct such a comparative analysis with financial support from research funds in their countries.[1] Now they would like to show the results of their work to the readers.

[1] In Russia, this financial support was provided by the Russian Humanitarian Research Foundation (project "Civilizational peculiarities of dreams in Russia and China" No. 14–23–21,001).

The original version of this chapter was revised: Affiliation has been updated in this chapter. The correction to this chapter can be found at https://doi.org/10.1007/978-981-16-2505-3_19

M. K. Gorshkov (✉)
Institute of Sociology of FCTAS RAS, Beijing, China
e-mail: 13263169197@163.com

P. Li and M. K. Gorshkov (eds.), *Life Expectations of the People*,
Research Series on the Chinese Dream and China's Development Path,
https://doi.org/10.1007/978-981-16-2505-3_2

Our team of authors based its work first and foremost on the everyday realities faced by the population of these two great nations, Russia and China, which determine their dreams to a large extent. However, we tried to go beyond a purely utilitarian approach to people's dreams because determination of the image of the desired future and its separate elements that exist in the views of the Russians and Chinese makes it possible to answer the fundamental question of whether the "Russian dream" and "Chinese dream" are alternative social projects on the macro- and microlevels (that is, on the level of "big" dreams about a given society and on the level of individual dreams about something very personal).

Such a study seemed especially relevant to us in view of the radical transformations that have taken place in the past three decades in Russia and China due to change in the proportion of planned and market components in the economy, with the countries choosing different ways of transitioning to the market. The niches our countries wanted to occupy in the globalizing economy were different as well.

Thirty years is a long period of time as the norms, values and motivations of the population amidst simultaneous globalization, modernization and marketization change quite quickly. This could not but help influence the dreams of the people of our countries. That is why we tried to understand in our analysis of the populations' dreams whether it is possible for each of them to combine the peculiarities of their national culture and marketization of social life along with integration in the global market economy as well as how great the civilizational differences between Russia and China are.

With this understanding and such interpretation of the "dream", its purposeful study through sociological methods becomes not only justified and interesting but also absolutely necessary. Is scientific sociological analysis of the "dream" possible without reliance on sociological data, in isolation from the wide and reliable empirical base? It seems it is hardly possible. That is why this book is based on numerous empirical studies conducted by RAS Institute of Sociology and the Institute of Sociology of the Chinese Academy of Social Sciences, as well as data from the statistics authorities of our countries.

The key study relating to Russia is the one conducted in cooperation with the Representation of the Ebert Foundation in Russia in March–April 2012, the All-Russian Sociological Study "Russian Dream: What Is It and Can It Be Realized?".[2] However, the Russian authors were not limited by the data of this study, and this book is also based on other empirical studies conducted between the 1990s and 2015. Such a wide empirical basis for analysis made it possible not only to determine the peculiarities of the "Russian social project" as an alternative to those offered as part of other cultural and civilizational traditions of the image of the desired future but also the degree of homogeneity/heterogeneity of Russians' ideas about the desired future

[2] During development of the program of study and in analysis and interpretation of its results, notions of the "Russian dream" and the "dream of Russian citizens" were used as synonyms. See more about the survey description and results of this study: *What do Russians dream about: Ideal and reality*. Eds. Gorshkov, M.K., Krumm, R., Tikhonova, N.E. Moscow: Ves Mir, 2013.

for themselves and for society in general, and also socio-political, socio-economic and socio-cultural consequences derived from the peculiarities of these ideas.

As for our Chinese colleagues, their chapters are also based on extensive empirical material, first and foremost, the results of the fourth "China Social Survey" conducted in June–October 2013 by the Institute of Sociology of the ChineseAcademy of Social Sciences. Li Peilin, renowned scholar and director of the Institute of Sociology of the Chinese Academy of Social Sciences, describes in detail how the idea of a comparative international study of what people in different countries dream about came to be. He also presents the objectives they wish to achieve through the study.

If we speak about the Russian participants of the project, the main objectives they tried to resolve in this book consisted of the following:

- Determine the basic elements of the "Russian dream" as the image of the desired future relating to society as a whole and to the future of individual Russians;
- Determine what is distinct about different age groups, professions and political sympathies when it comes to the Russian dream;
- Determine the factors that influence the different elements that make up the image of the desired future;
- Determine whether the "Russian dream" is an independent idea or one that is becoming increasingly similar to corresponding ideas in other civilizations, in particular, those that originated in the Chinese society.

Realization of these objectives was of recurrent nature and all the chapters of this book were more or less oriented towards their resolution. However, the logic of narration in the book is based on another principle which makes it possible to compare the situation in Russia and China in each considered sphere of "Russians' dreams" in association with the image of the desired future. In the opinion of the team of authors, this logic of narration makes it possible to see more clearly both the general and the specific aspects not only in the dreams of the Russians and Chinese but also in the factors that determine their peculiarities in relevant spheres. It is up to the reader to decide whether the authors have succeeded in this.

In conclusion, I would like to say that preparation of this book is another step on the path of cooperation between the Institutes of Sociology of the Russian Academy of Sciences and the Chinese Academy of Social Sciences, which has been ongoing for many years. The latest works as part of this cooperation were the monographs published in the Russian and Chinese languages in Russia and China that were later expanded and translated into English.[3] They were focused on the social structure of our societies and the situation of young people, and both works received a wide response. The team of authors of this book sincerely hope that the work offered to the reader following completion of another stage of cooperation will raise just as much interest.

[3] Social Stratification in the BRIC Countries: Changes and Perspectives (2011); Russia and China: Changes in the Social Structure of Society [in Russian] (2012); Handbook on Social Stratification in the BRIC Countries (2013); Russia and China: Youth of the 21st Century [in Russian] (2014).

References

Handbook on Social Stratification in the BRIC Countries. 2013. *Change and Perspective.* Singapore: World Scientific Publishing Co.

Russia and China: Changes in the Social Structure of Society. 2012. Eds. M. Gorshkov, Li Peilin, and Z. Golenkova. Moscow: Novy Chronograph. [in Russian].

Russia and China: Youth of the 21st Century. 2014. Eds. M. Gorshkov, Li Chunling, Z. Golenkova, and P. Kozyreva. Moscow: Novy Chronograph. [in Russian].

Social Stratification in the BRIC Countries: Changes and Perspectives. 2011. Eds. Li Peilin, M. Gorshkov, C. Scalon, and K.L. Sharma. Beijing, China: Social Science Academic Press. [in Chinese].

Chapter 3
Moving Towards a More Affluent Society

Di Zhu

It is the common aspiration of humanity to pursue an affluent and happy life. However, in modern times, the Chinese people have experienced many twists and turns in this pursuit. Aside from the constraints of the economic environment, there have been invisible shackles of ideological discipline: Is it hedonistic to pursue an affluent life? Are we taking the capitalist road? All of this controversy gradually disappeared in the minds of the Chinese people after Deng Xiaoping set forth the "Common Prosperity Theory;" "We adhere to the socialist road for the purpose of achieving common prosperity" (Deng Xiaoping 1993). In the past 30 years of reform and opening up, the living standards of the Chinese people have significantly improved, as has China's overall social and economic development. The report of the 18th Congress of the CPC stressed:

> We must adhere to the path of common prosperity, which is the fundamental principle of socialism with Chinese characteristics…We should adhere to the basic socialist economic system and distribution system, adjust the distribution pattern of national income, and strengthen secondary distribution, making great efforts to solve the problem of the larger income distribution gaps so that the fruits of development can benefit all the people more fairly, with steady progress towards the direction of common prosperity.

The Chinese Dream of "common prosperity" unites traditional ideology with new meanings, and encourages the Chinese people to pursue wealthy and happy lives. However, there currently exist significant differences in income levels among different sectors in different regions of China. Consumers are at a level of just being able to maintain their basic daily life, with heavy financial burdens that include housing, medical care and other expenses. Facilitating family development and improving the quality of life through expenditures in areas such as education, culture and leisure is still limited. Unreasonable income and consumption structures hinder the improvement of residential living standards and people's livelihoods. This affects

D. Zhu (✉)
Chinese Academy of Social Sciences, Beijing, China

P. Li and M. K. Gorshkov (eds.), *Life Expectations of the People*,
Research Series on the Chinese Dream and China's Development Path,
https://doi.org/10.1007/978-981-16-2505-3_3

life satisfaction and confidence of residents to a large extent, and results in a negative evaluation of overall social fairness and security. Inadequate income structures and job security are not conducive to social and economic development, which is significantly reflected in weak domestic consumer demands. In the executive meeting of the State Council in October 2014, Premier Li Keqiang stressed that consumption would be the major engine of economic growth, with huge potential for the development of China. He proposed focusing on improved consumption in six areas: (1) information, (2) green energy, (3) housing, (4) tourism and leisure, (5) education, culture and sports, and 6) retirement, health and housekeeping. (See note 1) The outcomes of the State Council meeting clarified the relationships among revenue restructuring, consumption expansion and the improvement of the security of people's livelihoods. Deeper reforms of the income distribution system would activate consumption, and thus improve economic quality and efficiency for the purpose of improving people's living standards and achieving common prosperity.

This chapter uses empirical data to analyze the income structure, consumption structure, life satisfaction, personal aspirations, and social evaluation of Chinese residents with rural-urban divisions and income groups as the main structure. At the end of this chapter, the author will, based on the empirical findings, propose recommendations for policies on how to improve social security, activate consumption and forecast the development trends of the future.

3.1 Consumption Structure of Urban–Rural Residents and its Development Trend

The China Social Survey collected family expenditure data from 2013. To be consistent with other analyses, this chapter refers to the expenditures of the survey year. In 2013, average annual living expenses were 60,379 yuan for all Chinese households, 74,271 yuan for urban households and 43,865 yuan for rural households. Compared with their total income, 61 percent of households had lower or equal expenses, and 39 percent of households had higher expenses. The income to expenditure ratio is relatively better among urban households, with only 33 percent having higher expenditure than income, while 46 percent of rural households had higher expenditure than income.

Living expenses and the composition of urban and rural households are shown in Fig. 3.1. In urban and rural households, the highest category of consumption was food (including eating out). In 2013, the average household expenditure on food was 15,102 yuan, with urban households spending an average of 18,035 yuan annually, and rural households spending an average of 11,534. The higher food expenditures of urban households might be caused by eating out more often and the higher costs of high quality or organic food. However, the proportion of food expenditures for urban households was slightly lower than that for rural households, 24 percent and 26 percent respectively.

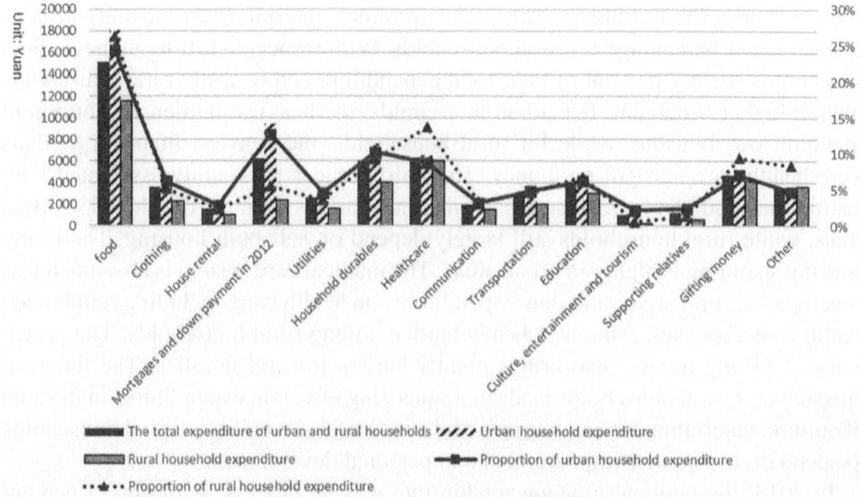

Fig. 3.1 Urban–Rural households living expenses and composition in 2013

In addition to food, other high expenditures for rural and urban families include mortgages and down payments, home durables (appliances, furniture, household vehicles, etc.), health care (medical care, hospitalization, medicines and other non-deductible expenses), gifting money (for weddings and funerals, as well as reciprocity), and education (tuition, incidental expenses, stationery, tutoring fees, school accommodations, etc.). The average household expenditures in these categories are 6,201 yuan for mortgages/down payments, 5,973 yuan for home durables, 6,267 yuan for healthcare, 4,743 yuan for gifting money, and 3,874 yuan for education. The lowest household expenditure category was culture, entertainment and tourism—the annual average spending was only 991 yuan for all households. The most significant difference in expenditures between urban and rural households was for food, household durables, and mortgages and down payments. In 2013, the average expenditure on mortgages and down payments was 9,406 yuan for urban households, and only 2,390 yuan for rural households. Such differences between urban and rural households are mainly the result of the different housing systems in urban and rural areas. The average expenditures for household durables was 7,487 yuan for urban households and 4,040 yuan for rural households. The gap reflects the different living standards and quality of life between urban and rural areas.

In terms of the composition of expenditures, the most significant difference between rural and urban households was mortgages and down payments, which accounted for 13 percent of urban households' total expenditures, yet only 5 percent of rural households' total expenditure. The proportion of expenditures spent on health care is also quite different between urban and rural areas, 9 percent and 14 percent respectively. Moreover, urban and rural households had different proportions of expenditures on culture, entertainment, tourism and gifting money. On average, 2 percent of urban household spending went to culture, entertainment and tourism, with an even lesser percentage for rural households. With respect to gifting money, urban households spent 7 percent of their total expenditures on it, while rural households spent a higher 9 percent. For urban households, the heaviest burden on household spending was housing, while for rural households, the heaviest financial burdens were health care and gifting money. These differences are mainly associated with institutional and ideological factors. Real estate markets are more developed in urban areas, while rural households still largely depend on self-built housing. Therefore, housing spending is higher in urban areas. The medical care system is also much less developed in rural areas, and thus expenditures on health care, including reimbursed health care expenses, remains a heavy burden among rural households. The prevalence of gifting money also brings greater burden to rural families. The financial pressures for rural households leads to a squeezing effect on expenditures in the area of culture, entertainment and tourism, and suppresses the ability of rural households to spend on life quality improvement and personal development.

In 2013, the national homeownership rate was 95 percent, with only 5 percent of the interviewed households reporting not having any family housing. The homeownership rate was 92 percent among urban households, which was 6 percent lower than that of rural households (98 percent). In terms of housing condition, the average per-capita housing space was 41 square meters among all households. Rural households had a larger average per-capital housing space (49 square meters) than urban households (34 square meters).

95 percent of urban and rural households became first-time home-owners after 1981. First-time home owners most commonly built their own homes. Self-built housing accounted for 69 percent of first homes, followed by the purchase of commodity housing (19 percent) or original public housing (5 percent). Other, though less common, ways of owning housings included purchasing rural private housing, limited property right housing and welfare housing. There were significant differences between urban and rural households in how they obtained their first house. For urban households, the proportion of self-built housing was 45 percent, purchased commodity housing was 35%, and purchased original public housing was 9 percent. For rural households, 95 percent of first housing was self-built housing, while purchases of rural private housing and commodity housing were each only about 2 percent. Such differences largely reflect the differences in the housing system and the housing market between urban and rural areas.

Overall, both urban and rural households benefited from their first homes; that is, the present value of their property was higher than the purchase/building price and the, with average appreciation of 190,000 yuan. Urban households in municipalities directly under the central government had the highest average appreciation rate of 1,050,000 yuan. Urban households living in provincial capitals saw their homes appreciate by 350,000 yuan on average. Urban households in prefectural and county-level cities ranked third, with their homes appreciating by 290,000 yuan on average. Households in counties or towns outside of the urban areas of prefectures and county-level cities ranked fourth, with average home appreciation of 230,000 yuan. Families living in rural areas profited the least from their first homes, with an average appreciation of only 100,000 yuan. This is in spite of the fact that the original purchase (or building) price for first homes in urban and rural areas was not significantly different. The average price was 160,000 yuan for urban households and 70,000 yuan for rural households. Therefore, in terms of housing appreciation, rural households were in a disadvantaged position because of institutional and market factors.

With respect to the composition of consumption trends among Chinese households from 2006 to 2013 (Fig. 3.2), the share of total household spending on food (including both eating at home and eating out) and education significantly declined. In 2006, the total share of household food spending was 34% for urban households and 29% for rural households. Urban households maintained a higher share of food spending until 2008, after which the proportion of urban and rural household food spending leveled out in 2011. By 2013, urban households were spending a lower proportion of household expenditures on food (24 percent) than rural households (26 percent) for the first time. Such changes suggest that living standards for urban households

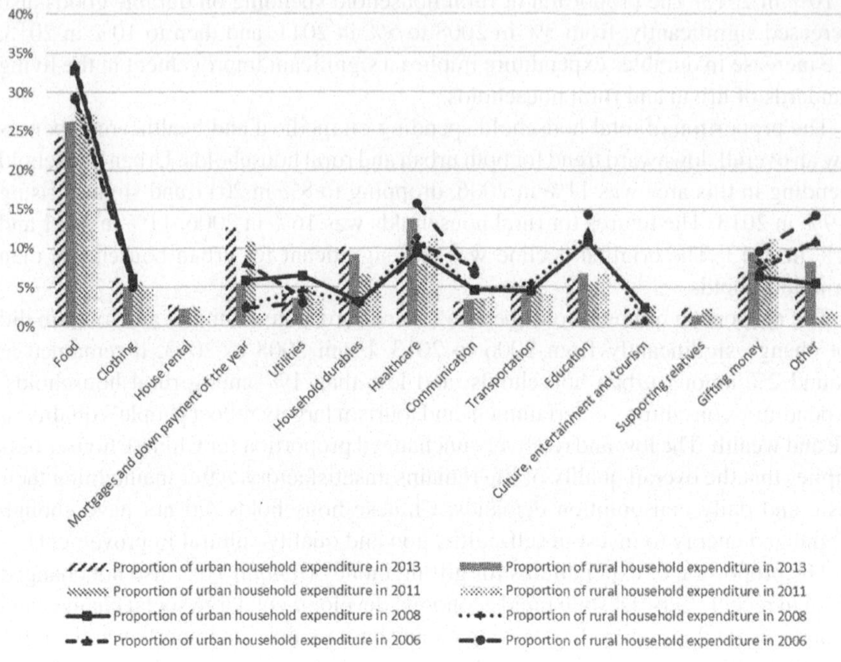

Fig. 3.2 Proportion and composition of living expenses in urban and rural households from 2006 to 2013 (*Note* There are some differences in the composition of living expenses in each wave, so the expenditure categories have different meanings. In 2006 and 2008, the "annual mortgage and down payment" category included mortgages and rent as one variable in the survey. In 2006, only power costs were surveyed in terms of utility fees. In 2006, the "communication fee" included communications and transportation expenses as one variable in the survey. To make the expense categories consistent across waves, expenditures on "daily necessities" and "residential renovation and decoration" were removed from the 2008 and 2011 surveys)

largely improved. However, increases in expenditures in other areas, such as home purchases and home durables, might be another reason for the changing proportion of urban household spending. From 2006 to 2013, the proportion of expenditures on education declined from 12 to 6% among urban households, and from 14 to 7% among rural households.

In urban households, there was a significant increase in the proportion of expenditures on home purchases and home durables, as well as a significant increase in the proportion of expenditures on home durables among rural households. In 2006, the proportion of total urban household expenditures on mortgages and down payments was 8%. This increased to 11% in 2011 and 13% in 2013. This trend was consistent with the booming development of the urban housing market and sharp increases in housing prices since 2008, and reflects the economic pressure of housing purchases on urban families. During the same period, the proportion of spending on home purchases among rural households grew as well, yet still only increased to 5 percent by 2013. Urban household spending on durable goods (appliances, furniture, vehicles and other purchases) increased from 3% in 2008 to 7% in 2011, and then increased to 10% in 2013. The proportion of rural household spending on durable goods also increased significantly, from 3% in 2008 to 5% in 2011, and then to 10% in 2013. The increase in durables expenditure implies a significant improvement in the living standards of urban and rural households.

The proportion of total household spending on medical and healthcare expenses saw an overall downward trend for both urban and rural households. Urban household spending in this area was 11% in 2006, dropping to 8% in 2011 and slightly rising to 9% in 2013. The figures for rural households was 16% in 2006, 11% in 2011 and 14% in 2013. The original decline was less significant for urban households than rural households.

The proportion of household spending on culture, entertainment and tourism did not change significantly from 2006 to 2013. From 2008 to 2013, it remained at around 2% among urban households, and less than 1% among rural households. Expenditures on culture, entertainment and tourism largely reflect people's quality of life and wealth. The low and relatively unchanged proportion for Chinese households implies that the overall quality of life remains unsatisfactory. After maintaining their basic and daily consumption demands, Chinese households did not have enough capital and energy to invest in self-cultivation and quality cultural improvements.

The proportion of expenditures for gifting money (*renqing*) has also not changed much in recent years. Despite rapid economic development, large social change, and changes in ideology and values, gifting money has remained an important and unique aspect of Chinese culture. Compared with urban households, rural households had a higher proportion of spending on gifting money. Gifting money includes money spent on weddings and funerals, as well as reciprocity (such as gifts and cash). For urban households, the proportion of household spending on gifting money was 7% in 2006, 6% in 2008, 9% in 2011, and 7% in 2013. For rural households, the percentages were 10%, 8%, 11%, and 9% for the same years.

3.2 Life Satisfaction and Personal Aspirations of Urban and Rural Residents

Whether the respondents were satisfied with life depended not only on their abstract and general feelings about life, but also their specific social and economic experiences. We use the term "happiness" (well-being) to evaluate overall life satisfaction. Then, based on the respondents' feelings about their economic and social lives, we evaluate satisfaction related to specific life aspects and the differences from overall satisfaction. The analyses in Sect. 2 and 3 are based on data from the 2013 China Social Survey.

The happiness index in the CSS 2013 included six statements to which recipients responded "strongly disagree," "disagree," "do not quite agree," "relatively agree," "agree," and "strongly agree." Each response was assigned a point value of 1 to 6, with "strongly disagree" assigned the lowest value of one, and "strongly agree" the highest value of 6. "Not sure" and missing values were assigned zero points. The six statements include: (1) "Overall, my life is very close to my ideal," (2) "My living conditions are very good," (3) "I am satisfied with my life," (4) "I have got the important things that I want in life," (5) "Even if my life could start all over again, I have no wish to change it," and (6) "Overall, I am a happy person. Adding up the points, the lowest and highest scores measuring Chinese residents' happiness were 0 points and 36 points, with a mean score of 21 points. In general, overall happiness was high among Chinese residents, 75 percent of whom responded affirmatively to the question, "Generally, I am a happy person." There was no significant difference in happiness levels between urban and rural residents, both of which averaged a happiness score of 21 points.

However, high-income and middle-income groups were generally happier. 87% of high-income earners and 82% of the middle-income earners agreed with the statement that "overall, I am a happy person," while only 75% of the lower-middle-income group and 66% of the low-income group agreed to the same. In terms of the happiness score, the survey showed that the higher the income, the higher the level of happiness. The high-income group had the highest average score at 23. The lowest score in the high-income group was 8 points, far above the 0 score for other income groups. The average score for the middle-income and lower-middle-income groups was 22 points and 21 points respectively. The low-income group had the lowest score at 20 points, which was lower than the average score for all Chinese residents. This suggests that, at China's current stage of development, happiness is closely associated with income.

The CSS 2013 measured life satisfaction according to seven aspects: education level, health status, social life, family relationships, family economic status, leisure and entertainment, and overall self-assessed satisfaction. Respondents were asked to score these aspects on a 10-point scale, from "very dissatisfied" (1 point) to "very satisfied" (10 points). The average score for Chinese residents' overall self-assessed satisfaction was 7 points, suggesting that they were relatively satisfied with their lives. The lowest and highest scores were 1 point and 10 points. The difference between urban and rural residents in overall satisfaction was not very significant. The average life satisfaction score for Chinese residents across the seven aspects was 45 points, with the lowest score of 0, the highest score of 70, and a standard deviation of 10 points. Although the survey showed that Chinese residents generally have high life satisfaction, the internal variation among respondents was large. Compared with rural residents, who had an average score of 44 points, urban residents had a slightly higher average satisfaction score of 46 points. Life satisfaction was positively associated with income. The high-income group had a higher average life satisfaction score of 52 points, with the lowest score among them being 21 points. This is vastly different than the lowest score of 0 among other income groups. Next to the high-income group, the middle-income group had an average life satisfaction score of 49 points. The average life satisfaction scores of the lower-middle-income and low-income groups were 45 points and 42 points respectively.

Figure 3.3 shows the overall life satisfaction of urban and rural residents based on the various seven aspects. Relatively speaking, "family relationships" were the aspect Chinese residents were most satisfied with, averaging 8.2 points. This is followed by "health and social life," with an average score of approximately 7 points. Both urban and rural residents had the lowest level of satisfaction with their own education, which averaged 5.4 points. "Leisure and recreation" and "family economic status" had the next lowest satisfaction levels, with an average score of 6 points. Except for "social life", rural residents had lower satisfaction scores for all other aspects than urban residents. The results reflect rural residents' dissatisfaction with their life situation and the aspiration for change. The development gap between urban and rural areas is also implied in the survey results. The results support the need for government action to improve the living standards of rural residents and enhance their confidence in life.

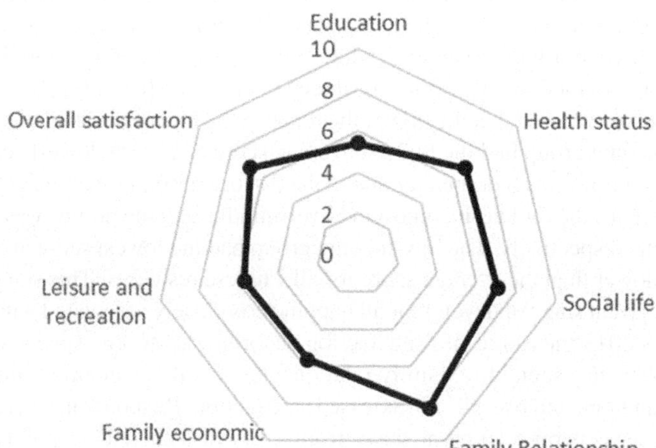

Fig. 3.3 Overall and individual aspects of life satisfaction among urban and rural residents

The high-income and middle-income groups showed a similar level of life satisfaction. As shown in Fig. 3.4, these groups had higher life satisfaction in all aspects, especially in terms of family economic status, leisure and recreation, and health status. The high-income group, middle-income group, lower-middle-income group and low-income group respectively scored an average of 7.4, 6.4, 5.5 and 4.9 points for family economic status satisfaction; 7.0, 6.3, 5.6 and 5.2 points for leisure and recreation satisfaction; and 7.6, 7.2, 6.8 and 6.2 points for health status satisfaction. The different income groups also showed similar levels of satisfaction for family relationships and social life.

Figure 3.5 shows the personal future expectations and desires of urban and rural residents across nine categories: (1) family health and prosperity; (2) improvement

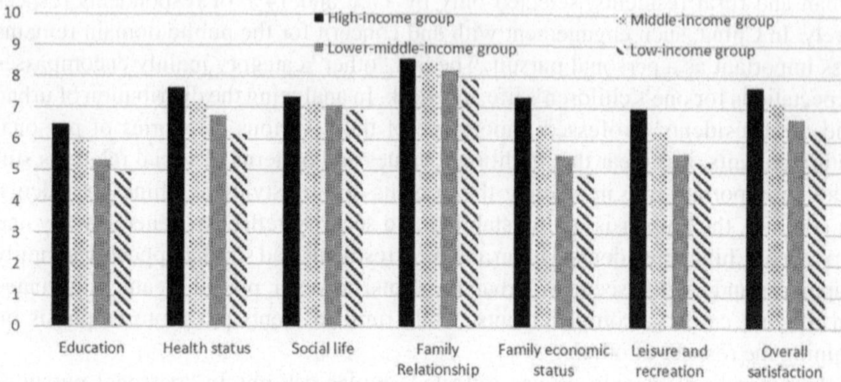

Fig. 3.4 Life satisfaction of different Income groups

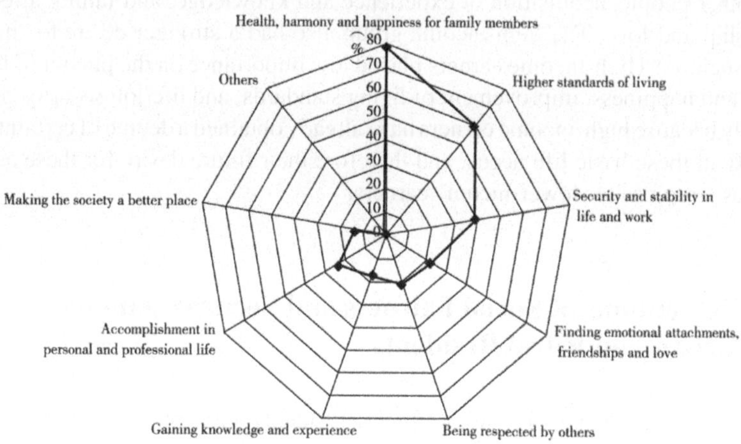

Fig. 3.5 Distribution of personal pursuits among urban and rural residents

of living standards; (3) life and job stability and security; (4) life and career achievements; (5) family affection, friendship, and love; (6) respect from others; (7) acquisition of knowledge; (8) making society better, and (9) other. The first three categories -family prosperity, improved living standards, and job security were ranked the highest among Chinese residents' personal pursuits and desires at 79%, 60%, and 39% respectively. Such results reflect the concentrated desire of Chinese residents to improve family happiness and life security. The second most concentrated categories of personal pursuits were life/career achievements at 23%, family affection, friendship, love at 22%, and respect from others at 21%. This reflects the traditional Chinese values of a hard work ethic and importance of family, and a social model that emphasizes relationships with others. The acquisition of knowledge and desire to make society better ranked relatively lower as desired personal pursuits among urban and rural residents, selected only by 17% and 14% of respondents respectively. In China, such engagement with and concern for the public domain remains less important as a personal pursuit. The last "other" category mainly encompasses expectations for one's children's life and work. In analyzing the distribution of urban and rural residents' professed importance of these various categories of personal future pursuits, it is clear that traditional values and patterns of social relations still play an important role in shaping the pursuits and lifestyles of Chinese residents. In addition, the emphasis on life stability and security reflects a general worry and anxiety of Chinese residents. Urban and rural residents had similar appeals for family happiness and job/life security. Urban residents, however, placed greater importance on life and career accomplishments, while rural residents put more emphasis on gaining the respect of others.

In general, all income groups reflected similar patterns in "personal pursuits" as that shown in Fig. 3.5, with a few key differences. The high-income group was more likely than other income groups to pursue life and career achievements, respect from other people, acquisition of experience and knowledge, and family affection, friendship and love. The high-income group also had a stronger desire to "make a better society." High-income earners placed less importance on the pursuit of family health and happiness, improvement of living standards, and life/job security. This is possibly because high-income earners have already obtained a degree of certainty and stability in these basic life needs, and therefore their future desire for these aspects is not as strong as for lower-income earners.

3.3 Perceptions of Social Fairness and Security Among Urban and Rural Residents

The focus of this chapter is to study Chinese residents' perceptions of social fairness and security. The CSS 2013 questioned respondents on their perceptions of fairness in many aspects of social life, using a 1 to 4 point scale representing "very unfair," "not very fair," "relatively fair" and "very fair." As shown in Fig. 3.6, Chinese residents

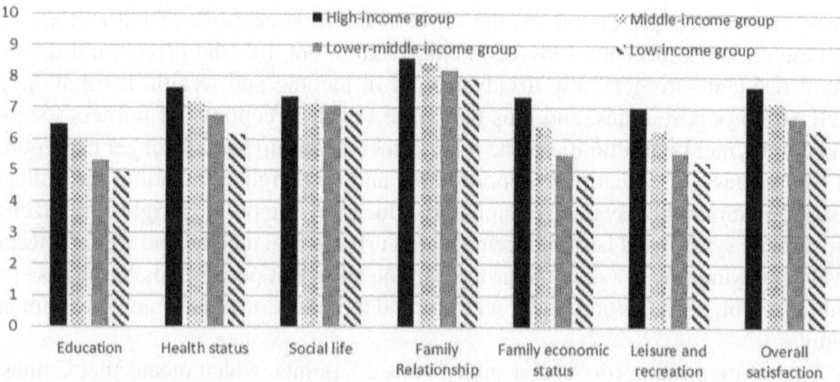

Fig. 3.6 Perceptions of societal fairness among urban and rural residents across income groups (*Note* 1 = very unfair, 10 = very fair)

on average scored 2.5 points for their overall evaluation of social fairness, which falls between "not very fair" and "relatively fair." Rural residents had a relatively higher average score of 2.5 points, while urban and town residents scored an average of 2.4 points. Not a single social aspect was rated as "relatively fair" (3 points) by either urban or rural residents. However, compulsory education and public health were more likely to be thought of as relatively fair with an average of 2.5 points. The college entrance examination system, pensions and other social security benefits, the political rights of citizens, the judicial system and law enforcement, work and employment, and wealth and income distribution were all perceived to be "not very fair" with an average of 2–2.5 points. Respondents considered the most unfair aspects of social life, averaging 1–2 points, to be income and welfare inequality across different regions and sectors, the selection process for CPC and government cadres, and rights and welfare in urban and rural areas. There were no significant differences between urban and rural residents in these perceptions. Comparatively, urban residents scored slightly higher than rural residents in their evaluations of the fairness of the college entrance examination system and employment opportunities. Rural residents scored higher in their evaluations of the fairness of medical care, pensions and other social security benefits, and the selection of CPC and government cadres. Overall, Chinese residents' feelings of fairness in all aspects of social life were not quite optimistic.

The relationship between income and the perception of fairness is more complex. As shown in Fig. 3.6, the lower the income, the higher the overall perception of the fairness of society. The average score was 2.5 points for the low-income and lower-middle-income groups, 2.46 points for the middle-income group, and only 2.34 points for the high-income group. Yet in terms of job and employment opportunities and wealth and income distribution, the high-income group had the highest feelings of fairness, followed by the middle-income group, and then the lower-middle-income and low-income groups. The majority of residents in high-income and middle-income groups are urban residents, with rural residents accounting for only 3 percent in these income groups. Therefore, the differences in perceptions of fairness among income classes reflect not only economic factors, but also the urban-rural divide. Rural residents are generally disadvantaged in income and wealth distribution as well as job opportunities, and thus they have lower perceptions of fairness for job and employment opportunities. The middle-income group had a stronger perception of the fairness of educational opportunities and civil rights, including the college entrance examination system, compulsory education, the political rights of citizens, the judicial system and law enforcement, and urban–rural income and welfare. Relatively speaking, the low-income group had the strongest perceptions of fairness for public health, pensions and social security, and the selection of CPC and government cadres.

The average rating for "social safety" was 2.8 points, which means that Chinese residents generally view their environment to be between "not very safe" and "relatively safe." Rural residents had a slightly higher evaluation of overall social safety (2.9 points) than urban residents (2.7 points). Chinese residents felt that personal property and personal safety were the most safe (above 3 points), while medical care, traffic, labor conditions, and the ecological environment were considered relatively safe (2–2.5 points). Personal information, privacy and food safety were considered to be relatively unsafe (2–2.5 points). The results show that Chinese residents worry more frequently about privacy issues and unsafe food, and worry less about the safety of their person and property. Urban residents generally felt their social environment to be less safe, and gave negative evaluations for safety across a variety of aspects, particularly food safety, labor safety, personal information and privacy security, and the ecological environment. Problems in these areas are generally more common in urban settings, and thus more relevant to the daily lives of urban residents.

There were greater differences across income groups with respect to perceptions of social safety than there were for perceptions of social fairness. The higher the income, the lower the general sense of security. This trend holds true for both overall perceptions of safety, and perception of safety across individual social aspects (shown in Fig. 3.7). The largest difference between income groups was the perception of food safety. The higher the income, the lower the evaluation on food safety. Middle-income and high-income groups gave food safety an average of 2 points, reflecting an overall feeling of "not very safe." This was a lower average score than that of urban residents. Lower-middle income groups gave an average rating of 2.4 points, while low-income groups gave food safety an average score of 2.6 points, which was similar to that of the average score of all rural residents. Such a pattern suggests that higher income groups are more worried about food safety, while lower income groups are not quite as sensitive to food safety issues, likely because basic living security is a more pressing concern. Additionally, higher income groups had lower safety evaluations related to personal information security and privacy, ecological and environmental security, and medical safety.

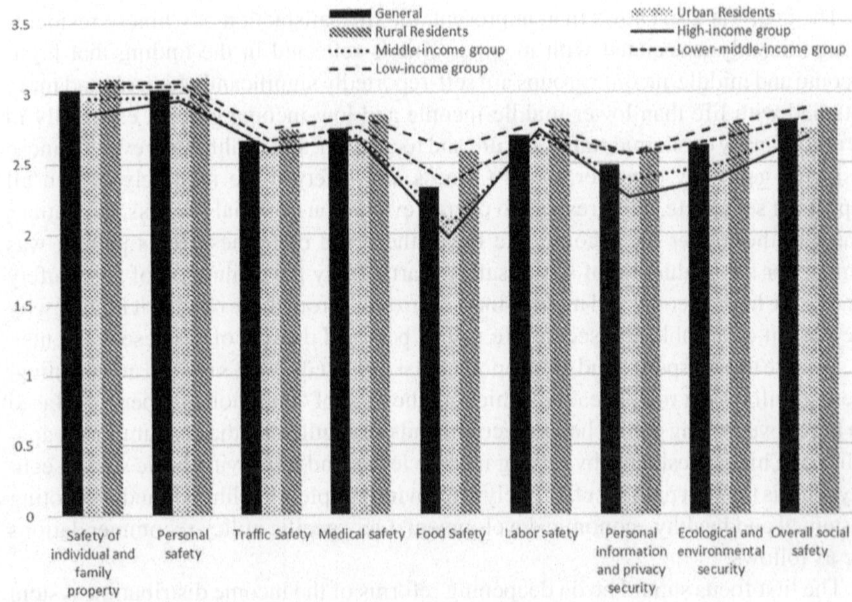

Fig. 3.7 Evaluation of societal safety among urban–rural residents across income groups (*Note* 1 = very unsafe, 2 = not very safe, 3 = relatively safe, 4 = very safe)

3.4 Summary and Outlook

The survey reveals the income and consumption structure of Chinese urban and rural residents, and how income distribution relates to the perception of life satisfaction. Analysis of the survey results illuminate two main characteristics of the income distribution in China. First, China's low-income and lower-middle-income population is extremely large, accounting for more than 70 percent of China's total population. Second, the income gap is also quite large, as shown by the fact that the average income and the average income growth rate for high-income earners is much higher than those of other groups. Therefore, a key goal for readjusting the income distribution structure is to significantly increase the income of low-income and lower-middle-income earners, and to expand the proportion of the middle-income group. A positive aspect of the consumption structure trends is the decline in the proportion of food expenditures as a percentage of household spending, and the increase in the proportion of household spending on durables. This suggests a significant improvement in household living standards. However, the increasing proportion of household spending on down payments and mortgages, the decline in education expenditures, and low spending rates on culture, education, and leisure—thus suppressing demand-remain a great concern in the overall consumption structure of Chinese households.

The analysis also shows that, at present, the life satisfaction of Chinese residents is significantly associated with income. This is reflected in the finding that high-income and middle-income groups are self-reportedly significantly happier and more satisfied with life than lower-middle-income and low-income groups, especially in terms of family economic status, leisure and recreation, and health. However, Chinese residents generally consider social fairness and safety to be relatively low in all aspects of social life. With respect to overall evaluation of social fairness, the pattern was that the higher the income, the lower the sense of fairness. This pattern was similar for the evaluation of social safety, particularly the evaluation of food safety among the high-income and middle-income groups. From these results, it is clear why the pursuit of a stable and secure life is the "personal dream" of Chinese residents.

Despite the prosperity and development that followed China's reform and opening, there is still a long road ahead to achieving the goal of "common prosperity." Based on the above findings, this chapter recommends strengthening the consumption capability of Chinese residents by raising income levels and improving basic social security. This is the best path for effectively improving people's livelihoods and promoting sustained and healthy economic development. Our specific policy recommendations are as follows:

The first focus should be on deepening reforms of the income distribution system through adjustments to the income distribution structure, promoting a rate of income growth that is faster than GDP growth, raising disposable incomes, and continuing large-scale poverty reduction efforts. Additionally, improving the employment situation for college graduates and the new generation of migrant workers will help promote upward mobility for lower-middle-income earners and expand the the middle-income group.

The second focus should be on improving the social security system, stabilizing commodities and housing prices, and promoting the construction of a social assistance system for the purpose of relieving financial pressures.

The third focus should be on improving the consumption environment and enhancing consumer confidence through product safety legislation.

The fourth focus should be on guiding and cultivating quality of life by encouraging educational, cultural and recreational consumption, promoting green consumption concepts, encouraging spiritual pursuits and cultivating "responsible" consumers.

In 2013, China's GDP growth rate was approximately 7.7%, the per-capita GDP was $6,995 USD, (See note 1) and the actual growth rate of per-capita GDP was about 7.1% (excluding natural population growth factors). (See note 2) According to criteria set forth by the World Bank in 2015, (See note 3) countries with a per-capita gross national product (GNP) between $4,125 USD to $12,746 USD are considered middle-to-high-income countries. A report by the People's Bank of China predicts that China's GDP growth is likely to slow to 7.4% in 2014 and 7.1% percent in 2015. (See note 4) If we assume that China's GDP is quite close to its GNP, and assume that the future per-capita GDP can maintain an average annual growth rate of around 7 percent, then China's per-capita GNP in 2020 will be approximately $11,232 USD (without consideration of changes in the exchange rate). This is still lower than the threshold for high-income countries, which is marked by a per-capita GNP of $12,746 USD or above. Provided a 7% growth rate can be maintained, the per capita GDP of China could reach $12,860 USD as early as 2022 (without consideration of changes in the exchange rate), which will place China in the ranks of high-income countries. If the annual per-capita GDP growth rate is less than 7%, assuming conservatively 6.5%, then the per-capita GDP in 2020 is projected to be $10,870 USD and $13,130 USD in 2023 (without consideration of changes in the exchange rate). According to these preliminary estimates, a slowdown in economic growth will not significantly delay the timing for when China crosses the threshold into the category of a high-income country, and thus China still has space to improve the speed of economic development on the basis of adjusting the economic development structure and deepening reforms of the income distribution system.

In 2013, urban per-capita disposable income increased by 7%, rural per-capita net income increased by 9.3%, and national per-capita disposable income increased by 8.1%. (See note 1) Overall, residents' income growth kept pace with GDP growth. During the 10 years from 2003 to 2012, after adjusting for inflation, the per-capita disposable income of urban residents and per capita net income of rural residents retained an average annual growth of 9.3% and 8.4% percent respectively. (See note 2) If future economic growth slows down and average annual income growth drops to 7% for urban residents and 8% for rural residents, the per-capita disposable income of urban residents and per-capita net income of rural residents are expected to reach 43,284 yuan and 15,246 yuan respectively in 2020 (from the 2013 baseline of 26,955 for urban residents and 8,895.90 for rural residents, per data from the 2013 National Bureau of Statistics). Even if income growth is affected by a slowdown in economic development, the per-capita income of urban and rural residents in 2020 is still expected to be double that of ten years ago, when the average income rates for urban and rural residents were 19,109 yuan and 5,919 yuan respectively (2010 National Bureau of Statistics).

Indeed, the greater challenge is adjusting the income distribution structure. Based on CSS2013 data, if China can control the income growth rate of the high-income group and accelerate the income growth of the low-income and lower-middle-income groups, China can achieve an "olive distribution pattern" (larger in the middle and smaller on each end) in which a greater proportion of the Chinese population, i.e. up to 40% of urban residents, are in the middle-income group (Li Peilin and Zhu Di 2015). In this more appropriate income distribution structure, domestic demand would be more powerful, life satisfaction would significantly increase, and there would be greater confidence in future economic and social development. It would also represent a step toward achieving the Chinese Dream of "common prosperity."

References

Deng, Xiaoping. 1993. *Selected Works of Deng Xiaoping*, vol. 3. China, Beijing: People's Publishing House. [in Chinese].

Li, Peilin, and Di Zhu. 2015. Make Efforts to Develop and Olive-shaped Distribution Pattern: An Analysis Based on Data from the Chinese Social Survey from 2006–2013. Social Sciences in China 37 (1): 45–65. [in Chinese].

Chapter 4
Towards a Prosperous Society: Expectations and Reality

N. E. Tikhonova

In everyday understanding, a dream is usually an ardent wish that brings people happiness the moment it comes true. The sociological understanding of a dream, however, goes beyond that, in which a dream is not just a projection of a desired future, but a source of motivation and an incentive. This approach allows researchers to obtain a population's vision of a desired future, while at the same time determining what things people lack that are significant for them.[1]

> Respondents' dreams, or life aspirations, may be analyzed on several different levels. The first is the "macrolevel," which encompasses what people desire for their society, the type of social structure they would like to see in their country, and what kind of society they would like to live in. These particular aspects of the "Russian Dream" will be covered in more detail in further chapters of this book. Second and just as important is the "microlevel," which focuses on what individuals wish for themselves. This level mostly comprises thoughts about the ideal job and family, the quantitative and qualitative features of desired living standards, etc. Even though respondents' aspirations may vary greatly, and the set of desires they list may be impacted by the precise wording of a question,[2] certain patterns can still be discovered in

[1] That said, it is vital to note that these "significant things" are not easily attainable, and getting hold of them is not a simple, regular task. As a matter of fact, this is what makes people dream in the first place, instead of merely meeting certain day-to-day goals as part of our routine.

[2] For instance, when asked open-ended questions about their dreams, respondents shared various wishes "for a better society" less often than when asked close-ended questions that contain direct references to societal life. The same person might also give slightly different answers when asked what he dreams about overall and when asked what he would wish for in a fantastic situation (e.g. if they met a genie, had a magic wand, etc.). The nature and scope of these deviations are described in detail in: O chem mechtayut rossiyane? (What do Russians dream about?).

The original version of this chapter was revised: Affiliations have been updated in this chapter. The correction to this book can be found at https://doi.org/10.1007/978-981-16-2505-3_19

N. E. Tikhonova (✉)
HSE University, Moscow, Russia

Institute of Sociology of FCTAS RAS, Moscow, Russia

P. Li and M. K. Gorshkov (eds.), *Life Expectations of the People*,
Research Series on the Chinese Dream and China's Development Path,
https://doi.org/10.1007/978-981-16-2505-3_4

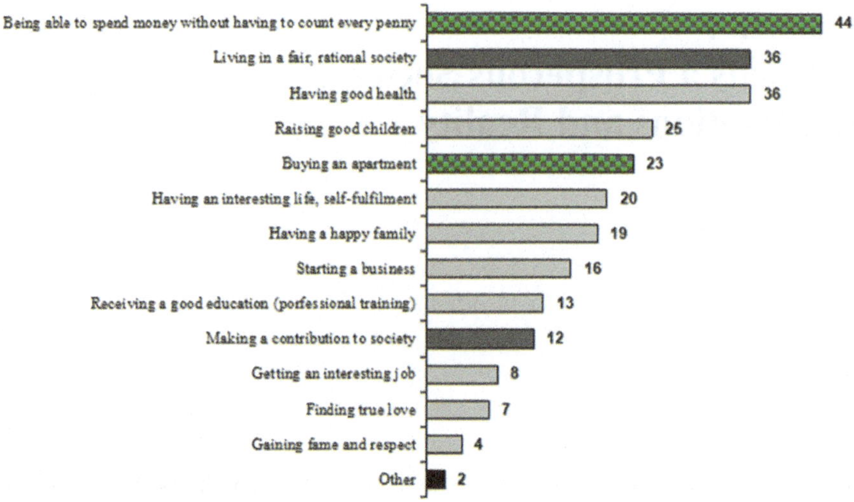

Fig. 4.1 What do Russians dream about? (2012 data, percentage of those who have a dream, based on a close-ended multiple-choice question with up to three possible answers; arranged by percentage of people who share a given dream)[3]

Russian citizens' attitudes towards the objects of their dreams. Namely, we can determine the ratio between macro and microlevel dreams, calculate Russians' general tendency to dream, and describe their thoughts on dreams.

Figure 4.1 shows that most Russians tend to express microlevel life aspirations, although macrolevel (society-related) desires are also quite prominent. Having a dream is a cultural norm for Russians. This is proved by several survey findings: only 13% of Russians said that they did not have a dream, and over three quarters of the nation's adult population believe that "life cannot be complete without dreams, and you must dream, even though your dreams may sound impossible." Only 24% say that "dreams do not have any practical purpose; you must dwell only on the day-to-day happenings of the real world".

In addition, Fig. 4.1 shows that "being able to spend money without having to count every penny" is one of the most common life aspirations of Russian citizens. Having one's own apartment or house is also a popular; it is mentioned by about one in every four Russians who have a dream. Overall, about one-half of all respondents list various material benefits as among their three most ardent life desires (54% to be more precise, as two-thirds of those who wish for their own place to live also dream about being able to spend money freely). This is not a small figure, but not a large one, either, taking into account the actual living standards in Russia. These findings are hardly sufficient to form a solid conclusion that Russian society has

[3] In the figure, macro- and microlevel dreams are highlighted in different colors; among the latter, special emphasis is paid to dreams that are related to the material aspect of everyday life.

turned into a consumer society.[4] Furthermore, as much as 40% of all respondents mention a macrolevel, society-related dream among their three main desires, and one in every eight respondents desire to make a useful contribution to society (in spite of aggressive media coverage of commodification ideals).

It is worth mentioning that other studies by IS RAS also confirm that a substantial share of the population in Russia does not focus solely on their personal interests. For instance, in February 2014, 41% of Russians expressed a firm belief that one should sacrifice one's own well-being for the good of the society and the nation, while 59% adhered to the opposite point of view, stating that personal interests should be every individual's priority. Even though at that time two-thirds of the population confessed that they were not ready to compromise their well-being to benefit the rest of the nation, 34% said that this was a risk they were willing to take.[5] Moreover, the population's stoic reaction and heightened sense of national unity after Western countries imposed sanctions against Russia following the annexation of Crimea prove that the Russian people underestimated rather than overestimated their capacity to make sacrifices for the greater good.

Other research also shows that only half of all Russians consider material values to be important. For example, in 2012, when respondents were asked an open-ended question about what they would wish for if granted three wishes by a genie, exactly half of the respondents (among respondents who wished for anything at all) provided responses related to wealth and material well-being. Yet these were often wishes for the well-being of the respondent's children rather than for personal prosperity. Moreover, the concept of "well-being" spanned a whole range of different meanings among different social groups. While some Russians said that, if they chanced to meet a genie, they would wish for things like "wealth," "lots of money," "fortune," "win the lottery jackpot," and even "luxury items: my own private island, a yacht, or a manor," others stated that they would merely ask the genie to help them "meet their daily needs," get a "good wage," or "not have to count every penny". In addition, there were frequently very specific responses regarding material wealth, as many people said they would ask the genie for an apartment, a house, a car, etc. (Fig. 4.2). Moreover, the share of Russians who would rather ask the genie for some tangible assets, such as money, an apartment, a car, etc. (56% in all) was roughly equal to the share of Russians who were more or less focused on material wealth, as mentioned above (54%).

---

[4] The concept of a "consumer society" was first introduced in the 1920s by Erich Fromm. This type of society has been subsequently analyzed in a wide range of works, Jean Baudrillard's *La société de consommation* being the most prominent. Today, scholarly research primarily regards a consumer society as a type of society where consumption is elevated to the status of life's greatest value, becoming the main aspect of an individual's personal fulfillment and bringing about a corresponding set of norms and a certain lifestyle.

[5] Based on research from the "Middle Class in Modern Russia," which was carried out by the Institute of Sociology RAS in February of 2014, $n = 1600$. Sample was stratified. Stratification was performed by economic regions of the Russian Federation in accordance with the Rosstat's [Russian Federal State Statistics Service] method (excluding the Kaliningrad Oblast); respondents from every region were further stratified by gender, age, and settlement type.

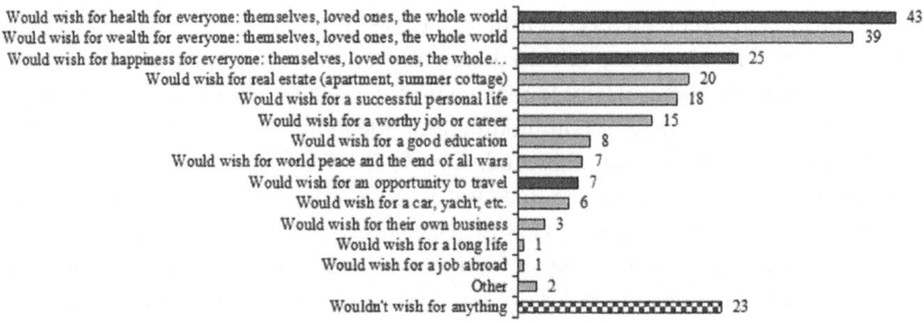

Fig. 4.2 What would Russians wish for if they met a genie, 2012[6] (Open-ended question where respondents were allowed to select up to three answers; arranged by wish popularity)[7]

The other group of respondents, representing almost half of all Russians aged 18–55 (44–46%, depending on the sampling method) wished solely for intangible things. Of course, this does not necessarily imply that everyone within this group is a complete and utter altruist, but it still demonstrates that for them, material benefits are less significant than other life aspirations.

What are the reasons behind the choices made by Russians who are inclined to prioritize material wealth in one way or another? Does the popularity of the desire for wealth and well-being mean that Russian society has begun its slow but steady progress down the path to consumerism? Or is it a mere question of survival, which has become crucially important for some Russians in their constant struggle against hunger and deprivation, starting with the omnipresent shortages during Soviet times, and continuing through the trials of the 1990s, when most of the population had to tighten their belts just when shops finally started filling their shelves with merchandise? What is the true cause of the past decade's consumption boom?

To find answers to all these questions, we will now look at income levels and living conditions across Russia, analyze the consumption structure (especially the availability of various household items and relevant spending priorities), and determine how social and economic status influenced respondents' answers.

First, we shall explore the relationship to income level. As of October 2014,[8] the median value of the average monthly income of Russian households amounted to 14,000 rubles for the majority of the population (based on respondents' self-reporting). Back in early 2010, when the nation had just emerged from the 2008–2009 financial crisis, this figure was as low as 7,500 rubles. In other words, the

[6] Aggregated data measuring responses to an open-ended question, which, translated from Russian, ran as follows, "Now imagine that you have become the master of a genie, who is ready to grant three of your wishes. Please write down what you would wish for."

[7] The figure uses different colors to highlight the tangible and intangible values, as well as responses by those who would not wish for anything.

[8] The income status data is based on the monitoring survey, which was carried out in October and November of 2014 by the Institute of sociology RAS and involved a nation-wide sampling of 4,000 people representing the population of every region and stratified by gender, age, and settlement type. The survey was funded by a Russian Science Foundation grant (Project No. 14–28-00,218).

nominal median income increased 1.87 times in that four-year period. The average income, in turn, increased even more (1.88 times), from 8,954 rubles in early 2010 to 16,820 rubles in October 2014. Even if we account for inflation, this still means that the population's real income experienced a significant boost. Notably, the income pattern revealed by sociological research corresponds to statistical data reflected by the Russian Federal State Statistics Service.[9]

We must also bear in mind that the average income level is based on dramatically heterogeneous figures, as the incomes of Russian residents differ greatly across the country and in various population groups. For example, as of October 2014, the bottom 10% of the population (i.e. those with the lowest average monthly income) earned no more than 7,000 rubles per capita, while the top 10% earned at least 30,000 rubles per capita.

Figure 4.4 shows that even among those who are included in social surveys, there is an enormous gap between the average per capita income of the top and bottom 10% of the population: in October 2014, the top 10% earned nine times more than the bottom 10%. Furthermore, if instead of deciles we compare the top and bottom 1% of respondents (In Russia 1% of the population is almost as many as 1.5 million people), the gap between the average incomes of their respective households turns into a precipice: the top 1% earn 40 times more than the bottom 1%. Additionally, the income of the wealthiest Russians (about 3–5% of the population) is not accounted for, since they generally are not included in survey samples.

It is important to note that the increase in income inequality, even among those respondents who are included in social surveys, is only so sharp in the upper income decile. The average per capita income of respondents in the 10th decile is only two times higher than the income of respondents in the 9th decile (Fig. 4.4). Overall, if we take a look at the colossal, almost sevenfold, leap in income in the top decile (Fig. 4.3) and the vast difference in the top 3–5% of the population (who are not covered by surveys) and the rest of Russians, we discover that the income distribution in the country resembles a hyperbola.

Data from the Russian Federal State Statistics Service also reveals that income distribution in Russia is highly uneven. For example, in 2013 the modal and median

9 This is an important fact to consider, as the nominal value of the population's real income differs greatly if we look at surveys and official statistics. For example, even in 2013, the figures provided by Russian Federal State Statistics Service were somewhat higher than the survey data for October 2014 (with the median monthly income reaching 19,151.4 rubles per capita, and the average income reaching 25,928.2 rubles (Russian Federal State Statistics Service. Official website. Table "The population's average, median and modal income in 2013, across Russia and in separate regions" (in Russian). Updated on 26.01.2015 (http://www.gks.ru/free_doc/new_site/population/bednost/tabl/1-2-6.htm). This is hardly surprising, however, given that the state statistical bodies do not base their data solely on the money that people actually receive (which is what respondents refer to when they evaluate their income), and make certain additional calculations. What is more, the Russian Federal State Statistics Service takes into account the income of the upper 3–5% of the population; since these people usually are not included in mass surveys, this also contributes significantly to the difference in the research findings, especially concerning the average income.

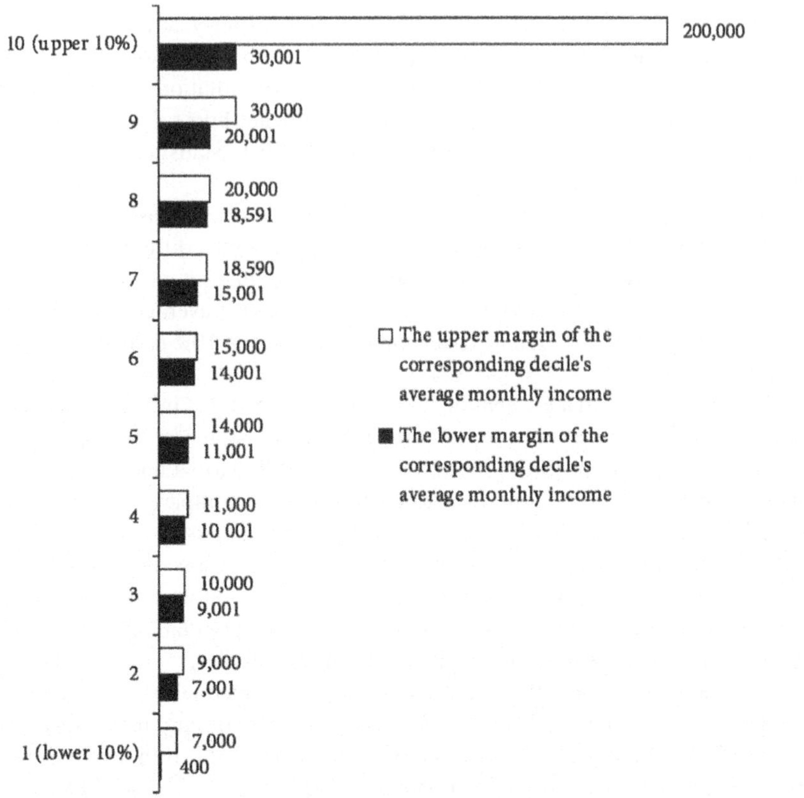

Fig. 4.3 Russians' estimates of their average monthly income across various Deciles, 2014, Rubles

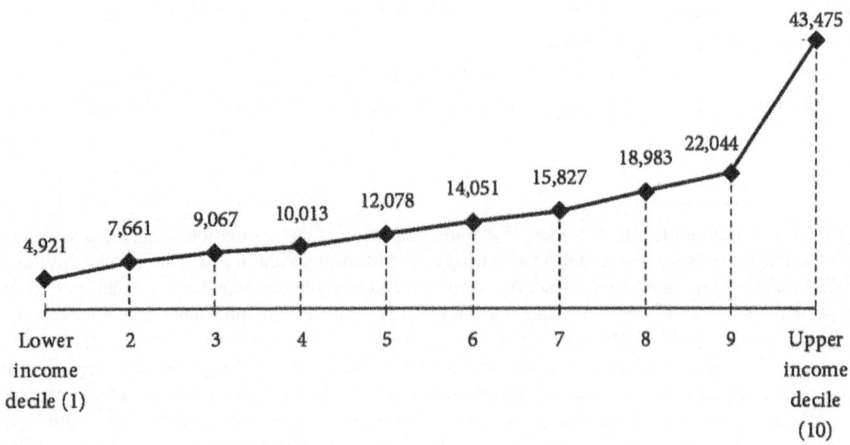

Fig. 4.4 Russians' average per capita income across various Deciles, 2014, Rubles

Table 4.1 Distribution of the population's total financial income, 1980–2013, %[11]

Year	Across 20-percent population groups:				
	first (lowest income)	second	third	fourth	fifth (highest income)
1980	10.1	14.8	18.6	23.1	33.4
1985	10.0	14.6	18.3	23.1	34.0
1990	9.8	14.9	18.8	23.8	32.7
1995	6.1	10.8	15.2	21.6	46.3
2000	5.9	10.4	15.1	21.9	46.7
2005	5.4	10.1	15.1	22.7	46.7
2010	5.2	9.8	14.8	22.5	47.7
2013[a]	5.2	9.8	14.9	22.5	47.6

[a]Preliminary data

income in the country amounted to 40.3% and 73.9% of the average income respectively.[10] Uneven income distribution is precisely what causes such a striking discrepancy between the modal, average, and median income: up to 60% of Russians receive as little as 29.9% of the population's total earnings. The tendency of the income distribution to form a hyperbola keeps growing over time (Table 4.1).

All these facts show that Russians' persistent desire for wealth is no accident, and that the economic status of their households is not as idyllic as it might seem from the aggregated data that reflects the increase of their income over the past few years. At the same time, it must be noted that the wish to live "without having to count every penny" is not necessarily linked to personal earnings and income dynamics, which yet again demonstrates that Russian culture is not characterized by an obsession with material wealth. That is to say, the dream to live in plenty is just as popular among households that have been enjoying positive financial dynamics over the past few years as it is among those who report experiencing a downward trend. The dream of wealth is shared by only 30% of those who consider their financial status to be good, whereas among respondents with a negative assessment of their financial status this share increases to 44%, but still remains under 50%.

Empirical evidence shows that the importance of tangible assets as an object of desire is influenced not by the person's income level per se, but rather by the conclusions the person makes when comparing his own income with the situation in the local society, i.e. the living standards of his social surroundings. Consequently, Russians are more concerned about their social status, which is mostly defined in

[10] Russian Federal State Statistics Service. Official website. Table "The population's average, median and modal income in 2013, across Russia and in separate regions" (in Russian). Updated on 01/15/2015 (http://www.gks.ru/free_doc/new_site/population/bednost/tabl/1-2-6.htm).

[11] Russian Federal State Statistics Service. Official website. Based on the findings of the Service's random sampling research, which covered household budgets and the macroeconomic aspect of the population's earnings. Table "Distribution of the total financial income across 20-percent population groups and the main factors of social and economic disparity. Time series" (in Russian). Updated on 26.01.2015 (http://www.gks.ru/free_doc/new_site/population/bednost/tabl/1-2-2.htm).

Russia by personal wealth,[12] rather than about consumption as such. Thus, it stands to reason that over 50% of respondents whose incomes are lower than 1.5 times the local median inevitably wish for material wealth, regardless of the question's wording. At the same time, if we turn to groups where the household's average monthly income is higher than 1.5 times the median (and more so in groups with incomes two times higher than the median), we will discover that most respondents do not mention tangible values at all. Therefore, the differences in this respect are qualitative rather than quantitative.

Interestingly enough, when we switch from the abstract notion of wealth to more specific tangible desires (such as an apartment, a house, or a car), the gap between various income strata is almost completely bridged. When it comes to specific items, most differences stem from other factors, namely the person's consumption specifics and needs, which are defined by their ambitions, social identity, and other individual characteristics, including age. For instance, the wish for certain material possessions (excluding real estate) is expressed by 8% of respondents under 25, 7% of respondents from the 26–30 age group, 5% of those aged 36–45, and only 2% of respondents who are aged 46–55. The contrast is just as striking when we take a look at another issue that is far more relevant for most Russians, owning one's own apartment or house. This aspiration is shared by 31% of people under 25, 27% of people aged 26–30, 15% of those aged 36–45, and only 10% aged 46–55. But even so, this remains one of the most popular dreams in every age group.

So, why do Russians wish so ardently to have their own place to live, and why do so many of them consider housing to be a dream and not a routine task? A review of housing in modern Russia reveals that the majority of the population resides in two or three-bedroom apartments (Fig. 4.5). But at the same time, quite a few Russians live in communal apartments or municipal residential facilities, own only part of a house, are forced to rent, or even do not have a place to live at all and stay with their acquaintances. These categories make up as much as 16% of the population. In addition, many young people have no choice but to live with their parents, even though they would like to move out, and formally they are considered to be members of a household with their own living premises.

There is also another type of housing deprivation, apart from the lack of one's own place to live: housing density. Today, only 2% of Russians have no more than 6 square meters per person at their disposal; however, the share of those whose households have a housing space of no more than 10 square meters per person is still quite substantial, reaching 14%. Taking into account that only respondents who had at least 12 square meters per person assessed their living conditions as at least satisfactory, we can infer that almost a quarter (24%) of all Russians lives in premises that predetermine dissatisfaction with their living conditions. As for housing space that more or less fits current European standards (i.e. over 30 square meters per person), this is a luxury that only 11% of the survey respondents can afford. Even 20

[12] Tikhonova (2014).

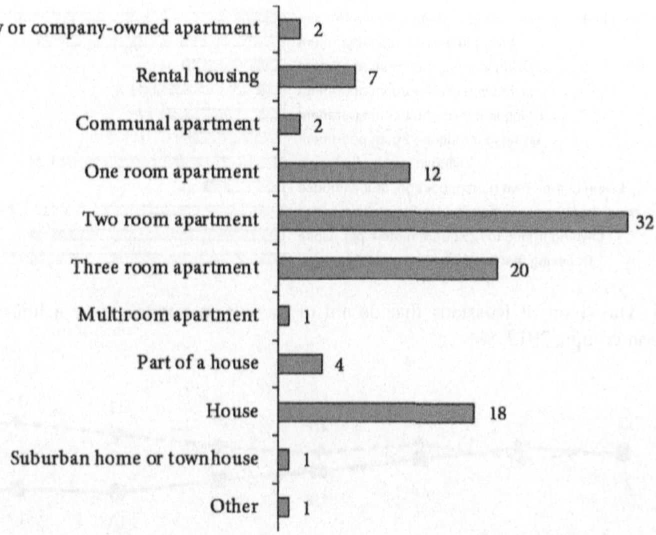

Fig. 4.5 Types of premises occupied by various population groups, 2014, %[14]

square meters per person are only available to less than half of all Russians (47%[13]). It is also very important to remember that the vast majority—nearly 60%- of people whose household space reaches 30 square meters per person or more are over the age of 50. This means that for most people with this amount of space, it is likely because their children have moved out, leaving them all alone in a rather spacious "nest." Moreover, these "nests" are mostly located inside old buildings or in rural areas. The proportion of other age groups with such low density living space is relatively small (about 11–17%), gradually beginning to increase with age.

Combining the two deprivation factors of lack of personal premises and high household density, objectively at least one in every five Russians suffer from housing deprivation. Moreover, 4% of the population suffers from both forms of housing deprivation, and that is without taking into account young adults and middle-aged people who, while living in satisfactory conditions, are forced to share a household with several generations of their relatives, as they have no other choice in the current economy.

If a person suffers from objective housing deprivation, this dramatically increases the likelihood the person will have a negative subjective opinion of their premises as well. However, the subjective and objective notions of housing deprivation do not always match. For instance, only 16% of those who do not have their own place to live (be it private or public housing) consider their living conditions to be good,

[13] Here, it must be specified that if we account for the wealthiest Russians (who are not included in mass surveys and who enjoy far better living conditions than the vast majority of the population), we may conclude that this group actually amounts to one half of the country's population.

[14] Data on Russians' living conditions are based on the "Middle Class in Modern Russia" research, which was carried out by the Institute of Sociology RAS in February of 2014.

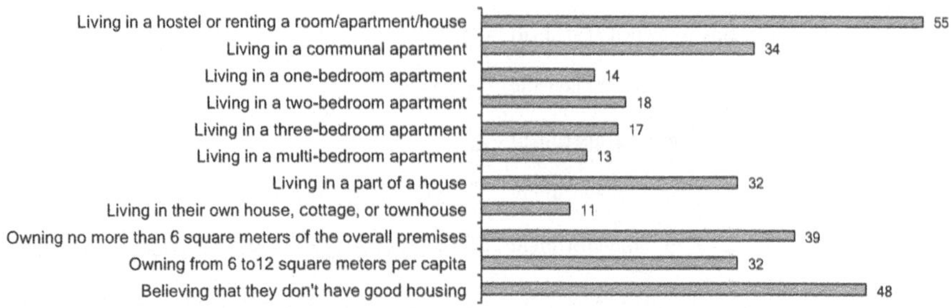

Fig. 4.6 The share of Russians that dream of having an apartment or a house across various population groups, 2012, %

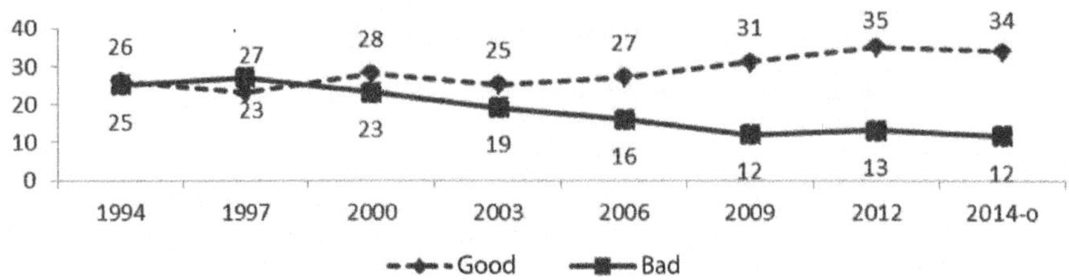

Fig. 4.7 Share of Russians who assess their living conditions as "good" or "bad:" percentage (%) dynamics from 1994 to 2014[15]

while the same opinion is shared by as much as 42% of those who have their own house or apartment. Assessment of living conditions as satisfactory is expressed by an equal number of respondents from both groups (53%), whereas the shares of negative responses differ drastically (31% and 5% respectively). Living conditions are most commonly rated as "bad" by respondents who live in communal apartments (43%). Household density also has a significant impact on the subjective notion of housing deprivation. Among those whose living premises measure no more than 6 square meters per person, 41% of respondents assess their living conditions as bad. Yet in all these cases, negative opinions are expressed by a relative minority of every population group. Moreover, the subjective assessment of one's living conditions influences expectations about the ideal home just as much as the objective factors of lack of personal premises or high-density living conditions (Fig. 4.6).

It is important to note that Russians' general level of satisfaction with their living conditions has noticeably trended upward over the 1990s and the early 2000s. That said, the main changes in Russians' attitudes towards their housing situation has occurred roughly over the first five years of the twenty-first century. In contrast, satisfaction levels in most recent years have been at a virtual standstill (Fig. 4.7).

The Russian Federal State Statistics Service also reports a rapid improvement of living conditions in the country up to the mid-2000s, with subsequent stagnation over

[15] The survey also offered another option, "satisfactory", which is not featured in the figure. Consequently, the total sum is less than 100%.

the latest years. For instance, the Service's findings show that in 1995 the national average housing space reached 18.0 square meters per capita. By the late 2000s, the figures grew by 4.6 square meters, reaching 22.6. Later on, the trend continued, albeit at a much slower pace. Today, the average housing space in Russia amounts to approximately 23 square meters per capita. Housing in rural areas is slightly more spacious than in cities (24.7 square meters per capita vs 22.9 square meters per capita). The quality of housing in Russia has also improved greatly over the past two decades; the share of living premises with running water has increased from 71 to 80%, while the share of those with central heating has leaped from 68 to 84%, and the share of those with a hot water supply has climbed from 55 to 66%, etc.[16]

Quite naturally, all of the above has had a tangible impact on Russians' satisfaction with their living conditions. Even so, we must once again stress that the aspirations of living in a place of one's own are still relevant for one-third of the population. Moreover, an even greater number of Russians state that they would immediately acquire real estate if they suddenly came across a large sum of money (in 2014, the share of such response reached 41%). This means that on the one hand, the majority of Russians who are in need of better living conditions believe that having their own apartment or house is actually just a dream (given the financial constraints) and do not even consider including it on their actual checklist; but on the other hand, there are those who want to buy an apartment, even though they do not consider this wish a "dream."

Now let us analyze the current characteristics of consumption among the Russian population. It is widely known that there are two general priority areas of consumption, leaning either towards purchasing services (entertainment, education, health and recreation, etc.) or towards purchasing goods. As a rule, these two categories complement one another in various proportions. We can understand what Russians consider to be more important (goods or services) if we review the corresponding consumption dynamics and analyze the nature of pent-up demand.

First, we shall study consumption of services. Figure 4.8 reveals that despite the growth in prosperity up to 2008 and income stabilization from 2010 to 2014, fewer and fewer Russians used paid healthcare, education, and health improvement services. Foreign travel is the only service type that has actually grown more popular over the past decade.[17] Furthermore, when we look at the use of social services that are considered important from a human development potential point of view, we discover that a mere decline in popularity is by far an incomplete picture. Starting from 2003, there has been a dramatic spike in the number of those who do not use

[16] Russian Federal State Statistics Service. Official website. Table "Household Amenities" (in Russian). Update on 02.02.2015 (http://www.gks.ru/free_doc/new_site/population/jil-f/jkh43.htm). However, empirical evidence shows that amenities do not really influence a person's desires about having a place to live, and they most definitely do not impact these desires nearly as much as housing space or, most importantly, living in one's own house or apartment.

[17] That said, it appears that the wish to travel abroad has already come true for the majority of people who used to consider it very important. At any rate, only 7% of all Russians have counted traveling among their top three wishes.

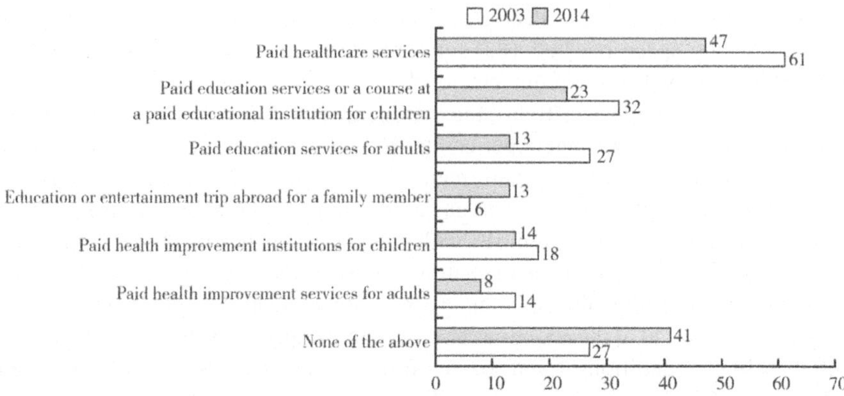

Fig. 4.8 Dynamics of paid social services consumption by Russians, 2003 and 2014, %

any of these services at all. These dynamics confirm a significant shift in Russians' consumption preferences over the past decade.

Data gathered by other research centers also confirms that Russians tend to pay increasing attention to the material side of life. For example, when asked what they would do if they won a million dollars, about one-third of the respondents (33%) said that they would prefer to spend the money on real estate, cars, or luxury items, while only 21% opted to use at least some of their winnings to cover various social services.[18]

This brings forth another question: how well do Russians fare in terms of the aforementioned material goods, in which Russian attach so much importance that they are willing to give up investments not only in their own welfare, but also in that of their children?

Sociological data shows that the day-to-day environment of Russian citizens has diversified greatly over the past fifteen years. In terms of household appliances, the average Russian lives in truly new conditions compared to the early 2000s (see Table 4.2).

Table 4.2 shows that the set of essential durable goods has expanded greatly over the course of thirteen years, and that by 2014 the variety of appliances and devices has soared to a median of 9 types per household and an average of 8.6 types per household. It also reveals quite a few other important factors that define the specific features of the consumption structure in Russia and explain the way consumption has evolved.

For instance, the past few years have witnessed the emergence of a new consumption standard, which has redefined both the property requirements of a household as a whole and the needs of separate household members. When applied to households in general, this new standard includes state-of-the-art kitchen appliances, which used to

[18] Based on a survey by the Romir Research Holding (April 2012, nation-wide representative sampling, 1,500 respondents over 18) (http://www.romir.ru/studies/343_1338408000).

Table 4.2 Various durable goods owned by Russians, 2003 and 2014, %[19]

Durable goods	2003	2014
First category of durable goods: *household appliances*		
Refrigerator	99	98
Color television	96	98
Vacuum cleaner	85	91
Cell phone	25	91
Washing machine (incl. semi-automatic models)	87	86
Microwave, food processor, grill, or any other kitchen appliance	44	73
Satellite dish	2	31
Air conditioner	2	15
Dishwasher	2	9
Second category of durable goods: *digital devices*		
Computer or laptop	22	71
Digital video or photo camera	9	47
Tablet or iPad	-	27
iPhone or smartphone	-	29
Third category of durable goods: *cars, including*		
Domestic models	33	29
Foreign models	8	30
Total number of car owners	*40*	*54*

be a rarity, and even cars (interestingly enough, more often than not, these are foreign rather than Russian models). Now that cars have become somewhat run-of-the-mill, it is hardly surprising that only one in every twenty Russians (i.e. a relatively small share) dreams of owning a car. Evidently, the vast majority of those who once wished to buy a car have successfully managed to do so, seizing the moment in those years when incomes were growing and banks were offering more and more tempting car loans. Now Russian society has simply split into those who advocate for and those who oppose car ownership.[20] The evolution of this new consumption standard is also evidenced by a boost in the number of Russians who own air conditioners, satellite dishes, and dish washers (even though overall, their share amounts to a mere third of the population, meaning that these particular goods are just starting to pave their way into Russian households).

[19] Arranged by 2014 data. Highlighted segments signify that the share of Russian households that own corresponding appliances has increased manifold over the past few years.

[20] Thus, it is only logical that 99% of those who dream of buying a car already have at least one and wish to buy a car for another member of their household who does not yet have one. In turn, if we look at the respondents who make up the group that dreams about having a car of their own, it becomes apparent that most of them are under 35 and have a low income.

Turning from households to individuals, we discover that owning a cell phone, a computer, and digital video equipment has already become part of the norm. A sizable share of the Russian population also owns iPads, tablets, iPhones, and smartphones. In due time, these devices will soon be considered "essential" property, alongside computers and cell phones.

Table 4.2 also provides explicit evidence that Russian consumers prefer more complex technology, especially digital devices and innovative appliances that transform their day-to-day routine and make their lives more enjoyable (these include air conditioners, dishwashers, or satellite dishes). As of late, these household appliances have been the most actively purchased, with the share of households that own them increasing manifold. And that is not all; preferences for high-end technology also become apparent in the selection of traditional items like TV sets. Before 2007, the overwhelming majority of customers who shopped for TV sets chose traditional color TVs, whereas over the period from 2007 to 2012, the ratio between traditional TVs and LCD and plasma screen TVs reached 26:45. By 2013, this same ratio changed to 1:12.

Thus, the past few years have seen significant improvements in Russians' living conditions, and consumers have begun surrounding themselves with new household items. One can even go as far as to say that, in a way, the nation has experienced a "consumption boom." But we must bear in mind that this "boom" did not have the same effect on all the social groups in Russia, and impacted Russians' desires for well-being in a number of diverse ways. For instance, while in the first income decile the median number of different types of household durables is five items per household, in the uppermost (tenth) income decile this figure increases to as many as twelve types per household. The same trend can be observed when comparing various social groups based on the relation of their income to the median income in their type of settlement. For example, a glance at the 2014 data reveals that in groups where income is no higher than one-half of the local median, the average number of durable goods per household was 7.78 types. The figures were slightly higher in groups with incomes ranging from half a median to a full median, but the rise in the number of item types was barely significant (8.0 types per household). At the next income level (up to 1.5 times the local income median), the average number of item types per household was 8.84. In households with incomes of 1.5 to 2 times the local income median, the figure climbed to 9.11 item types. And finally, at the topmost income level, the average figure skyrocketed to an impressive 10.68 item types per household. This shows that only those Russians whose income exceeds two times the local income median can actually afford a vast variety of household items. On the other hand, lifestyle consumption differentiation is still visible at the point when income levels pass the median. Still, a great share of households that fall below the median income level are virtually denied consumption options. This factor alone becomes an obstacle for the formation of a consumer society in Russia.

Quite naturally, if people do not earn more than half the median income and cannot even afford basic kitchen appliances or a computer for their child, they will not concern themselves with lofty material ideals quite as often. They instead aspire to meet daily survival goals and gain access to whatever may aid them in doing so,

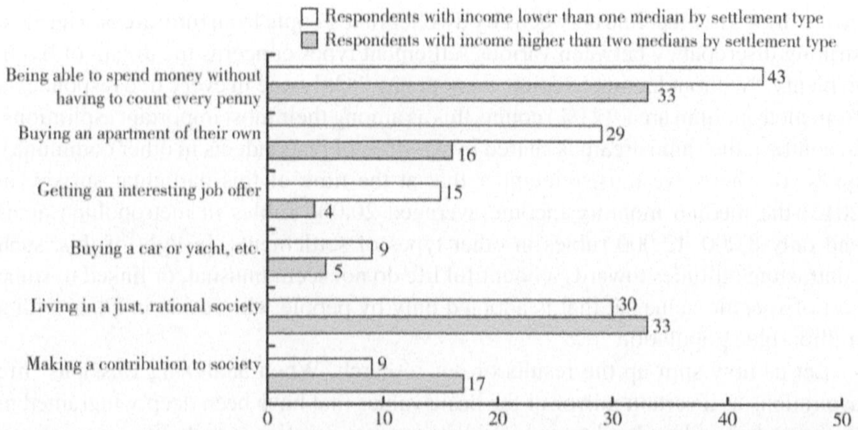

Fig. 4.9 The popularity of certain dreams in the lowest and highest income groups in Russia, 2012, %

such as achieving a good (well paying) job (Fig. 4.9). At the same time, it is interesting to review aspirations that are connected to personal life but are not strongly linked to income. As it turns out, these types of aspirations occur at almost exactly the same rate across all income groups, even polar opposites. For example, when it comes to dreaming of an interesting life, the shares of respondents from the lowest and highest income groups differ by a mere one or two percent (21% and 20% respectively). The same is true of dreams to start a business (15% and 16% respectively) and raise good children (25% and 24%), among quite a number of others.

Thus, the life aspirations of Russian citizens do not differ quite as much, even in polar opposite income groups. This yet again validates our previous finding that, important though material values are, for many Russians they are still not a dominant part of their value system. What is more, this indicates that the national culture, in particular the set of norms and standards that shapes Russians' dreams, still remains highly homogeneous in many respects. Of course, individual circumstances, including financial status, do bear some weight in a Russian citizen's notion of an ideal life, but the influence is still minimal and does not touch the core of Russians' life aspirations, even within polar opposite income groups (i.e., in a review of social groups en masse).

This consensus, this integral unity of national culture, as reflected in Russians' life aspirations, also becomes apparent when we analyze the specific features of desires across various social groups that are singled out according to some other criteria than income. Though in this case Russians' desires are also somewhat affected by day-to-day issues, the differences that arise are still not substantial. Instead, they merely reflect the specific life circumstances within a given social group, and do not reveal any fundamental, quintessential contrast in Russians' basic value sets. For instance, studies of life aspirations in different settlements show certain nuances that distinguish respondents who live in metropolitan areas from all others. However they do not draw a distinct line between city dwellers and people from rural areas. The most striking discrepancy between various settlement types concerns the dream of living in plenty, "without having to count every penny." Only one in every five respondents from metropolitan areas (21%) counts this as among their most important aspirations. In contrast, the same dream is shared by 41–46% of respondents in other community types. But here, we must remember that at the time of this particular survey (in 2012) the median monthly income averaged 20,000 rubles in metropolitan areas and only 8,000–12,000 rubles in other types of settlements. In light of this, such contrasting attitudes towards a bountiful life do not seem unusual, or linked to some sort of specific value set that is adopted only by people who reside in cities with a million-plus population.

Let us now sum up the results of our research. When analyzing Russians' life aspirations as a certain mirror of the basic values that have been deeply ingrained in their mindset and are hard or impossible to put into practice in daily life, one may say that the foundations of Russian national culture still remain highly homogeneous. No matter which principles we use to divide the Russian population into a number of social groups, the main "dream set" remains almost unchanged, even though the popularity of every specific dream fluctuates somewhat, depending on individual circumstances. Even dreams of a material nature, which are more typical to financially disadvantaged groups, do not differ dramatically if compared to the desire for certain material assets that are expressed within groups with the greatest financial advantage.

These homogeneous life aspirations, however, do not mean that Russians' basic values and corresponding wishes are always exactly the same. To the contrary, one may even say that Russian society is polarized, splitting into two roughly equal groups that share opposite priorities and wishes. Slightly more than a half of all respondents (54–56%) prioritize material assets over other aspects of life. This is hardly surprising. After all, Ronald Inglehart's theory[21] stipulates that a population's priorities are predetermined by social and economic status; the fewer goods people have at their disposal, the more emphasis they put on material values and goals. But even if the situation improves and they gain access to more goods, their value set does not transform overnight. Changes like this need time. This theory also provides a wholesome explanation for Russians' widespread inclination to dream about the material benefits of life.

It is rather surprising, however, that around 50% of Russians do not even mention material values while describing their dreams, irrespective of the generally unsatisfactory quality of life across the country, and of their own objective financial status. Furthermore, while calculating the share of people who are more or less focused on obtaining material value, we have accounted for those who wish to have their own place simply because they do not have it at all (bearing in mind that "having your own roof over your head" is among the most vital necessities of a human being). However, if we do not account for this group, the paradoxical nature of the Russian mindset will become even more apparent, as the figures will then show that even less than half of the country's entire population (46–48%) is focused on material values.

[21] Inglehart and Welzel (2011).

Thus, research reveals that about half of the Russian population does not wish for material benefits. Of the half that do, only a little more than 40% dream about having more money. These findings substantiate the theory that the norms and values of Russian culture are still more focused on intangible assets, as they have always been. In most cases, Russians' motivations are still not too affected by the ongoing trend of commodification, and to the extent that they are, material priorities are largely accompanied by other, intangible values. Only a small share of Russians (5%) has "nothing but money" on their minds.

While attempting to interpret Russians' microlevel dreams (i.e. dreams related to their day-to-day life) it is also crucial to bear in mind that there are two completely different processes currently influencing the proliferation of desires for material benefits. For some Russians (that is, the majority of those who dream of living in plenty), these wishes reflect the burning issue of survival, the objective challenges that Russians face when looking for housing, and the scant amount of household appliances they can afford. For others, i.e. the people that are seemingly well-to-do, wishes for material objects are influenced by the fundamentally new standard of living that is emerging in Russia, with consumption patterns mimicking those in more developed countries. This latter population group is the only one that can be described in terms of consumption society ideals and values gaining a foothold in Russia. At the same time, even within this group, the increasing consumption is overwhelmingly "thing-focused." That is, people are willing to go to any lengths to acquire new durable goods, even if it means sacrificing investments into their own personal development. This is an important factor to consider when analyzing the future social and economic development of Russia, as well as the country's competitiveness in the international arena. This approach to consumption greatly accelerates the growth of the trade sector, which mostly imports goods from abroad, but stunts the development of the social service sector, which operates almost entirely within the country.

All of the above allows us to conclude that so far, Russians are not falling under influences of the processes that have been in place for the past few years, including the growing priority of material values and wealth, the commercialization of non-commercial sides of life, the expansion of consumption opportunities, and the introduction of new consumption standards across various social strata. On the one hand, this is connected to the peculiarities of Russian national culture; on another, the modest lifestyle of most Russians greatly hinders the rise of a full-fledged consumer society and the strengthening of the corresponding norms and values. In addition, the consumption fever that has evidently been affecting Russians over the past two decades is mostly nothing more than a psychological reflex that followed a lengthy period of deprivation (first, during Soviet times when there were notorious shortages, and subsequently during the 1990s, when stores started filling up with goods but the people had no money to buy them with). However, when we look at a small share of the population (mostly upper middle-class city-dwellers), we witness the first inklings of a consumption society, characterized by a number of tell-tale signs, including commodification, the promotion of purchasing diverse ranges of goods as part of a successful lifestyle, and more. Yet, this process has barely begun, and the general notion that Russian society is turning into a consumption society is still premature.

References

Inglehart, R., and C. Welzel. 2011. Modernization, Cultural Change and Democracy: The Human Development Sequence. Moscow, Novoye Izdatelstvo. [Cited by the Russian translation.].
Tikhonova N.E. 2014. Russia's Social Structure: Theories and Reality. Moscow: Novy Khronograf. [in Russian].

Chapter 5
Developing a Society of Stable and Secure Employment

I. O. Tyurina

According to the results of the national census in 2010, nearly 66 million people (or 91%) of economically active Russian citizens aged 15–72 were employed in the economy. During the years since the previous national census in 2002, the economic activity of Russians increased by 6.1%. This growth was due to the increase in the share of the working population and simultaneous reduction in the number of unemployed.[1] Official statistics (Table 5.1) also report that even at the height of the 2008–2009 global financial crisis, which inevitably led to consequential job cuts, the national labor market remained rather "vigorous." This did not change even during the latest Russian crisis of 2014–2015.

Moreover, according to the 2010 census, the vast majority of those employed in economic activity—61.6 million people or 94%—worked as wage workers. Compared with 2002, the number of wage workers increased by 5.8%. The number of employers hiring wage workers for their operations amounted to 1.4 million at that time (in 2002, there were 923,000).[2] As of March 2015, the related figures have slightly altered, though no fundamental changes have occurred—the number of wage workers employed in economic activity employment amounted to 66.6 million

[1] *Demoscope Weekly* (2011).
[2] *Demoscope Weekly* (2011).
[3] Russian Federal State Statistics Service. Official website. Population Survey on Employment Issues—2015. Table "Structure of the Employed Population According to Status at the Main Job" and "Employed Population According to Status at the Main Job" (http://www.gks.ru/bgd/regl/b15_30/Main.htm).

The original version of this chapter was revised: Affiliation has been updated in this chapter. The correction to this chapter can be found at
https://doi.org/10.1007/978-981-16-2505-3_19

I. O. Tyurina (✉)
Institute of Sociology of FCTAS RAS, Moscow, Russia

P. Li and M. K. Gorshkov (eds.), *Life Expectations of the People*,
Research Series on the Chinese Dream and China's Development Path,
https://doi.org/10.1007/978-981-16-2505-3_5

Table 5.1 Economically active population of the Russian Federation, 2001–2015, thousand people[4]

Figures	2001	2003	2005	2007	2009	March, 2015
Economically active population, including:	71,411	72,835	73,811	75,060	75,658	76,148
employed in the economy	65,124	67,152	68,603	70,814	69,285	71,645
unemployed	6288	5683	5208	4246	6373	4503

Note According to sampling population survey on employment issues

people (92.9%) and 0.9 million people were counted as employers (the others were self-employed).[3]

Translated into the language of sociology, these official statistics indicate that almost all Russians go to work and spend most of their lives working. Moreover, for the majority of Russians, a job means not only money, but also self-affirmation, the opportunity to feel wanted, to realize their ideas, and also, an opportunity to communicate with colleagues. Only few are willing to give up all of the above mentioned. This is indicated, in particular, by the results of a survey of the economically active population of the Russian Federation over 18, conducted in October 2008 by the research center of SuperJob.ru portal. According to this survey, the prospect of receiving a salary without working attracted only a quarter of respondents, while 66% were definitely not ready to give up their job.[5]

Thus, one's *job is one of the most important areas of daily life for Russian citizens and consistently ranks among their most important priorities.*[6] Russians' desires of all kinds relate to the search for the ideal job, as well as identification of areas of professional activity which Russian citizens consider dream jobs for themselves or their children. What is this "dream job" for Russians?

First, one should note that *the task of creating a society of stable and secure employment in the country as a whole has already been successfully implemented, and stable and secure work for Russians is rather a stan*dard than an ultimate dream. Year to year unemployment rates, according to data from the Russian Federal State Statistics Service, are quite low (Table 5.1). Even in the context of the 2014–2015economic crisis, less than 30% of Russians identified unemployment as among the five most disturbing problems in Russia.[7] Moreover, though in these difficult conditions half of the employed expected to become unemployed within the next year, in context of

[4] Work and employment in Russia. [Trud i zanyatost v Rossii]. 2011: Statistics digest. M.: Russian Federal State Statistics Service (Rosstat), 2011. p. 31 and also: Russian Federal State Statistics Service. Official website. Population Survey on Employment Issues—2015. Table "Economically Active and Economically Inactive Population Aged 15–72" (http://www.gks.ru/bgd/regl/b15_30/Main.htm)

[5] Ref.: http://www.hr-life.ru/news/1721.

[6] See e.g.: Anikin (2009), Tikhonova (2010), Tyurina (2011).

[7] 2015 data is based on the second wave of the monitoring survey, which was carried out in April of 2015 by the RAS Sociology Institute and involved a nation-wide sampling of 4000 people, who represented the population of every region and were subdivided by gender, age, and community

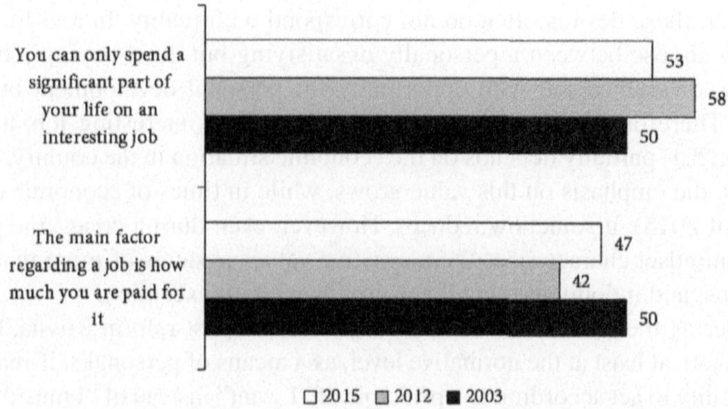

Fig. 5.1 Specific features of attitudes of Russians 55 and under towards a job, 2003, 2012, 2015, %

the crisis, three-quarters of those who had lost their job almost immediately found a new one, according to a survey in April 2015. So even in this difficult period, stable employment remained for the vast majority of the population.

In terms of working conditions, the situation in Russia has also been improving gradually, although it is still absolutely necessary to continue the struggle for the improvement of labor safety. According to statistics, the occurrence rate of fatal industrial injuries between 2001 and 2013 in the Russian Federation fell by half—from 15 to 8 people per 100,000 workers. The occurrence rate of non-fatal industrial injuries reduced even more significantly—from 482 to 159 people per 100 thousand workers for the same period.[8] However, these results are partially due to the fact that in the last quarter of the century, the share of office and commercial employment has increased while the number of employees engaged in more dangerous manual labor industries, including manufacturing, transportation and construction, has decreased.

Despite the relatively satisfactory situation with employment stability and worker safety in Russia, topics related to one's job have not disappeared from the life aspirations of the country's residents. In 2012, one in every four Russians of working age included a job-related desire among their three major personal life aspirations. For most of the respondents, it was a dream of initiating their own business, but one-third dreamed of landing a "good job."

What do Russians mean by a "good job?" According to the stereotypes which are typical for Russian citizens, "a dream job" should provide an opportunity to fulfill one's potential (Fig. 5.1) while at the same time pay enough money so that one's family can live comfortably. In other words, a "dream job" is a kind of "business hobby" that not only brings moral satisfaction, but also a decent income.

type. The survey was funded by a Russian Science Foundation grant (project No. 14–28-00,218, project leader M.K. Gorshkov).

[8] Ref.: Russian Federal State Statistics Service. Official website. Section "Labor Market, Employment and Wages". Table "Indicators of Decent Labor" (http://www.gks.ru/wps/wcm/connect/rosstat_main/rosstat/ru/statistics/wages).

However, these desires often do not correspond with reality. In real-life, people often must choose between a personally unsatisfying but good-paying job, and an interesting, diversified job with opportunity for personal development but that is low-paid. Therefore, the prevalence of the value on an interesting job, as can be seen in Fig. 5.1, partially depends on the economic situation in the country. In stable conditions, the emphasis on this value grows, while in times of economic crisis (as in spring of 2015), it somehow reduces. However, even during crises, the presence of such a mindset characterizes the normative values systems of more than half of all Russians, and it dominates in all age groups without exception.

Considering the above data, it can be stated that in post-reform Russia, Russians perceive a job, at least at the normative level, as a means of personal self-realization, an opportunity to act according to a principle of "I want" instead of "I must." In other words, a job is a means of obtaining satisfaction sometimes even without any strong relation to the level of remuneration.

One should note that even such potential differentiating factors as place of residence, type of settlement and social and professional affiliation have almost no effect on this perception of a job. Russians at the normative level focus primarily on the desire to have an interesting job, almost completely irrespective of the above-mentioned characteristics. The only exception is wage workers, in which wages factor much more importantly than the nature and content of the produced work. Representatives of other kinds of employment focus primarily on having an interesting job. Heads and deputy heads of enterprises and institutions place the lowest value on salary amount. Roughly 70% of them are convinced that the extent to which their job is interesting is a much more important factor. Specialists in positions requiring higher education have similar ideas.

A rather significant factor influencing the standard attitudes of Russians toward their job is their education level (Fig. 5.2).

As Fig. 5.2 shows, the emphasis on having an interesting job increases with the level of education. Those with higher education, especially those with two higher education degrees, have the highest rates of valuing interest over income when it comes to a job. For those who value income as the primary factor in a job, the opposite trend holds true.

Assessment of one's personal financial situation significantly and rather reasonably affects the choice in this situation. The more well-off a Russian feels, the more he or she will agree that the main priority in choosing a job should be the level to which the job interests them (67, 58, and 48% in the groups assessing financial security as "good", "satisfactory" and "bad" respectively as of 2012). A decrease in level of wealth increases the share of those who emphasize income as a primary factor in selecting a job (33, 42, and 52% respectively).

However, when it comes to real-life circumstances, and not just general attitudes, Russians' daily preferences in choosing a job show that most Russians take off their "rose-colored glasses" and "come back to earth." As Fig. 5.3 shows, when we transition from a question of "should" to actual personal situations, Russians place much more significance on the role of a good income. However, the content of the job in this case still remains important for most.

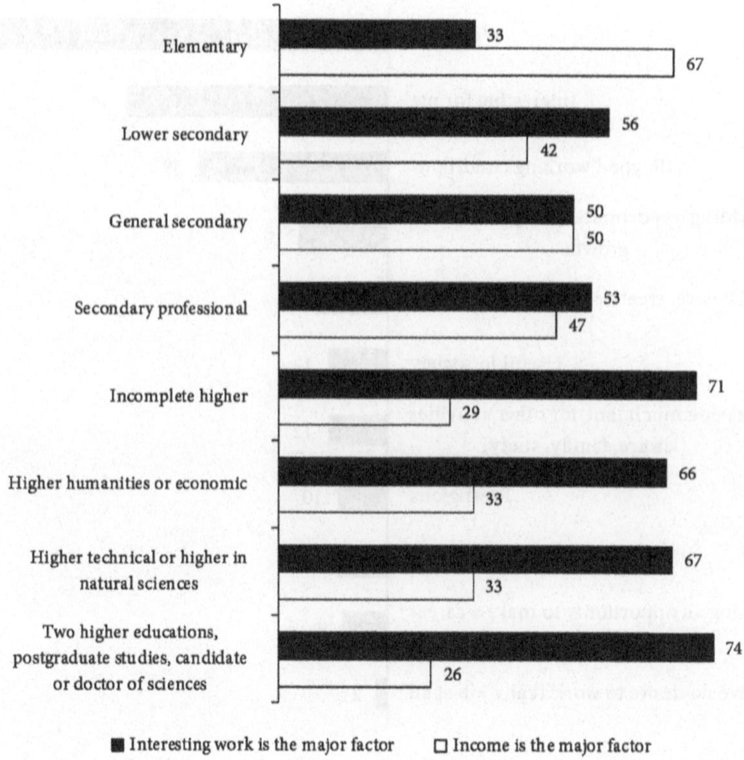

Fig. 5.2 Specific features of attitudes towards jobs of Russians aged 55 and under based on education level, 2012, %

According to the perspectives of Russian survey respondents, the ideal job is defined by three main characteristics: salary, content-involving the predetermined capability of the work to be interesting- and good working conditions. In other words, the majority of Russians dream of having a well-paying job that is interesting to them and is carried out in a comfortable environment. The prevalent desire among Russians to be well-paid for one's work does not depend on gender, age or place of residence (Table 5.2).

Data in Table 5.2 show that while general trends are similar, the significance of each of the three criteria for the ideal job varies among different age and community groups. The emphasis on high income is more specific for rural residents. While urban residents acknowledge the importance of a well-paying job, they are less demanding in this respect. The pattern is similar situation when it comes to good working conditions. The distinct territorial differentiation of quantitative and qualitative employment figures that is common in the modern Russian labor market is thus reflected in the collective consciousness of Russians. Data provided in Table 5.2 more clearly demonstrates the presence of tight and depressive segments within the modern Russian labor market, which sharply limit employment opportunities and

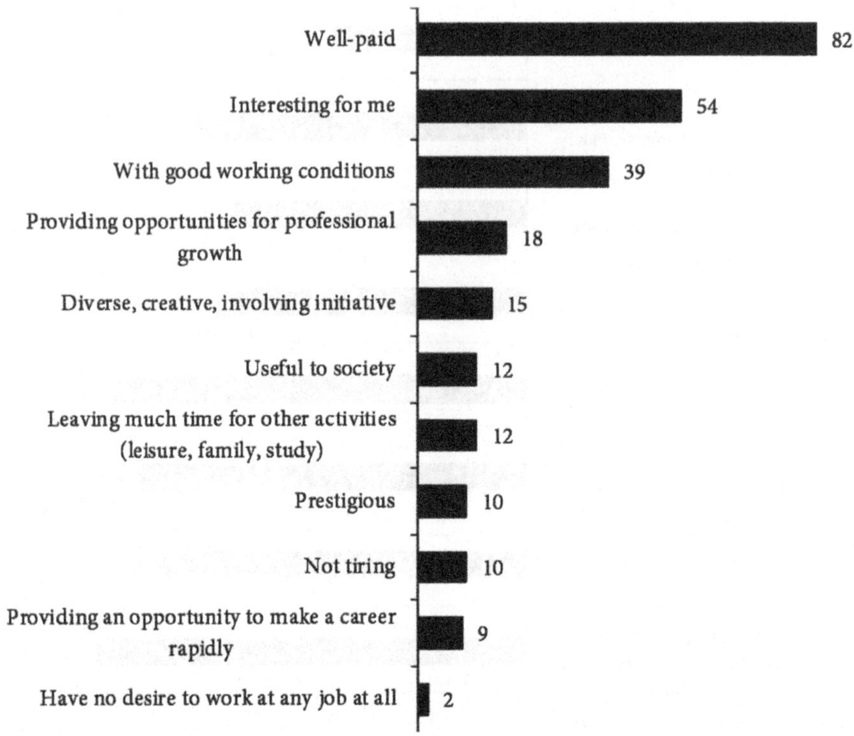

Fig. 5.3 What is an ideal job according to Russians age 55 and under, 2012, % (up to three answers were allowed)

the availability of high-paying jobs. The data presented in Table 5.2 also suggests that the requirements for the ideal job differ among older and younger generations, making age another differentiating factor. As one ages, the importance of rapid career and professional growth, as well as the "prestige" of a job, decreases while demand for better working conditions grows.

Some typical deviations in the general rating of the criteria for an ideal job are also found across different social and professional groups. For instance, entrepreneurs typically put forward high income (81%) and an ability to generate interest (56%) as two key conditions an ideal job. "Usefulness to society," is the third top ranked criterion for entrepreneurs (31%), while good working conditions and prestige are tied for fourth position, each valued by 25% of respondents in this professional group. People employed in trade and consumer services, to the contrary, consider working conditions more significant and therefore rank this second (50%) in importance after a good income (85%). Semi-skilled workers, such as students at technical schools, colleges, high schools and lyceums students, pay much more attention to the prestige factor than to working conditions. For this reason, prestige is the third top characteristic for the ideal job for this group (23%). The importance of career opportunities at the workplace is slightly higher than the average overall rate for heads and deputy

Table 5.2 Characteristics of the "ideal job" by representatives of different social groups, 2012, % of relevant groups of Russians age 55 and under (up to three answers were admitted)

What requirements should be met by an ideal job?	**Age**			
	18–25	26–35	36–45	46–55
Interesting for them	**66.1**	**53.0**	**48.0**	46.2
Provides an opportunity for rapid career advancement	14.6	7.3	6.6	4.4
Provides opportunities for professional growth	23.7	22.5	13.4	11.6
Diverse, creative, involves initiative	15.6	14.1	16.0	14.8
Useful to society	10.4	10.5	14.6	14.1
Well-paying	**77.1**	**82.3**	**84.2**	83.7
Has good working conditions	**29.9**	**34.8**	**44.5**	47.9
Prestigious	15.8	10.9	7.8	5.4

(continued)

Table 5.2 (continued)

Leaves time for other activities (leisure, family, study)	10.8	14.1	9.4	16.0
Not tiring	7.5	9.8	10.8	11.6
What requirements should be met by an ideal job?	**Gender**			
	Male		Female	
Interesting for them	**51.8**		**55.5**	
Provides an opportunity for rapid career advancement	10.9		6.4	
Provides opportunities for professional growth	17.1		18.9	
Diverse, creative, involves initiative	13.6		16.4	
Useful to society	12.8		11.8	
Well-paying	**80.7**		**82.5**	

(continued)

Table 5.2 (continued)

Has good working conditions	**37.4**	**40.0**
Prestigious	10.0	10.4
Leaves time for other activities (leisure, family, study)	10.4	14.2
Not tiring	9.8	9.9

Requirements of the "Ideal Job" by Representatives of Different Social Groups, 2012, % of Relevant Groups of Russians Age 55 and Under (up to three answers were admitted)

What requirements should be met by an ideal job?	**Localities**						
	City with a population over 1 million	City with a population of 500,000–1 million	City with a population of 250,000–500,000	City with a population of 100,000–250,000	Town with a population of under 100,000	Urban settlement	Rural settlements
Interesting for them	**48.9**	**63.6**	**58.2**	**53.3**	**58.5**	50.5	50.3
Provides an opportunity for rapid career advancement	11.0	10.2	7.7	11.3	6.2	4.5	7.7

(continued)

Table 5.2 (continued)

Provides opportunities for professional growth	24.3	20.3	16.5	22.7	18.5	19.8	10.6
Diverse, creative, involves initiative	15.2	17.6	25.3	22.0	11.8	14.4	12.7
Useful to society	12.3	15.0	6.6	19.3	8.1	8.1	14.1
Well-paying	**74.3**	**78.1**	**85.7**	**88.0**	**81.5**	78.4	86.9
Has good working conditions	**35.0**	**40.1**	**35.2**	**30.7**	**39.2**	39.6	44.1
Prestigious	9.4	8.6	11.0	12.7	7.8	9.0	12.7
Leaves time for other activities (leisure, family, study)	14.7	15.0	16.5	6.0	12.9	13.5	10.6
Not tiring	10.7	3.2	11.0	8.7	9.0	6.3	13.3

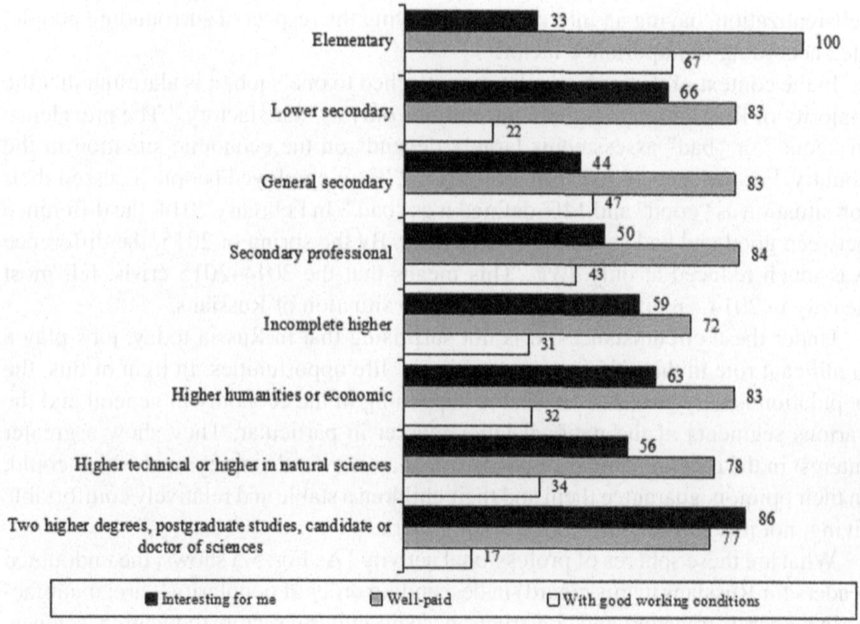

Fig. 5.4 Characteristics of the ideal job among Russians aged 55 and under based on education level, 2012, %

heads of enterprises and institutions, specialists in positions requiring higher education, the self-employed, as well as students of higher and secondary educational institutions (29, 7, 18, 21, and 32% respectively).

Education level also has a significant impact on the ideal job criteria as rated by Russians. While there is overall dominance at the normative level of emphasis on income and the "interesting nature" of work (Fig. 5.4), higher education increases the importance of the interesting nature of work as the top criterion of an ideal job. As a result, the share of those who believe that the work should be interesting is slightly higher in higher-educated groups than the normal rate common to all Russians in general. Among those who have two higher degrees (i.e. postgraduate degree like a master's degree or doctoral degree) this characteristic significantly "shoots ahead," leaving behind both income and good working conditions. Moreover, highly educated Russians are more likely to appreciate jobs that provide opportunities for professional growth.

One more aspect is worth attention—as noted above, one's job is a sufficiently high priority for Russians. In a March 2015 survey, one's job scored a 3.9 point average on a 5-point scale of importance (where 5 points stood for "very important" and 1 point "not important at all"). Only aspects such as financial well-being, life in a fair and reasonably organized society, health and friends scored higher among a total of eighteen measured life aspects. In this survey, one's job outscored family, self-realization, having an interesting life, having the respect of surrounding people, etc., according to importance factor.

In the context of the high significance attached to one's job, it is alarming that the majority of Russians assess their current jobs only as "satisfactory." The prevalence of "good" or "bad" assessments largely depends on the economic situation in the country. For instance, in the spring of 2015, 27% of employed people assessed their job situation as "good" and 14% defined it as "bad". In February 2014, the difference between good and bad assessments was 33%. By the spring of 2015, the difference was much reduced at only 13%. This means that the 2014–2015 crisis, felt most heavily in 2014, significantly affected the job situation of Russians.

Under these circumstances, it is not surprising that in Russia today, jobs play a significant role in the polarization of citizens' life opportunities. In light of this, the population is very sensitive to what is happening in the economy in general and the various segments of the national labor market in particular. They show a greater interest in the types and areas of professional activity and employment which could, in their opinion, guarantee them and their children a stable and relatively comfortable living, not just substantial and interesting work.

What are these spheres of professional activity? As Fig. 5.5 shows, the undoubted leaders for Russians in this regard -in descending order of popularity—are: manufacturing, energy, transport and construction, socio-cultural sectors (education, science, health and culture), and finance, marketing, consulting, followed by jobs in state and municipal government.

The distribution of respondents by area of activity in which they are engaged at the present time looks rather curious (Fig. 5.6). Comparing the data from Fig. 5.6 with the ratings of activity areas considered desirable work, a certain mismatch between jobs that are "available" and "desirable" is revealed.

With rare exceptions, personal preferences regarding various spheres of employment remain almost unaffected by characteristics such as gender, age, place of residence and occupation. However, some distinctions among various groups in this area can still be identified. For instance, young people aged 18–25 are more likely to desire a job in finance, credit, insurance, marketing, etc. areas (26%), while Russians aged 46–55 prefer employment in manufacturing, energy, transport and construction areas (28%). In general, the share of those who desire a job in the manufacturing industry increases with age, while those who desire a job in finance or consulting decreased with age. In this sense the findings are rather consistent with the realities of the modern Russian labor market, where the youth focus mainly on areas where there is already a personnel surplus. The manufacturing industry, despite its demand for professional workers, remains beyond the sphere of interest.

In terms of gender distribution, men are more likely to desire work in certain sectors such as manufacturing, energy, transport and construction (43%); army, police, security and other law enforcement agencies (16%); and information technology and communications (15%). Women are more likely to dream of a career in the sphere of education, health, science and culture (36%); as well as finance, credit, marketing, etc. (18%).

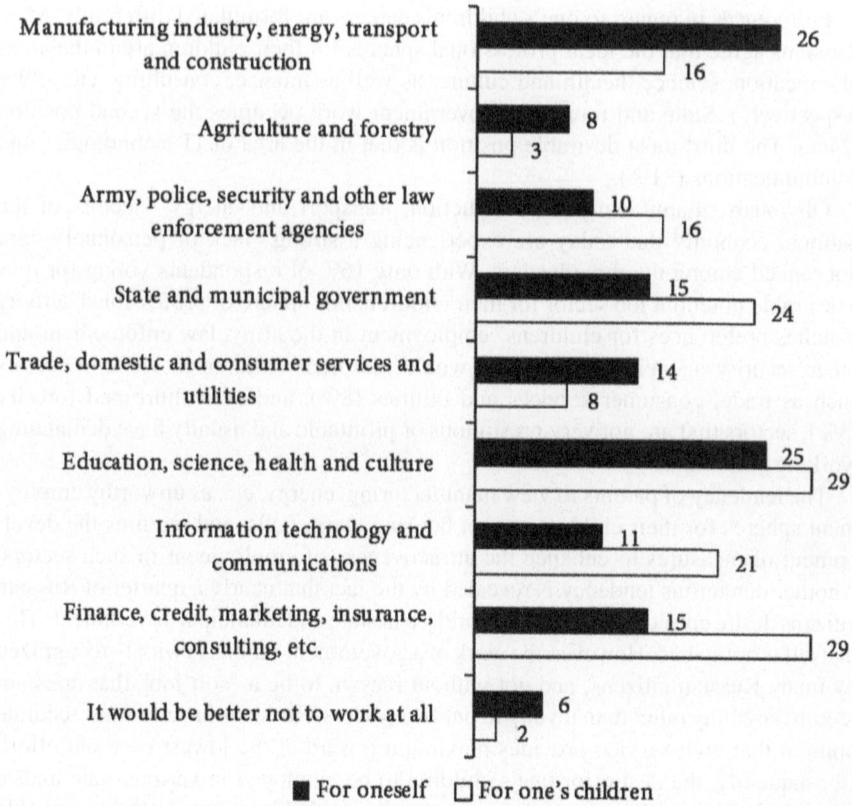

Fig. 5.5 Spheres of professional activity which Russians consider desirable to work in for themselves and their children, 2012, % of Russians aged 55 and under (*Note* Up to three answers were allowed when choosing "personal desires" and "preferences for children". The figure does not account for those who responded "I am not sure")

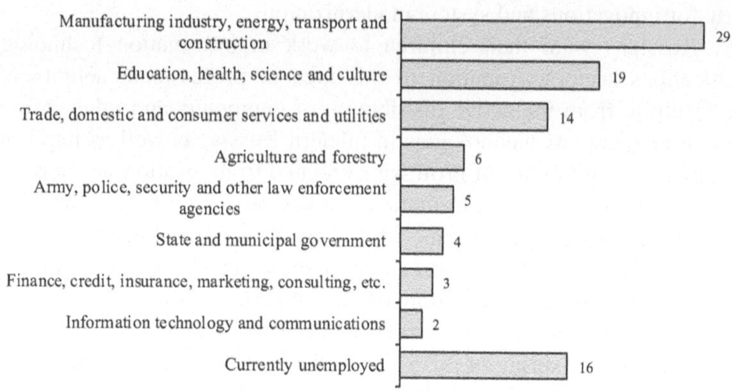

Fig. 5.6 Distribution of the Russians in the spheres of professional activity, self-esteem, 2012, % of Russians up to 55 inclusive (*Note* The figure does not account for those who responded "Other")

Preferences in regard to one's children's careers are formulated differently. Most Russians agree that the ideal professional spheres for their children are in the areas of education, science, health and culture, as well as finance, consulting, etc. (29% respectively). State and municipal government work occupies the second position (24%). The third most desirable position is that in the area of IT-technologies and communications (21%).

Obviously, manufacturing, construction, transport and energy—sectors of the national economy that today are experiencing a strong "lack of personnel"—are not ranked among the three leaders. With only 16% of respondents voting for it as a desirable potential job sector for their children, this sphere of professional activity matches preferences for childrens' employment in the army, law enforcement and other security agencies. Even fewer would like their children to work in sectors such as trade, consumer services and utilities (8%), and agriculture and forestry (3%), sectors that are not very prestigious or profitable and usually have demanding working conditions.

The tendency of parents to view manufacturing, energy, etc. as unworthy employment spheres for their children cannot but ring alarm bells, and requires the development of measures to enhance the attractiveness of employment in such sectors. Another dangerous tendency is revealed by the fact that nearly a quarter of Russian citizens desire employment for their children in state and municipal government. This in itself is not so bad. However, the work of a government official is widely recognized by many Russian citizens, and not without reason, to be a "soft job" that does not require anything other than loyalty to one's superiors. Russians have a rather accurate opinion that civil service provides maximum reward at the lowest cost and effort. Consequently, the desire for one's children to be employed in various state and/or municipal administrative structures is generally guided by a simple and reasonable (of course, on the individual level) formula: "One may work in government service, receive a guaranteed salary, social status, a certain power and be responsible for nothing." In this regard one cannot but agree with the common opinion of national experts: a society whose members on a mass scale seek to get to the civil service is not ready for innovations and system modernization.

Many Russians want their children to work in information technology and communications sectors. Attention to this area of professional activity is quite natural, resulting from the active distribution of computers and other information and telecommunications technologies in modern Russia, as well as the growth of the prestige and profitability of professions related to innovation development and creative work. Realizing that information is a key resource of the future has influenced the choice of Russian citizens: while only 11% of respondents desired a job in the sphere of IT-technologies, this share increases nearly by half (21%) when it comes to similar preferences regarding one's children.

How do Russians view their own achievements in areas related to their professional activities? Even in the spring of 2015 (i.e. in the midst of the economic crisis), the majority of employed Russians (52%) defined their ability to realize themselves in their profession as "satisfactory," 30% described it as "good" and 18% as "bad." Yet, Fig. 5.7 shows that the ability to engage in prestigious and interesting work is

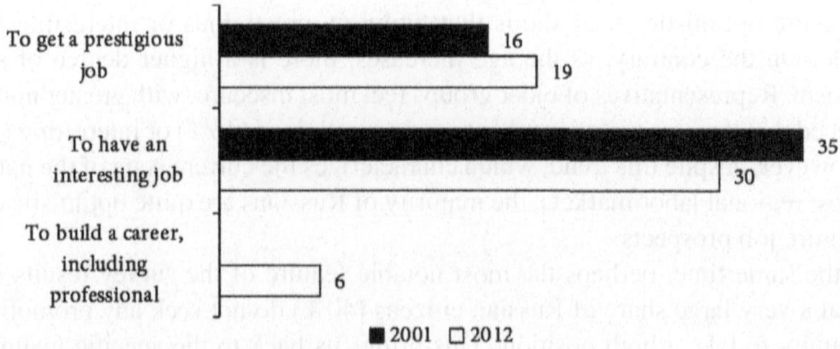

Fig. 5.7 Dynamics of professional achievements (areas in which Russians have already achieved what they want to achieve, according to self-assessments), 2001/2012, % of Russians 55 and under (*Note* In 2001, the question did not include the desire to "build a career")

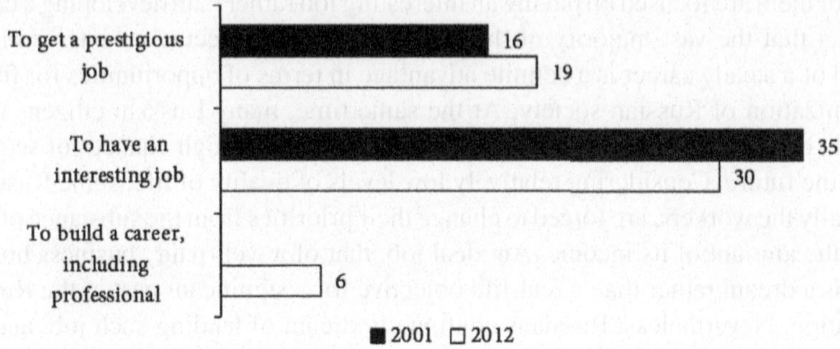

Fig. 5.8 Dynamics of professional achievements (areas in which Russians believe they can achieve, according to self-assessments) % of Russians age 55 and under, 2001/2012 (*Note* In 2001, the question did not include the desire to "build a career")

specific to a relative minority of Russians. One may note that in 2001 the situation was similar.

Success in the search for an interesting and prestigious job is determined by a combination of socio-demographic, socio-economic and geographical factors. For instance, the majority (three-quarters) of entrepreneurs with wage workers as employees consider their job to be both prestigious and interesting. For heads and deputy heads of institutions, the majority evaluated their jobs as interesting, while almost half also considered their jobs as prestigious.

While Russians in other fields of work have skeptical attitudes toward their achievements in securing prestigious and interesting jobs, over a third of them (37%) still believe that they are capable of eventually achieving career success (Fig. 5.8).

The younger generation prevails amongst Russian citizens with an optimistic attitude towards their future achievements, especially those aged 18–25. In general, the age factor significantly determines the degree of optimism of Russians regarding opportunities to get a prestigious and/or interesting job. The younger the respondent is, the more optimistic he or she is that finding a prestigious or interesting job is possible. On the contrary, as the age increases, there is a higher degree of social pessimism. Representatives of older groups feel most insecure, with greater numbers convinced that they are no longer able to get a prestigious (46%) or interesting (34%) job. However, despite this trend, which characterizes the current state of the national and most regional labor markets, the majority of Russians are quite optimistic about their future job prospects.

At the same time, perhaps the most notable feature of the survey results is the fact that a very large share of Russian citizens (40%) do not seek any promotion or opportunity to take a high position. This brings us back to the specific features of Russian attitudes regarding their dream job with the characteristics described at the beginning of this chapter.

In summary, the results of our review reveal with surprising steadiness what can be considered a national feature of Russians with respect to their attitudes towards jobs: Many of them are focused on having an interesting job rather than developing a career. The fact that the vast majority of the population aims to secure an interesting job instead of a steady career is a definite advantage in terms of opportunities for further modernization of Russian society. At the same time, many Russian citizens at the moment do not consider their job interesting job, nor have high chances of securing one in the future. Considering relatively low levels of quality of life, some Russians, especially the workers, are forced to change their priorities from the substance of their job to the amount of its income. An ideal job, that of a well-paid "business hobby," remains a dream rather than a real-life objective for a significant part of the Russian population. Nevertheless, Russians continue to dream of landing such job, and this desire is even larger when it comes to their preferences regarding their children. This should be taken into account when developing public policy, in particular, industrial and investment policy of the Russian state.

References

Anikin, V.A. 2009. Job in the Lives of Russians. *Sociological Studies* [Sotsiologicheskie issledovaniya]. Issue 12: 48–55. [in Russian].

Economic activity of the population. 2011. *Demoscope Weekly*. Electronic version of the "Population and society" newsletter. Issue 491–492 (December): 19–31. http://www.demoscope.ru/weekly/2011/0491/perep01.php. [in Russian].

Russian Federal State Statistics Service. Official website. Population Survey on Employment Issues—2015. Table "Economically Active and Economically Inactive Population Aged 15–72". http://www.gks.ru/bgd/regl/b15_30/Main.htm.

Russian Federal State Statistics Service. Official website. Population Survey on Employment Issues—2015. Table "Structure of the Employed Population According to Status at the Main Job" And "Employed Population According to Status at the Main Job". http://www.gks.ru/bgd/regl/b15_30/Main.htm.

Russian Federal State Statistics Service. Official website. Section "Labor Market, Employment and Wages". Table "Indicators of Decent Labor". http://www.gks.ru/wps/wcm/connect/rosstat_main/rosstat/ru/statistics/wages.

Tikhonova, N.E. 2010. *Social and Cultural Modernization: Stage and Prospects Evaluation: Is Russian Society Ready for Modernization?* [Sotsiokulturnaya modernizatsiya: otsenka etapa i perspektiv // Gotovo li rossiyskoe obshchestvo k modernizatsii?], ed. M.K. Gorshkov, R. Krumm, and N. E. Tikhonova, 90–92. Moscow: Ves Mir. [in Russian].

Tyurina, I.O. 2011 Transformation of the Labor Market and Employment Relations. In *Twenty Years of Reforms Through the Eyes of Russians: The Experience of Long-Term Sociological Measurement* [Dvadtsat let reform glazami rossiyan: opyt mnogoletnikh sotsiologicheskikh zamerov], ed. M.K. Gorshkov, R. Krumm, and V.V. Petukhov, 95–128. Moscow: Ves Mir. [in Russian].

Work and employment in Russia in 2011. *Statistical Yearbook 2012*. Moscow: Rosstat. [in Russian].

Chapter 6
Moving Towards a More Content Society in Life and Work

Chunling Li

The "China Dream" is not only the collective dream of becoming a powerful country, but an individual dream of every Chinese person to pursue personal happiness, of which a specific reflection is to live and work in contentment (Li 2013). In modern society, work constitutes the most important aspect of one's life, with one's job serving as a link between personal life and social life. A stable and satisfactory job provides individuals not only with basic economic security, but also a sense of accomplishment and happiness. An equally important dream for millions of Chinese people today is to have a spacious and comfortable residence. This is the number one dream especially for many urban young people, as satisfactory housing has become a materialized indicator of happy family life. Therefore, "happy home" and "happy work" have become the twin foundations of the individual's "China Dream." This chapter analyzes the employment, living conditions, social security, and job satisfaction situation for Chinese people, and the impact job satisfaction has on one's individual sense of happiness, for the purpose of understanding what the "China Dream" is from the individual level.

6.1 The Status of Employment and Unemployment

Employment stability is the most fundamental factor influencing the evaluation of individual work as job insecurity and high unemployment risk affects both job and life satisfaction. According to the 2013 China Social Survey, 74.5% of the Chinese population age 18–60 years have jobs, while 25.5% do not work. Among the unemployed, the highest proportion are students, accounting for nearly one-third (30.7%) on the non-working population. 13.8% of the remaining unemployed are retirees or

C. Li (✉)
Chinese Academy of Social Sciences (CASS), Beijing, China

P. Li and M. K. Gorshkov (eds.), *Life Expectations of the People*,
Research Series on the Chinese Dream and China's Development Path,
https://doi.org/10.1007/978-981-16-2505-3_6

Table 6.1 Employment and unemployment rate of labor force aged 18–60 years (%)

	Employment situation	Reason for unemployment	
Holding a job	80.8		
Jobless	19.2	Work disability	8.8
		Retirement	11.1
		Homemaker	38.0
		Unemployed student after graduation	3.8
		Others	38.3
Total	100		100
	Estimation of unemployment rate	Estimation method of unemployment rate (questions in questionnaire)	
Unemployment rate 1	14.4	If you now have a job, can you go to work in two weeks? (Answer "Yes" is defined as unemployment)	
Unemployment rate 2	7.5	Do you still intend to work? (The answer "Yes" is defined as unemployed)	
Unemployment rate 3	3.9	Are you currently looking for a job? (The answer "Yes" is defined as unemployed)	

those with disabilities, 26.7% are homemakers, 29.2% are unemployed for various other reasons. Excluding students, the proportion of employment and unemployment among those aged 18–60 years is 80.8% and 19.2% respectively, with 42.1% of unemployment resulting from various reasons and underemployed graduates (see Table 6.1).

Table 6.1 shows the estimated unemployment rate of the labor force aged 18–60 years based on three different ways to define unemployment. The International Labor Organization (ILO) defines unemployment as "people with labor ability looking for a job (i.e. the jobless rate 3 in Table 6.1). According to this definition of unemployment, the unemployment rate of the labor force aged 18–60 years in 2013 was 3.9%, which is quite low in comparison with other countries (International Labor Organization 2015). However, in terms of the general understanding of unemployment, the proportion of unemployed people in China is far greater than 3.9%. There are 14.4% (Unemployment rate 1) of people who have the ability to immediately obtain jobs but could not obtain jobs, and 7.5% of people (Unemployment rate 2) would like to have jobs but obtained no jobs. This shows that, in current Chinese society, while the strictly defined unemployment rate is not high, the hidden unemployment is more significant.

The group at most risk of unemployment is young people and women (International Labor Organization 2013). Figure 6.1 compares the proportion of groups across ages and genders with "no jobs" and unemployment. In the female labor force, the proportion (29.1%) with "no jobs" was triple that of men (9.6%). Women

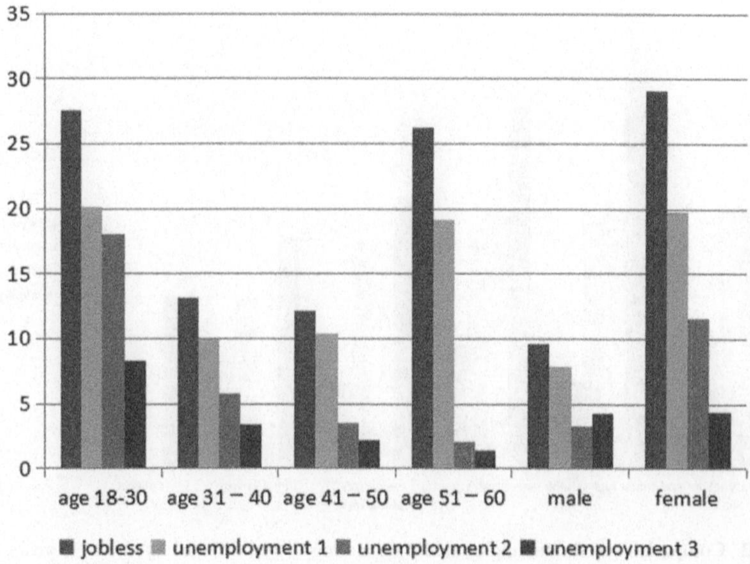

Fig. 6.1 The unemployment rate of groups across ages and genders (%)

accounted for 19.8% of those with the ability to work immediately but could not obtain employment, which is 2.5 times the rate of men. Women accounted for 11.6% of those who wanted to work but were not working, which is 3.5 times that of men. However, the proportion of women who were looking for jobs (4.3%) was similar to that of men (4.2%). This shows that although there is no big difference between men and women under the strictly defined unemployment rate, far greater numbers of women are "invisibly" unemployed. Many women with the capability and desire to work have had to withdraw from the labor market to raise families due to the competitive pressures of employment and gender discrimination in the labor market.

Figure 6.2 shows that the highest percentage of the Chinese population with "no jobs," for each of the three measures of unemployment, belongs to young people aged 18–30 years. 27.6% of 18–30 year olds in the labor force did not work, with 20.1% of those having the ability to immediately obtain jobs but could not obtain jobs (jobless rate 1), 18.1% wanted to work but did not work (jobless rate 2), and 8.3% were looking for jobs but did not find jobs (jobless rate 3). The 31–40 year and 41–50 year age groups (middle-aged people) faced the lowest risk of unemployment, with the share of those with "no jobs" and the unemployment rate at less than half of that of the 18–30 year age group. Among these two "middle-age" groups, the proportion with "no jobs" was 13.1 and 12.1% respectively. Those with the ability to immediately obtain jobs but could not obtain jobs accounted for 9.9 and 10.4%, those who wanted to work but did not work were 5.8 and 3.5% respectively, while those looking for a job accounted for only 3.4 and 2.2% separately. For the 51–60 year old age group (senior people), while a high percentage had no jobs (26.3%), only 2.1%

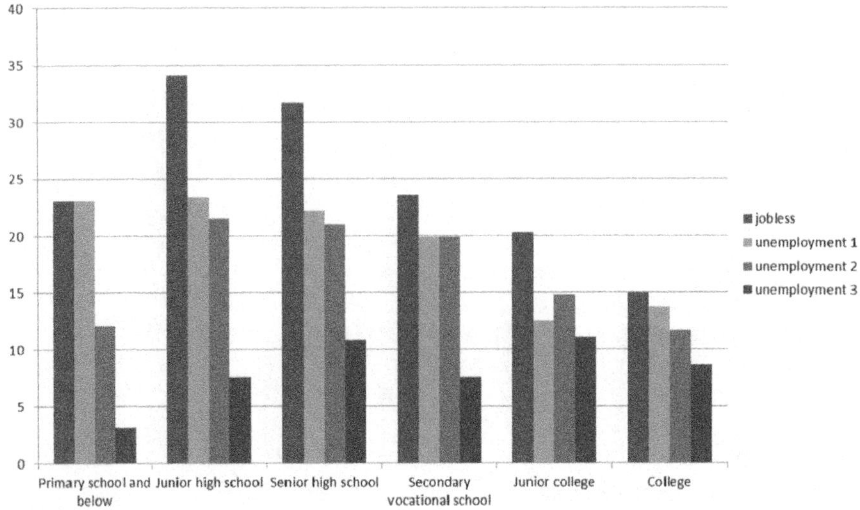

Fig. 6.2 Comparison of the unemployment rate among the labor force aged 18–30 years across educational levels

still wanted to work, and only 1.4% were looking for jobs. This data indicates that China's current unemployment problems mainly concentrate on young people.

For the 18–30 year age group, the unemployment risk varies according to different levels of education and culture. In general, the lower the educational and cultural level, the higher the risk of unemployment. The exception is those with primary school education and lower level of culture. Those with just a junior high school education have the highest proportion of joblessness in this age group, accounting for 34.1%. In other words, more than one-third of junior-high graduates have no jobs after graduation. They are closely followed by senior high school graduates, nearly a third (31.7%) of whom do not have jobs after graduation. Graduates from technical secondary and vocational schools, while considered to have the same secondary educational level as senior high schools, have a far lower rate of "joblessness" than that of senior high school graduates. 20.3% of junior college graduates and 15% of university graduates also "do not work". Surprisingly, graduates of primary schools and lower education levels are not the group with the highest risk of unemployment. Their proportion of joblessness (23.1%) is much lower than that of junior and senior high school graduates, but similar to that of technical secondary and vocational school graduates. Their unemployment rate is also the lowest of the aforesaid groups, with only 3.1% (unemployment rate 3) looking for jobs. Quite different from the trend for "joblessness", lower educational and cultural levels do not indicate a higher unemployment rate. For graduates who have both the ability to obtain and job and desire to work but do not work (unemployment rate 1 and unemployment rate 2), we see higher proportions of joblessness for junior and senior high school graduates than junior college and university graduates, but slightly lower rates than technical secondary school and vocational school graduates. However, there is not much difference in the proportion of graduates who are looking for jobs (unemployment rate 3) among graduates with different education and cultural levels, except for graduates with primary school education or lower. The unemployment rate is 7.6, 10.8, and 7.6% respectively for graduates of junior high school, senior high school, and technical secondary school or vocational high school. The unemployment rate for junior college and college/university graduates is 11.1 and 8.7% respectively. This indicates that although youth with low educational and cultural levels have a high rate of joblessness, they have no urgent intent to find jobs. Less than a quarter of jobless junior high school graduates are looking for jobs, while only one-third of jobless graduates from senior high schools, technical secondary schools and vocational school are looking for jobs. However, more than half of junior college and university graduates are looking for jobs because they have a stronger need or willingness for employment.

6.2 The Higher Job Satisfaction

The personal desire of many Chinese people—and an indispensable part of the China Dream—is not just to find work, but to find a satisfactory job. Figure 6.3 shows the job satisfaction of Chinese employees according to eight aspects on a scale of 1–10, from least satisfactory (1 point) to most satisfactory (10 points). The overall average

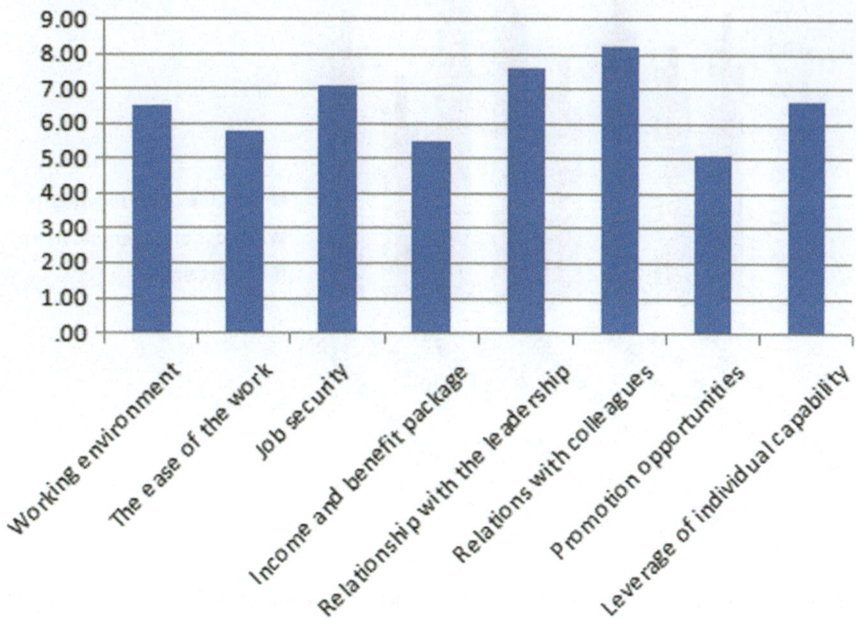

Fig. 6.3 Job satisfaction levels of people aged 18–60 years

score of the satisfaction evaluation across all eight aspects exceeded 5 points, which indicates that people are generally satisfied with their jobs. Among the eight evaluation aspects, the two aspects with the highest scores were "relationship with the leaders" and "relationships with colleagues," with an average rating of 8.2 points and 7.6 points respectively. Chinese people attach great importance to relationships because a good interpersonal relationship is a very important factor impacting job satisfaction and personal happiness. The two aspects with lowest scores were "promotion opportunities" and "income and benefits", rated at 5.1 points and 5.5 points respectively. This indicates that people are less satisfied with their own income and career prospects.

Employment stability has a significant impact on job satisfaction. Figure 6.4 compares the job satisfaction of three different types of employment groups: those with "possible joblessness", those with "stable employment" and those with "uncertain employment or joblessness" in next six months. Employees with "possible joblessness" had the least amount of job satisfaction, followed by those with "uncertain employment or joblessness." Employees with "stable employment" had the highest level of job satisfaction.

Education level also affects people's job satisfaction. Figure 6.5 shows that, in general, the higher the education level, the higher job satisfaction. This appears most

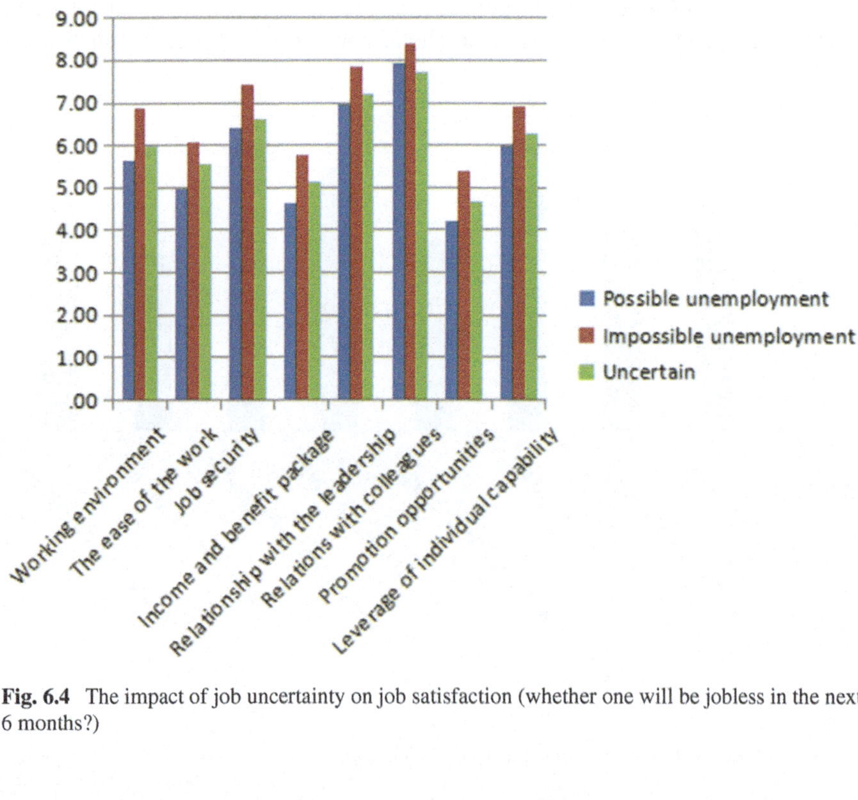

Fig. 6.4 The impact of job uncertainty on job satisfaction (whether one will be jobless in the next 6 months?)

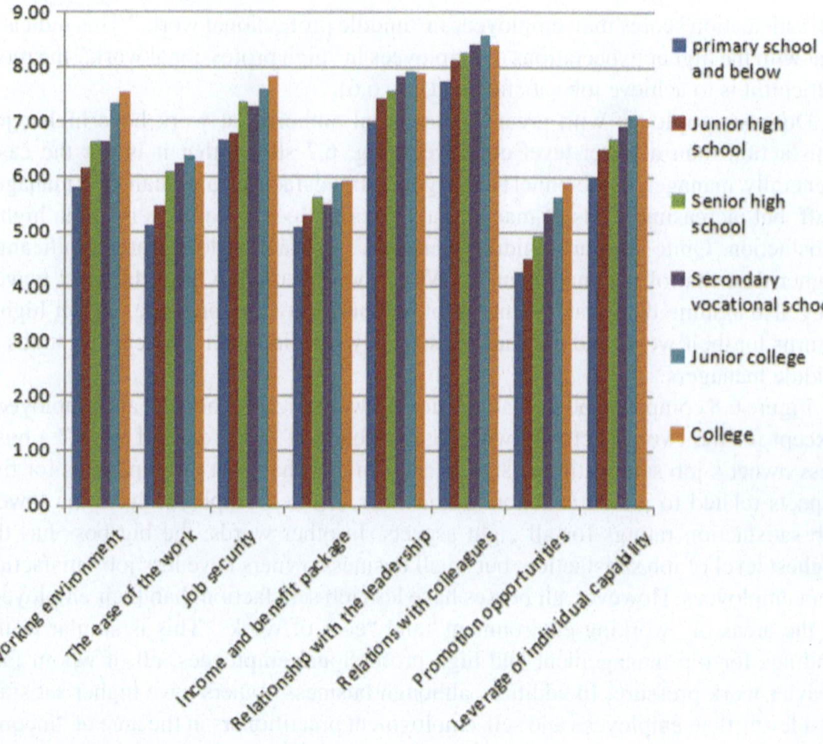

Fig. 6.5 The impact of educational levels on job satisfaction

prominently in the three aspects of "promotion opportunities", "leverage of individual capability" and "working environment." However, higher education does not appear to correlate with a higher evaluation of one's "income and benefit package." Employees with higher levels of education generally have higher expectations for income and benefits. Even if their actual incomes are higher than that of the employees with lower levels of education, their satisfaction levels may not always be higher. Additionally, with respect to relationships with leadership and colleagues and evaluation of "the ease of work," employees with college educations do not show higher satisfaction than those with lower educational levels. This indicates that employees with higher levels of education are satisfied with their own working environment and development prospects, but feel high levels of pressure and competition in their work, and have greater difficulty dealing with interpersonal relations.

One's professional level has a similar effect on job satisfaction as that of education level. The higher one's professional or technical level, the higher the satisfaction with "leveraging of individual capability" and "promotion opportunities." However, higher education levels do not indicate greater satisfaction in the aspects of "the ease of work" and "personal relationships." It is particularly noteworthy that in five of the eight rating aspects, employees in "high professional work" have lower average job satisfaction scores than employees in "middle professional work." This indicates that with the higher expectations of employees in "high professional work," the more difficult it is to achieve job satisfaction (Fig. 6.6).

Does an employee with greater managerial authority at work have higher job satisfaction than a lower-level employee? Fig. 6.7 shows that it is not the case. Generally, managerial personnel have higher job satisfaction rates than their managed staff, but increasing levels of managerial authority does not always result in higher satisfaction. Quite contrary, middle managers' satisfaction levels are significantly higher than that of top management. While those at the top have the most power, they also assume the greatest amount of responsibility and pressure, expect higher returns for their work, and thus are not so easily satisfied with their current status as middle managers.

Figure 6.8 compares the job satisfaction between owners (bosses) and employees. Except for the two aspects of "working environment" and "ease of work," a business owner's job satisfaction is significantly higher than that of employees for five aspects related to job satisfaction. Meanwhile, the self-employed have the lowest job satisfaction ratings for all eight aspects. In other words, the big boss has the highest level of job satisfaction, but small business owners have less job satisfaction than employees. However, all bosses have less job satisfaction than their employees in the areas of "working environment" and "ease of work." This is similar to the findings for top management and high professional employees, all of whom face heavier work pressure. In addition, although business owners have higher satisfaction levels than employees and self-employment practitioners in the area of "income and benefits package," the average score is still less than 6 points, indicating that the

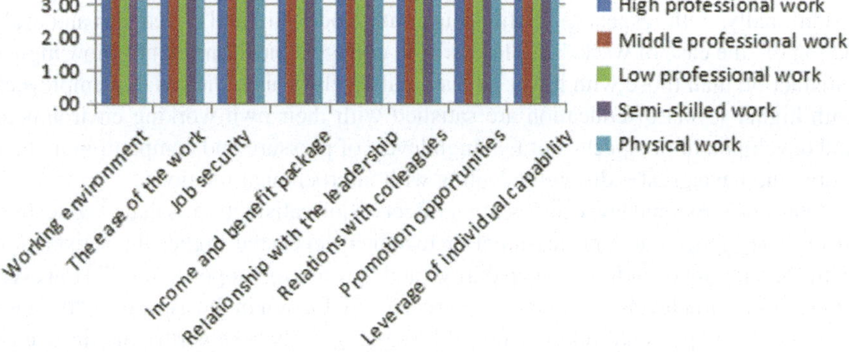

Fig. 6.6 The impact of professional and technical levels on job satisfaction

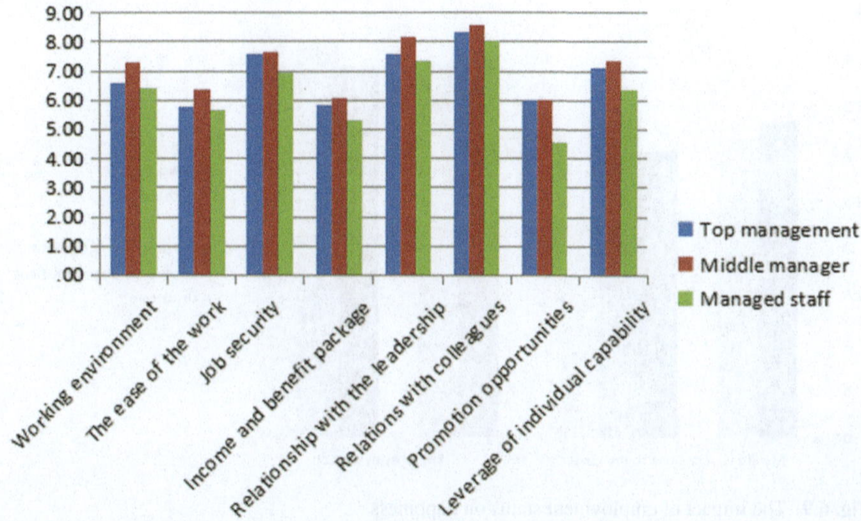

Fig. 6.7 Comparison of job satisfaction among managerial personnel and managed staff

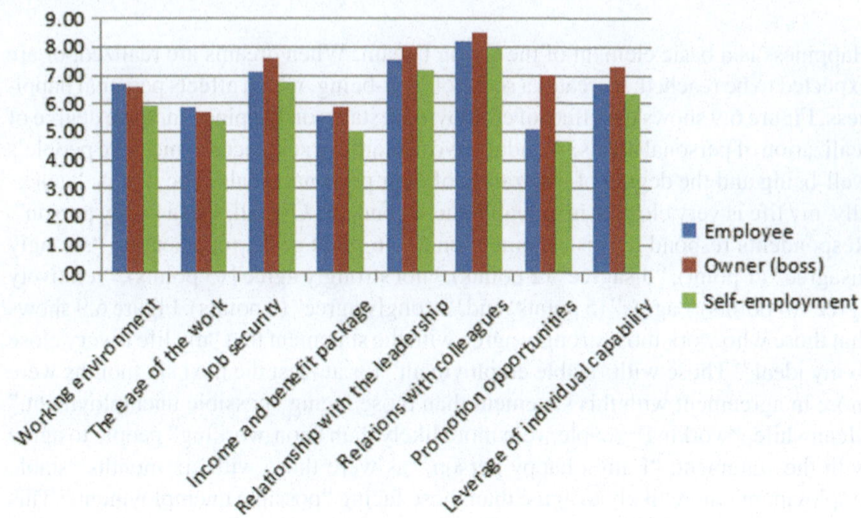

Fig. 6.8 Comparison of job satisfaction between employers and employees

bosses are not very satisfied with their income. Meanwhile, bosses have much higher satisfaction levels than employees and the self-employed in terms of "promotion opportunities," with an average score of slightly more than 7 points. This indicates that they have higher expectations for their career prospects and look forward to earning more money.

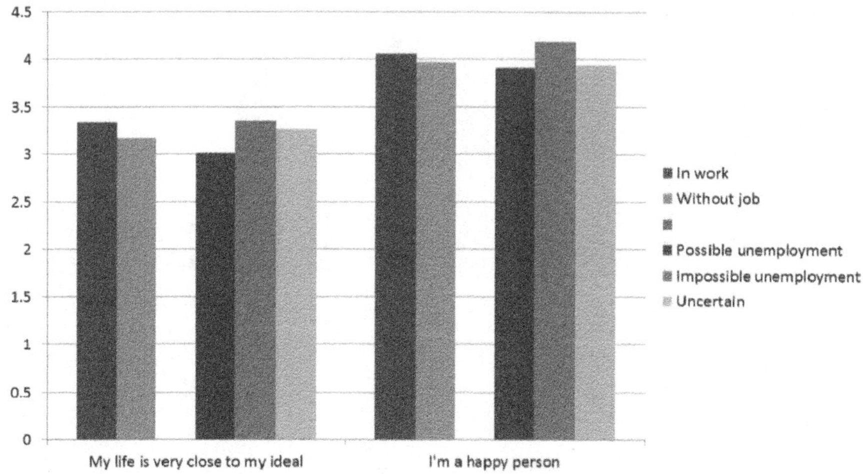

Fig. 6.9 The impact of employment status on happiness

6.3 The Impact of Employment and Jobs on Happiness

Happiness is a basic element of the China Dream. When dreams are realized, or are expected to be reached, it creates a sense of well-being, which affects personal happiness. Figure 6.9 shows the effect of employment status on happiness and the degree of realization of personal ideals. We adopt two declarative sentences to measure people's well-being and the degree of realization of their personal ideals. The first is: "generally, my life is very close to my ideal." The second is: "Overall, I'm a happy person". Respondents respond to this statement on a 1–6 point scale, representing "strongly disagree" (1 point), "disagree" (2 points), "not strongly agree" (3 points), "relatively agree" (4 points), "agree" (5 points) and "strongly agree" (6 points). Figure 6.9 shows that those who work most strongly agree with the statement that "my life is very close to my ideal." Those with "stable employment" for at least the next six months were more in agreement with this statement than those facing "possible unemployment." Meanwhile, "working" people were more likely than "non-working" people to agree with the statement, "I am a happy person," as were those with six months "stable employment" more likely to agree than those facing "possible unemployment." This fully reflects that a stable job can make people feel happier and more able to realize their dreams.

Job satisfaction also affects individual happiness and the degree to which one feels they are achieving their goals. Table 6.2 lists the correlation coefficients in the eight aspects of job satisfaction, indicating the affect these aspects have on people's happiness and realization of life goals and personal ideals. The data shows that the eight aspects of job satisfaction have affected people's happiness and realization of life goals. Among the eight categories of job satisfaction, satisfaction with "income and benefits package" has the greatest impact on one's assessment that "my life

Table 6.2 The impact of job satisfaction on happiness (Pearson correlation coefficient table)

	My life is very close to my ideal	I am a happy person
Working environment	.213*	.197*
The ease of the work	.158*	.159*
Job security	.127*	.137*
Income and benefits package	.251*	.172*
Relationship with the leadership	.101*	.160*
Relations with colleagues	.098*	.183*
Promotion opportunities	.127*	.098*
Leverage of individual capability	.185*	.219*

Note Sig.* = .000

is very close to my ideal," followed by "working environment" and "leveraging of individual capability." Agreement with the statement, "I am a happy person" is most greatly impacted by satisfaction with "leveraging of individual capability," followed by "working environment" and "relationships with colleagues." This illustrates that individual happiness is likely to be improved if people's personal values are embodied in their work and if they feel comfortable in their working environment and have good interpersonal relationships. Thus, the life aspirations pursued by Chinese people has come to include satisfactory income levels, finding work that best utilizes one's personal ability and that provides a comfortable working environment.

6.4 Improving Social Security

Social Security is an essential guarantee to maintain social justice, promote social stability and development, and also offer basic assurance for realizing the "China Dream." In recent years, the government has attached great importance to social security and vigorously promoted the construction of the social security system in order to improve the existing imbalance between urban and rural residents in enjoying social security benefits. The 2013 National Survey (see Table 6.3) indicates that 61.4% of urban and rural residents enjoy social security insurance, an increase of 21.3% from the year 2011, making it the fastest growing social security program promoted

Table 6.3 Rate of social security coverage for urban and rural residents (%)

	Social security coverage rate in 2011						Social security coverage rate in 2013					
	Cities and towns		Rural area		Total		Cities and towns		Rural area		Total	
	Frequency	Rate of enjoyment	Frequency	Rate of enjoyment	Frequency	Rate of enjoyment	Frequency	Rate of enjoyment	Frequency	Rate of enjoyment	Frequency	Rate of enjoyment
Pension Insurance	1938	53.4	855	25.4	2793	39.9	2062	63.3	2468	59.9	4530	61.4
Medical Insurance	2933	80.5	3031	89.7	5964	84.9	2827	86.7	3841	93.3	6668	90.4
Unemployment insurance	686	19.0	72	2.1	757	10.8	686	21.1	125	3.0	811	11.0
Industrial Injury Insurance	678	18.8	128	3.8	806	12.2	688	21.1	168	4.1	856	11.6
Maternity Insurance	416	11.6	44	1.3	460	6.8	504	15.5	94	2.3	598	8.1
Urban and rural minimum living allowance	145	4.1	150	4.5	295	4.5	107	3.3	196	4.8	303	4.1

in recent years. Currently, national health insurance coverage is growing, reaching 90.4% of the population in 2013, an increase of 5.5% from 2011. However, other areas of social security are developing much more slowly, including unemployment insurance, industrial injury insurance and maternity insurance, which only cover approximately 10% of the population. More specifically, 11% of the population has unemployment insurance, 11.6% have work injury insurance, and 8.1% have maternity insurance. In addition, the urban and rural minimum living security system—a financial relief system for low-income urban or rural residents or people living in difficulty—currently covers 4.1% of urban and rural residents. In recent years, the rapid development of the rural endowment insurance system has expanded coverage of rural residents from 25.4% in 2011 to 59.9% in 2013.

There is still a large gap between urban and rural areas in terms of social security coverage, which the government is taking various measures to narrow. The 2013 survey data shows that urban residents have higher coverage than rural residents with respect to pension insurance (3.4% higher), unemployment insurance (18.1% higher), industrial injury insurance (17% higher) and maternity insurance (13.2% higher). However, rural residents have a slightly higher coverage rate for medical insurance than that of urban residents.

Another weakness of the current social security system is the huge population of migrant workers from rural areas, which is a significant factor in the social security gap for urban employment. These migrant workers often face unstable employment, low income levels and lack of social support, and discrimination in various aspects of employment and social life. They are thus the most in need of social security support. Due to the long-term impact of the household registration system, many migrant workers cannot join the local social security system or must suspend their social security for greater job mobility. In recent years, local governments have taken a number of measures to facilitate the entry of migrant workers into the local social security system, with remarkable results. However, there is still a gap in social security coverage between migrant workers and non-agricultural household employees. Figure 6.10 shows that the residents with non-farm employment accounts have significantly higher coverage rates for pension insurance (21.5% higher), unemployment insurance (26% higher), industrial injury insurance (21.1% higher) and maternity insurance (16.3% higher) than that of migrant workers.

6.5 Achieving the "Dream Dwelling"

Achieving one's "dream dwelling" is a specific feature of the China Dream for urban and rural residents. In the survey, 18.8% of respondents expressed the desire to "improve dwelling" when they were asked "what personal aspirations do you most want to achieve in the next 5–10 years?" The share of the population who identified this as one of their life goals followed "improvement of income" and "family safety and health." From the survey results, the current family homeownership rate was 93.5%, a 1.9% increase over the year 2011, when urban households homeownership

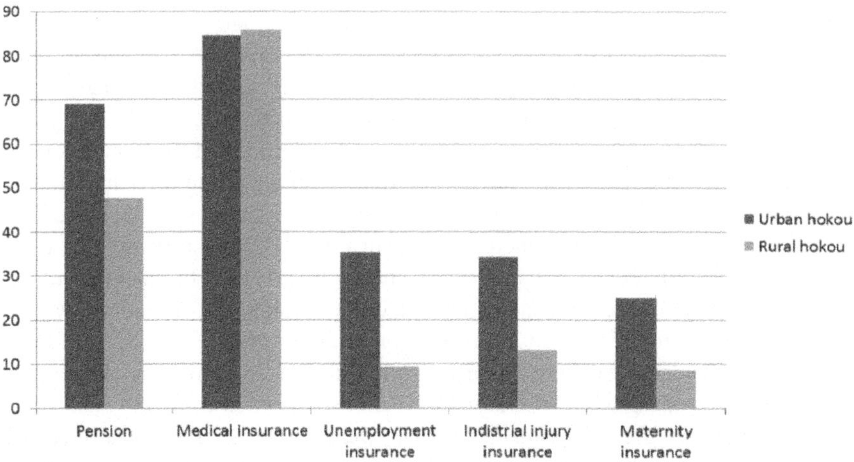

Fig. 6.10 Comparison of social security coverage rate between agricultural and non-agricultural accounts in the urban labor force aged 18–60 years (%)

was 89.6%. The survey also showed that 18.6% of families have two or more houses, an increase of 3.5% in comparison with the year 2011. In 2013, urban and rural residents had an average per capita floor space of 47.3 m^2, an increase from the 42.0 m^2 average in 2011. However, there is still a high percentage of people who face difficulty in achieving their "dream dwelling." In response to the survey question, "what of the following issues of life aspects did you or your family experience in the last 12 months?" 38.9% identified "poor housing conditions with no ability to build/afford housing." Usually, people think that housing difficulties mainly exist in urban areas, but the survey results show that there was a higher proportion of rural residents (40.9%) identifying this concern than urban (37.1%).

Homeownership rates for Chinese families has typically been high, but as urban real estate prices continue to rise, there has been an increase in the proportion of tenants who rent their homes. The 2013 survey data (see Fig. 6.11) shows that 70.8% of urban residents live in their own houses, while the remaining 29.2% are renters (except for a few of people who live in dormitories, or live together with relatives and friends). The highest proportion of rental housing is occupied by young people. Figure 6.11 shows the younger the age, the lower the homeownership rate and the higher the home rental rate. The oldest age group, 61–70 years, has a homeownership rate of 85.3%, while the youngest age group, 18–30 years, has a home ownership rate of only 60.6%. Conversely, the youngest age group of 18–30 years has a housing rental rate as high as 35.6%, while the oldest age group of 61–70 years has a rental rate of only 12.4%. In megacities such as Beijing, Shanghai and Guangzhou, there is a higher proportion of young renters, reaching approximately 60% of all young employed people, according to the Beijing Youth Population Survey in 2014. The situation in rural areas is much different, with over 90% of rural residents across all ages living in their own houses. In addition, more studies have shown that urban

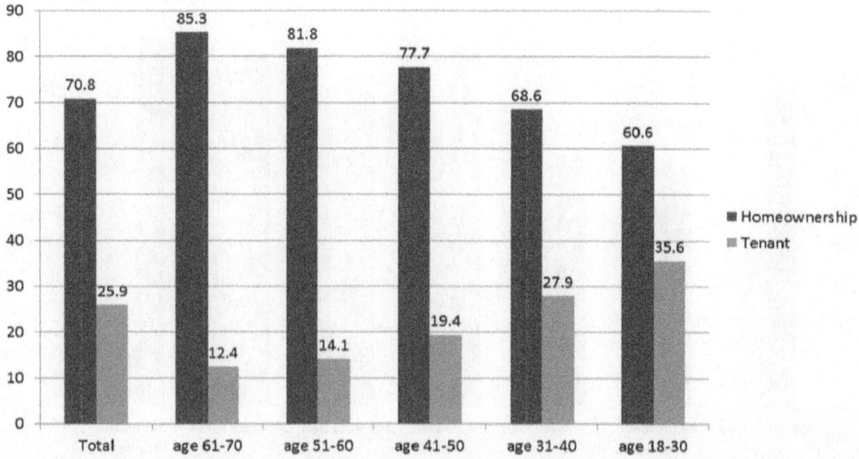

Fig. 6.11 The proportion of homeownership vs tenancy among urban residents across age groups (%)

homeownership rates are vastly different among different provinces, which has significantly and negatively impacted the housing-price-to-income ratio, the proportion of migrants, and the unemployment rate. Homeownership rates are positively and significantly affected by the proportion of the population over 65 years, the proportion of married people and family sizes (Wang and Zhang 2014).

The improvement of living conditions for urban and rural residents is reflected not only in homeownership rates and housing space, but also in the improvement of housing facilities. There are two factors that promote improved living facilities. The first is the effort of governments to vigorously promote the construction of urban and rural infrastructure, extend water, electricity and gas supply facilities from large and middle-sized cities to small towns and rural areas. The second factor is the steady improvement in income levels of urban and rural residents that provide the financial ability to buy or build housing with improved facilities. Figure 6.12 shows that 81.5% of urban and 42.9% of rural residents live in multi-storied houses. Nearly all urban and rural families have separate toilets and kitchens, but while nearly all urban families have tap water and separate bathing facilities, only two-thirds of rural families do. Gas facilities in rural areas are also still relatively low, requiring further government promotion efforts.

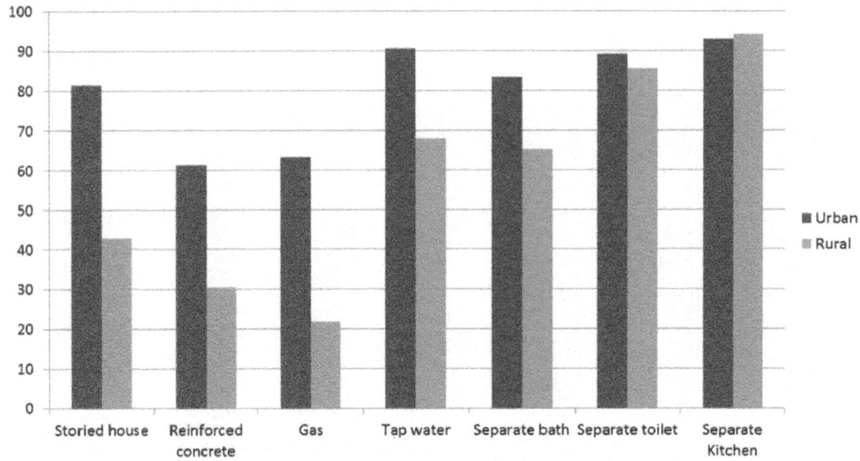

Fig. 6.12 Residential house facilities of urban and rural residents

6.6 Summary

It is an important component of the China Dream to have a stable and satisfactory job, as this affects an individual's well-being and realization of life goals. Compared with many countries which are still dealing with the impact of the financial crisis, Chinese people now have more employment opportunities, a relatively high degree of employment stability, low unemployment risk, and middle-to-high job satisfaction rates, all of which provide a good foundation for the purpose of realizing the China Dream. However, young people and women remain at higher risk of unemployment, and have high jobless unemployment rates. More people can be helped in their pursuit of the China Dream by providing education and skills training to low-educated youth in order to promote their employment, and by reducing gender discrimination in the labor market to encourage women to return to the field of employment.

Helping Chinese people achieve their "dream dwelling" requires more efforts. Even though the vast majority of Chinese families own their own houses with greatly improved space and facilities, many Chinese people are not satisfied with their current living conditions and want to improve their living conditions as quickly as possible. In particular, a large number of urban youth live in rental houses, and are working hard to achieve the dream of home ownership.

References

International Labor Organization: Global Employment Trends for Youth 2013. 2013. http://www.ilo.org/global/research/global-reports/global-employment-trends/youth/2013/lang--en/index.htm.
International Labor Organization: World Employment and Social Outlook—Trends 2015. 2015. http://www.ilo.org/global/research/global-reports/weso/2015/lang--ja/index.htm.
Li, Yabin. 2013. Properly Treat the Relationship Between 'Chinese Dream' and "Individual Dream: Interview with Li Jie, the Chair Specialist in the Project of Marxism Research and Building." *Guangming Daily* (May 9): 2. [in Chinese].
Wang, Renyang, and Hui Zhang. 2014. Inter-provincial Difference on Homeownership Rates of Urban Households in China and Its Influential Factors: Research Based on the 'Sixth National Population Census' Data. *China Real Estate* 6: 3–10. [in Chinese].

Chapter 7
Moving Towards a Harmonious Society with More Affluent Families

Yi Zhang

Whether a person has a happy family is a major component of overall happiness. In childhood, parental love and the degree of marital harmony among one's parents profoundly impact one's quality of family life. In youth, the family support system directly affects one's educational achievement. After marriage in adulthood, the relationship between spouses is the major determinant of one's family well-being. In old age, the support from family members brings filial obligations full circle. In short, the degree of harmony and happiness in one's family life is not only a major component of happiness, but also a typical "dream" of a Chinese person or a family.

To build an all-around well-off society is the basic goal of the Chinese dream in the first place. In the process of building a moderately prosperous society, what happens to middle-class families, working families and peasant families? What problems still exist in the family structure, household size, household consumption and household financial burdens? These are major social problems that need to be tackled. In the article, "Study on Family Life Ritualization of the 19th Century British Middle Class," Li Baofang described the food, clothing, and housing situation, among other aspects, in the family life. The following analysis describes the basic family life and changing trends of current Chinese middle-class families, working families and peasant families. The intent of this analysis is to provide a theoretical and practical basis for the development of family policy.

Y. Zhang (✉)
Chinese Academy of Social Sciences, Beijing, China

P. Li and M. K. Gorshkov (eds.), *Life Expectations of the People*,
Research Series on the Chinese Dream and China's Development Path,
https://doi.org/10.1007/978-981-16-2505-3_7

7.1 Recognition of Family and Household Size

According to weighted analysis of the data from the 2013 CGSS questionnaire, middle-class families account for 31.6% of the Chinese population (including "old middle class families" such as small owners and self-employed households, which comprise 13.9% of the population). "Working class" families account for 33.6% of the population, and peasant families account for 34.8%.

In academia, some people regard people who eat and live together as a "household," while others only count family members that have a blood and marriage relationship and share common economic life and balance of payments as a single household. When discussing household size, the following needs to be considered: For Chinese people, family members with blood and marriage relationships and that live together are universally considered family household members. However, due to population movements, "living together" is difficult to define. Although a simple concept in theory, in practice, defining household size in this way creates a lot of problems. For example, boarding school students live with their parents on weekends, but usually live at the school. These students sometimes eat and live together, and sometimes do not. Some migrant workers work in the city and eat and drink at the site during the day, but go home to sleep at night. That is to say, they live together but do not eat together. The vast majority of respondents feel that these people should be their family members. Therefore, "identity household size" is greater than "actual household size".

Because there is a large gap between households defined by "eating and living together" and self-identified households recognized by interview, our analysis uses "common income and expenditure" to define the actual household size. That is, in our research, accounting for common income and expenditure, household members with blood and marriage relationships that have been living together for a long time or regularly are defined as "the actual household" members, with "household size" calculated as the sum of the actual household members. The sum of household members recognized by the interviewees outside these parameters is defined as "identity family size."

As shown in Table 7.1, the average actual household size of middle-class families is 2.53 people, and the median is 2 people. But the average identity household size of middle-class families is 4.28 people with a median of 4 people.

For working families, actual household size is 2.49 people, with a median of 2 people. The identity household size is 4.28 people with a median of 4 people. In other words, the identity household size of working class families is the same as that of middle-class families.

For peasant families, the actual household size is 2.96 people with a median of 3 people. The identity household size is 4.87 people with a median of 5 people.

In general, the actual household size of middle-class families is less than that of working families, and the household size of working families is less than that of peasant families. But why is the household size of working-class families actually less than that of the middle-class families in our survey? There are a few reasons: First,

Table 7.1 Actual household size and identity household size

Class	Statistical indicators	Actual household size	Identity household size
Middle-class families	Number of samples (piece)	2305	2299
	Mean (person)	2.53	4.28
	Median (person)	2.00	4.00
Working-class families	Number of samples (piece)	2452	2447
	Mean (person)	2.49	4.28
	Median (person)	2.00	4.00
Peasant families	Number of samples (piece)	2543	2535
	Mean (person)	2.96	4.87
	Median (person)	3.00	5.00

Note 2013 data from the 2013 GSS survey

China's family planning policy stipulates that a couple can only have one child in urban areas. Namely, the family planning policy is the same for both working-class and middle-class families. Second, part of the Chinese working-class are migrant workers who originally come from peasant families. A large part of these people have left their original domiciles and moved to urban areas to work for their living. Thus many have formed mobile families. Even for migrant workers with family members in the city or town, the actual household size will be smaller. In fact, this dynamic explains the reason why the identity household sizes of working-class families is equal to that of middle-class families.

7.2 Household Income and Expenditures and Family Housing Occupancy

7.2.1 *Household Income and Expenditures*

An important aspect of family life is the per capita family income and consumption status, which determines the family's living standards and to some extent, the potential for future family development. Because the household size of middle-class and working-class families is smaller, and that of peasant families larger, we use family income per capita to compare household consumption expenditures per capita:

Table 7.2 shows that the average per capita household income of middle-class families in 2012 was 43,831.42 yuan. To an extent, income determines consumption, and thus the per capita consumption level of middle-class families was the highest,

Table 7.2 Total household expenditures and income among different socio-economic classes

Socio-economic class	Statistical indicators	Household annual consumption expenditures per capita	Annual household income per capita	Consumption/income
Middle-class families	Number of samples (N)	2028	2035	
	Mean (yuan)	34,840.06	43,831.42	79.49
Working-class families	Number of samples (N)	2100	2127	
	Mean (yuan)	23,820.75	29,207.54	81.56
Peasant families	Number of samples (N)	2306	2325	
	Mean (yuan)	13,948.64	14,653.71	95.19

Note The data in the table reflects the income and expenditures in 2012; data comes from the GSS survey of 2013

reaching 34,840.06 yuan. The per capita annual income of working-class families was 29,207.54 yuan, with annual per capita consumption expenditures reaching 23,820.75 yuan. The per capita annual income of peasant families was 14,653.71 yuan, with annual per capita consumption expenditures reaching 13,948.64 yuan. The data shows that the per capita household income and per capita household expenditures of middle-class families are higher than those of working families, and those of working families higher than those of peasant families.

According to the proportion of income from consumption, middle-class families account for 79.49%, working-class families account for 81.56%, and peasant families account for 95.19%. That is to say, if you want to stimulate consumption, it is necessary to improve the income level of the lower classes.

It should be noted that according to the data in the statistical bulletin of the People's Republic of China, the per capita net income of rural residents in 2012 was 7,917 yuan, and the per capita disposable income of urban residents was 24,565 yuan. The annual per capita income of peasant families reflected in our sample survey data was 14,653.71 yuan, which is much higher than 7,917 yuan released by the Bureau of Statistics. The reason for this is that there are differences between the two statistical indicators: the household per capita net income released by the National Bureau of Statistics excluded family business expenses and productive fixed assets after depreciation and taxes. Our calculations are based on the household per capita income reported by the survey respondents (Table 7.3).

With self-assessed reporting, household expenditures tend to be expanded while household income is often underreported due to fears in showing one's true wealth. Therefore, to a certain extent, the household "income < expenditures" ratio will be expanded among households reflected in the sample survey. Because of this, according to the self-assessment of middle-class families, "income > expenditure"

Table 7.3 Self-assessed economic income and expenditures of families in 2012 (%)

	Middle-class families	Working-class families	Peasant families
Income > expenditures	36.61	31.59	18.95
Break-even	33.78	34.64	30.75
Income < expenditures	29.61	33.77	50.30
Total	100.00	100.00	100.00
Engel coefficient	33.60	40.00	39.18

Source 2013 GSS survey data

accounted for 36.31%, "break-even" was 33.78%, and "income < expenditure" was 29.61%.

For working-class families, 31.59% reported that their "income > expenditure," 34.64% reported "break-even," and 33.77% reported "income < expenditure."

For peasant families, the answer "income > expenditure" accounted for 18.95%, "break-even" was 30.75%, and "income < expenditure" was 50.30%.

Obviously, if more than 50% of peasant households had incomes that were less than their household expenditures, the speed in which China's rural social and economic situation has improved would not be so fast. Nevertheless, only a small percentage of middle-class families reported that "income < expenditure," followed by working-class families, with the highest percentage among peasant families.

As part of the survey of income and expenditures among various households, we also calculated the Engel coefficient of family consumption for all classes, namely, the percentage of food consumption as a share of total household consumption. As the last row of Table 7.2 shows, the Engel coefficient of middle-class families was 33.60, that of working-class families was 40.00, and that of peasant families was 39.18.

7.2.2 *Family Homeownership Status*

Since China's reform and opening up, Chinese family housing conditions have gradually improved. While in the past, the National Bureau of Statistics has released the per capita housing area of urban and rural residents, relevant authoritative data for housing space based on the family as a unit is scarce. By the end of 2012, China's urban per capita housing area reached 32.9 square meters, and the rural per capita housing area was 37.1 square meters.

What is the per capita number of housing for China's residents? According to our 2013 survey data, middle-class families with no house (0 suite) represented 5.18% of the population, those with at least one house (1 suite) comprised 73.91%, those with two houses (two suites) accounted for 17.90%, and middle-class families with three or more houses made up 3.01%.

Table 7.4 Homeownership status of different families (%)

Number homes of homeowners	Middle-class families	Working-class families	Peasant families	Column subtotal
0 suite	5.18	6.51	1.57	4.37
1 suite	73.91	76.45	83.87	78.24
2 suites	17.90	14.95	13.53	15.38
3 suites and more	3.01	2.09	1.02	2.01
Line subtotal	100.00	100.00	100.00	100.00

Source 2013 GSS survey data

Among working-class families, 6.51% had no house, 76.45% had one house, 14.95% had two houses, and 2.09% had three or more houses. Among peasant families, 1.57% had no house, 83.87% had one house, 13.53% had two houses, and 1.02% had three or more houses (Table 7.4).

Among all interviewees, 4.37% of the population do not own a home, 78.24% has one house, 15.38% have two houses, and 2.01% have three or more houses. Because there is no historical data to compare with, purely analyzing whether Chinese families own houses or not reveals that most of the population owns a home, fulfilling the objective of "home ownership." This can be proved from the other side: China's housing market prices have soared in recent years. But if the flow of the population continues to accelerate, the proportion of housing development on the housing market will maintain unchanged. However, if growth of the floating population is limited, the trend of rising home prices will not continue to soar.

Of course, the population we survey might be different from the full spectrum of housing needs. After all, conducting a "household" survey increases the number of respondents "with a house" to a certain extent, and also increases the likelihood that there will be an elevated proportion of respondents in the elderly population. Although the samples were weighted during the processing of the data, the problem of uneven age distribution may still exist.

Even taking into account the above factors, we still believe that the housing situation in China has greatly improved following China's reform and opening up. In the future, the housing problems of Chinese families will no longer center around the issue of home ownership, but the quality of housing and structural problems of the housing market resulting from population movement. In this latter regard, the flow of the rural population to urban areas, including the flow from small towns and cities to the middle-size cities, has led to the rapid growth of the urban population and thus greater demand for housing. However, for smaller cities and areas with slow population growth or negative growth, the housing market will suffer from long-time weakness.

7.3 Problems in Family Life

Different families with different incomes, living environments, needs and abilities to meet their family's consumption demands will have different perspectives on their most challenging problem in their family life. In the 2012 survey, families felt the most serious problem affecting family life was "rising prices affecting the standard of living."

China's prices have been rising steadily since 2009. Because the wage growth index is less than the inflation index, all Chinese families -middle-class, working-class, and peasant- expressed deep feelings about the negative impact of rising prices. For example, 69.26% of middle-class families asserted that inflation affected their lives, while 72.63 and 63.06% of working-class and peasant families respectively agreed that rising prices affected their lives.

If incomes rise at a faster rate than prices, the negative impact will be relatively small. But because of the limited revenue growth rate, there was a relatively high percentage of families that agreed to the subjective statement, "owing to low family income, daily life is difficult." 36.38, 45.70 and 58.79% of middle-class, working-class, and peasant families subscribed to this sentiment, respectively. It is evident from this data that the lower one's class status, the greater the chance of experiencing this problem. Peasant families were 22% more likely to experience this problem than middle-class families. Therefore, how to improve the income level of farmers' families is still the main measure for improving family life. In addition, new members of working-class households are mainly migrant workers—predominantly migrant workers who have moved from rural areas. In this case, the income level of working-class families living in the city is quite fragile in terms of resisting price increases. Thus, working-class families have a strong subjective sense that, "owing to low family income, daily life is difficult" (Table 7.5).

As previously described, Chinese people typically have homes. In fact, in rural areas, homesteads are evenly assigned according to the number of married sons in a family (in some villages, homesteads are also assigned to married daughters, but this is a relatively low proportion). In this case, the rural population typically has access to homesteads and housing (except in very special circumstances), but there are wide gaps in the quality of housing. Even in towns and cities, owning a house does not mean that the quality of housing has reached the level of consumers' satisfaction. It is expected that in the future, the percentage of replacement housing will be relatively high. Therefore, the Chinese government has launched a renovation plan to rebuild the city's shantytowns. After many years of renovation, in 2015, construction of affordable housing for low-income residents reached 7.4 million planned units, with 5.8 million units in shantytowns. Because of this, the number of Chinese families who felt that, "in spite of poor housing conditions, I cannot build/afford house" increased to 36.26% for middle-class families, 40.49% for working-class families, and 42.20% for peasant families. It should be noted that along with rising income levels, each family's expectations for housing quality will certainly increase, so middle-class families' expectations for housing quality will be higher than that of

Table 7.5 Family experiences of the following life problems in 2012 (%)

Problem encountered	Occur or not	Middle-class families	Working-class families	Peasant families
Price rises are affecting the standard of living	No	30.74	27.37	36.94
	Yes	69.26	72.63	63.06
Low family income leads to difficulties in everyday life	No	63.62	54.30	41.21
	Yes	36.38	45.70	58.79
Poor housing conditions, unable to build/buy a house	No	63.74	59.51	57.80
	Yes	36.26	40.49	42.20
Cannot bear the high costs of household "goodwill" spending	No	71.24	72.61	64.47
	Yes	28.76	27.39	35.53
Cannot bear the overload work	No	74.63	73.39	76.87
	Yes	25.37	26.61	23.13
Unemployed, unemployment or unstable work	No	75.97	68.55	68.35
	Yes	24.03	31.45	31.65
The cost of children's education is too high, unbearable	No	76.70	77.42	76.44
	Yes	23.30	22.58	23.56
Disciplining children is difficult, very tiring	No	77.78	78.80	81.01
	Yes	22.22	21.20	18.99
Big medical spending, unbearable	No	76.44	75.62	63.89
	Yes	23.56	24.38	36.11
The heavy burden of supporting the elderly	No	88.96	87.17	87.00
	Yes	11.04	12.83	13.00
Discord in the family relationship	No	95.64	94.95	95.66
	Yes	4.36	5.05	4.34

Source 2013 GSS survey data

working-class families, and that of working-class families will be higher than that of peasant families. Housing quality pertains not only to housing location, but also to the quality of construction and availability of basic public services in the community.

China is still very much a relationship-based society. In order to maintain close relationships between people, ordinary investments in other people, i.e. "goodwill" spending, will be relatively large. In this respect, 28.76% of middle-class families, 27.39% of working-class families and 35.53% of peasant families, felt "they could not bear the high household goodwill spending." Because peasant families live in small villages, and goodwill spending is more important in a close-knit relationship-based society, peasant families had a stronger sense of this problem.

The percentage of middle-class, working-class, and the peasant families who felt "unbearably overloaded with work" was basically the same at 25.37%, 26.61% and 23.13% respectively. In the cities, rapid social and economic development, long overtime hours, and other factors have exhausted many middle-class and working-class families. In the countryside, because most young people have moved to the city, the labor force is mostly comprised of the elderly, with the same sense that their physical labor is "too much." Another problem relating to work is "unemployment or unstable work." Typically, as the new labor population gradually declines, the pressures of joblessness and unemployment will gradually weaken. However, because of frictional unemployment and structural unemployment problems, pressures are increasing on account of an increase of the human capital in the labor force. In addition, China is still in a state of transition from a planned economy to a market economy. The stable working arrangements from the planned economy period will change because of competition in the new market economy. As a result, nearly every Chinese family fears work instability. Among those surveyed, 24.03% of middle-class families, 31.45% of working-class families, and 31.65% of peasant families felt this pressure. Working-class and peasant families felt this pressure at a higher rate than middle-class families.

In Chinese culture, the achievements of one's children is a large component of the concept of family happiness. So, in families with minor children, the cost of investment in schooling and education is a higher percentage of total household spending. We found that the percentage of middle-class, working-class, and peasant families who felt that "the cost of the children's education was too high" was 23.30%, 22.58% and 23.30% respectively. The proportion of Chinese families who felt that "disciplining children is difficult and very tiring, was also 22.22%, 21.20% and 18.99% respectively. In general, family problems related to children's education and discipline were very similar across the different socio-economic classes.

Although reform of the medical system has been ongoing for a long time, many families still feel "seeing a doctor is difficult and expensive." 23.56% of middle-class families, 24.38% of working-class families, and 36.11% of peasant families identified "big medical spending" as a family concern. Here, peasant families tend to feel the burden of "big medical spending" much more acutely than middle-class and working-class families. An important reason for this may be that the medical resources in cities are superior to those in rural areas. When farmers have a relatively serious disease, they must transfer to the city for treatment. However, in accordance with the provisions of the new rural cooperative medical insurance system, the reimbursement ratio for transfer treatment is progressively reduced according to whether one transfers to a county hospital, a city hospital in the province, or a hospital outside the province. This increases the treatment cost to a certain extent.

Surprisingly, the percentage of families who experienced "the heavy burden of supporting the elderly" was still low for middle-class families (11.04%), working-class families (12.83%) and peasant families (13.00%). It is worth noting that different types of families may feel different support pressures: For the elderly in middle-class families, the greatest need may be family service support; for the elderly in working-class families, both family service support and financial support may be needed; but for the elderly in peasant families, the greatest need may be financial support, because at present, the average pension of the vast majority of the rural elderly population is a mere 55 yuan per person per month. Although pensions increased to 70 yuan in 2015, the increased amount is still subject to the negative effects of inflation.

Even more notable is the relatively low share of Chinese families that cite "discord in the family relationship" as a problem in family life. Only 4.36% of middle-class families, 5.05% of working-class families and 4.34% of peasant families noted this as a problem. Influenced by collectivism and family altruism, China's family ties among all socio-economic classes are still relatively harmonious.

7.4 Community Support Networks

People living in society always encounter risk of some kind or another. How Chinese people address risks or difficulties when they occur reflects the "strong relationship" feature of Chinese society, and also the structural features of community support networks.

As shown in Table 7.6, 81.11% of middle-class families responded "yes" when asked whether they would seek help from their family members when "difficulties" arose. Correspondingly, 85.82% of working-class families and 87.12% of peasant families also replied "yes." This indicates that Chinese people, regardless of their socio-economic status, regard the "family" as the biggest resource for help in times of difficulty. Compared with middle-class and working-class families, peasant families had the highest probability of asking for help from their families.

Compared with traditional rural society, an important trend in China's social change is the emphasis on the network of personal relationships. When asked whether they would seek help from friends and other private networks in the face of difficulty, 76.54, 75.74 and 65.87% of middle-class, working-class, and peasant families, responded "yes" respectively. Although the majority of all families replied that they would seek help from "friend and other personal networks," middle class families had a higher share of "yes" respondents than working-class families, and working-class families had a higher share than peasant families.

Table 7.6 Who Chinese people turn to for help in the face of difficulties (%)

	Family member		Friends and other private networks		Relatives and clan		Neighborhood or village committee		Work unit	
	No	Yes	No	Yes	No	Yes	No	Yes	No	Yes
Middle-class families	18.89	81.11	23.46	76.54	61.66	38.34	75.69	24.31	82.77	17.23
Working-class families	14.18	85.82	24.26	75.74	60.11	39.89	73.55	26.45	79.40	20.60
Peasant families	12.88	87.12	34.13	65.87	51.40	48.60	59.65	40.35	97.83	2.17

Source 2013 GSS survey data

With the increase in the degree of modernization of Chinese society, extended family and clan support for individuals is not only lower than support from a "family member", but also lower than support from "friends and other private networks," ranking third. Only 38.34% of middle-class families, 39.89% of working-class families, and 48.60% of peasant families responded that they would ask their relatives and clan for help. Here, the share of respondents from middle-class and working-class families was lower than that of peasant families. This may be because the peasant's extended family is relatively concentrated in a relatively fixed community, while the living location of extended family members of middle class and working-class families are scattered. Thus, a peasant may be more inclined to rely on family and clan relationships. 24.31% of middle-class families, 26.45% of working-class families and 40.35% of peasant families responded that they would ask their neighborhood or village committee for help during a time of difficulty. As can be seen here, there are more people who have a sense of dependence on their own "village committee" among peasant families.

Before China's reform and opening up, Chinese society had a strong "working unit system" that acted as a social support system. However, with the social changes resulting from reform and opening up, the percentage of the population who consider turning to their working unit for help when they encounter difficulties has greatly reduced, down to 17.23% for middle-class families, 20.60% for working families and only 2.17% for peasant families. The vast majority of peasant families under the household responsibility system have no "work unit" to depend on, with the exception of a very small number who are employed by agricultural enterprises. Thus, most peasant families are self-reliant on the family unit. Although middle-class and working-class family members are in the workplace on a daily basis, the relationship between these organizations and their staff has gradually evolved into an employment relationship. The "unit system" has transformed into for-profit organizations, and thus economic rationalism has weakened the relationships between employees and their organizations to the extent that people do not identify the "working unit" as an important source of help in times of difficulty. Because of this, whether it is a business organization or a public institution, a company with middle-class or working-class employees, it is necessary to focus on culture and corporate responsibility to build an enterprise or institution into a relatively warm place.

Because the family plays a very important role in Chinese life, respondents consistently replied "yes" to the question, "do you regard family health, unity, happiness and harmony as your greatest desire in the next 5–10 years?" As shown in Table 7.7, 75.85% of middle-class family members, 75.83% of working-class family members and 79.52% of peasant family members responded yes to this question.

Table 7.7 Family health, unity, family happiness and harmony as the greatest desire in the next 5–10 years (%)

	No	Yes	Total
Middle class family members	24.15	75.85	100.00
Working-class family members	24.17	75.83	100.00
Peasant family members	20.48	79.52	100.00
Line subtotal	22.88	77.12	100.00

Source 2013 GSS survey data

Table 7.8 The ideal number of children among different classes (%)

	Your ideal number of children when the family planning policy, family income, and health conditions are not considered					Total
	Childless	One child	Two children	Three children	Four children and more	
Middle-class families	1.11	16.58	78.21	2.74	1.37	100.00
Working-class families	0.99	20.31	73.22	3.73	1.76	100.00
Peasant families	0.33	13.96	74.75	7.36	3.60	100.00
Subtotal	0.77	16.99	75.01	4.87	2.36	100.00

Source 2011 GSS survey data

7.5 Conclusion and Discussion

7.5.1 *Middle-Class and Working-Class Families Have Similar Household Sizes, While the Size of Peasant Families Is Larger*

Reduction in family size is being affected by both population movement and the decrease in number of children. Under China's social transition, families have condensed into nuclear families, and the reduced number of household children is a key determinant of "actual household size." In the 2010 GSS survey, we asked respondents specifically about their fertility goals, with the results shown in Table 7.8. From this data, the ideal number of children of married adults in China has been greatly reduced. Whether couples are from middle-class, working-class, or peasant families, most want to have two children. Fewer middle-class families desired "three children" or "four or more children," than working-class families, and fewer working-class families desired greater numbers of children than peasant families. While some business owners have broken the one-child policy in highly-publicized media reports, the ideal number of children tends to decrease with the increase of social status. With the transformation of China's social structure, it is believed that China's future fertility rate is on a long-term downward trend—which will reduce actual household sizes.

However, as described above, the "identity" household size of Chinese families is also relatively large. While the survey did not study the structure and make-up of identity households in depth, and thus cannot detail the specific sources of household members, via interviews we discovered that subjectively identified family members often include parents. More specifically, a husband often identified his biological parents as family members, but gave less recognition to his parents-in law as family members. Similarly, a wife also often recognized her family members, including her parents, as family members, but gave less recognition to her parents-in-law in identifying family status. Many parents with adult children also tended to think of sons as family members, but fewer thought of adult daughters as family members.

7.5.2 *The Higher the Social Status, the Higher the Consumption Ability and Lower Ratio of Consumption to Income*

Although many emphasize changes in consumption structure as a more accurate reflection of people's standard of living, consumer spending still depends on income. Because of this, the consumption ability of middle-class families is far higher than that of working-class and peasant families. But the ratio of consumption to income is far higher for peasant families than middle-class families. As this ratio gradually narrows for peasant families in the future, and increases for middle-class families, the spending power of Chinese families will gradually increase. For now, raising the incomes of peasant and working-class families, is a prerequisite for expanding the scale of Chinese household consumption.

Household consumption—especially consumption of consumer durables- is a key factor in the quality of life for families, along with housing. According to our survey, the homeownership rate among Chinese adults has greatly improved; families that did not own a home accounted for only 4.37% of adults, while more than 15.38% of families had two houses. Both middle-class and working-class families had basic "housing." Therefore, families' future housing problems will primarily relate to changing houses, for improved quality of housing and also following the flow of population movement. For example, structural challenges in the housing market remain as migrant workers move from the countryside into the city, or families move from small cities to big cities.

Because the homeownership rate of middle-class families is higher than that of working-class and peasant families, and also because the majority of peasant family homes are self-built (the price of a self-built house is much lower than urban housing), the property gap (regarding homes as property) between middle-class, working-class, and peasant families is relatively large.

7.5.3 *Rising Prices Have a Serious Negative Impact on Household Consumption and Family Life of Each Household*

The quality of life for families across all socio-economic classes is greatly reduced in the face of inflation. The good news is that most families report harmonious family relationships, and thus are able to support dependent family members. Adults, especially adults over the age of 35, tend to have siblings. Although pension pressures borne by each adult child in the family is growing, families are generally able to bear the financial burden. In the future however, after the one-child generation enters adulthood, pension pressures will gradually emerge. At this point, all will face a variety or pension pressures regardless of social class.

With the increase in living standards, "human expenditures" in China has become a very heavy financial burden for many families. Because of limited wage growth for peasant families, expenditures for weddings, birthdays, New Year, funerals and so on, are becoming increasingly hard to bear for farmer families.

China is a fast-growing society. The acceleration of the social rhythm and corresponding social pressures has placed stress on middle-class, working-class and peasant families. Roughly a quarter of families across every socio-economic class expressed concerns with "heavy workloads" and "unstable work."

China is still a society in which every family holds high hopes for its children, so the problems of unbearably high education expenses and difficulty in disciplining children can't be ignored. Until now, the family still serves a very important educational function. In spite of a significant increase in government education spending throughout the country, the family's financial burden for education spending has also increased with the rise in commodity prices. The costs of specialty education and remedial teaching outside the school has become particularly unbearable.

Finally, for peasant families, in the event of family member sickness—particularly when a family member suffers from a serious illness- the economic pressure can be unbearable. Healthcare reform has been ongoing for many years, but the problem of "expensive and difficult medical treatment" ultimately still has not been solved.

7.6 Family Members and Personal Friends Are Still the Main Social Support Network for Chinese Families

Families across all socio-economic strata consider family and friends to be the main sources for help in the face of difficulty. Although support from one's clan and relatives has declined, they still constitute a part of the support network. The major support role that "working units" used to play has declined in the process of marketization. But for the peasant families, villages and communities still play a strong support role.

2.6 Family Members and Personal Friends Are Still the Main Social Support Network for Chinese Families

Chapter 8
Towards a Society of Modern and Successful Families

Yu. P. Lezhnina

Over the past 20 years, Russia has undergone a dramatic transformation that has affected, among other phenomena, relationships within families, changing many aspects thereof. For instance, there has been a significant shift in the age when Russians get married and start a family. The forms of marriage and parenthood have changed as well; nuclear families are becoming more spread out, for example.[1] These changes mostly stem from processes that are typical to social and cultural[2] modernization, such as greater emphasis on individual freedom and rationality, greater divergence of people's life paths and lifestyles, and higher relevance of self-expression, etc.

How do all these processes shape the modern Russian family? What does it take for Russians to consider their family life to be successful? What is their idea of a "dream family?".

First and foremost, it is worth pointing out that today, family has not lost its importance for Russians, remaining a crucial value for the vast majority of the population. Practically everyone in Russia (99%) expresses the belief in the importance

[1] Ref. Gurko (2008).

[2] To learn more about the current status and future prospects of modernization in Russia, please refer to such research as: Gotovo li rossiyskoye obschestvo k modernizatsii (Is Russian Society Ready for Modernization [2010]).

[3] Please refer to, e.g.: Rossiyskaya povsednevnost v usloviyakh krizisa (Russian everyday life during a crisis [2009]).

The original version of this chapter was revised: Affiliations have been updated in this chapter. The correction to this book can be found at https://doi.org/10.1007/978-981-16-2505-3_19

Yu. P. Lezhnina (✉)
HSE University, Moscow, Russia

Institute of Sociology of FCTAS RAS, Moscow, Russia

P. Li and M. K. Gorshkov (eds.), *Life Expectations of the People*, Research Series on the Chinese Dream and China's Development Path,
https://doi.org/10.1007/978-981-16-2505-3_8

of family. Interestingly enough, for most Russians, family comes before many other values, including one's job.[3] The prioritization of the family in the Russian value set is continually confirmed by research.[4] Russians widely define themselves as part of their families as separate communities (56%); this figure means that Russians' sense of unity with the family roughly equals that of people living in countries known for their conservative family attitudes, such as Germany (59%) or Poland (57%).[5] Overall, this type of self-definition is the most wide-spread in Russia—as it often is for people in other countries.[6] That said, Russians' family ties are becoming less close; traditional extended families are fading into the background, and the notion of "kinsfolk" is gradually losing its importance. Almost a quarter of the Russian population does not count their relatives among the people they socialize with in their free time (excepting those relatives who live in the same household). On average, only 79% of Russians keep in touch with their relatives, with women (82%) doing it more often than men (76%).[7]

At the same time, while having a family is very important, it is not considered a life aspiration for most Russians, as a happy family and good children is either something they already have or something that is so easy to achieve that one does not dream about it. According to 2012 data,[8] a pessimistic attitude towards successfully starting a family and raising children one could be proud of is expressed only by 9% and 6% of Russians respectively. The complete lack of desire to have a happy family and good children is expressed only by 1% and 2% respectively. Meanwhile, exactly one half of all Russians (50%) claim that they already have a happy family, while 42% firmly believe that they will be able to start one in the future (see Table 8.1). This explains why only 23% of Russians count having good children among the three main things they dream about, while only 17% say the same about having a happy family (these figures amount to 25 and 19% of those who shared their dreams in 2012). It is interesting to note that people who live in the countryside dream about having a happy family with good children slightly more often than city-dwellers (26% and 19% and 21% and 16% respectively).

[4] Please refer to, e.g.: Kartzeva (2003), Varlamova et al. (2006), Mitrikas (2004), Is Russian society ready for modernization (2010).

[5] Results of a national identity research, carried out in 2003 as part of the International Social Survey Program (ISSP). This figure reached 63% according to the findings of a nation-wide representative sampling study carried out by the IS RAS in 2014 and titled "Modern Russian Middle Class: 10 years later" (In this study, 1,600 people were selected as representatives of various gender, age, local, social, and professional groups; hereinafter, this study will serve as the primary source of 2014 data, unless stated otherwise).

[6] Mitrikas (2004).

[7] The findings of the nation-wide topical representative sampling study "Is Russian society ready for modernization?", carried out by the IS RAS in 2010. For more information, please refer to: Gotovo li rossiyskoye obschestvo k modernizatsii (Is Russian society ready for modernization? [2010]). Hereinafter, this study will serve as the primary source of 2010 data, unless stated otherwise.

[8] Hereinafter, unless stated otherwise, the 2012 data is based on a nation-wide topical representative sampling study "What Russians dream about: the ideal and reality", carried out by the IS RAS in 2012.

Table 8.1 Russians' achievements in starting a family and raising children, 1994–2012, %

	2003	2008	2010	2012
Successfully starting a happy family				
Have already achieved their goals	52	52	52	50
Have not yet achieved their goals, but are confident that they will be able to do so	32	32	36	40
Would like to achieve their goals, but are doubtful if they will ever be able to do so	14	13	11	9
Do not have any goals whatsoever	2	2	1	1
Successfully raising their children and teaching them to be good				
Have already achieved their goals	34	37	38	36
Have not yet achieved their goals, but are confident that they will be able to do so	57	53	52	56
Would like to achieve their goals, but are doubtful if they will ever be able to do so	7	7	7	6
Do not have any goals whatsoever	2	3	3	2

Note The table does not account for those who responded, "I am not sure". The data reflects responses from people aged from 18 to 55

Consequently, we can see that Russians treat a happy family as something easily accessible and achievable—an item on a checklist rather than a dream. Essentially, it could be said that "a modern family is one of the projects that a person works on throughout their life,"[9] alongside career and personal growth.[10] Only 13% of those who have a happy family (12% of respondents residing in cities and 17% of those residing in the countryside) and 23% of those who plan to start one (regardless of the place of residence) treat family life as a dream, appreciating it for what it is and striving to preserve it.

Is Russians' certainty in the possibility of having a happy family actually true to life? As of 2014, 68% of men and 56% of women across Russia were officially married. The discrepancy in figures can be explained by the fact that the overall number of Russians males is lower than the number of females. In addition, if we compare the statistics among women from urban and rural communities, we discover differences in terms of the number of single women (14% and 10% respectively), divorced women (13% and 10% respectively), and widows (14% and 11% respectively). As there are fewer males than females, rural women prefer to stay married for as long as possible. This makes it easier to run a household, and supports the traditional patriarchal values that are quite common in rural communities.

Family is treated as a dream mostly by those who have not been able to start one yet. This desire is expressed by 22% of Russians that have never been married and 26% of unmarried Russians that are in a long-term relationship. These figures

[9] Zdravomyslova (2006).

[10] Chernova and Shapokovskaya (2010).

are significantly lower among Russians that are married, divorced, or widowed, or have a common-law spouse (from 14 to 16%). In turn, when it comes to treating having a family as a goal (that has not been achieved yet), this opinion is shared by 94% of Russians that have never been married, 88% of unmarried Russians in a long-term relationship, 77% of divorced, and 50% of widowed Russians. Finally, this figure reaches 20% among Russians that are officially married, and 59% among those who have a common-law spouse. This may look like proof that common-law marriages are generally unhappy, but in truth, such unions are simply rarely regarded by Russians as "proper" families.[11]

It is worth bearing in mind that in countries that have already undergone the second demographic transition, common-law marriages have stopped "being a deviant form of an intimate relationship, becoming a commonplace variation of the norm."[12] This in turn has weakened the traditional notion that a proper union is ensured by an official marriage.[13] For example, a survey by the Russian Federal State Statistics Service[14] shows that as of the Fall of 2009, common-law marriage was the first stable relationship for one in every four women (26%) and one in every three men (32%) younger than 25. However, in older age groups, the share of common-law marriage as the first relationship was significantly lower. Among women and men aged 25–29, it amounted to 12% and 14% respectively. At the same time, the vast majority of second long-term relationships were common-law marriages. About 46% of women and 53% of men aged 30–34 did not register their second marriage officially. Even among women and men over age 40, the figures reached 38% and 47% respectively. In addition, 15% of women and 20% of men who made their first serious commitment at the age of 25 or older opted for common-law marriage. Among those who started their second long-term relationship at this age, the share of common-law marriages soared to about a half (51% among women and 47% among men).

When analyzing the traditional family's transformation over the past years, it is also worth mentioning that, according to the aforementioned study by the Russian Federal State Statistics Service, the number of first marriages that started out as official unions has been steadily shrinking. For women, the figures decreased from 72% pre-1990 to 50% in 2005—2009, and from 78 to 49% respectively for men. What is more, between 1990 and 2005, the average amount of time between making a commitment and registering it as a marriage (in the case of marriages where the couple has postponed formalities until later) increased from 11 months for women and 9 months for men to 30 and 28 months respectively. It is quite possible that this change was the result of the turmoil of transformation within Russian society,

[11] We have already come across this phenomenon in previous studies, such as, for instance, Gotovo li rossiyskoye obschestvo k modernizatsii (Is Russian society ready for modernization? [2010]).

[12] Nezaregistrirovanniye braki: semya i deti (Common-law marriages: family and children)—07/24/2008 (http://bd.fom.ru/report/cat/famil/civ_marr/d082924); Zakharov (2006) etc.

[13] Zdravomyslova (2006).

[14] Brief overview of the Family and Birth Rate random sampling survey (http://www.gks.ru/free_doc/2010/family.htm). This random sampling survey was carried out in 30 Russian regions in September and October of 2009. The study featured responses from 1,999 people (881 man and 1,118 women under 45).

which led to feelings of insecurity about the future and doubts whether an "official" start to a family was worthy. This assumption is supported by the fact that as the situation stabilized, the figures plummeted once again, returning to 11 months for both genders in 2005–2009. It is interesting to note that most of the people who responded to the Russian Federal State Statistics Service survey (61% of women and 63% of men) stated that they believe it is necessary to officially register a first marriage. A significant number of respondents (57% of women and 58% of men) also added that it is desirable to register a second marriage. That said, most Russians also tended to note that before making their marriage official, a couple should first live together for a couple of years, testing out if their feelings for each another are true[15] (this opinion was expressed by more than one-third of all respondents regarding the first marriage and by more than a half of all respondents regarding the second marriage).

All of the above may be considered as evidence that there is a new "typical" (although not yet dominant) marriage pattern emerging: the first marriage is preceded by the couple living together for a while, taking some time to officiate their relationship. In the case of the second marriage, the couple tends to postpone formalities even further. This means that Russians now view common-law marriage as a logical stage that precedes life as an officially married couple; in the case of the first marriage, the common law stage may be shorter than in the case of the second marriage (when the couple may spend their entire life together as common-law spouses). Such a pragmatic attitude towards marriage is likely to have been prompted by, at least in part, the upward dynamics in the age of Russians at first marriage. According to Russian Federal State Statistics Service data, in 1980 the groom and the bride were under age 25 in 62 and 71% of first marriages respectively; in 1990 these figures shrank to 53 and 65%; in 2000, they amounted to 45 and 60%, and in 2013, to a mere 25 and 39%.[16]

What part does family play in fulfilling another important goal—having a baby and raising it? How has the transformation of the family affected Russians' behavioral strategies and expectations in this area?

Procreation strategies and parent–child relationship models are another key transformation aspect that shapes the modern family. In today's Russia, this aspect of family life is mostly characterized by an increase in the parents' average age at first birth, a decrease in the number of children, and a shift to planned pregnancies and responsible parenting.[17] Only 2% of Russians do not wish to have good children, while over one-third (36%) believe that they already have them, more than a half (56%) are confident that they will be able to raise their children well, and 6% say that they would love to have children and give them a good upbringing, but have little chance to succeed in doing it. In turn, good children are a dream for only 23% of

---

[15] Other, far less popular responses included, "You should register a marriage before moving in together," and "You should register a marriage as soon as you move in together."

[16] Calculations based on: Marriages classified by age of the groom and the bride / http://www.gks.ru/free_doc/new_site/population/demo/demo33.xls.

[17] Chernova and Shapokovskaya (2010).

all Russians and 21% of those who already have children. Thus, Russians consider children to be a highly important value, while at the same time believe that having a child (just as having a family in general) is an achievable goal rather than an aspiration. This goal usually turns into a more immediate aspiration once people get married (this includes common-law marriages). 25% of married couples and 29% of common-law couples confess that they would love to have good children. Among divorced and widowed Russians, this figure is slightly less, reaching 22% and 20% respectively, while in the case of single Russians and those who are unmarried but have a long-term partner, it amounts to 19% and 14% respectively.

We must highlight that having children remains an important social norm for Russians. Many people count raising a child among their essential values (the most important value for women and the second most important value for men, with respective average scores of 4.88 and 4.81 out of 5). According to the 2009 random sampling survey by the Russian Federal State Statistics Service, the significance of having children rivals only that of achieving wealth and well-being (which is the most important value for men and the second most important value for women, with scores of 4.85 and 4.80 out of 5).[18] Interestingly enough, 88% of married Russians who consider themselves successful parents also believe that they have succeeded in creating a happy family. This opinion is significantly less widespread among those married Russians who think that they do not have good children yet but may achieve this goal in the future: only 67% of them believe that their family is happy. The connection between having a good family as a whole and having good children becomes even more apparent as relationships deteriorate; the corresponding figures amount to 93 and 81% among married Russians with good family relations and 78 and 49% among those with satisfactory family relations.

In addition, Russians appear to have a pretty well-defined notion of how many children there should be in one family. The 2014 data shows that, from Russians' point of view, the current ideal number of children per family is just one, the median value being 1 and the average value being 1.16—this is applicable even to those parents who could financially afford to have more children. These figures, however, also reflect the significant input of those respondents who would prefer to be child-free; overall, only 55% of Russians say that they want to have children. Out of this latter group, 10% would like to have one child, 30% would like to have two children, and 15% would like to have more than two children. Thus, the ideal number that is prevalent among those who actually want a child is two. At the same time, 75% of Russians currently have children: about one third (34%) of the adult population has one child, another third (34%) has two children, and 7% have more than two children. Considering this data, we may arrive at the conclusion that many Russians who already have children have more children than they would like or have even ended up having children even though they did not want to. This means that the children of about one in every five Russians were unwanted.

[18] Brief overview of the Family and Birth Rate random sampling survey (http://www.gks.ru/free_doc/2010/family.htm).

In urban areas, 72% of the population have children, with 37% having more than one child. In rural communities the figures are slightly higher at 82% and 49% respectively. It must be noted that "accidental" or undesired children are quite a common occurrence everywhere. In the cities, people who actually end up having children are 1.3 times more prevalent than those who have expressed a wish to have children; in the countryside, this figure reaches 1.7. In other words, unwanted pregnancies occur much more often in rural communities than in urban ones.

The desire to have children, especially several children, is lessening with time. For instance, according to a survey conducted by the Russian Federal State Statistics Service[19] carried out five years earlier (in the fall of 2009), the number of Russians who were considering having children was slightly higher. 58% of women and 51% of men said they would like to have two children, while 25% of women and 26% of men expressed a wish to have three children. However, when it came to actually planning a pregnancy, only 47% of women and 50% of men wanted to have two children, and as little as 8% and 11% respectively wanted to have three children. In other words, this survey shows that in 2009, the average number of children that Russian women and men wished to have was 2.28 and 2.38 respectively, while the average planned number was 1.72 and 1.90.[20] Thus, in just a few years' time, the demographic plans of Russia's population underwent a significant change.

What is more, the Russian Federal State Statistics Service data indicates that the key obstacles that prevent both women and men from having as many children as they would like are mostly of an economic nature. In particular, these economic hurdles include money troubles (indicated by 85% of both women and men), economic insecurity (82% of women and 83% of men), and housing problems (63% and 65% respectively).[21] Apparently, the chronic nature of these issues in modern Russia is leading to the gradual acceptance of fewer children per family as the new norm. All things considered it is hardly surprising that the wealthiest part of the population expresses a wish to have more children than the national average. The desire to have more children than average is also characteristic of those Russians who are absolutely certain that this is one of life's greatest values (i.e. those who dream of raising good children), as well as of families where spouses get along well with one another.

Consequently, the majority of modern Russian families are certain that having children is a norm. They believe that there have to be children in the family, and that children cement their parents' union and give family life more meaning, make it more successful and fill it with happiness. Even so, children, just as a family in general, tend to be an item on life's checklist rather than a dream. What is more, the Russian population is experiencing a steady rise in the number of people who do not consider children to be a part of their life's plan. Meanwhile, the attitude of those

---

[19] Brief overview of the Family and Birth Rate random sampling survey (http://www.gks.ru/free_doc/2010/family.htm).

[20] Official statistics show that in 2005, the aggregate birth rate began to gradually increase, starting out at 1.6 and reaching 1.9 by 2009.

[21] Taking into account such responses as "Obstacle" and "Great obstacle". To learn more about the factors that influence Russians' reproductive activity, see also: Gurko (2014).

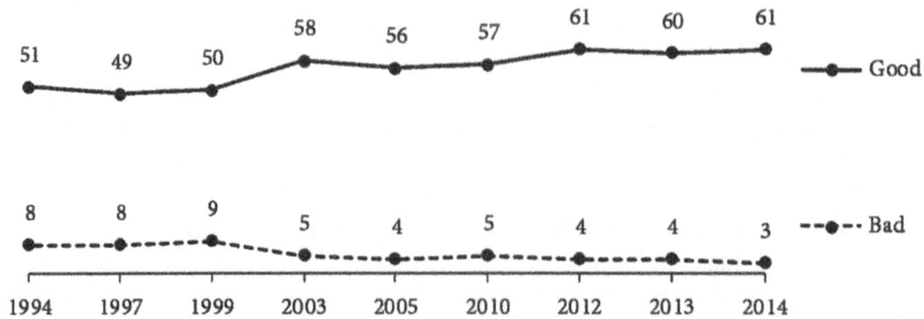

Fig. 8.1 Russians' evaluation of their family relations, 1994–2012, % (*Note* The figure does not feature responses by those who assessed their family relations as "satisfactory" ore those who responded "I don't know")

who still believe that it is necessary to have children is also changing; an increasing number of people believe that one child per family is enough, although this point of view has not yet become a mainstream norm in modern Russia.

It is important to bear in mind that this change of attitude towards children does not stem from deteriorating family relations. Overall, 61% of Russian families are on good terms with one another. Only 4% of Russians describe their family relations as bad, while merely 18% say that they have family problems, and 9% say that they are experiencing problems bringing up their children. Furthermore, the situation has been improving throughout the entire past decade. This could be the result of higher standards of quality of life, since both Russian[22] and foreign research[23] has consistently shown that material wealth and satisfaction with one's social status have a direct impact on family relations. Almost all (90–93%) Russians who identify their social and financial status as good claim to get along with their family members. Among those who assess their status as satisfactory, the figure is slightly higher than half (53–57%). In turn, among those who have a negative opinion of their financial and social status, the share of good family relations drops below 50% (49% and 30% respectively).

It should also be noted that members of urban communities, where the quality of life standard is generally higher, give a slightly better evaluation of their family relations than people who live in rural areas. A positive attitude towards family relations is expressed by about two-thirds (63%) of the urban residents but only a half (56%) of rural residents (Fig. 8.1).

Ironically enough, there are instances when people may consider their families to be happy even though they have had a rocky relationship with their family members. In 2012, the response "I already have a happy family" was chosen by 86% of Russians with good family relations and 61% of Russians with satisfactory ones. This same answer was also selected by 13% of Russians with bad family relations, while 48%

---

[22] Is Russian society ready for modernization? (2010), Russian everyday life during a crisis (2009), and other studies.

[23] Liu and Chen (2006), Aseltine and Kessler (1993), Adele (2004).

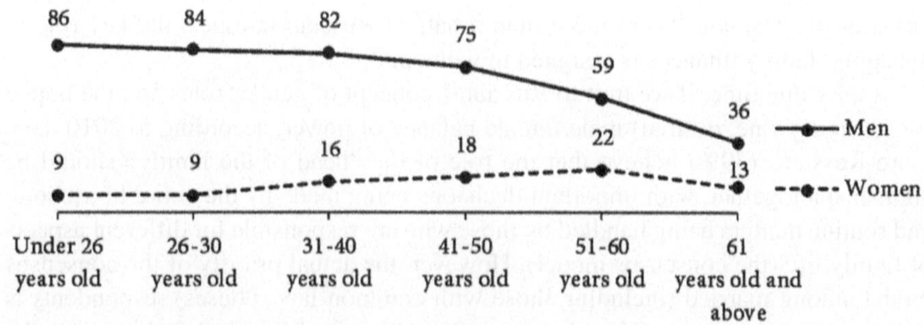

Fig. 8.2 Self-identification as the family breadwinner among men and women in different age cohorts (Responses by Married Russians, including those in Common-Law Unions), 2014, %[26]

of respondents with bad family relations believed that their families still had a chance to live happily.[24] This implies that today, when starting a family, few Russians treat a supportive relationship as one of their main goals—or, at any rate, they do not believe that this is a must.

Additionally, one must not forget that gender roles have also begun to shift in the process of modernization. For example, men are no longer the sole family breadwinners (i.e. family members with the highest income[25]); on the contrary, the share of male breadwinners is decreasing, while the number of female breadwinners keeps growing. This trend is especially prominent in the 30-plus age group, where women are beginning to return to the labor force after delivering and taking care for their babies (Fig. 8.2). It appears that children have the greatest impact on female employment, as 66% of married women who are raising minors confess that their earnings do not make a substantial contribution to the family budget; in the case of child-free households, this is true only for 48% of women. Meanwhile, male breadwinners still continue to be dominant, considerably outweighing the females. For instance, according to 2014 data, 70% of married men and 16% of married women (including those with common-law spouses) say that they are the ones with the highest income in the family. It should be noted that in some cases, both genders confess that they are unsure who is the family breadwinner; but even so, only 10% of married men agree that their income is smaller than that of their family members, or at any rate confess that they do not contribute substantially to the family budget (in cases where it is hard to determine who supports the family the most)—while the same is true of 59% of married women.

Thus, men continue to enjoy a confident lead in the race for the title of breadwinner, while women are more likely to apply their potential for leadership to heading the household, as they take control of the family budget and reserve the right to carry

[24] The figures are derived from responses by married Russians, including those who have common-law spouses.

[25] This issue is discussed in more detail by I.M. Kozina (see Kozina 2000).

[26] The figure does not represent those who responded “other” (i.e. cases when neither the respondent nor other family member is the breadwinner).

out strategic planning[27]—in more than a half of Russian families, the key role in managing family finances is assigned to women.[28]

At the same time, if we turn to Russians' concept of gender roles and the hoped for (or at any rate, desired) male/female balance of power, according to 2010 data, more Russians (39%) believe that the role of the "head of the family" should be abolished altogether, with important decisions being made by the entire household, and routine matters being handled by those who are responsible for different aspects of family life (the consensus model). However, the actual priority of the consensus model among married (including those with common-law spouses) respondents is slightly different—about 35%. In turn, 38% of married Russians believe that the role of the head of the family should be assigned to the oldest male (or, if there is none, the oldest female)—in other words, they lean towards the so-called paternal family model. This model is slightly less popular among the Russian population in general—it is supported by 34% of respondents, making it 5% less popular than the consensus model. When it comes to other models of power balance in the family, the views of married Russians do not really differ from the views of Russians in general. For instance, about one in every five Russians (and 20% of those who are married) prefers a rational approach to choosing the head of the family, pointing out that important decisions should be taken by the person who has the best grasp of the current situation and displays the best ability to make choices with the household's best interests in mind (the pragmatic model). The smallest number of respondents has opted for the utilitarian model, which dictates that the role of the head of the family must be assigned to the person making the greatest contribution to the family budget. This opinion is shared by a mere 7% of the total population, and 7% of married Russians. Most women (44%) favor the consensus model, while most men (45%) favor the paternal one.

It should be noted that the notion of ideal role assignment may change as a person gets married. As pointed out above, the paternal model is in greater demand among married Russians (both those who are married officially and those who have common-law spouses), while the consensus model is preferred by the population in general (Fig. 8.3).

Furthermore, the level of disagreement between the two genders on the matter of allocating roles within the family is the lowest among those who are officially married.[29] It could be that after getting married, both men and women (but mostly women) change their views on the subject. The highest level of disagreement between men and women occurs among divorced respondents and common-law spouses, exceeding 50%. Such dramatic inconsistency of opinions in these two particular

---

[27] Lytkina (2004).

[28] Ref.: Lezhnina (2009).

[29] To determine the level of disagreement between men and women, the following procedure was taken. For each relationship type, the modulus of difference between the share of men and women among the supporters of a given family model was found. The sum of the modulus revealed the degree of disagreement: 45% for single men, 36% for officially married men, 54% for divorced men, 45% for widowers, and 59% for men with common-law spouses.

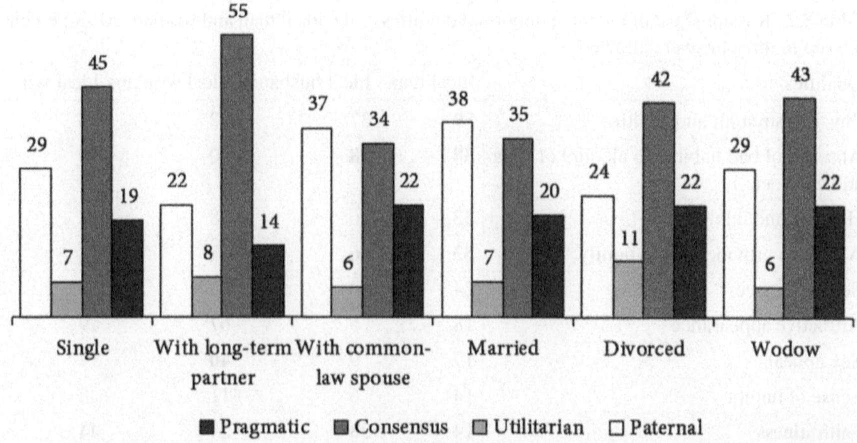

Fig. 8.3 Notion of the ideal family model among Russians with different marital status, 2010, %

social groups heralds a high risk of marriages falling apart, and in the case of common-law unions, of refusing to officially register a marriage due to disagreements over the distribution of duties, power, and chores within the family.[30]

The perceived notions of role distribution in the family is closely linked to ideas of the dream family and the ideal man/woman and spouse. Traditional gender concepts in Russian culture is closely connected to family and childbirth, which links the gender roles of men and women per se to the gender roles of husband and wife. However, as relations within Russian society grow more complex, these concepts are shifting, especially in large cities.

Most Russians believe that the ideal man (see Table 8.2) should be strong and healthy (59%), have no bad habits (38%), be able to provide for his family (33%), and have a high IQ (33%).[31] Physical strength and health are mentioned as the most important traits of the ideal man by both men and women (67% and 53% respectively). We note that some women are ready to overlook the lack of strength if the man has an attractive appearance, which women pay attention to slightly more often than men (21% and 13% respectively). Women also place more emphasis than men on bad habits (42% and 33% respectively), while the ability to provide for the family is the third most important quality of the ideal man from the female point of view (35%). Men, in turn, believe that it is not that important for the ideal man to provide for the family (33%), putting slightly more emphasis on being smart (35%). Therefore, one can conclude that in drawing the portrait of the ideal man, women pay greater

---

[30] See also such research as *M.G. Gorlach.*Genderny aspekt semeyno-rolevogo dissonansa (The gender aspect of family role dissonance // Sotsis. 2002. Issue 1; Lytkina (2004).

[31] A 2015 study by the Levada Center (nation-wide representative sampling with 1,600 respondents) reveals a similar image of the ideal man. The line-up of desired qualities is slightly different, however: a high IQ and ability to provide for the family have been pointed out as significant traits by no less than a half of the respondents (59% and 50% respectively). For more information, please refer to: http://www.levada.ru/13-02-2015/kachestva-kotorye-muzhchiny-i-zhenshchiny-tsenyat-drug-v-druge.

Table 8.2 Russians' list of the most important qualities of the ideal man and woman, 2012, percent (%) (up to three answers allowed)[32]

Qualities	Ideal man	Ideal husband	Ideal woman	Ideal wife
Physical strength and health	**59**	**37**	12	13
Absence of bad habits (no alcohol or drug addiction, etc.)	**38**	**38**	20	19
High IQ and intellect	**33**	16	18	11
Ability to provide for the family	**33**	**56**	2	4
Self-assurance	24	13	13	7
Attractive appearance	18	5	**67**	29
Sex appeal	17	9	**40**	17
Sense of humor	14	6	11	5
Faithfulness	14	**38**	24	**44**
Resolve	12	7	2	2
Thrift and practicality	12	21	22	**47**
Affection for children	7	31	24	**55**
Kindness	6	6	14	17
An easy-going, agreeable personality	4	5	21	20

attention to qualities that are, in one way or another, connected to family life, while men are more inclined to treat the ideal man and the ideal husband as two separate entities.

The main traits of the ideal man do not differ substantially per social group –the difference is more of a quantitative than a qualitative nature. That is, the contrast between the preferences across various social groups is based more on additional brush strokes than on the overall portrait of the ideal man. For instance, young people put more emphasis on male attractiveness (24% of responses by Russians under 25 and 14–17% of responses by other age groups) and sexual prowess (20% of responses by Russians under 35 and 10–15% of responses by other age groups). Those who live in metropolitan areas also tend to consider attractiveness important to a somewhat greater extent (this option is favored by 24% of city dwellers and 14–15% of people from other communities), while giving lower priority to an absence of bad habits (30% and 34–43% respectively) and the ability to provide for the family (24% and 28–37% respectively). Those Russians whose parents do not have a university education value thrift and practicality slightly more than other groups (17% and 7–12% respectively).

The popularity of such characteristics as physical strength, a healthy lifestyle, the ability to provide for the family, faithfulness, thrift, affection for children, and kindness (which are traditionally linked to man's role as the "master of the house", husband, and father) is primarily typical of rural areas, where the traditional notions

[32] The list is arranged from the most important male quality to the least. The qualities selected by no less than one third of the respondents (33%) have been highlighted in bold.

of gender are carefully preserved. When asked to select three key qualities of the ideal man, 21% of rural community members opted for a set (all three) of traditional masculine traits that are part of Russian culture, while only 11% of residents of metropolitan areas did so. Quite the opposite, almost a half of all respondents (49%) in metropolitan areas, where there is low prevalence of traditional values in the traits of the ideal man, picked no more than one quality from the "traditional" list (whereas in rural areas this share amounts to 34%). The lower importance of "traditional" traits is also common among young adults under 35, 44% of whom picked no more than one traditional trait. In other age groups, this rate ranged from 37 to 39%. Respondents from metropolitan communities tend to lean more towards other features of the ideal man, which reflect the emergence of a new male stereotype and gender role; these features include attractiveness (24% in metropolitan areas and 14% in rural communities), sex appeal (19 and 16% respectively), and a high IQ (32 and 27% respectively). Consequently, by comparing the concepts of the ideal man in rural and metropolitan areas, we gain a better understanding of the way a man's gender role is evolving in modern Russian culture, and the way traditional notions of gender are steadily becoming more blurred.

Most Russians believe that an ideal woman must be first and foremost attractive (67%) and sexually enticing (40%).[33] Interestingly enough, men and women agree on this (69 and 48% of responses from men and 66 and 34% of responses from women). When it comes to the third most important quality of the ideal woman, men name faithfulness (31%), while women name affection for children (27%). The excessive number of respondents who consider attractiveness and sex appeal to be key female qualities signifies that the perception of the ideal woman in modern Russia is more homogeneous than the perception of the ideal man. This portrait of the ideal woman also shows that most people, especially men, view the role of a woman separately from the role of a wife, what is not typical of traditional gender concepts.

In this context, it is important to understand the changes that are occurring not only in terms of gender roles as such, but also in terms of husband's and wife's duties in the family. The descriptions of the ideal husband and the ideal wife prove that Russians' understanding of family as a whole implies two clearly defined gender roles: generally, the wife is not expected to perform the same function as her husband, and vice versa (Table 8.3). That is, the husband should be the breadwinner, ensuring the family's wealth and well-being, and act as the strong and healthy "protector" of the hearth. The wife, in turn, "looks pretty" and uses her kindness and easy-going personality to cement family relations (the shares of people who believe that the corresponding traits are necessary for the ideal husband and the ideal wife are three to eleven times greater than of those who do not). In addition, it is the wife who plays the key role in raising children and doing household chores (here, the figures differ

[33] And even though most respondents that took part in the aforementioned Levada Center survey believe that the key female traits should include thrift (49%) and an attractive appearance (41%), the same study shows that the ideal female lover should be sexually enticing (60%) and attractive (59%), which mirrors the evaluation of the ideal woman in the IS RAS survey.

twofold). This means that in order to become an ideal wife, a female must master completely different skills than those required of an ideal woman.

When talking about the ideal husband, members of large urban communities give more preference to traits that allow the wife to feel comfortable around him, i.e. faithfulness (51% in metropolitan areas, 41% in regional capitals, and 33–37% in local centers and rural areas) and an easy-going personality (11% in the largest cities and 3–4% in other communities). In turn, those who live in other areas favor an absence of bad habits (26% of responses by members of metropolitan communities and 40% of responses by members of other communities) and thrift (which is singled out as an important trait of the ideal husband by 15% of Russians that live in metropolitan areas and 19–25% of Russians who live elsewhere).

Respondents from metropolitan areas also put psychological comfort into the foreground when selecting character traits for the ideal wife, far more so than Russians from other communities. Their favored responses include kindness (29% in metropolitan areas, in contrast to 16% elsewhere), intelligence (18% and 7–11% respectively), and faithfulness (56% and 38–46% respectively). In turn, they put far less emphasis on thrift (41% and 46–51% respectively), a healthy lifestyle (13% and 18–20% respectively), affection for children (43% and 52–59% respectively), and attractiveness (20% and 29–33% respectively).

Thus, we can conclude that so far, Russians' notions of the ideal husband and the ideal wife still correspond to the traditional concepts of these roles. By analyzing the set of most important traits for the ideal husband and wife, we can deduce that the family is a microcosm that the spouses must together protect (through their faithfulness), support (through household chores), and expand (through giving birth to children and raising them). For many Russians, the dream family largely reflects traditional cultural values. Of course, this does not mean that actual family models cannot differ—they do, due to the great variety of real-life circumstances. Furthermore, family models are continuing to undergo gradual change. Nevertheless, the profound perception of the ideal family is still preserved. At the same time, certain groups (especially people from metropolitan areas and the younger generation) are coming up with their own image of the dream family, that of a comfortable environment where both spouses' personal qualities ensure a stable, harmonious, and enjoyable relationship. This indicates a surge of new perceptions related to gender roles in the modern Russian family.

In general, traditional gender roles are still deeply rooted in Russians' minds. Since these roles are more or less function-oriented overall, this poses a new question: is there a place for emotional attachment and love in modern Russians' lives? Generally speaking, in Russian culture love has never been the sole basis for starting a family. All the same, love has always been a crucial value for Russians, and an object of pursuit for many. Today, however, even young people no longer dream about love, aspiring instead to enjoy financial security, improve their health, and live in a fair society. Only 6% of Russians dream about finding love, which amounts to only 7% of those who dream about anything at all. Among women, these figures increase to 8% and 9% respectively, including a mere 15% of the 16–25 age group. Furthermore, finding true love ranks a low 12th among Russians' top 14 life goals.[34] Having a good family ranks 4th, being a desire for 17% of the overall Russian population and for 19% of those Russians who confess that they have dreams (taking into account that every respondent could choose up to three options).

It is quite striking that as recently as the early 2000s, only 5% of all Russian women, aged 17–50, said that finding true love was not one of their goals.[35] Two-thirds of all women believed that love matches were more lasting than marriages of convenience. Furthermore, a mere seven years ago, in 2006, 57–70% of Russians under the retirement age said that love was important to them.[36]

Turning now from the concept of love to the more general notion of a successful personal life, when asked what they would wish for if they found a "genie's bottle," only 18% of Russians wished to be socially successful (about 24% of those who would make any wish at all). This wish was generally expressed more among women (23% vs 13% of men), those not yet married (37% of singles, and 28% of people with long-term partners who aren't their spouse), and those whose primary socialization occurred in metropolitan areas (23%; the figure reaches 20% in large cities and 14–18% in other communities).

A happy Russian family is usually characterized by a comfortable environment, in particular a stable relationship between the spouses, which includes their sex life. Good family relations and an active sex life prompt Russians to assess their success in creating a happy family in a more positive way. Although it is interesting to note that almost no one mentions having a good sex life as one of their life aspirations -even though it apparently plays an important role in ensuring a married couple's happiness- 84% of married Russians who enjoy their sex life believe that they already have a happy family. This opinion is expressed strikingly less often by those who are merely satisfied with their sex life (67%). We must note that having a good sex life does not come easily to most Russians, even for younger people. Today, only 44% of Russians rate their sex life as "good," while as many as 12% rate it as "bad." Moreover, women have a negative opinion on the subject twice as often as men (16% and 8% respectively). Odd as it may seem, the situation is the most dire in the largest cities; in metropolitan areas, only 44% of married people (including

[34] Overall, the list of dreams and aspirations includes: making a contribution to society and to Russia's national development; receiving a good education and training for a prestigious job; living in a just, rational society; buying an apartment or a house; starting a business; raising good children; achieving prosperity and being able to spend money without having to count every penny; enjoying good health; having an interesting life and becoming a successful individual; having a happy family; getting an interesting job offer; finding true love; becoming beautiful and attractive; and gaining fame and respect.

[35] Based on the nation-wide topical study entitled "Zhenschina novoy Rossii: kto ona? Kak zhivyot? K chemy stremitsya?" (The new Russian woman: who is she? How does she live? What drives her?) (for more information, please refer to Zhenschina novoy Rossii: kto ona? Kak zhivyot? K chemy stremitsya? (The new Russian woman: who is she? How does she live? What drives her?)—M.: ROSSPEN Publishers, 2002), which was carried out by the Institute of Comprehensive Social Research RAS in March 2002. The data reflects responses from 1,406 women aged from 17 to 50.

[36] Varlamova et al. (2006).

Table 8.3 Evaluation of sex life by different groups of Russians, 2012, %

	Good	Satisfactory	Bad
Age			
16–25 years old	71	28	1
26–35 years old	66	33	1
36–45 years old	51	44	5
46–55 years old	38	51	11
Income			
Less than 1 local median	49	44	7
1–2 local medians	55	40	5
More than 2 local medians	64	35	1
Family relations			
Good	78	20	2
Satisfactory	11	80	9
Bad	22	35	43

Note Based on responses by married Russians, including those who have common-law spouses

those with common-law spouses) believe that they had a good sex life, while 51% of married respondents in other communities expressed this belief.

Things are slightly less bleak for unmarried Russians with a long-term partner. While a high sex life rating was provided by 54% of married respondents and 49% of respondents with a common-law spouse, the figure goes up to 62% for unmarried respondents with a long-term partner. For single, divorced, and widowed respondents, this figure reaches 37%, 19%, and 18% respectively. At the same time, one-third of young married Russians (i.e. 29% of Russians under 25 and 34% of Russians aged 26–35), while generally satisfied with their marriage, rate their sex life as satisfactory or even bad. Respondents' attitudes towards their sexual activity is influenced by a high level of economic wealth and a good environment in the family (Table 8.3), which in general, provides good soil for nourishing personal relations, including one's sex life.

We should note that an unsatisfactory sex life does not mean that a person considers their family to be unhappy. As many as 46% (!) of married Russians who rate their sex life as bad believe that they have a happy family. In turn, only 59% of respondents who are confident that their family is happy rate their sex life as good, while 3% of the same category even say that their sex life is unsatisfactory.[37]

To conclude, love towards one's partner and an enjoyable sex life increase psychological comfort and foster a feeling of well-being. At the same time, Russians do not

[37] Other research has already highlighted the fact that even young Russians believe that sexual satisfaction is not a must-have for happy family life; see, for example, *L.F. Borusyak*. Lyubov, seks, partnerstvo: oriyentatsii moskovskikh studentov (Love, sex, partnership: Preferences of Moscow students) // Vestnik Obschestvennogo Mneniya: Dannye. Analiz.Diskussii (The Russian Public Opinion Herald. Data. Analysis. Discussions). 2011. Vol. 108. Issue 2.

regard these aspects of family life as something crucial to happiness—even though there is no doubt that they introduce harmony and stability to family and marriage.

Overall, research indicates that family still remains an independent value in modern Russia. At the same time, modernization, along with resulting diversification of social relations, is transforming the institution of the family and bringing forth new practices and norms, such as common-law unions, delayed first marriages and first childbirths, the proliferation of nuclear families and a weakening sense of kinship, fewer desired number of children, etc. In this context, a happy family and good children are becoming one of life's present goals rather than an aspiration. In turn, social and psychological comfort within the family is still desirable, but for most of the Russian population, this is not an essential condition for family happiness.

As interpersonal relations undergo modernization, the interaction between men and women is gradually changing as well. It is no longer an aspiration to achieve love and harmony in one's personal life (including sex life), although these aspects do contribute greatly to marriage stability. At the same time, however, the lack of love and good sex life does not necessarily jeopardize a family's well-being and happiness.

Irrespective of the above, the general notion of family that Russians envision in their dreams (including relations between the spouses) still reflects traditional values of Russian culture. That is, despite active social and demographic modernization, which has diversified the relations between men and women, Russians' preferred family model preserves traditional values and common gender roles (with the man as the breadwinner and the woman as a mother and the keeper of the hearth). This leads to the conclusion that the basic foundations of the family value system are still present in Russian society. These foundations are the most vulnerable in metropolitan areas, where life is growing increasingly more complex and dynamic, forcing people to apply new standards to their concept of family.

References

Adele, H. 2004. How Poverty Is Pushing Families into Divorce. Sydney Morning Herald Online. http://www.smh.com.au/articles/2004/03/24/1079939718989.html.

Aseltine, R.H., and R.C. Kessler. 1993. Marital Disruption and Depression in a Community Sample. *Journal of Health and Social Behaviour* 34 (3): 237–251.

Chernova, Zh. V., and L.L. Shapokovskaya. 2010. Young Adults as Spouses, Partners, and Parents. Discourse directives and practices in modern Russia [Molodiye vzrosliye: supruzhestvo, partnerstvo i roditelstvo. Diskursivnye predpisaniya i praktiki v sovremennoy Rossii]. Laboratorium. *Russian Review of Social Research.* Issue 3. [in Russian].

Gurko, T.A. 2008. *Marriage and Parenthood in Russia [Brak i roditelstvo v Rossii].* Moscow: Institute of Sociology RAS [in Russian].

Gurko, T.A. 2014. *Spouses' Reproductive Planning* [Reproduktivniye plany suprugov]. *Sociological Studies.* Issue 9. [in Russian].

Is Russian Society Ready for Modernization [Gotovo li rossiyskoye obschestvo k modernizatsii]. 2010. *Is Russian Society Ready for Modernization,* ed. M.K. Gorshkov, R. Krumm, N.E. Tikhonova. Moscow: Ves Mir. [in Russian].

Kartzeva, L.V. 2003. Family Model During the Transformation of Russian Society [Model semyi v usloviyakh tranformatsii rossiyskogo obschestva]. *Sociological Studies*. Issue 7. [in Russian].

Kozina, I.M. 2000. What Defines a Person as a Breadwinner? [Chto opredelyaet status kormiltsa semyi?]. *Sociological Studies*. Issue 11. [in Russian].

Lezhnina, Yu. P. 2009. Family in Russians' Everyday Life [Semya v povsednevnoy zhizni rossiyan]. *Russian everyday life during a Crisis: A View of Sociologists* [Rossiyskaya povsednevnost v usloviyakh krizisa], ed. M.K. Gorshkov, R. Krumm, and N.E. Tikhonova. Moscow: Alpha-M. [in Russian].

Liu, R.X., and Z.-Y. Chen. 2006. The Effects of Marital Conflict and Marital Disruption on Depressive Affect: A Comparison Between Women In and Out of Poverty. *Social Science Quarterly* 87 (2): 250–271.

Lytkina, T. 2004. Housework and Distribution of Power Between Genders in the Family [*Domashny trud i gendernoye razdeleniye vlasti v semye*]. *Sociological Studies*. Issue 9. [in Russian].

Mitrikas, A.A. 2004. Family as a Value: Current Status and Future Possibility of Value Choice in European Countries [Semya kak tsennost: sostoyaniye i perspektivy tsennostnogo vybora v stranakh Evropy]. *Sociological Studies*. Issue 5. [in Russian].

Russian Everyday Life During a Crisis [Rossiyskaya povsednevnost v usloviyakh krizisa]. 2009. Russian Everyday Life During a Crisis, ed. M.K. Gorshkov, R. Krumm, and N.E. Tikhonova. Moscow: Alpha-M. [in Russian].

Varlamova, S.N., A.V. Noskova, and N.N. Sedova. 2006. The Place of Family and Children among Russians' Life Goals [Semya i deti v zhiznennykh ustanovkakh rossiyan]. *Sociological Studies*. Issue 11. [in Russian].

Zakharov, S. 2006. Marriage in Russia: History and Present [Brachnost v Rossii: istoria i sovremennost]. *Demoscope Weekly*. Issue 261–262 http://demoscope.ru/weekly/2006/0261/tema04.php. [in Russian].

Zdravomyslova O.A. 2006. Family: From the Past to the Present [Semya: iz proshlogo – v budusche]. Proceedings of the Online Conference "Gender Stereotypes in Modern Russia" 01.05.06–07.07.06. http://ecsocman.hse.ru/text/16209413.html. [in Russian].

Chapter 9
Moving Towards a More Equitable and Just Society

Wei Li

The Chinese ideal of social justice dates back to ancient times, from which the main ideological components of social justice can be traced. These components include no scarcity or uneven distribution of wealth, care and social assistance for the weak, merit-based rather than social-based cultivation of talent, and the election of wise and capable officials for public posts.[1] The "Western Learning" social reform movement that occurred during the late Qing Dynasty was born out of the interaction between the European Enlightenment and the traditional Chinese ideal of "Great Harmony." This social movement was built on the ideals of Kang Youwei, who believed in a "whole world united as one, with no class distinctions, and equality for everyone." He also believed that "all people are equal masters." In the late nineteenth and early twentieth century, socialist ideology was introduced to China. "Building a political system of dictatorship by peasants and workers, eliminating the system of private property, and gradually realizing a communist society" became the highest aims of the Chinese Communist Party.[2] The founding of People's Republic of China in 1949 fostered the gradual establishment of a socialist system. Although social inequalities cannot be completely eliminated, the state-owned economy and planning system have maintained a situation where differences in social wealth have been quite small.

Chinese society has experienced great social changes since China's reform and opening up in 1978. While marketization reform accelerated economic growth, it also brought about the polarization of social classes and growing inequality in the distribution of social wealth. According to data from the National Bureau of Statistics and estimations of some scholars, China's Gini coefficient, the standard economic measure of income inequality, was 0.2797 in 1978. After year-by-year growth, it

[1] Zhu (2011).

[2] The Declaration of the Second National Congress of the Communist Party of China.

W. Li (✉)
Department of Social Development, Chinese Academy of Social Science, Beijing, China

P. Li and M. K. Gorshkov (eds.), *Life Expectations of the People*,
Research Series on the Chinese Dream and China's Development Path,
https://doi.org/10.1007/978-981-16-2505-3_9

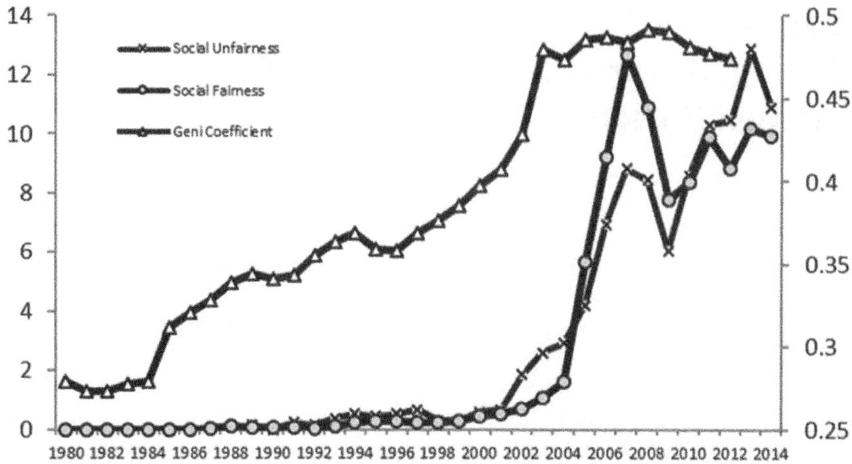

Fig. 9.1 Comparison of China's Gini coefficient (measuring income inequality) and keyword trends relevant to social fairness in *Chinese Academic Journals* between 1980 and 2014

exceeded 0.4 in 2000, reaching its highest point at 0.491 in 2008, before gradually falling to 0.469 in 2014. The rising level of income inequality aroused a sense of social injustice, resulting in stronger appeals for social justice. Taking statistics on the distribution of keywords such as "social fairness" and "social injustice" in literature published by the Chinese Knowledge Resource Integrated Database between 1980 and 2014 and comparing them with variations in the Gini coefficient in corresponding years we find the following: (1) for over 30 years, the Gini coefficient (representing income inequality) and the frequency of references to social fairness in academia (including the keywords "social fairness" and "social inequality") grew in step with one another, indicating to a certain extent that the social reality of growing economic inequality has triggered more attention to the idea of social fairness; (2) academia did not pay much attention to social fairness in the last 20 years of the twentieth century, yet attention increased sharply in the early twenty-first century, when China's Gini coefficient exceeded 0.4; (3) there was less attention to social inequality than social fairness until 2010, when the growth rate in the use of the term exceeded that of social fairness, indicating that people are currently more concerned with social inequality than social fairness (Fig. 9.1).

To understand the public's attention to social fairness during China's social change and to further analyze the Chinese public's evaluation of social fairness and sense of justice, the author utilized four national survey datasets of the China Social Survey (CSS) conducted by the Chinese Academy of Social Sciences Institute of Sociology between 2006 and 2013.

9.1 Changing Trends in the Public's Assessment of Social Fairness

In the CSS conducted in 2006, 2008, and 2013, respondents were asked, "what do you think of the degree of fairness in the following fields of society at present?" There were 11 specific fields listed, including compulsory education and the college entrance examination system, as well as the overall situation of social fairness. The possible answers were "very fair," "relatively fair," "relatively unfair," and "very unfair." Table 9.1 shows that the proportion of positive assessments of overall fairness (the share of "very fair" + "relatively fair" responses) among rural and urban residents was about 60%, with no great change between 2006 and 2013. In terms of the specific fields, there were ups and downs as well as a certain steadiness in the public's assessment of fairness. The public's assessments of fairness in compulsory education and the college entrance examination system were among the highest and most stable, ranking in the top three in all three years of the CSS surveys. This suggests that the public feels positively towards the field of education on the whole. The public's assessments of fairness in the salaries offered among different regions and

Table 9.1 The Chinese public's positive assessment of social fairness[a]

	CSS 2006		CSS 2008		CSS 2013	
	%	Rank	%	Rank	%	Rank
Compulsory education	76.7	1	85.9	1	82.2	1
College entrance examination system	71.4	2	74.1	2	68.0	3
Political rights actually enjoyed by citizens	62.0	3	65.6	4	50.4	5
Administration of justice and law enforcement	55.1	4	53.0	5	46.3	6
Public health	49.9	5	66.9	3	68.1	2
Work and employment opportunity	44.4	6	41.2	8	41.7	7
Wealth and income distribution	40.2	7	28.9	11	33.4	9
Pension and other social security benefits	37.5	8	50.4	6	57.7	4
Election of party and government cadres	34.4	9	47.7	7	35.3	8
Payment among different regions and industries	33.6	10	38.1	10	29.9	11
Rights and treatment between urban and rural areas	29.0	11	39.9	9	30.2	10
Overall assessment of social fairness	62.3		69.2		60.4	

[a]Positive assessment of social fairness is the summation of the percentages of "very fair" and "relatively fair"
(*Note* a=.000)

industries, along with the equality of rights between rural and urban areas, scored the lowest, ranking at the bottom three in all survey years. This reveals the public's strong discontent with the income gap among different industries and regions, as well as between urban and rural areas. In comparison, the fairness evaluation of social security such as public health and pensions increased over the survey years. The evaluation of public health rose from fifth place (49.9%) in 2006 to third place (66.9%) in 2008, and finally to second place (68.1%) in 2013. The fairness evaluation of pensions rose from eighth place (37.5%) in 2006 to sixth place (50.4%) in 2008, to fourth place (57.5%) in 2013. Such patterns of change reflect the public's affirmation of a series of beneficial policies aimed at improving people's livelihood and social security over the past eight years. At the same time, the public's fairness evaluation substantially declined in the following fields: the political rights of citizens ranked third (62.0%) and fourth (65.6%) in 2006 and 2008, but dropped to fifth (50.4%) in 2013; the administration of justice and law enforcement also declined from fourth place (55.1%) in 2006 to fifth place (53.0%) in 2008 to sixth (46.3%) in 2013; property and income distribution declined from seventh place (40.2%) in 2006 to last place (28.9%) in 2008, before rising slightly to ninth place (33.4%) in 2013. Evaluations of "work and employment opportunity" and "election of party and government cadres" consistently ranked in the lower middle over the course of the three surveys; the former ranked sixth (44.4%) in 2006, eighth (41.2%) in 2008 and seventh (41.7%) in 2013, while the latter ranked ninth (34.4%) in 2006, seventh (47.7%) in 2008 and eighth (35.3%) in 2013. In general, the public's assessments of fairness were highest in the field of education, increased with respect to people's livelihood and social security, and declined in the fields of politics and public power, and remained lowest in the area of income inequality.

We will further explore the internal structure of a "fair society" by comparing the assessments of different aspects of social fairness with the overall assessment of social fairness. By calculating the correlation coefficient between social fairness in the eleven fields with the overall assessment of social fairness using data from CSS 2013, we see that the fields with the greatest impact on the overall assessment of social fairness include the administration of justice and law enforcement (with a Pearson correlation coefficient of 0.487), the election of party and government cadres (with a Pearson correlation coefficient of 0.475), and the political rights actually enjoyed by citizens (with a Pearson correlation coefficient of 0.454). The fields with the second largest impact included the rights and treatment between urban and rural areas (0.437), and pensions and other social security benefits (0.432). The fields with the third largest impact were wealth and income distribution (0.407), work and employment opportunities (0.402), public health (0.400), and salary differences among regions and industries (0.386). The least impactful fields were the college entrance examination system (0.271) and compulsory education (0.250) (see Table 9.2). Such results suggest that although the public's fairness assessment of education is high, it has the least impact on the overall assessment of social fairness. The true determinants of overall social fairness lie in politics, social security and income distribution.

Table 9.2 Correlation coefficients between evaluations of social fairness in different fields and assessment of overall social fairness

Social fairness assessment by field	Pearson correlation coefficient	Sample size
Administration of justice and law enforcement	.487[a]	8225
Election of party and government cadres	.475[a]	8359
Political rights actually enjoyed by citizens	.454[a]	8604
Rights and treatment between urban and rural areas	.437[a]	8875
Pension and other social security benefits	.432[a]	9051
Wealth and income distribution	.407[a]	9138
Work and employment opportunity	.402[a]	8961
Public health	.400[a]	9280
Payment among different regions and industries	.386[a]	8651
College entrance examination system	.271[a]	8422
Compulsory education	.250[a]	9349

[a].000

Confirmatory factor analysis shows that the sense of social fairness in the above eleven fields can be simplified into four dimensions: (1) political fairness, which includes political rights actually enjoyed by citizens, the administration of justice and law enforcement, and the election of party and government cadres; (2) economic fairness, including wealth and income distribution, salary differences among regions and industries, and rights and treatment between urban and rural areas; (3) security fairness, including pensions and other social security benefits, work and employment opportunities, and public health; and (4) education fairness, including the college entrance examination system and compulsory education. The Pearson correlation coefficient between each of these four dimensions of fairness and the assessment of overall social fairness are, in descending order, 0.401 for political fairness, 0.368 for economic fairness, 0.332 for security fairness and 0.189 for education fairness. This more concisely reflects the Chinese population's assessment of overall social fairness prioritized in order of politics, economy, security and education (Fig. 9.2).

An interesting finding is that the higher the assessment of one of the four fairness dimensions, the less important and impact this dimension has on the evaluation of overall fairness. Figure 9.2 shows that the average positive assessment value (by percentage) of each of the four dimensions is ranked as follows: education (67.5%), security (54.8%), politics (51.1%) and economy (42.6%). But the impact of each of these dimensions on the overall assessment of social fairness (correlation coefficient) shows an opposite trend. The overall assessment of current social fairness is like an upright funnel, the center is located at a lower position than the edge. Using this metaphor, the dimensions of political and economic fairness are at the center, while the dimension of education is at the periphery of overall social fairness.

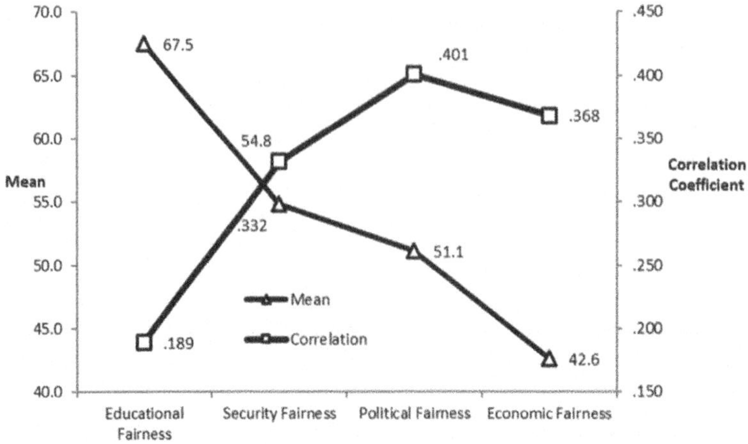

Fig. 9.2 Correlation coefficient between average values of four dimensions of fairness and assessment of overall social fairness

9.2 Group Analysis of Social Fairness Assessment

Next we will explore which social groups had positive and negative assessments of the current social fairness situation. Previous research shows that there are two interpretations of people's assessments of social fairness or sense of fairness. The first one is the objective perspective, which argues that one's sense of social fairness is a reflection of social inequality. As a result, respondents with higher socio-economic status and a better distribution position will feel society is fairer than respondents with lower socioeconomic status.[3] According to this theory, urban residents, respondents with a higher income, a high educational level and high occupational status should have a higher assessment of social fairness. The second interpretation comes from the theory of social reference, which argues that the public's sense of fairness arises from a comparison with a particular reference or past experiences in their own lives. Thus, when people's situations are better than the reference object or past living standards, they will have higher sense of fairness.[4] Based on the two perspectives, and leveraging data from the CSS 2013, we analyzed whether the sense of fairness for each of the four dimensions of fairness varied among socio-demographic characteristics, gender, urban and rural residency, age, political affiliation, education, income, occupation, subjective identity of social status, changes in living standards, and so on. Statistical analysis shows that there is no gender difference in the assessment of social fairness, yet clear differences exist among different socio-demographic groups.

[3] Kluegel and Smith (1981), Ng and Allen (2005).

[4] Wang (2011), Meng (2012).

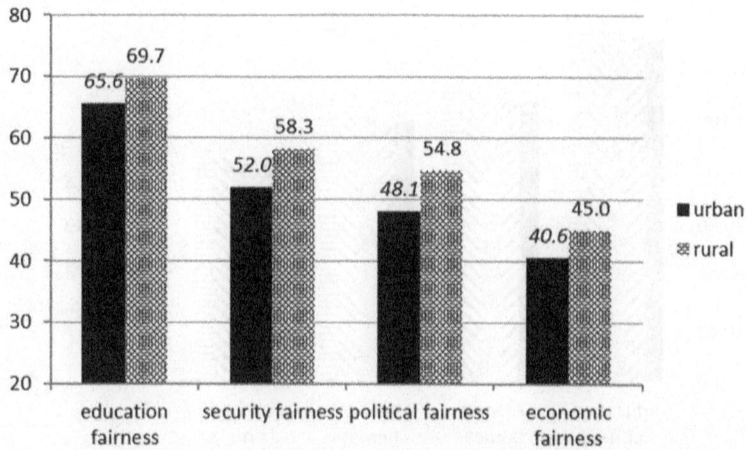

Fig. 9.3 Rural and urban residents' assessment of social fairness (mean)

(i) Urban and Rural Residency

Statistical results show that rural residents had a higher sense of social fairness in all fields compared to urban residents (Fig. 9.3). Calculated using a hundred-mark system, rural residents were 4.1 points higher than urban residents in their assessments of education fairness (69.7 vs 65.6), 6.3 points higher in that of security fairness (58.3 vs 52.0), 6.7 points higher for political fairness (54.8 vs 48.1), and 4.4 points higher for economic fairness (45.0 vs 40.6).

(ii) Age

Statistical results show that the age of respondents is positively related to their assessment of social fairness, with older people having a stronger sense of social fairness. Taking the example of fairness in education, the average assessment value was 65.5 for respondents under 30 years old and 66.5 for those between 30 and 39 years old. For respondents between 40 and 49 years old it increased to 67.2, and reached over 69 for those over 50 years old. The fairness assessment for the dimensions of security, politics, and economy also increased with age (Fig. 9.4). Since the CSS 2013 is a cross-sectional survey, differences in the assessment of fairness might represent generational differences.

(iii) Political Affiliation[5]

Statistical results show that for education fairness and political fairness, Chinese Communist Party members and ordinary people had higher assessments than members of the Communist Youth League. In terms of education fairness, CCP members and ordinary people respectively scored 67.0 points and 67.8 points on average, while members of the Communist Youth League scored 64.1 points on

[5] Due to small sample size, analysis of political affiliation excluded the democratic parties in China.

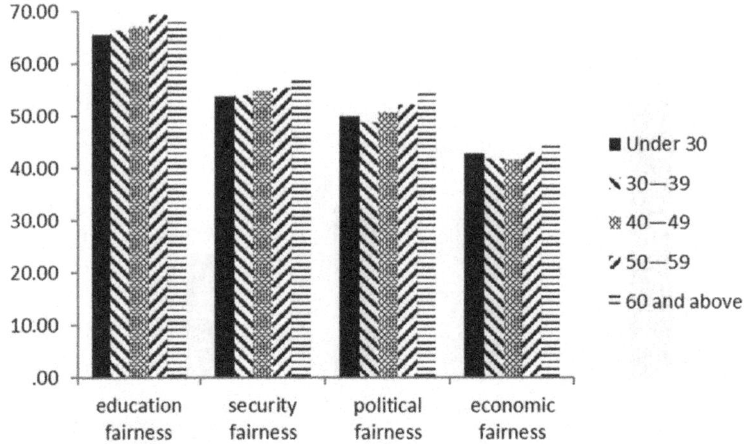

Fig. 9.4 Assessment of social fairness by age group (mean)

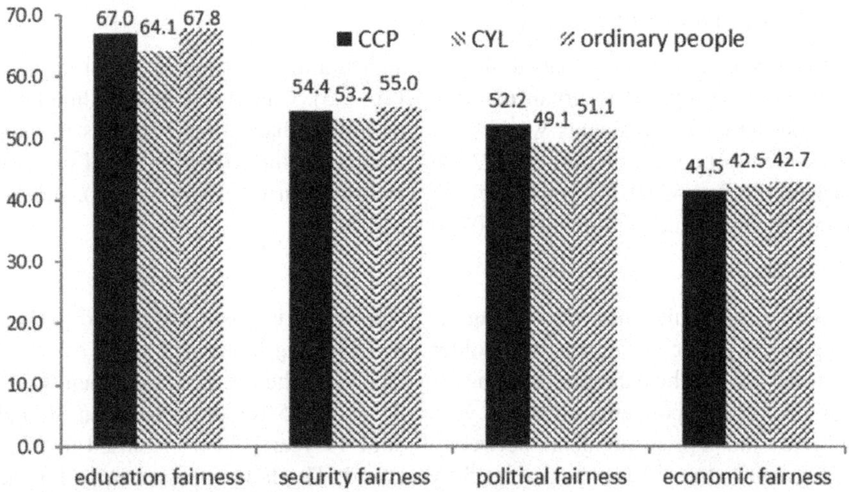

Fig. 9.5 Assessment of social fairness by political affiliation (mean)

average. In terms of the assessment of political fairness, the average values of CCP members and ordinary people were 52.2 points and 51.1 points respectively, for members of Communist Youth League it was 49.1 points. Respondents with different political affiliations had similar assessments of security fairness and education fairness (Fig. 9.5). However, such results might be due to the age of respondents rather than political affiliation; members of the Communist Youth League are younger compared with CCP members and ordinary people, and younger people have a lower sense of social fairness than older people.

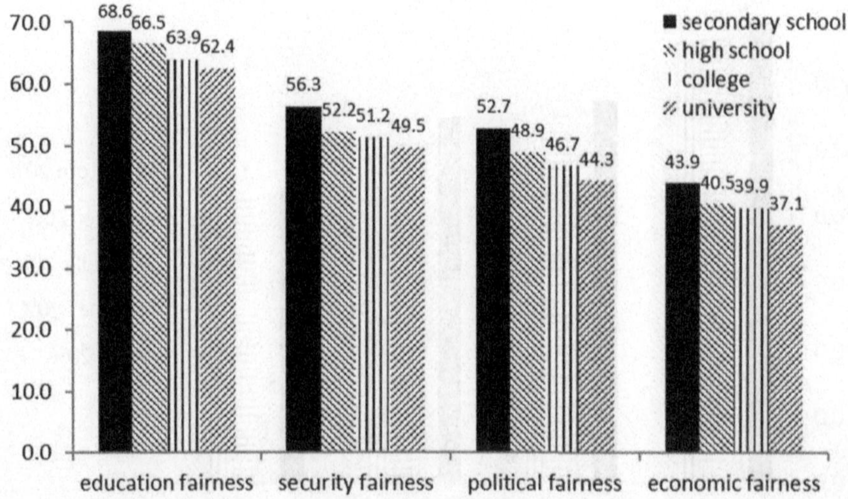

Fig. 9.6 Assessment of social fairness by educational level (means)

(iv) Educational Level

Statistical results show that the public's assessment of social fairness in different fields was negatively associated with educational level (Fig. 9.6). Taking the example of education fairness, the average fairness assessment score was highest among people with junior middle school or below education (68.6), followed by those who graduated from senior high school (66.5) and graduates of junior college (63.9). The lowest score came from those with a bachelor's degree and above (62.4). There was a 6.2 point difference between the highest and lowest scoring groups. This pattern is similarly reflected in the fairness assessments in the other three fields. Educational differences in assessment of political fairness was the largest. The group with the highest average score (junior middle school) had 8.5 points more than the group with the lowest average score (Bachelor's degree or above).

(v) Income

Statistical results show that family income per capita had an obvious negative impact on the assessment of social fairness in all fields (Fig. 9.7). Among the five groups divided by family income per capita, the bottom 20% scored highest in the assessment of social fairness on average, while the top 20% scored the lowest on average. Taking the example of political fairness, the average score of the bottom 20% income group was 55.1 points, followed by 52.8 points from the lower-middle income group, 50.9 points from the middle income group, 49.5 points from the higher-middle income group, and 47.7 points from the top 20% income group. The lowest income group's score was 7.4 points higher than that of the highest income group.

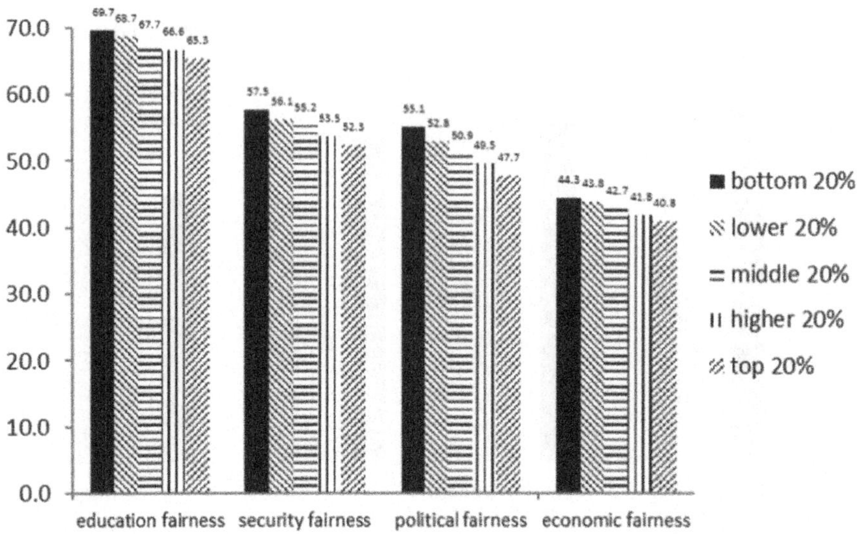

Fig. 9.7 Assessment of social fairness by income group (means)

(vi) Occupation

Statistical results show that agricultural workers had the highest assessment of social fairness in all fields, and the differences among other occupational groups were not large (Fig. 9.8). Taking the example of security fairness, the average score of the fairness assessments of agricultural workers was 58.8 points, while that of other occupational groups ranged between 51 and 54 points. With respect to political fairness, the average score of agricultural workers was 55.2 points, while that of other occupational groups ranged between 46 and 49 points. In comparison, clerks and professionals had the lowest fairness assessments in all fields. Agricultural workers' high assessment of fairness is consistent with the assessments of rural residents and lower educated respondents, as shown above.

(vii) Self-Identified Socioeconomic Status

In the survey, we asked respondents about their self-identified socioeconomic status relative to other local people. The statistical results show that self-identified socioeconomic status does have a correlation to the assessment of social fairness. Specifically, respondents who considered themselves to have middle to high socioeconomic status in comparison with other people had higher assessments of social fairness than those who considered themselves to have low to lower-middle socioeconomic status. For instance, the average overall fairness scores of people with high, higher-middle and middle socioeconomic status were 52.9 points, 53.8 points and 53.4 points respectively; the average scores of people with lower-middle and low socioeconomic status were 49.8 points and 49.1 points. In terms of the assessment

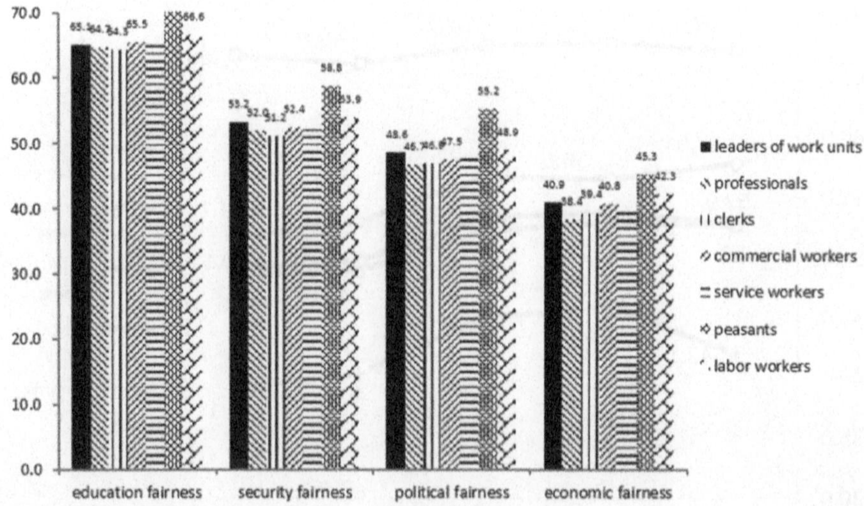

Fig. 9.8 Assessment of social fairness by occupational group (mean)

of social fairness in specific fields, self-identified socioeconomic status did not seem to have much impact in the assessment of education fairness, however, it was positively associated with the assessments of political fairness and security fairness. The middle and upper-middle socioeconomic groups had the highest assessment of economic fairness (46.0 points and 45.0 points respectively), followed by those with high socioeconomic status (42.1), lower-middle socioeconomic status (40.4 points) and low socioeconomic status (39.1 points) (Fig. 9.9).

(viii) Changes in Living Standard

In the survey, we asked respondents about changes in their standards of living in the last five years, whether their living standard had improved, declined or remained unchanged in the past five years. The results show that changes in living standard were significantly associated with the assessment of social fairness. Respondents with improved living standards in the past 5 years had a substantially higher assessment of social fairness than those with unchanged or decreased living standards. Specifically, for those with a significantly improved living standard, the average social fairness assessment score was 55.0 points, followed by 52.1 points for those with a slightly improved living standard, and 49.1 points for those with an unchanged living standard. For those with slightly and significantly decreased living standards, the average social fairness assessment scores were 45.5 points and 43.4 points respectively. The influence of changes in living standards on the perception of social fairness is reflected in both the assessments of overall fairness and assessments in each of the four dimensions, with slightly smaller differences for the assessments of education fairness (Fig. 9.10).

From the above analysis, we can draw some conclusions:

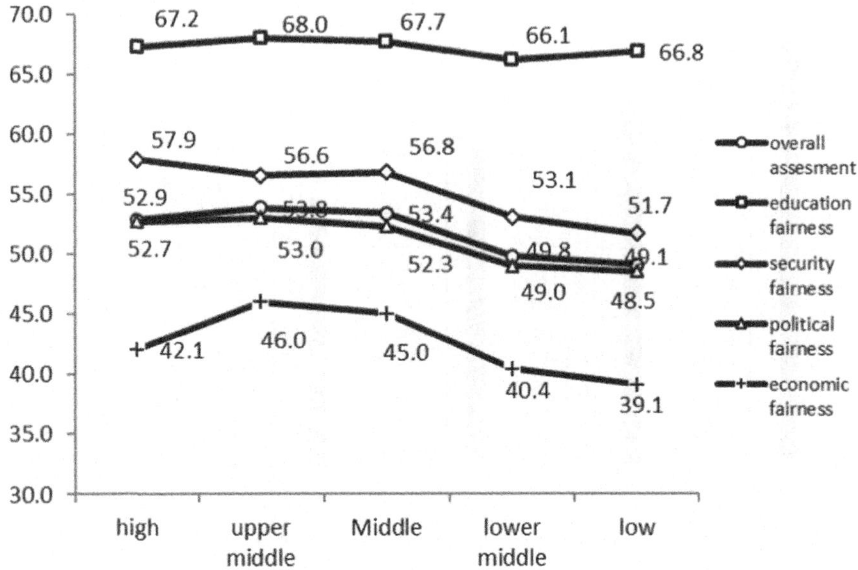

Fig. 9.9 Assessment of social fairness by self-identified socioeconomic status (mean)

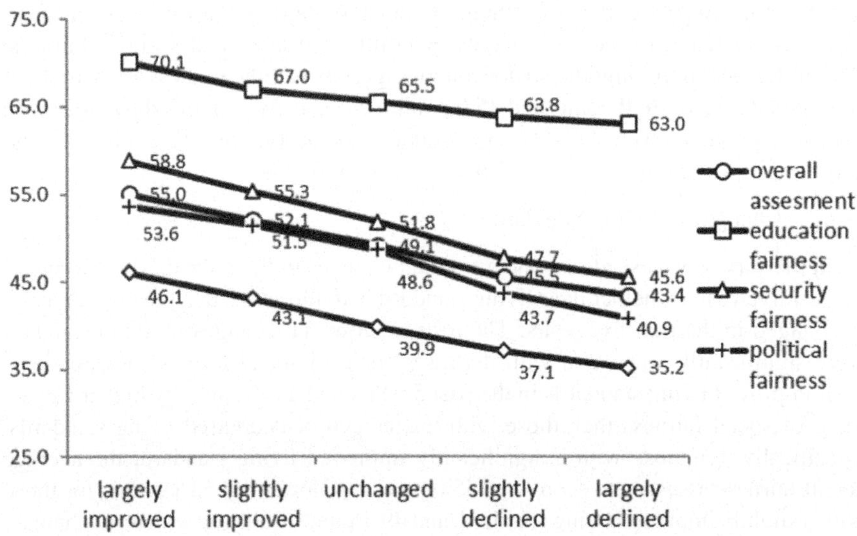

Fig. 9.10 Assessment of social fairness based on changes in living standard (mean)

1. At present, there are differences in the assessment of social fairness among different social groups. Respondents who had a high assessment of social fairness were mainly of lower social classes. Most were rural residents, over 50 years old, with a low educational level and low income, and engaged in agricultural work. In comparison, higher social groups had a low assessment of social fairness. Most were urban residents, young, with a high-level education and higher income, and engaged in non-agricultural work. Aside from demographic factors such as age and generation, differences among groups in their social fairness assessments were clearly related to social stratification and socioeconomic status.
2. It is worth noting that socioeconomic status was negatively associated with assessments of social fairness. Social groups with a lower socioeconomic status had higher assessments, and social groups with higher socioeconomic status had lower assessments. Such results suggest that in China today, the normally adopted logic of "unequal status = social injustice" is not appropriate for interpreting group differences in the sense of social injustice, and therefore other mechanisms must be adopted.
3. Another competitive interpretation is the influence of perceptions of social reference. Social reference indicators, such as self-identified socioeconomic status and changes in living standards, had a significant influence on the sense of social fairness, the latter of which had the more obvious impact. However, the reference framework is different between the two indicators: self-identified socioeconomic status is based on referencing oneself to other people around, which is a horizontal comparison, while changes in living standard is based on reference to one's past situation or the rate of change between oneself and others, which is a longitudinal comparison. As long as one's situation improves at a faster rate in comparison with other people, people have a stronger sense of social fairness, even from a disadvantageous socioeconomic position. This phenomenon is just the opposite of "relative deprivation," as proposed by S.A. Stauffer, and could be termed "relative gain."
4. An increase in the sense of "relative gain" derives mainly from continuous improvement in the living standards of rural residents Fig. 9.11 shows that 78.1% of rural residents reported that their standard of living had improved in the last five years (slightly improved + largely improved), which is 8% higher than that of urban residents. This suggests that rural residents had a higher sense of "relative gain" than urban residents. If we divide rural and urban residents into different groups by family income per capita, rural residents had a higher sense of "relative gain" than urban residents in all five income groupings. The gap between rural residents and urban residents in the sense of "relative gain" among different income groups was 8% (70.8 vs. 62.7%), 16, 13, 11 and 12% (92.6 vs. 76.6%). Among the group with relatively higher incomes, rural residents had a stronger sense of "relative gain" than urban residents.

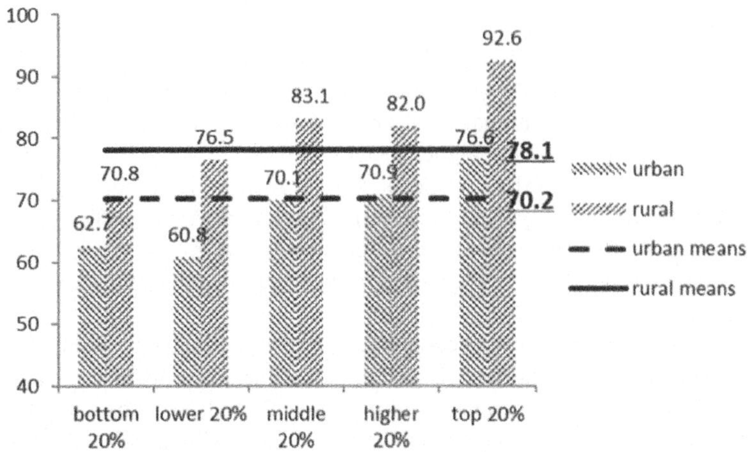

Fig. 9.11 Sense of "relative gain" for urban and rural residents by family income per capita (%)

9.3 Assessment of Social Fairness and Social Attitude

The public's sense of social fairness is not an isolated social-psychological phenomenon, but is related to other factors and attitudes such as interpersonal trust at the individual level, social security and social approval at a societal level, and satisfaction with the government and national identity at the political level. All these factors form a set of social mentality indicators.

(i) Assessment of social fairness and social trust

Social trust is the recognition of general interpersonal relationships within a society, and serves as an important index of social cohesion. The 2013 CSS survey used seven indicators to measure the social trust of the public, including: (1) "People are willing to help others in most cases;" (2) "Most people can be trusted;" (3) "In most cases, people care only about themselves;" (4) "I am very cautious in interactions with other people;" (5) "Most people will try to treat people equally as far as possible;" (6) "Most people will take advantage of others at the first opportunity;" and (7) "The trust among people around me is relatively good at present." Respondents were asked to assign a value of 1–4 for each question, with lower values indicating less social trust. A scale of social trust with values ranging from 4 to 28 was constructed by adding the results of these seven indicators together. The survey results showed that the average value on the social trust scale was 19.05, or about 59.3% when coverted into a percentage. Statistical analysis of this result shows that the sense of social fairness is moderately correlated with social trust. The Pearson correlation coefficient between social trust and assessment of fairness was 0.306. For each dimension of social fairness, the correlation between social trust and political fairness was the highest (0.294), followed by security fairness (0.266), economic

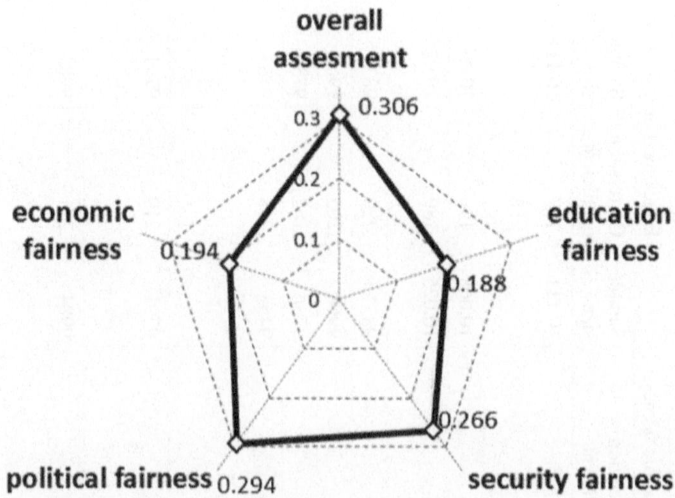

Fig. 9.12 Correlation between sense of social fairness and social trust (Pearson R)

fairness (0.194) and education fairness (0.188). This indicates that an increase in social fairness is helpful in improving social trust (Fig. 9.12).

(ii) Assessment of Social Fairness and Sense of Social Security

A population's sense of social security is the overall reflection of people's attitudes towards whether a society is safe, and is embodied by an individual sense of security. This sense of social security not only reflects perceptions of public security, but also indicates the degree of stability in individual life and society. Nine aspects of social security were measured in the 2013 CSS survey, including: (1) "individual and family property safety;" (2) "personal safety;" (3) "transportation safety;" (4) "medical safety;" (5) "food safety;" (6) "work safety;" (7) "safety of personal information and privacy;" (8) "ecological environment safety;" and (9) "overall situation of social security." Each aspect was given a value from 1 to 4, with higher values indicating a stronger sense of social security.

Results from statistical analysis show that the assessment of social fairness has a moderately positive correlation with a sense of social security (Table 9.3). In other words, the assessment of social fairness increases with the sense of social security. The correlation coefficient between the assessment scores for overall fairness and overall social security was 0.415. The correlations between the sense of social security and each dimension of social fairness were, in descending order: political fairness (0.366), security fairness (0.348), economic fairness (0.302) and education fairness (0.271).

(iii) Assessment of Social Fairness and Awareness of Social Conflict

Table 9.3 Correlation analysis between assessment of social fairness and sense of social security[a]

Social security	Total score		Political fairness		Security fairness		Economic fairness		Education fairness	
	Correlation coefficient	Sample size	Correlation coefficient	Sample size	Correlation coefficient	Sample size	Correlation coefficient	Sample size	Correlation coefficient	Sample size
Individual and family property safety	.249	10,111	.210	10,111	.224	10,111	.158	10,111	.197	10,111
Personal safety	.244	10,068	.204	10,068	.225	10,068	.153	10,068	.190	10,068
Transportation safety	.283	10,025	.252	10,025	.232	10,025	.206	10,025	.189	10,025
Medical safety	**.387**	9831	**.340**	9831	**.364**	9831	.261	9831	.229	9831
Food safety	**.366**	9968	**.335**	9968	**.313**	9968	.268	9968	.205	9968
Work safety	.284	9736	.241	9736	.256	9736	.203	9736	.182	9736
Safety of personal information and privacy	**.331**	9463	.288	9463	.284	9463	.239	9463	.218	9463
Safety of ecological environment	**.344**	9791	**.306**	9791	.299	9791	.242	9791	.219	9791
Overall social security	**.415**	9984	**.366**	9984	**.348**	9984	**.302**	9984	.271	9984

[a]All correlation coefficients in the form have passed statistical tests, sig. < 0.0001

Awareness of social conflict reflects people's perception and assessment of current conflicts of interest among different social groups. In the 2013 CSS, we asked respondents about six kinds of conflicts of interest among different groups in current Chinese society: (1) the rich and the poor, (2) officials and ordinary people, (3) employers and employees, (4) different ethnic groups, (5) different religious groups, and (6) locals and migrants. The statistical results showed that the perception of conflicts of interest among different social groups was clearly associated with assessments of social fairness. That is, respondents who consider conflicts of interest among different groups to be severe have lower assessments of social fairness than those who do not. As shown in Fig. 9.13, for those who felt that there was "severe conflict" between the rich and the poor, the average assessment score for social fairness was 48.8 points, about 6 points lower than those who answered "not severe conflict" (54 points). Those who believed there was "severe conflict" between officials and ordinary people had an average social fairness assessment score of 46.5 points, 9.2 points lower than that of those who answered "not severe conflict" (55.7 points). These results show that if people consider a society to be fair on the whole, they will generally approve of current social interest distribution patterns, and will have less awareness of conflicts of interest among different social groups.

(iv) Assessment of Social Fairness and Social Approval

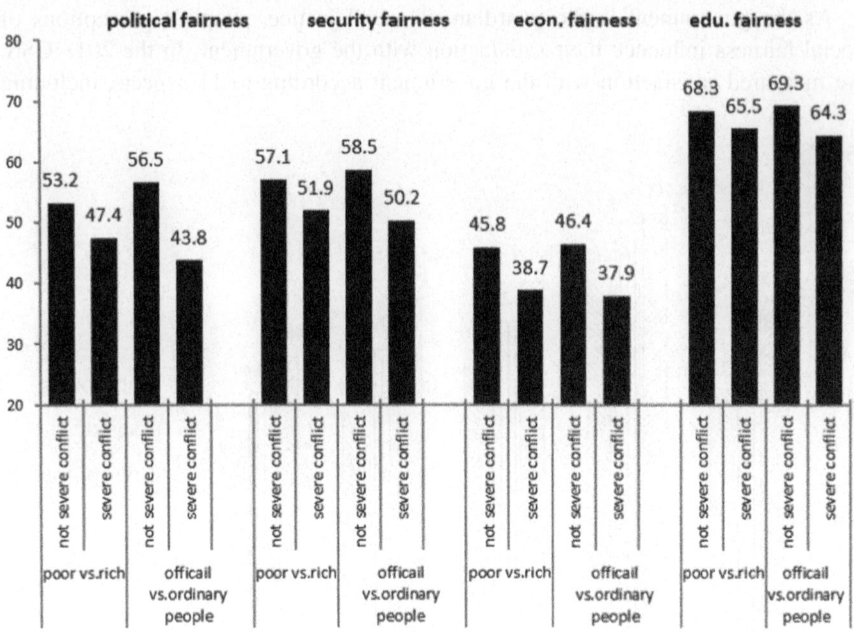

Fig. 9.13 Overall assessment of social fairness and awareness of conflicts of interest among different social groups (mean)

In the 2013 CSS, respondents were asked whether current Chinese society met their standard of a good society, which was taken as an indicator of people's social approval. The survey results showed that, on the whole, more than half of respondents (51.9%) considered current society to "fully meet" or "largely meet" their standard of "a good society." 31.2% chose "moderately meet," 15.1% chose "not quite meet" or "not meet," and 1.8% chose "hard to tell." The group that chose "fully meet" and "largely meet" were deemed to have approving attitudes, and the group that chose "not quite meet" and "not meet" were deemed to have disapproving attitudes for the purposes of analyzing the relationship between social approval and the assessment of social fairness. The statistical results showed that people with higher social approval had higher fairness assessment scores, and vice versa. As shown in Fig. 9.14, the average assessment score for social fairness was 55.9 points among those with approving attitudes, almost 15 points higher than those with disapproving attitudes (41). The pattern was similar for each dimension of social fairness. For education fairness, those with approving attitudes had an average score of 70.2, 10.7 points higher than those with disapproving attitudes (59.5 points); for political fairness, those with approving attitudes had an average score of 56.2, 19 points higher than those with disapproving attitudes (37.2 points). The differences in the scores for economic fairness and security fairness were 13.2 points and 14.4 points respectively.

(v) Assessment of Social Fairness and Satisfaction with Government

As the government is the guardian of social justice, people's perceptions of social fairness influence their satisfaction with the government. In the 2013 CSS, we measured satisfaction with the government according to 11 aspects, including

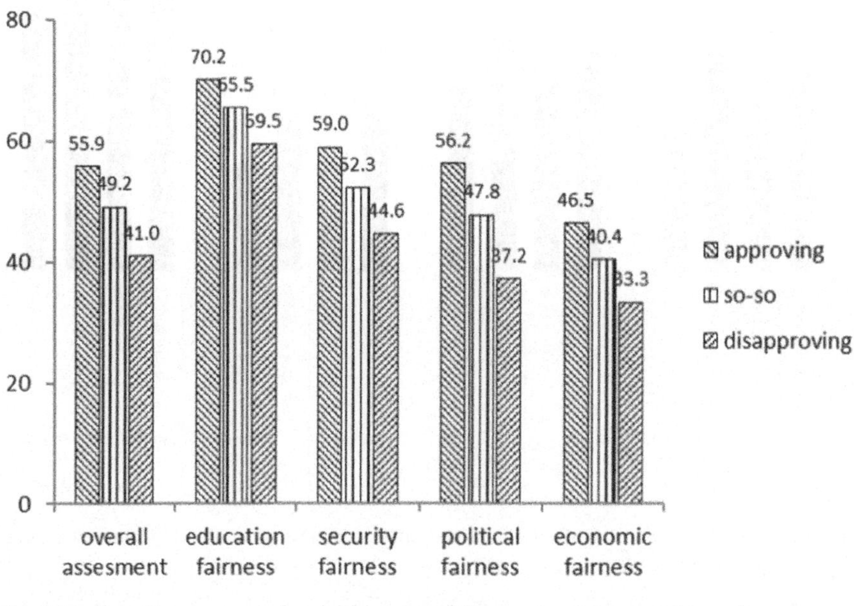

Fig. 9.14 Overall assessment of social fairness and degree of social approval (mean)

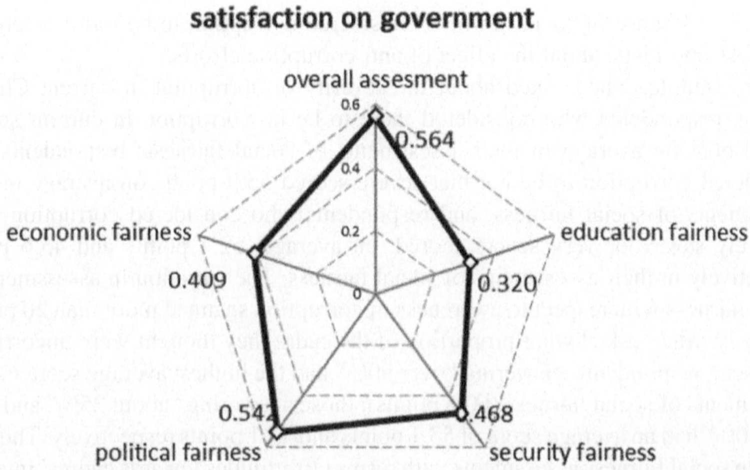

Fig. 9.15 Correlation analysis between assessment of social fairness and satisfaction with the government (correlation coefficient)

medical and health services, social security, compulsory education, and so on.[6] Each aspect was rated on a scale of 1 and 4, with higher scores indicating higher satisfaction with the performance of the government. An evaluation scale was constructed by adding the scores for these 11 aspects together, ranging from 11 to 44. The statistical results show that people's assessment of social fairness is related to their satisfaction with the government. Figure 9.15 shows that the Pearson correlation coefficient between the assessment of social fairness and government satisfaction was 0.564. Such a moderate correlation suggests that people's satisfaction with the government increases with their assessment of social fairness. The correlation coefficient between political fairness and satisfaction with the government was the largest (0.542), followed by security fairness (0.468), economic fairness (0.409) and education fairness (0.320).

Related to satisfaction with the government, the public's assessment of social fairness was influenced by their perception of corruption. In the 2013 CSS, we asked respondents a group of questions regarding the severity of corruption in Chinese society, their judgment of cadres' integrity, and the effect of anti-corruption efforts. The statistical results showed that the public's assessment of social fairness was obviously associated with social attitudes towards issues of corruption. Respondents

[6] The 11 aspects were: (1) provision of medical and health services; (2) social security; (3) compulsory education; (4) protection of the environment and pollution control; (5) fighting against crime and maintaining social safety; (6) honesty and abiding by the law, punishing corruption; (7) acting according to the law and fair law enforcement; (8) economic development and increasing individual income; (9) provision of low-rent and affordable housing for lower-middle income earners; (10) greater employment and increased employment opportunities; and (11) government information publicity and transparency of government's work.

with a lesser sense of social fairness considered corruption to be more severe and were less optimistic about the effect of anti-corruption efforts.

For example, when asked about the severity of corruption in current Chinese society, respondents who considered there to be no corruption in current society scored 66.8 on average in their assessments of social fairness; respondents who considered corruption to be not that severe scored 55.9 points on average in their assessments of social fairness; and respondents who considered corruption to be relatively severe or very severe scored, on average, 52.1 points and 45.6 points respectively in their assessments of social fairness. The variation in assessments of social fairness with respect to awareness of corruption spanned more than 20 points. Similarly, when asked what proportion of the cadre they thought were uncorrupted at present, respondents answering “over 90%” had the highest average score in their assessments of social fairness (60.8 points); those answering “about 25%” and “less than 10%” had an average score of 53.1 points and 43.1 points respectively. The variation in social fairness assessments with respect to attitudes towards cadres’ integrity spanned about 18 points. In addition, respondents who had higher assessments of social fairness were more optimistic about the outcomes of anti-corruption efforts. Those considering the effect of anti-corruption actions by the party and government to be “very obvious” and “relatively obvious” scored an average of 57 points and 54 points respectively in their assessments of social fairness, while those answering “not quite obvious” and “not obvious” scored an average of 49.3 points and 40.7 points respectively in their social fairness assessments (Fig. 9.16).

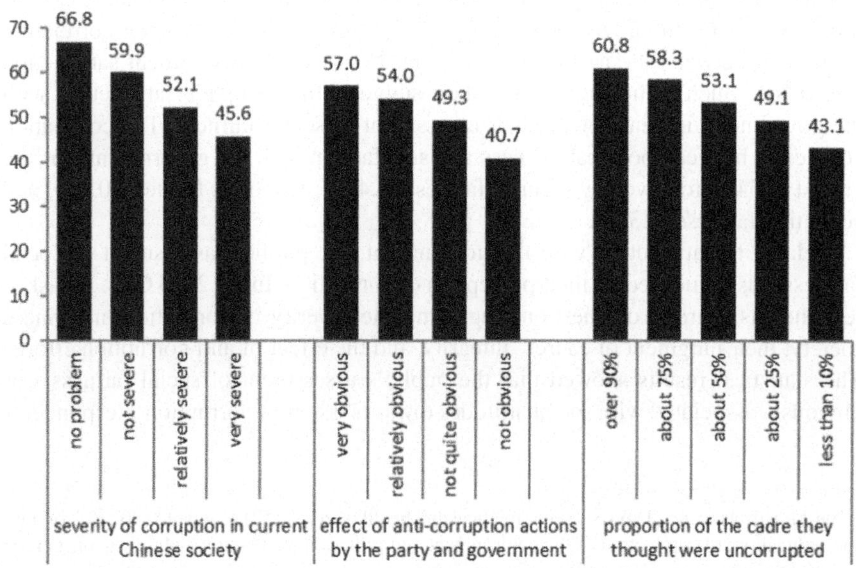

Fig. 9.16 Correlation analysis between assessment of social fairness and attitude towards anti-corruption efforts (mean)

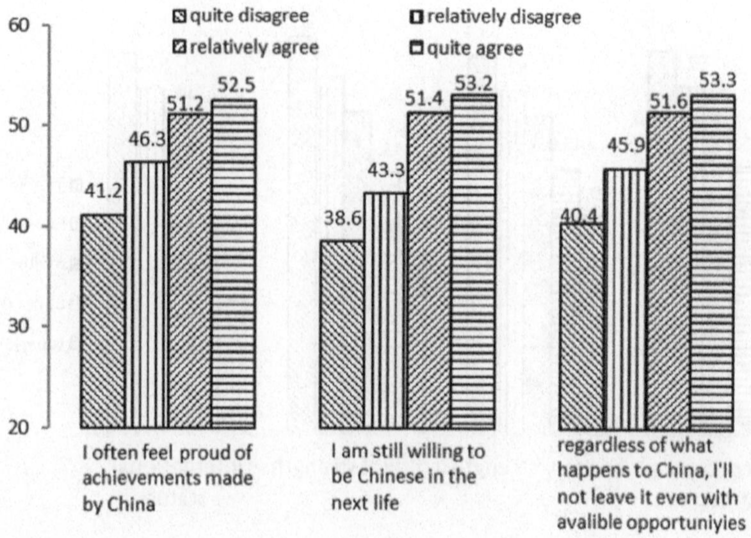

Fig. 9.17 Correlation analysis between assessment of social fairness and national identity (mean)

(vi) Assessment of Social Fairness and National Identity

The public's assessment of social fairness directly affects their identity with and assessment of the nation. In the 2013 CSS, we used three statements to measure the national identity of the public: (1) "I often feel proud of achievements made by China;" (2) "I am still willing to be Chinese in the next life;" and (3) "Regardless of what happens to China, I will not leave China even with available opportunities." The possible responses were "quite agree," "relatively agree," "relatively disagree" and "quite disagree." The statistical results showed that the assessment of social fairness is positively correlated with national identity. That is, respondents with higher national identity had higher fairness assessments, and vice versa. As shown in Fig. 9.17, respondents who chose "quite agree" in response to "I am still willing to be Chinese in the next life" had an average social fairness assessment score of 53.2 points, 14.6 higher than those who chose "quite disagree" (38.6 points). This pattern was similar with respect to the other two questions of national identity, with the variation in social assessment scores spanning more than 10 points.

In addition to national identity, we also measured the public's evaluation of economic strength, military strength, cultural strength, and international status according to five levels: superior, upper-middle, middle, lower-middle, and inferior. The statistical results showed that respondents who had higher assessments of China's international status tended to have a higher assessment of social fairness, and vice versa. For instance, respondents who considered Chinese economic strength to be "superior" scored an average of 55.9 points in their fairness assessments, 15.6 points higher than those who chose "inferior" (40.3 points). Similarly, respondents

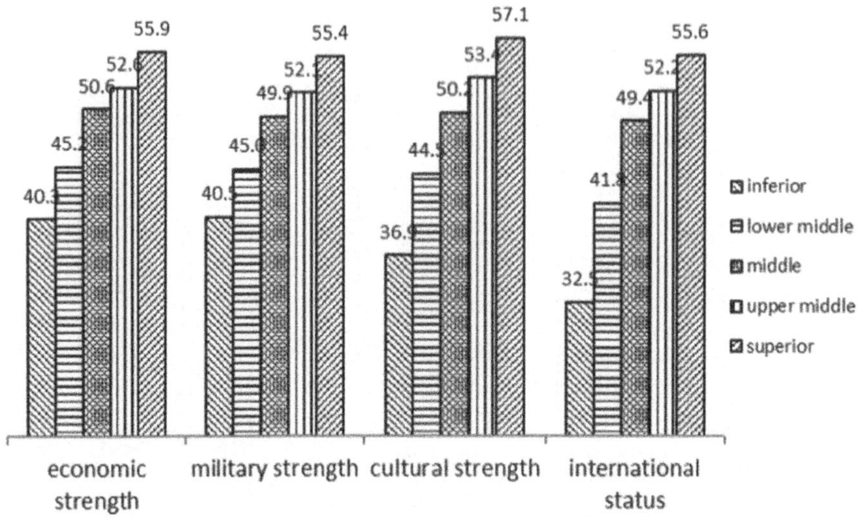

Fig. 9.18 Correlation analysis between assessment of social fairness and China's international comparison (mean)

who considered Chinese military strength to be "superior" and "inferior" had an average score gap of 15 points (55.4 points vs. 40.5 points) in their social fairness assessments. In terms of Chinese cultural strength and international status, this gap was even larger, at 20.2 points and 23.1 points respectively (Fig. 9.18).

We make the following conclusions from the above analysis:

1. In the past 10 years, the Chinese public's overall assessment of social fairness was stable and relatively good, with about 60% of respondents considering China's current society to be fair. Respondents rated education fairness the highest, followed by security fairness, political fairness and economic fairness.
2. In the past 10 years, there was no great change in the assessment of fairness in the field of education, but there was great improvement in the field of social security. In the economic and political fields, the assessment rates declined. The assessment of economic fairness and political fairness are more likely to affect people's overall assessment of social fairness.
3. There are group differences in the assessment of social fairness. Social groups with lower socio-economic status had higher assessments of social fairness, and vice versa. The lower class, mainly comprised of rural residents, had a strong sense of "relative gain," which played an important role in their positive assessments of social fairness.
4. Moreover, the assessment of social fairness affects a series of social attitudes. The sense of social fairness is closely associated with: interpersonal trust at the individual level; awareness of social security and social approval at the societal level; and satisfaction with the government and national identity at the political level. Guaranteeing equal rights to citizens, reducing gaps in income and social

treatment, promoting the construction of a clean government, maintaining the fairness and justice of current society, and strengthening the sense of social fairness are all critical for the social development of China. Improving fairness in these fields is essential for realizing the great rejuvenation of the Chinese nation and the Chinese Dream.

References

Kluegel, James R., and Eliot R. Smith. 1981. Beliefs About Stratification. *Annual Review of Sociology* 7: 29–56.

Meng, Tianguang. 2012. Chinese People's Perception of Distributive Justice in Transitional China: Outcome Justice and Opportunity Justice. *Chinese Journal of Sociology* 32 (6): 108–134. [in Chinese].

Ng, Sik Hung, and Michael W. Allen. 2005. Perception of Economic Distributive Justice: Exploring Leading Theories. *Social Behavior and Personality: An International Journal* 33 (5): 435–454.

Wang, Fuqin. 2011. Perception of Distributive Justice of the Residents in Contemporary China's Large Cities: An Empirical Study Based on the Survey in Shanghai. *Chinese Journal of Sociology* 31 (3): 155–183. [in Chinese].

Zhu, Wendian. 2011. Understanding Justice in Harmonious Society from Traditional Culture. *Journal of Chongqing University of Science and Technology* (Social Sciences Edition) 15: 16–17, 27. [in Chinese].

Chapter 10
Towards Greater Equality and Justice

S. V. Mareeva

Justice is often defined as the attainment of what is fair and right. It is also often related to the concept of equality, in which everyone gets due reward in accordance with what they deserve.[1] Social justice has been a key issue in social philosophy since antiquity. Aristotle defines two particular forms of justice: rectificatory and distributive. Rectificatory justice implies the principal "equals should get equal." Distributive justice employs geometric proportions: what each person receives is proportional to his merit. During the Enlightenment, a new, liberal justice theory developed that was based on the premise that justice can be attained through the application of law. This new theory also involved the ideas of social contract, freedom from government intervention, and the priority of personal rights (T. Hobbes, J. Locke, J.-J. Rousseau, C.-L. Montesquieu). The concept was re-framed in the twentieth century by J. Rawles.[2] His theory of justice is based on two main principles: first, each person is to have an equal right to the most extensive basic liberty compatible with a similar liberty for others; second, social and economic inequalities are to be arranged so that they offer the greatest benefit to the least-advantaged members of society, and offices and positions must be open to everyone under conditions of fair and equal opportunity. According to Rawles, both a democratic government with a dominant private sector and market economy and authoritarian regime with the prevalence of state property can achieve the two principles. He gives preference to social justice over economic efficiency. However, even though Rawles' theory is based on the

[1] See for example: Abercrombie et al. (2006), Jary and Jary (1991).

[2] Rawls (1971).

The original version of this chapter was revised: Affiliations have been updated in this chapter. The correction to this book can be found at https://doi.org/10.1007/978-981-16-2505-3_19

S. V. Mareeva (✉)
HSE University, Moscow, Russia

Institute of Sociology of FCTAS RAS, Moscow, Russia

P. Li and M. K. Gorshkov (eds.), *Life Expectations of the People*,
Research Series on the Chinese Dream and China's Development Path,
https://doi.org/10.1007/978-981-16-2505-3_10

priority of rights and freedoms, it has often been criticized by liberal philosophers (by M. Friedman[3] and F. Hayek[4] in particular).

The idea of justice has always played an important role in the Russian socio-cultural model. Is it still true today? If so, what is, according to Russians, personal and social justice? What social structure suits their understanding of justice the most? Does it imply any forms of inequality? Here we will try to answer these questions with the help of recent national survey data obtained by the Institute of Sociology of the Russian Academy of Sciences.[5]

Surveys shows that justice is still an important concept for Russians in terms of how they see the future of the country. When asked about their idea of an ideal future in 2014, most Russians (53%) named exactly the aspects connected with a fair and just society: social justice, equal rights for all, a strong state that takes care of its citizens. Other options were less popular: 33% of the respondents said they dreamed of Russia becoming a superpower again, 29% strived for human rights, democracy and freedom of expression, 28% wanted stability and sustainable development without revolutions or calamities, and less than 20% chose other options, including the idea of a free market with minimal state intervention (12%) and rapprochement with the West (8%). The results show that the Western social model is not currently perceived in Russia as a model for an ideal society. However, the idea of a just, fair society can become a consolidating factor for the Russian population.

The share of those who strive for social justice varies across different social groups. It is not very common among young people (18–21 years old)—only 38% of the respondents in this age group chose this option when talking about their perceptions of the ideal future for Russia; at the same time, it was selected by every second respondent aged between 26 and 50, and by 65% of the 60+ group. However, there is no strong correlation between the drive for justice and the respondents' education or income level, or type and size of settlement they came from (despite some quantitative differences, no direct correlation was found). On the whole, regardless of certain quantitative differences between social groups, the idea of justice is still a core component of the Russian dream of an "ideal society."

Moreover, the wish to live in a just and rational society was the third most popular "personal" dream expressed by Russians during the 2012 survey, falling, at 33%, just behind the second most popular wish to have good health (also about 33%). The most popular desire was to be wealthy and have an opportunity to live without counting every penny.[6] Those who expressed wanting to live in a just society differed from the

[3] Friedman (1962), Friedman and Friedman (1980).

[4] Hayek (1982).

[5] We will refer to the following all-Russian representative surveys conducted by the Instituteof-Complex Social Research and the Institute of Sociology of the Russian Academy of Sciences: What Russians Dream About (March 2012, $n = 1751$); Poverty and the Poor in Modern Russia (April 2013, $n = 1600$); Middle Class in Modern Russia (February 2014, $n = 1600$). All survey samples represented population of the country by region, and on regional level—by type of settlement, age, and gender (except for the 2012 survey, which did not include respondents over 55 years of age). Hereafter we will refer to the surveys by their date.

[6] Survey sample only included the respondents younger than 55 years old.

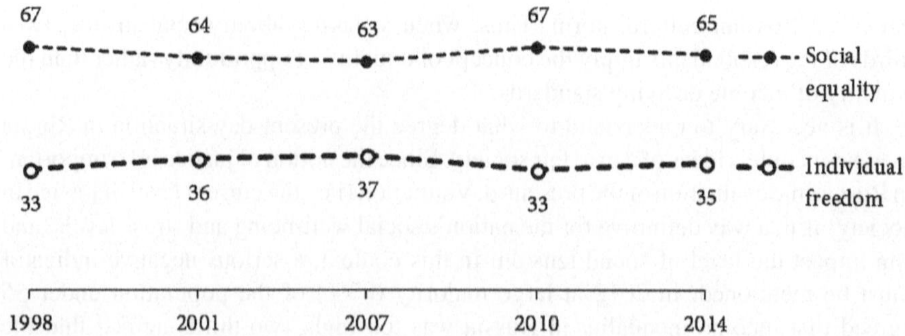

Fig. 10.1 Social model preference dynamics (social equality vs individual freedom), 1998–2014, % of those who gave an answer to the question

rest in their understanding of what an ideal society should look like—they more often said that it is important to have a strong state that can bring order (24 vs 15% among others) and to restore national traditions and values (27 vs 20% respectively). This means that there might be no consensus among Russians about what social justice actually implies.[7] Here, we analyze how the respondents' views differ in this respect and how, according to them, the idea of justice is related to various forms of social inequality.

First of all, it is interesting to look at which social model is more popular among Russians: the model of social equality or a societal model based on individual freedom (see Fig. 10.1).

Figure 10.1 shows that the nation's perceptions have been rather stable in this respect. In the past 15 years, the share of those who preferred the social equality model remained at about 65% (among those who answered the question), while those who prefer individual freedom make up about one-third of Russian society.

This does not mean that freedom is not important for Russians (on the contrary: according to survey data, two-thirds of the population agree that life is meaningless if there is no freedom); this means that the issue of equality (which is related to justice) is perceived as a pressing one for modern Russian society. Russians are not committed supporters of full equality, yet a social model based on individual freedom does not seem to be too appealing to them either, since many of them associate individual freedom with permissiveness and overindulgence (which is not surprising, considering that in 2011, 64% of Russians said that freedom was, in their opinion, an opportunity to be one's own master).

However, while striving for equality, Russians more often mean the equality of opportunity (68% of the respondents in 2013) than about equality of income (32%). These ratios have been rather stable in the past decade across all age groups, despite minor fluctuations. Therefore, we can say that preference for social equality is a

[7] See, for example, post-hoc analysis based on WVS, Levada-Centre, Public Opinion Foundation, WCIOM, and IS RAS data: Urnov (2012).

persistent Russian cultural norm. Thus, when speaking about social justice, two-thirds of the respondents imply the concept of equality of opportunity rather than the equality of income or living standards.

It is necessary to understand to what degree the present-day situation in Russia matches people's ideas of a just, fair society. Since the notion of justice is so important in Russia, the evaluation of the present-day situation (i.e., the current level of justice in society) is in a way definitive for the nation's social well-being and stress levels, and can impact the level of social tension. In this context, a serious negative indicator must be mentioned: in 2012, a large majority (83%) of the population under 55 agreed that income inequality in Russia was too high, two-thirds agreed that the system of property distribution was unfair, and the same share agreed that people were inadequately rewarded for their skills and qualifications. Nearly half of Russians (54%) also believed that they personally received inadequate remuneration due to being over-qualified or working in arduous conditions (see Fig. 10.2).

In other words, Russians strive for social justice but they don't think that the modern Russian society they live in is a just one. The population is very sensitive to excessive income differentiation and illegitimate inequality in terms of property

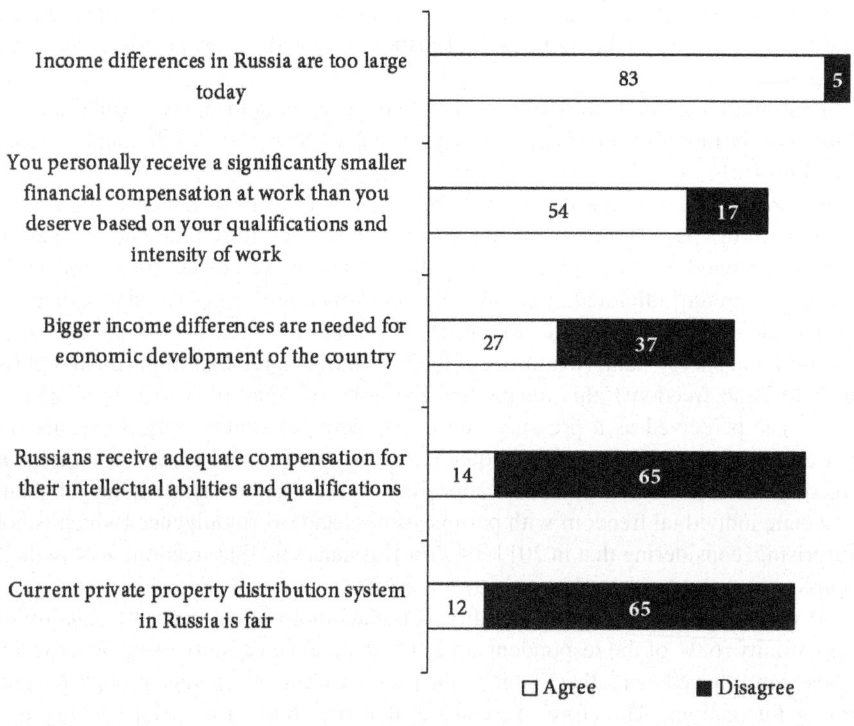

Fig. 10.2 Income distribution and property distribution as perceived by Russians, 2012, %[8]

[8] The figure does not reflect answers "Partly agree, partly disagree" and "Don't know"; based on a respondent sample of those younger than 55 years of age.

distribution. All social groups, irrespective of their own living standards and personal well-being, perceive the existing forms of social inequality as unjust. In 2012, for example, 59% of those earning twice the median income for their settlement type agreed that the existing system of property distribution was unfair, and 85% said that income inequality was too high. Some of the respondents stated that their living standards had worsened in the three years prior to the survey, others—that their living standards had improved. Yet, 83% of the people in both groups agreed that there was excessive income differentiation in the country. So, when asked whether the situation in Russia is just and fair or not, people gave answers based not only on their personal interests but also on their idea of social justice, which is fundamental to how they see the future of the country.

In actuality, the Russian people's perception of income inequality is not unrealistic; according to Rosstat [Russian Federal State Statistics Service] data, in 2013 the Gini coefficient measuring income distribution in Russia reached 0.418 (versus 0.397 in 2002), while the decile ratio grew from 14% in 2002 to 16.2% in 2013.[9] At the individual level, these statistical facts are reflected in feelings of deep and, moreover, unjustified and unfair inequality.

However, such perceptions cannot be interpreted as a result of alleged "egalitarianism" among Russians. Nearly half of the survey respondents (49% in 2013) believe that inequality is inevitable, natural and can be justified (only 20% of the respondents disagreed with this statement, and 31% didn't answer the question). Russians don't actually want to "divide everything between everybody," instead, they seek a system that would enable equal opportunities for all and maintain reasonable levels of inequality. Generally, Russians express high tolerance for forms of income inequality that they find reasonable and justified, for example, inequality caused by professional efficiency or education. In 2013, 74% of the respondents agreed that those who work faster and harder should receive higher remuneration, and 63% of the respondents believed that educational level was an important factor determining one's remuneration. However, 65% of respondents also believed that this inequality was acceptable only in a situation of equal opportunities to earn. In other words, Russians want to live in a society based on equality of opportunity (see Fig. 10.3).

We can conclude that the Russian socio-cultural model is marked by high tolerance towards inequalities caused by legitimate and reasonable factors, provided that everyone has equal opportunities (lines 1–4 in Fig. 10.3). Additionally, the data highlights what, according to public opinion, should be the remuneration level of highly qualified professionals or executives. Their remuneration, according to the respondents in 2014, should be about 4.7 times higher than national average (In 2006, this number was 4.9). Considering that there are poor people, whose earnings are well below national average, and rich people, who earn much more than highly qualified professionals, this means that the ideal society for Russians would still be highly differentiated, and that Russians perceive income inequality caused by education, qualification and efficiency as legitimate, fair, and even essential for efficient economic growth.

---

[9] Rosstat data (http://www.gks.ru/free_doc/new_site/population/urov/urov_32g.htm).

Speaking of more specific inequality types, i.e., housing and pension inequality, Russians seem to be less tolerant. This is probably due to the fact that this type of inequality is considered to be unjustified. Still, there are more people who are ready to accept this inequality than those who are not. 52% of Russians agree that wealthier people should be able to afford better housing (19% disagree) and 48% agree that it is fair that those with higher salaries receive higher pensions (21% disagree). However, unequal access to healthcare services seems totally unacceptable for Russians, irrespective of their level of income. However, the respondents who reported to be in good health turned out to be more tolerant towards healthcare inequality. That is not surprising, considering that in 2013, 19% of all respondents and 40% of those who needed medical help stated that they had recently encountered a situation when they couldn't receive certain medical services or buy certain medicines due to financial problems. As mentioned above, good health is one of the three most common "personal" dreams in Russia. When asked about their dreams in 2012, nearly one-third of the respondents chose having good health among multiple possible options. When presented with the open-ended question on what they would wish for if they met a genie, 43% of the respondents said they would wish for good health

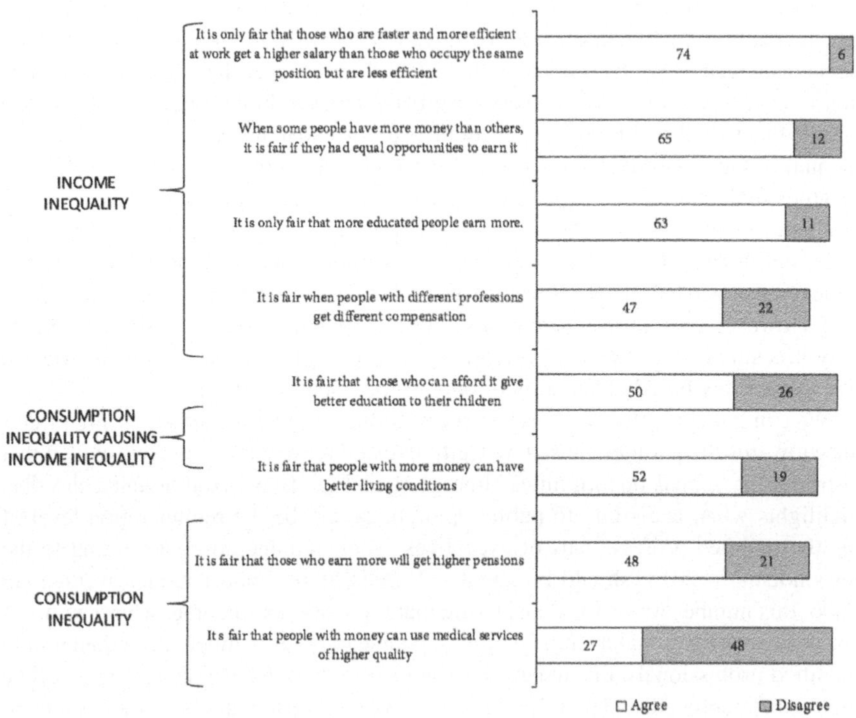

Fig. 10.3 Tolerance towards different forms of inequality in Russia (2012, 2013), %[10]

[10] The figure does not reflect answers "Partly agree, partly disagree" and "Don't know".

for themselves and their families. This reveals not only the high significance and acuteness of the problem of health among Russians, but also that a significant share of population does not see any real opportunities to solve their health problems and are forced to literally "hope for a miracle."

Income inquality as a result of educational level occupies an intermediate position. On the one hand, educational level is perceived as a valid reason for income inequality; on the other hand, educational inequality can be seen as a consequence of income inequality. Therefore, there is no consensus on whether it is fair that children of wealthier families get a better education; half of the respondents believe it is fair, 26% disagree. There were no differences between parents and those without children, which means that respondents drew upon their cultural norms rather than personal interests in answering the question. Moreover, 12% of Russians mention having better education among their three main personal dreams; when presented with the open-ended question on what they would wish for if they met a genie, 8% of the respondents said they would wish for better education too (2012).

Framing is also particularly important here. When asked directly: "Is it fair that wealthier people should be able to afford better education for their children than low-income people?" (2013), only 16% of the respondents agreed and 60% disagreed. This means that quality education is a sensitive issue in Russia. High tolerance towards inequality collides with the ideal of educational equality because a good education is perceived as the main social lift that provides justification to social inequality as such.

Such justice/inequality perceptions are not situational, i.e., this is not a reaction to the 2009–2010 economic crisis. Comparison of 2006 and 2012 data shows that social inequality perceptions are rather stable in Russia. People have become a little more tolerant towards the property distribution system (up to 12% in 2012 from 6% in 2006, although most Russians still believe it is unfair). The percentage of those who thought they were inadequately rewarded at work declined from 61 to 54% (still, this is nearly half of the population). The share of those who thought that income inequality is too high remained nearly the same (85% in 2006, 83% in 2012), so people are likely dissatisfied with inefficient state policy in this respect. They have also become less tolerant towards inequality of access to good healthcare (35 vs. 27%), which might be due to a general decline in the quality of medical services provided. On the whole, we can conclude that the problems with excessive inequality, according to the population, are not being solved. Even with the increased share of those who are satisfied with their personal earnings, the feeling of injustice in Russian society remains dominant among the country's population and is becoming chronic (Table 10.1).

Intolerance towards high inequality in modern Russia is not only due to the fact that it is excessive and unreasonable, but also because there are no opportunities for social mobility or increasing personal prosperity. Academic literature describes this phenomenon as "the tunnel effect."[12] Social lifts and legitimate ways

[11] For comparability reasons, only the under-55 share of the 2006 sample was analysed here.

[12] Hirschman and Rothschild (1973).

Table 10.1 Social inequality perception dynamics in Russia, 2006 and 2012, %[11]

Statements the respondents agreed with	2006	2012
It is fair that people with money can use medical services of higher quality	35	27
It is fair that those who earn more will get higher pensions	43	43
It is fair that people with more money can have better living conditions	53	46
It is fair that those who can afford it can provide a better education to their children	53	50
It is fair is some people have more money than others, given that they had equal opportunity to earn	67	70
The current private property distribution system in Russia is fair	6	12
Russians receive adequate compensation for their intellectual abilities and qualifications	17	14
Bigger income differences are needed for economic development of the country	24	27
You personally receive a significantly smaller financial compensation at work than you deserve based on your qualifications and intensity of work	61	54
Income differences in Russia are too large today	85	83

of improving one's situation actually legitimize the already existing inequality in the eyes of the people. However, the situation in Russia is the opposite: the channels of social mobility are closing, making people more dissatisfied with excessive and unreasonable inequality. When talking about social dynamics in Russia, most of the respondents say the situation has either remained the same or improved only for the lucky few. Overall, they believe that only wealthier people are getting safer in their situation, while everyone else has less and less access to social lifts. The share of those who saw improvement in any spheres has declined dramatically; the share of those who didn't see any changes or thought that the situation had only got worse has increased (see Fig. 10.4). In terms of quality improvements in life and the channels that could contribute to these improvements (education, entrepreneurship, professional activity), the situation in the eyes of the population appears to be quite alarming, resulting in increased intolerance to the current system of illegitimate and excessive inequality.

How do Russians perceive justice/inequality at the personal and social level? How do these levels correlate? Data shows that Russians tend to emphasize social backlash resulting from inequality more than their personal situation. This only proves that the negative perception of Russians towards high income differentiation and the need to reduce it is based not only on their personal situation, but on the concept of a just and fair society and social justice as a key component for a society they would wish to live in.

Overall, 71% of the respondents said income inequality was the most acute inequality issue at the social level, 47% at the personal level (2013). Inequality in access to healthcare, good housing, good jobs, and education followed. Only 14% of the population said they were not personally affected by any type of inequality, and a mere 4% believed there were no acute inequalities in Russian society (Table 10.2).

Perceived inequality intensity differs by type of residence though average figures remain stable. People suffer most from income differentiation (40% in metropolitan cities, 50% in rural areas) and inequality of access to healthcare no matter where they live (though urban citizens of metropolitan cities feel it to a lesser extent; 28% compared to 40% of the respondents in rural areas and small towns) (Table 10.3).

We can also trace the interrelation between micro- and macro-level perceptions of inequality by looking at how people imagine the actual and ideal social structure in Russia, and their own place in it (see Fig. 10.5).

The table in Fig. 10.5 shows that Russians perceive the current reality as being completely opposite to their ideals. Most see the existing social structure as a pyramid (57%) or as a structure built on a contraposition between the numerous poor and the rich few (28%). At the same time, Russians are more likely to choose a model with a high proportion of the middle strata (i.e. middle class societies) as the ideal model. Although 40% of Russians would like to live in a society where differences between social positions are small, most of them (60%) want to live in a highly differentiated society, but one that is based on a different distribution system than in modern Russia, which would provide the conditions for a mass middle-class and not mass low-income groups.

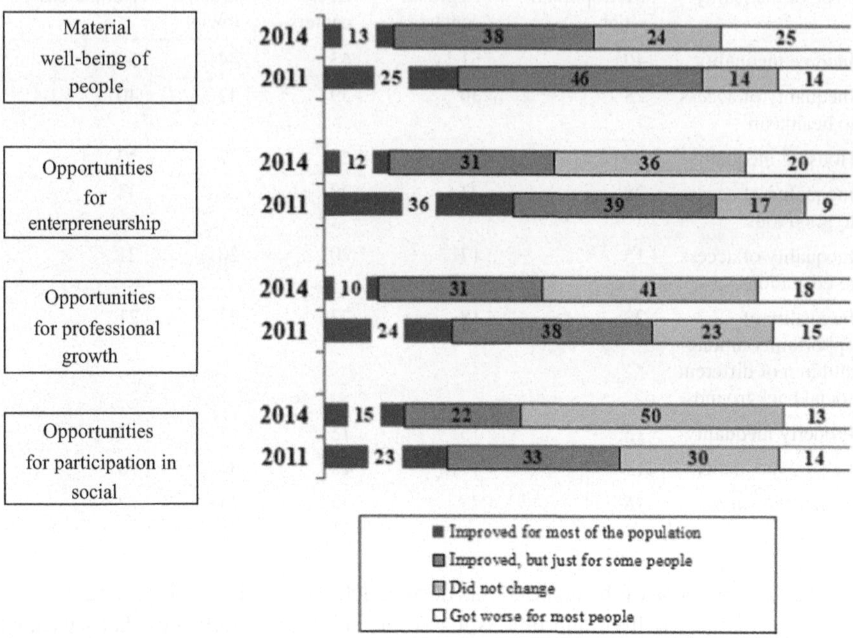

Fig. 10.4 Social perception dynamics, 2011–2014, %[13]

[13] Based on the following survey data: Civil Activism: New Public Policy Actors ($n = 1600$, March 2014, IS RAS); 20 Years of Reforms through the Eyes of Russians ($n = 1750$, April 2011, IS RAS). Both surveys were designed following the same nationally representative sampling model.

Table 10.2 Most acute types of inequality in Russia at the social and personal level, 2013, % *(respondents could choose up to three answers)*

Type of inequality	Most acute at social level	Most acute at personal level
Income inequality	71	47
Inequality of access to healthcare	47	38
Housing inequality	38	28
Inequality of access to good jobs	32	28
Inequality of access to education	28	19
Inequality of opportunity among children of different social backgrounds	27	21
Property inequality	16	13
Leisure inequality	10	11
None of the above	*4*	*14*

Table 10.3 Most acute types of inequality at personal level, by type of residence, 2013, % *(respondents could choose up to three answers)*

Type of inequality	Metropolitan cities	Regional centers	Local centers	Small towns	Rural areas
Income inequality	40	51	43	44	50
Inequality of access to healthcare	28	36	39	42	40
Housing inequality	26	31	26	27	27
Inequality of access to good jobs	28	23	28	28	34
Inequality of access to education	15	17	20	20	21
Inequality of opportunity among children of different social backgrounds	23	18	23	23	21
Property inequality	15	13	13	14	13
Leisure inequality	17	11	10	9	10
None of the above	*18*	*13*	*15*	*13*	*12*

The fact that 60% of the respondents desire such a societal model, even in the face of current perceived high and unreasonable differentiation, indicates that Russians do posses high tolerance for inequality. Russians actually perceive inequality to be an inherent feature of the present-day economic system rather than a "necessary evil." However, inequality today is, according to Russians, often too deep and unjustified by legitimate reasons—that is why they prefer models based on a strong and numerous

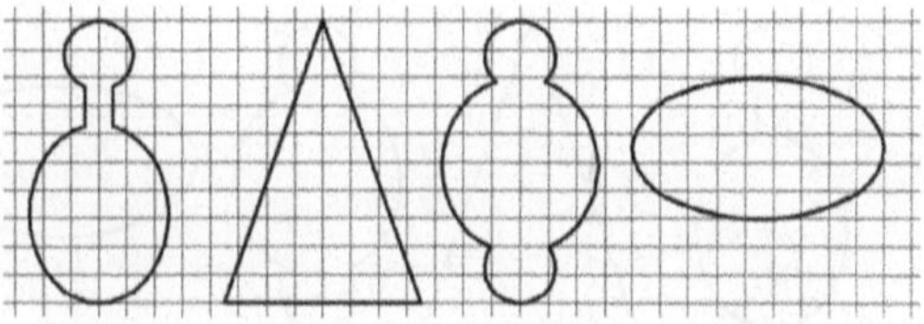

Chosen, % of the respondents				
	Model 1	**Model 2**	**Model 3**	**Model 4**
As an ideal model:	9	20	**31**	**40**
As an actual model:	**28**	**57**	12	2
Difference:	−19	−37	19	38

Fig. 10.5 Russians' idea of the actual and ideal social structure of Russian society, 2012 (*respondent sample no older than age 55*)

middle class as the ideal. This correlates with the fact that most Russians do not aspire for high social positions; instead, they would prefer to occupy middle ones.

We turn now to the subject of how Russians see their own position in society. It has already been mentioned before that over 50% of Russians think they are underpaid considering their qualification and labor conditions. This figure used to be even higher and has decreased over the last several years, yet it still remains significant. The same is true for how people evaluate their social status; most believe it should be higher than it is at the moment. The gap between the actual and ideal social position amounts to an average of 2.5 points (out of 10), depending of the social structure preferred by the respondents (see Fig. 10.6).

It is interesting that most people think that by rights they should be in the middle (5.7–6.4 out of 10), irrespective of the model they have chosen as the ideal one. Those who went for models 1–3 in Fig. 10.5 evaluated their actual social position at 3–4.6 and the fair social position at 5.7–6.3. Those who preferred model 4 (lowest social differentiation) scored 3.2 and 5 respectively.

Therefore, there is no reason to say that Russians hold excessive demands and expectations. Still, they generally believe their social position is lower than what they deserve, and dream of a fairer society with lower income inequality based on legitimate factors; however, in such a society they wish to occupy not the highest, but middle position.

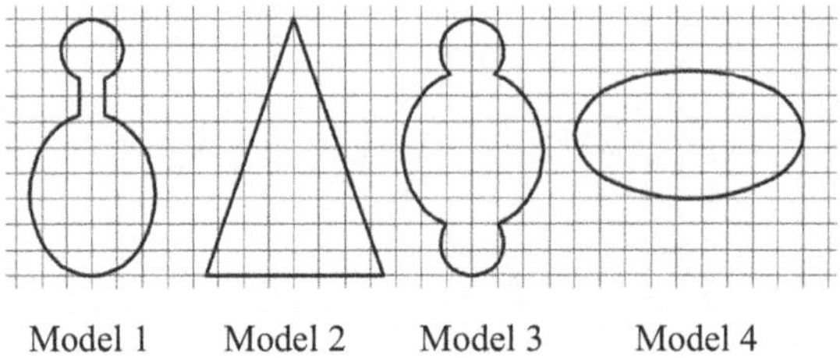

Average self-evaluation				
	Model 1	**Model 2**	**Model 3**	**Model 4**
Actual social position	**3.8** out of **10** points	**3.0 out of 10**	**4.6 out of 10**	**6 out of 10 (3.0 out of 5)**
Fair social position	**6.3** out of **10**	**5.7 out of 10**	**6.2 out of 10**	**6.4 out of 10 (3.2 out of 5)**

Fig. 10.6 Russian's evaluation of their actual and ideal social position, 2012 *(respondent sample no older than 55)*

Table 10.4 Ideal social security system as perceived by Russians, 2014, %

Social security systems	%
The state should only protect the unemployable (senior citizens, the disabled, orphans)	11
The state should also support some other disadvantaged groups (the unemployed, low-income families with children, etc.)	32
The state should support all low-income people	51
Social security should be the prerogative of employers	2
People should be able to deal with their problems themselves, without relying on the state	4

Data shows that the reality in Russia does not match people's dreams of an equal society, as current Russian society features high social differentiation based on illegitimate factors. Moreover, they are becoming less tolerant toward inequality due to lack of social lifts or other mechanisms that would allow them to overcome the handicap of inequality. It is not surprising that most Russians believe that the state should be the main actor in the fight for justice. This conclusion is supported by the data on social security ideals presented in Table 10.4.

Table 10.5 Best economic system for Russia, as perceived by Russians, 2014, %

Economic systems	%
Capitalism, free market competition, private property	17
Capitalism, partially planned market economy with elements of socialist principles	25
Socialism, planned economy with market elements	31
Socialism, planned economy, state property	22
Other/Don't know	5

Despite the lack of consensus on which target groups should receive social support, most Russians agree that it should be provided by the state. Only 2% think social security should be the prerogative of employers, and 4% think that people should be able to deal with their problems themselves. However, those who believe in state support do not call for the steep demands of a paternalistic social system, but believe that under the current circumstances of unjust distribution and deep illegitimate inequalities, it is the state who should take the first step to change the situation. Even though the share of those who believe that the state should support all low-income earners is inversely related to the respondents' income, it is clear that the desire for an active state role in providing social protection is typical for more than just the potential target group. It is a certain cultural norm for all Russians, which reflects their perception of a just society in which the state has an active role. Moreover, Russians think that the role of the state should be more prominent not only in social protection but in the economic system as well (see Table 10.5).

The majority of the population would prefer to live in a society with an economic system regulated more by the state then by the free market. 22% actually want to live in a planned, socialist economy, and 31% want to live in a planned economy with market elements. Less than half of the respondents (42%) think that capitalism and the free market, with or without planned economy elements, would be the best option for Russia. Other survey data supports these results; for example, according to a 2013 Levada-Centre poll, 45% of Russians agreed that all large enterprises should belong to the state, and 48% agreed that the most important enterprises for the country should belong to the state while the rest may stay private.[14] In other words, Russians share a specific norms and values system, which implies strong state participation in all spheres.

Russians in general do not believe that Russian society will actually become just and fair. When asked whether today's children would eventually live in such a society, 54% of the respondents answered "unlikely" while 14% answered "impossible." This can be explained by the fact that most Russians do not believe that certain elements of social justice (equality of opportunity, equal protection under the law, social protection) are actually feasible (see Table 10.6). Only 9% of the respondents think that Russian society has become more equal under Putin, nearly one-third

---

[14] Russians' Political Views. Levada-Centre, press-release (July 29, 2013). http://www.levada.ru/29-07-2013/politicheskie-vzglyady-rossiyan.

Table 10.6 Perceived probability of eventual social justice in Russia, 2013, %

Today's children will live in a society where the following ideals are true:	Yes/Very likely	No/Unlikely
Justice	32	68
Equal protection under the law	31	68
Social security	34	66
Equality of opportunity	29	71

(32%) think the opposite, and 58% haven't noticed any significant changes (2013). The ideal of social justice is very important for Russians, and they believe that the state should be the main force in the struggle for higher equality. Therefore, the lack of perceived change in the situation may lead to further social discontent and unrest. In the end, people might reconsider the importance of the state in their value system.

In summary, the idea of social justice is a unifying idea for the country's population. Though the understanding of the concept differs across different social groups, it bears some universal elements shared by people of varying social positions and financial well-being, including equality of opportunity, the active role of the state in economic and social systems, and reasonable income differentiation (based on education level and professional efficiency). This is indicative of a stable national social ideal, which inherently implies active state participation. Despite the fact that Russians display high tolerance towards different types of inequality, they do not perceive the actual situation in Russia as fair. Income differentiation is believed to be unreasonable and too high. Moreover, Russians do not how the situation could change due to a lack of social mobility opportunities. This leads to further social tension and intolerance towards the present-day situation; the gap between the actual situation and the desired level of social justice is growing. This might eventually force Russians to reconsider the importance of the state in the value system shared by most of the population.

References

Abercrombie, N., S. Hill, and B.S. Turner. 2006. *The Penguin Dictionary of Sociology*. London: Penguin.

Friedman, M. 1962. *Capitalism and Freedom*. Chicago: University of Chicago Press.

Friedman, M., and R. Friedman. 1980. *Free to Choose*. New York: Harcourt.

Hayek, F. 1982. *Law, Legislation, and Liberty: A New Statement of the Liberal Principles of Justice and Political Economy*, New pbk. ed. London: Routledge and Kegan Paul.

Hirschman, A., and M. Rothschild. 1973. The Changing Tolerance for Income Inequality in the Course of Economic Development. *The Quarterly Journal of Economics* 87 (4): 544–566.

Jary, D., and J. Jary. 1991. *Collins Dictionary of Sociology*. London: Harper-Collins Publishers.

Rawls, J. 1971. *A Theory of Justice*. Cambridge: Harvard University Press.

Urnov, M. Yu. 2012. What Is Justice? An Attempt to Analyze Mass Opinion [Chto est' spravedlivost'? Popytka analyza massovykh predstableniy]. *Obshchestvennye nauki i sovremennost'* 5: 71–88 [in Russian].

Chapter 11
Towards a More Pluralistic Society: "I" and "We" in the Perception of the Population

L. M. Drobizheva

Since the times of M. Weber, sociologists have been looking for explanations to the peculiarities of national populations and methods of interaction that ensure the harmonious development of society. M. Weber and K. Marx thought that ethnic differences would be erased and lose social importance with the development of industrial society and the process of civilization. Globalization theorists (M. Castells) had the same line of thinking. The results have been ambiguous at different stages of history. On the one hand, industrialization, urbanization, and the rise of the information society has brought commonalities to the material and spiritual lives of people from different cultures and civilizations. On the other hand, the flow of human movement and expanding information space has strengthened comparisons and correlations of those striving to understand their identity. The new globalizing society has provided possibilities which were unavailable earlier, and network communications have strengthened contact and solidarity. The polysemy of these processes is especially evident in polyethnic countries.

Russia is an example of such a polyethnic country. During the latest All-Russian Census, more than 180 different ethnic groups were registered in our country: the majority (81%) are Russians at 111 million, over 5.3 million are Tatars, almost 2 million are Ukrainians, over 1.5 million are Bashkirs, 1.4 million are Chuvash, 1.4 million are Chechen, and there are many other ethnic populations totaling just a few tens of thousands.

The Russian federative state includes 85 constituents of the Federation, among which there are 21 republics named after population groups. The 22nd republic is Crimea. The Federation also comprises the Jewish Autonomous Region and four autonomous districts (also named after population groups). The ethnic and cultural

The original version of this chapter was revised: Affiliation has been updated in this chapter. The correction to this chapter can be found at https://doi.org/10.1007/978-981-16-2505-3_19

L. M. Drobizheva (✉)
Institute of Sociology of FCTAS RAS, Moscow, Russia

P. Li and M. K. Gorshkov (eds.), *Life Expectations of the People*,
Research Series on the Chinese Dream and China's Development Path,
https://doi.org/10.1007/978-981-16-2505-3_11

variety of the country is also demonstrated in the language variety registered by the census. There are 277 languages, vernaculars and dialects in Russia. 99.4% of the population speaks Russian, with 94% of Chechens, 86% of Kabardians, 86% of Yakuts and the majority of other ethnic formations also speaking their own national languages. 89 languages are used in education: 30 as languages of study and 59 as the studied languages (in comparison, there are on average 9–10 languages per one country in the rest of Europe).

The collapse of the Soviet Union, the national movements of the late 1980s and 1990s, and the large inflow of migrants (in recent decades, Russia has consistently ranked second or third in the world with the largest inflow of migrants after the USA and Germany) has resulted in an increasing ethnic consciousness for both Russians and people of other nationalities. It is no wonder that under these conditions, 78% of Russians said they felt connected to people of their same nationality when asked in a 2014 study (October–November) by the RAS Sociology Institute, "which of the groups listed below could you treat as 'we'?" An additional 28% answered that they felt connected "to a large extent" to people of their own nationality, and practically the same number of people referred to such connection with the local community. Among people of non-Russian nationalities, the importance of ethnic connection is even more pronounced at 83%. In the 2014 Fall study, 73% of Russians agreed with the statement, "in our times, a person has to feel a part of his nationality" (33% agreed completely and 42% agreed somewhat). At the same time, 50% answered that they "rarely thought about their national identity." In everyday existence, a person does not always feel or think about their nationality as one typically does not come across circumstances that remind one of ethnicity. At the same time, the majority of people consider themselves connected to some extent with their relevant ethnic community.

On a personal level, the relations between people of different nationalities are established at work, in neighborhoods, and among friend and family environments. Friendly individual relations between representatives of different nationalities often contrast with publicly strained ones. These interactions seem to be taking place in different spheres, where the public and the private spheres do not coincide.

In the past decade, the considerable inflow of migrants from other nationalities due to the collapse of the Soviet Union, particularly the inflow of the Vietnamese and Chinese to the eastern regions of the country, has created challenges. According to the 2002 All-Russian Census, there were 34,577 Chinese living in Russia. In the 2010 Census, this number fell to 28,943 persons. However, there is a much larger number of Chinese immigrants who have come to Russia after receiving a work permit. The majority of these migrants, 281,700 of them, was registered in 2008. In 2013, the registered number decreased to 71,200. Many of these migrants worked in Moscow or the Far East in the Primorye and Krasnodar Territory, engaging in construction, agriculture and fishing. Young people aged 18–39 made up 40% of the Chinese migrants.[1] They were characterized as hardworking employees. Ethnic agencies for recruitment and public services were working.

[1] Work and Employment in 2013 (2014).

Over Russia's period of transformation, there were also other ethnic and demographic trends in Russia that influenced ethnic relations. Among titular nations, the Russian republics named after the dominant ethnic group in that state, especially those in the North-Caucasian region, there is a higher share of ethnic groups due to higher birth rate in families of the nationalities that gave names to the republics, combined with the outflow of Russians.

At the same time, developing education stimulated an inflow of rural youth to republican cities. In more urbanized regions, young villagers could find a job or continue studying (such as in Tatarstan, Bashkortostan, partially in North Ossetia-Alania, Sakha [Yakutia]). However, in a number of North-Caucasian republics such as Tuva and Dagestan, the rural youth added to the urban unemployed, making communication between different ethnic groups more complicated. The Russians were better employed here and had good living conditions in cities. Naturally, the newcomers wanted to have the same conditions. Competition for workplaces increased.

Democratization expanded the possibilities of movement to large cities (with the end of the registration system) where it would be easier to find a job. The number of ethnic minorities in Moscow, St. Petersburg and other large cities increased. The number of Azerbaijani, Armenians and Georgians in Moscow increased especially quickly, by 4.8, 2.8 and 2.7 times, respectively.

The so-called "split market," in which non-residents of different nationalities receive different remuneration for the same kind of work, then appeared in Russia (such migrants are sometimes referred to by the German word "Gastarbeiter"). This caused discontent among native city residents, some of whom faced competition from non-residents willing to perform any work at low pay.

European countries and the USA also faced such an increased inflow of new migrants as a result of globalization. As not all migrants managed to adapt to their new home culture at once, they often lived and continue to live in relatively closed communities. This resulted in the appearance of "capsules" like China Town or Little Italy in Berlin, Toronto, London, and large US cities like the Russian-Jewish Brighton Beach area in New York. Specialists now refer to this phenomenon as "new ethnicity." The peculiarities in everyday behavior of newly arriving groups engendered reactions to their ethnic identity by the receiving majority.

After the Soviet Union collapsed, 25 million Russians found themselves beyond Russian borders. As the status of Russians in the republics underwent changes, the theoretical disputes of what defines a people, ethnos or nation acquired practical value in the Russian Federation. An understanding of these terms and their different meanings and connotations is important not only for a correct understanding of political and scientific texts but also for ethnopolitical and sociocultural processes in Russian and around the world.

New theories that explain the formation of ethnos, which contend that the actions of elites construct the historical ideas that serve as a basis for solidarity of ethnic groups, face more traditional "ontological" or primordialist theories about nations as historical communities with social and cultural characteristics, the most stable of which are the largest communities. Two directions are singled out in the primordialist theories of ethnos: evolutionary-historical and socio-biological. The evolutionary-historical school regards the nation-ethnos as a historically formed social community with a name, identity, cultural traits and language. Before the 1960s and 1970s, this original variant of primordialism dominated world science and was practically the only one in Russia. This school of thought is associated with J.G. Herder, or, more frequently, A. Smith, as the latter was interested in the history and evolution of ethnic groups, while in Russia we can mention Yu.V. Bromley. The second school, the socio-biological one, explains ethnicity as an "expanded related group", with an emphasis on natural proximity and natural relation (C. Geertz). Despite the initial dominance of primordial theories, it is impossible to explain the complexity of ethnic interests, feelings related to political mobilization, and social life in present-day society using primordialist approaches, especially the socio-biological approach. Instead, in order to explain the ethnic problems that manifested in social political life as a result of mass ethnic and racial movements in the 1970s and 1980s, social and cultural anthropologists turned to new ethnicity theories.

The constructivist theory interprets the nation and ethnic groups as communities united by common notions of culture, language, historical past and shared solidarity. We are not talking about the realia of culture or language but rather the ideas toward them, not about history but about historical memory often based on myths and traditions, real or imaginary. The myths and ideas about the ethnos are produced by the elites—writers, scientists, and politicians. Widely distributed education and the activity of mass media made it possible to get their ideas across to the broader public.

The history of present-day society provides a significant amount of material for constructivists to justify their ideas. The well-known Scottish kilt, which became a distinctive ethnic symbol of Scotland, is an example constructivists use. Though the kilt was invented by an Englishman, it was only thanks to the activity of Gaelic culture lovers that it became associated with Gaelic clans.

Ethnicity is mobile and changeable, it may be formed, which means it can be destroyed, too. This is the reason why relevant myths are invented. The best known and widely quoted constructivists in Russia are B. Andersen, E. Gellner, and V. Tishkov.

Constructivist theory raises a lot of disputes. If the elites are so omnipotent that they can ensure the necessary mobilization, let's say, of a separatist movement, why can't the leaders put on the brakes when the movements become violent and destructive? Why can people be united and mobilized even without mass media, for example, in the mountains of Abkhazia or the villages and mountainous regions of Chechnya? Everybody can read or hear texts communicated by leaders, but not everybody buys into certain ideas. Leaders' mobilization activities unite only those that have similar life experience and ideas.

Of course, it is important to know what can bring a group together and what cannot. Representatives of the instrumentalist school of thought define ethnos as a group unified by common interests (J. Rothschild, D. Horowitz, R. Brass). In the opinion of instrumentalists, ethnicity derives from the need to overcome alienation, the need to feel involved and have a community that understands you, and in some cases, the desire for equality and feeling of dignity. Instrumentalist thought is closely aligned to the concepts studied by ethno-sociologists and ethno-politologists.

However, in order to explain the reasons for ethnic mobilization, the direction of national movements, and solutions to resolve conflict, researchers must integrate all the approaches (L.M. Drobizheva, E.A. Pain).

In the Soviet Union, populations were divided into ethnic groups and nations. Nations consisted of the peoples that had their own statehood—unions and autonomous republics. In present-day theoretical concepts, Russian people are no longer classified by socio-economic formations and statehood. This division is no longer mentioned in popular and political literature, but it is still used in the public sphere.

The notion of the ethnic group is the widest. It is applicable to ethnos on the whole and in part. For example, we could talk about the Ossetians in general or the Ossetians living in Moscow or St. Petersburg. However, the use of the term "nation" has remained questionable for a long time. In the Russian tradition, just like in some other European countries like Germany, the term "nation" has been used to mean ethnos. The notion of the nation is still used in Germany in the meaning of the "people" (das Volk).

The use of the term "nation" in Russia was associated with ambiguity, but at the start of the twentieth century it came to denote an ethnic meaning. After the "right of the nations to self-determination" was proclaimed in the Bolshevist manifesto, this term also acquired a political meaning. If a people were called a nation, they had the right to self-determination stipulated in the constitution. With the upsurge in national movements, the right to self-determination acquired a special meaning.

Russian ethnologist-constructivists such as V. Tishkov understood this. Their proposals reduced the interpretation of the word "nation" to mean a state rather than an ethnic community, as is the case for Great Britain, France and a number of other countries. This understanding of the nation is also based in historical tradition. The term "nation" asserted itself at the end of the eighteenth century during the time of the Great French Revolution to denote a community of free citizens. The nation, being a sovereign, has the right to form its state. It was in this sense that the notion of the nation was defined in English. In Russia, the same meaning of the word nation is applied in a number of cases, for example "national income" and "national bank". However, in Russia it is possible to use "nation" to express the notions of "ethno-nation," "nationality," "people," and "ethnic group" as accepted all over the world.

With this in mind, the interpretation of the principle of the "right of nations to self-determination" was debated in the 1990s and 2000s. It is enshrined in the Charter of the United Nations and in the "International Covenant on Civil and Political Rights." Intellectuals in the republics of our country interpret these provisions as the right of peoples to self-determination in the meaning of ethno-nations. Those that understand the concept of a nation as co-citizenship think that self-determination of the political nation and understanding of the people as the citizens of state is implied. Self-determination of the people inside Russia may be realized through the formation of a republic that is still subject to the Russian Federation but gives national-cultural autonomy to this or that ethnic group.

Disputes became relevant as the Russian political elite has attempted to shape Russian civil identity in the past years. Every year since 2000, the Russian President has used his "Addresses to the Federal Assembly" to reference the formation of a single political nation and civil identity, using such terms as "we as a nation" or "we as the Russian nation." In 2000, the notion of "national" in this meaning was used in the Address 10 times, in 2007—18 times. In the 2011–2012 election campaign, V.V. Putin returned to this idea many times. It was especially actively referred to in 2014–2015 in connection with reunion of Russia and the Crimea.

The notion of ethnicity and ethnos is also widely used in presidential discourse. However, ideologists and politicians in republics also apply the notion of the nation to their people—Tatars, Yakuts, Tuvinians, Ingush, etc. For over 20 years, the notion of the nation had two meanings: one as a civil nation and the other as an ethnic nation.

In this context, V.A. Tishkov, the scholar that initiated the transfer of the notion of the political nation to the Russian scientific and political environment, declared: "Russia is the nation of nations."[2]

The essence of present-day national policy has become dual. On the one hand, it aims to secure the national interests of the Russian nation inside the country and in the international arena, and on the other hand it seeks to ensure the preservation and support among the diverse representatives of different nationalities and religions living in Russia.

In December 2012, the State National Policy Strategy of the Russian Federation through 2025 was adopted by Russian Presidential Decree. The Strategy takes into account many centuries of experience of the interaction between Russian nations and international experiences. The Strategy lays out the main aims of Russia's national policy: strengthening the Russian civil consciousness and solidarity of the multinational nation of the Russian Federation (Russian nation); preservation and development of the ethnic and cultural variety of Russian peoples; harmonization of international (inter-ethnic) relations; ensuring equality of rights and freedoms of the person and citizen regardless of race, nationality, language, and attitude to religion; and successful social and cultural adaptation and integration of migrants. In accordance with the Strategy, these aims have to be achieved on the basis of the constitutional principles of democracy, social justice, and respect for the national (ethnic) dignity of the citizens. The project of the Strategy was widely discussed. 3,500 adjustments and corrections were introduced in consideration of expressed opinions.[3] One of the vehemently debated issues related to the requirement of the republics to include the principle of the federal structure of the state in the text of the Strategy. It was finally included.

The policy is oriented in such a way that Russia does not reject European programs of tolerance and political correctness. Ethnic tolerance is understood as respect for the ethnic and cultural pluralism, and a positive or neutral attitude to the ethno-cultural

[2] Tishkov (2013a).

[3] Zorin and Astvatsaturova (2014).

and religious differences.[4] This signals readiness to accept others as they are and to organize interaction within the law. Russian policy agrees with protecting its national minorities, the interests of indigenous peoples, and regional languages. However, as Russian President said at the Valday Forum in September 2013: "the interests of the majority should not be forgotten, either...".[5]

The Russian accent in politics appeared in 2012 during the presidential election campaign. The pre-election article by V.V. Putin entitled, "Russia: National Issue," stated: "the great mission of Russians is to unite and tighten...with the language, culture, every possible kind-heartedness..."[6] This was V.V. Putin's evident answer to the growth of ethnic consciousness in Russia, and reflects the growth of patriotic moods and ethnic identity. 66% of Russians felt love and pride for their Motherland in 2014.[7] In 2011, 64% of Russians thought that "the state should first of all support the culture and religion of the majority of the country's population, the Russians." This political trend was supported by the youth just as actively as the middle and older generations. According to the IS RAS survey in October–November 2014, this opinion was supported by 70% of Russians. In the course of the IS RAS study titled, "20 years of reforms in the eyes of the Russians", in 2011[8] 82% of Russians said they never forget about their nationality. However, other ethnic groups had the same perspective; about 70% of Bashkirs and 81% of Tatars also joined the opinion "I never forget about my nationality."[9]

How does Russian society manage to keep the balance of mutual recognition and agreement in these conditions? Multiple factors have created a general background of communication between representatives of different nationalities that mitigates possible tension. These factors include the long historical tradition of life together, global events lived together, the veil of the historical memory of Soviet times dominated by the ideology of the "friendship of peoples", and the declaration of Russian leaders about the necessity of taking into account the interests of all nations. In addition, all citizens of the country, regardless of their nationality, feel that they have common goals, desires and ideas in their everyday lives. These common goals include ensuring equality of the citizens before the law (about 80%), as well as the beliefs that a person should have the right to defend his opinion even if the majority has another opinion (about 80%), and that Russia should be a great power (about 70%), etc.[10] In these views, the people of different nationalities have practically no statistically important differences.

---

[4] UNESCO Tolerance Principles Declaration. Approved by the Resolution 5.61 of UNESCO General Conference on 16.11.1995. URL: www.unesco.ru.

[5] Speech by V.V. Putin at the Valday Forum on September 19, 2013 (http://www.rg.ru/2013/09/19/stenogramma-site.html).

[6] Putin (2012).

[7] Public Opinion [Obshchestvennoe mnenie] 2014. M. 2015. p. 145.

[8] For more information, please refer to: Gorshkov et al. (2011).

[9] Drobizheva (2013, pp. 66, 72).

[10] Data of the project "What do the Russians dream about?".

Fig. 11.1 Similarities in the values of Russians and people of other nationalities, 2014, %[11]

All the other RAS Institute of Sociology studies show that the people of different nationalities have a lot of common values. For instance, it is clear from Fig. 11.1 that different ethnic groups have similar life objectives important to them. Of course, this similarity is not true for everything. For example, opinions differ as to the desire to see Russia the "empire that unites different nations." But overall, this desire is not that widespread among the Russians, though this group has relatively more supporters of the idea of empire among them.

Possible differences in the positions of representatives of different nations are shown by the following example. It is common knowledge that trust is an important aspect of personal and cooperative relations.[12] Our study in Moscow in 2014[13] showed that trust for one's surrounding people was expressed by 48% of Russian Muscovites and those of different ethnicities, including the Tatars. In the city of Tatarstan, 31% of Russians fully trusted Tatars, and 63% "rather trusted" them; among the Tatars, 33% fully trusted the Russians and 60% "rather trusted" them.[14] That is, mutual trust is almost the same among both groups in Tatarstan, but it is much higher than in Moscow.

Interethnic relations are surely influenced by the attitudes of the ethnic majority. We noted above the growing ethnic consciousness of the Russians as a pronounced tendency in recent years. At the same time, the studies also record their high level of openness: 73% share the opinion that the state should support the cultures and religions of all the peoples in Russia (the same quantity that agrees with priority support for the Russian culture). There were no noticeable differences in age and educational groups on this matter. The priority of support for Russian culture was more often mentioned by residents of megalopolises.

---

[11] Data of the monitoring study of IS RAS in October–November, 2014.

[12] Shtompka (2014).

[13] Project "Resource of interethnic concord in consolidation of the Russian society: common and peculiar in regional diversity", supervisor—L.M. Drobizheva.

[14] Drobizheva (2013, p. 362).

The Levada Center has long studied the attitude of the Russians to the motto of the nationalists, "Russia for the Russians." In 2014, this motto was supported by 54% of Russians. We also brought up this issue in our studies, with respondents often explaining: "Surely, Russia is populated by the Russians, the nature and the riches are for the Russian people." However, when the question was put differently in one of the surveys in a polyethnic Sochi district to read, "do you agree with the motto 'Russia only for the Russians?'", only 15% agreed. It is interesting to note in this connection that when the motto, "Russia for the Russians first and foremost, creation of the Russian national state," was offered as one of the possible response options to the question, "what do the Russians dream about?", only 14% selected it as a personal dream (about the same percentage as above). The so-called "Russian marches" with dominant anti-immigrant mottoes gathered up to 10,000 people in 2011, up to 20,000 in 2013, but no more than 4,500 in 2014, during the period of Russian national consolidation. 31% supported such marches in 2014 in Russia.[15] This is almost the same number of those who support Jean-Marie Le Pen in France, who declares that "France is for the French."

The mentality of the Russian nation is surely important for inter-ethnic peace, pluralism and tolerance in society. The position of the ethnic minority in many ways sets the tone for the nature of interethnic relations. One of the most important indicators of interethnic tolerance is the readiness for peaceful settlement of discrepancies and conflicts. The absolute majority of Russians and other nationalities think that violence in international and inter-religious disputes is inadmissible—81–84%, respectively.[16] This opinion also dominates in different age and social groups. However, there are fewer people that share this opinion among the residents of megalopolises, youth and people with secondary education (by 9–10%). However, in the republics, for instance, Bashkortostan or Tatarstan, there are far more who support non-violence, at 88–92%.[17]

According to surveys, the possibility of mass bloodshed on ethno-national grounds considerably decreased in 2014. In 2011–2012, 24% considered violence possible in the country, while 39–43% expected violence. Even fewer people (13% compared to 20–23%) considered violence possible in the place where the respondent lives. According to the Levada Center, interethnic tension in the city or region of residence was felt by no more than a quarter of the population in 2014.[18]

These fears are partly justified: 40% of Russians consider violence impossible if justice in relation to their people or belief is violated (Table 11.1). Nevertheless, as we see from Table 11.1, there are more of those that disagree with this opinion than agree (50% against 40%). There are slightly more people that oppose violence in

[15] Public Opinion [Obshchestvennoe mnenie] 2014. M. 2015. p. 145.

[16] The data of IS RAS monitoring, October–November, 2014.

[17] Drobizheva (2013, p. 343).

[18] Public Opinion [Obshchestvennoe mnenie] 2014. M. 2015.

Table 11.1 Opinions of Russians and other nationalities regarding the admissibility of violence if justice in relation to their people or belief is violated, 2014, %

Violence is admissible if justice in relation to my people or belief is violated	Russians	Non-Russians	Residents of Russia on the whole
Completely agree	16	14	16
Rather agree	24	24	24
Rather disagree	22	21	22
Disagree	27	24	27

groups with higher education (54%) and fewer among those with just a secondary education (42%).[19]

There are practically no differences as to admissibility of violence among the Russians and people of other nationalities. In Russian republics, admissibility of violence in Tatarstan, Bashkortostan, Sakha (Yakutia) ranges within 25–31%, with 36–47% believing that any methods may be used to protect the interests of their nation.

Thus, the intolerance threshold for violating the ethnic interests of the people, and more importantly, their dignity, are quite high. However, it should be noted that the attitudes toward intolerant actions are considerably milder. Under present-day conditions, the image of the "other" is focused on migrants from other cultures. Nevertheless, the majority disapproves of coercive actions in relation to them. Namely, 39% of Russians and 25% of representatives of other nationalities approve or "rather approve" of actions such as expulsion of individuals of certain nationalities from their city (village). However, the approval of this type of action strongly differs according to place of residence (Fig. 11.2).

As we see in Fig. 11.2, the willingness to undertake decisive action is the highest in megalopolises. The majority of those who do not approve of such actions are naturally found among those who could be expelled under certain conditions. Among those of Russian nationality, there are greater numbers who express discontent with the perception that non-residents "behave as masters on our land" and violate the established code of conduct. The same tendencies are seen in other countries, too. It is no mere chance that policies of multiculturalism have become subjects of deep debate in Germany, France, and Great Britain, all long-standing democracies. The situation in Russia is more difficult as the balance of tolerance needs to be regulated with regard to Russian peoples and immigrants who are ready to adapt to Russian society.

Attitudes towards minorities are an indicator of democracy. In this regard, the start of the twenty-first century has signaled an era of gradual adaptation by new migrants into Russian cities, and the adoption of legal measures against extremists that violate the rights of citizens. This demonstrates the possibility of resolving

[19] Here and further on, data from the Monitoring study of the IS RAS in October–November, 2014 is provided.

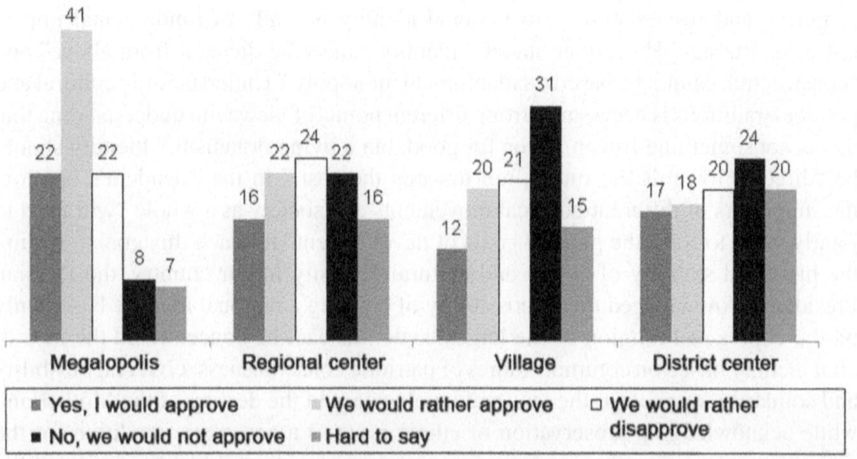

Fig. 11.2 Approval/disapproval of forced expulsion of representatives of some nationalities from the city (village) of residence according to different residential areas, 2014, %

complicated interethnic conflicts through negotiation and everyday communication. In most Russian regions, people mostly lived in peaceful communication among nationalities. Even in large cities like Moscow, St. Petersburg, and Ekaterinburg, where polls show ethnic conditions are the most complicated, the majority of the population engages in international communication through work collectives, neighborhoods, as well as friendly relationships. From 2005 to 2014, the Levada Center annually (except for 2012–2013) recorded no more than a quarter of the population that evaluated the interethnic relations in their city or region of residence as tense.[20]

State leaders and government authorities play a great role in supporting the climate of tolerant communication. We observe the desire of public leaders to oppose the all-Russian solidarity movement and pursue common goals, values and objectives to overcome lack of interethnic integration. One of their achievements is the formation of the Russian civil identity.

The creation of a national (civil) identity was launched under the scientific environment at the start of the 1990s. It has been actively stimulated by the President of the Russian Federation, V. Putin, since 2000. In practically every Annual Address to the Federal Assembly, he has referred to the problems that arise in the course of building the nation and national identity. At the Valday Forum in September 2013, V. Putin formulated the concepts of building a Russian identity and called on Russians to preserve their identity in the changing world. "For Russians and for Russia, the questions 'who are we?' and 'what do we want to be?' resound louder and louder in our society."[21] The goal was articulated: without a national identity "we cannot oppose the external and internal challenges…[and] gain success…the question of

[20] Public Opinion [Obshchestvennoe mnenie] 2014. M. 2015. p. 141.

[21] Speech by V.V. Putin at Valday Forum on September 19, 2013.

acquiring and strengthening our national identity is really of fundamental importance for Russia." He further stated: "identity cannot be dictated from above" and "construction cannot be based on ideological monopoly." Understanding cultural and political traditions is necessary "from different points of view with understanding that this is not something frozen, given for good, but a living organism." Identity should be "directed towards the future, not towards the past." In the President's opinion, the supporters of different political movements and society as a whole "will need to jointly work to form the general goals of development" to reach this goal.[22] Noting the historical stability of ethnic and cultural diversity in our country, the Russian President acknowledged the impossibility of creating a national identity based only on the ethnos and religion of the largest state. Instead, he concentrated the idea of civil identity based on common values of patriotic consciousness, civil responsibility and solidarity, respect for the law, and involvement in the destiny of the Motherland while acknowledging preservation of ethnic roots as a necessary condition for the country's unity. Strengthening this notion of the national civil identity is one of the main tasks and goals of the State National Policy Strategy.

Civil identity is the identity of a person within society, encompassing the idea of "who we are" and the feeling of solidarity and responsibility for the destiny of the country and lives of fellow citizens. Some scientists refer to civil identity as loyalty to the state and legitimacy of the power.[23] Others define it as "solidarity and everyday loyalty, the feeling of belonging to the same nation and recognition of the state as your own."[24] The second definition includes not only the state but also the entity, the nation. As the reader may see, we also incorporate responsibility of citizens in the affairs of the country into this notion, along with readiness to act in the name of the country's interests, trust for surrounding people, and manifestations of solidarity.[25]

Civil identity is surely sometimes connected with state identity. To assess Russian's notions of civil identity, we asked respondents in a number of Russian regions—first in expert and then in pilot (trial) surveys, and finally in representative studies in different regions of the country including Moscow, Tatarstan, and Sakha (Yakutia)—what unites them with the Russian citizens. The factor that scored the most votes in comparison with the others was the idea of a "common state," which was reflected in 60–85% of the answers. Among other unifying ideas, 35–60% of respondents mentioned such factors as native land, nature, language and culture. 30–40% mentioned responsibility for the destiny of the country. Customs, traits of character, etc. were mentioned by less than 10% of respondents. These evaluations naturally depend on the historical experience, place of residence, ethnic composition of the surroundings, and the outlook of people. Yet it is absolutely evident that Russian civil identity implies first and foremost state and civil identity.

---

[22] Ibid.

[23] Miller (2008).

[24] Tishkov (2013b).

[25] Drobizheva (2014).

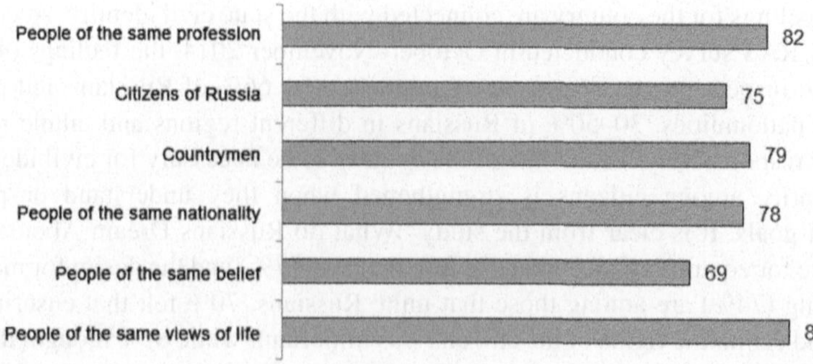

Fig. 11.3 Identities of Russians (where respondents feel considerably or somewhat connected), 2014, %

In our opinion, there are some circumstances that testify to the elements of civil identity in Russians. For example, in different constituents of the Federation, 30–40% of respondents mentioned "responsibility for the affairs in the country."[26] We also focused questions on the people and citizens rather than the state. For example, one of the survey questions was: "When we meet different people in our life, we easily find common language with some of them and understand them. Others do not become close to us, even though they live near. Russian citizens—can you say 'this is us' about them?" The majority of the answers indicated considerable or some kind of closeness to the citizens of Russia, which also testifies to the fact that Russian identity has an evident civil component.

Russian identity was formed or rather restored quite quickly in historical terms (historians V.A. Tishkov and A.I. Miller argue that Russian identity was present in the consciousness of Russians in the pre-Soviet period, too). After Russia was proclaimed an independent state at the start of the 1990s, the first polls in 1992 showed that just a quarter of Muscovites identified themselves as "citizens of Russia." Other polls, including the RAS Sociology Institute surveys of 2002–2008, the "Russian Monitoring of the Economic Situation and Health of the Population (RMEH)" polls conducted in 2006–2010, and the European Social Survey in 2006–2010, recorded civil identity in 63–68% of Russians. The latest RMEH survey in 2013 and IS RAS survey conducted in October–November 2014 recorded civil identity in 75–80% of respondents (Fig. 11.3).

The sense of civil identity is slightly higher in megalopolises and among more educated groups of the population. In the national republics where the studies were conducted in 2012–2013, the feeling of connection with Russian citizens was also higher than the average of the whole country: in Sakha (Yakutia) it was felt by 87% of Yakuts and 79% of Russians, in Tatarstan by 93% of Tatars and 94% of Russians, in Bashkortostan by 92% of Bashkirs, 91% of Russians, and 95% of Tatars.[27]

[26] Ibid., p. 132.

[27] Drobizheva (2013, pp. 59, 67, 72).

The feelings for the country are connected with the state civil identity. According to the IS RAS survey conducted in October–November 2014, the feelings of love, pride and respect for the country were expressed by 66% of Russians and people of other nationalities. 30–50% of Russians in different regions and ethnic groups consider responsibility for the fate of the country to be necessary for civil identity.

Solidarity among citizens is strengthened when they understand or pursue common goals. It is clear from the study "What do Russians Dream About?" that the desire for equality of all citizens before the law (77%) and the desire for material well-being (74%) are among those that unite Russians. 70% felt that ensuring the social and economic rights of the citizens was important, while 87% thought that the natural reaches must belong to the people or the state as its representative. 66% felt that "Russia has to be a great power with strong armed forces and influence all the political processes in the world." The last idea unites not only the Russians but also people of different nationalities, in different proportions and regions. The IS RAS survey conducted in October–November 2014 also found that this last idea unites Russians. It is important to note, however, that those who think that Russia should be a great power in most cases believes this should be accomplished mainly through a "developed present-day economy" (supported by 59% of Russians, 57% of other nationalities) and through a "high level of well-being" (53 and 52%, respectively).

Thanks to the monitoring studies of the RAS Institute of Sociology and studies in Russian republics, it is possible to show the dynamics of ideas about the desired nature of the Russian state from the standpoint of the role of ethnicity. In 1995, the majority of citizens (65%) agreed with the opinion that "Russia is the common home for many nations. All the Russian peoples must have equal rights, and none should have any advantages." 11% thought that Russia should be the state for the Russian people, and 14% thought that "Russians, being a majority, should have more rights as they are mainly responsible for the fate of the nation on the whole." In 2001–2007, the two last perspectives saw an increase in the number of supporters to 19% and 31%, respectively, or about double in number. Those who felt Russia should be a "common home for many peoples" fell from 61 to 50%. This shows a significant change since 1995. Though the majority of those polled still chose the inclusive position of Russia as "the common home for peoples," their numbers have fallen, and the share of those who support more rights for Russians in the state increased. At the same time, the share of those who believe that Russia should be a state for Russian people remained the same (Table 11.2).

It is also clear from Fig. 11.4 that the idea that the Russian majority should have more rights is just as popular among Russians as the idea that Russia should be the common home for many Russian peoples: 35 and 46%, respectively. However, the latter point of view is much more popular among representatives of other nationalities (70%).

It is also interesting that different Russian social groups showed a significant split in this respect, with age differences playing a significant role. For instance, among Russians over age 50, 56% share the opinion about Russia being a common home with equal rights of the peoples. Among those aged 18–30, only 43% held this view.

Table 11.2 Dynamics of the ideas of Russians about the desirable nature of the Russian State, 1995–2014, %

Views	1995	2007	2011	2014
Russia should be a country for the Russian people	11	16	14	9
Russia is a multinational country, but the Russians make up the majority, so they must have more rights	14	31	31	32
Russia is the common home for many peoples. All the Russian peoples must have equal rights, and none should have any advantages	65	48	47	50

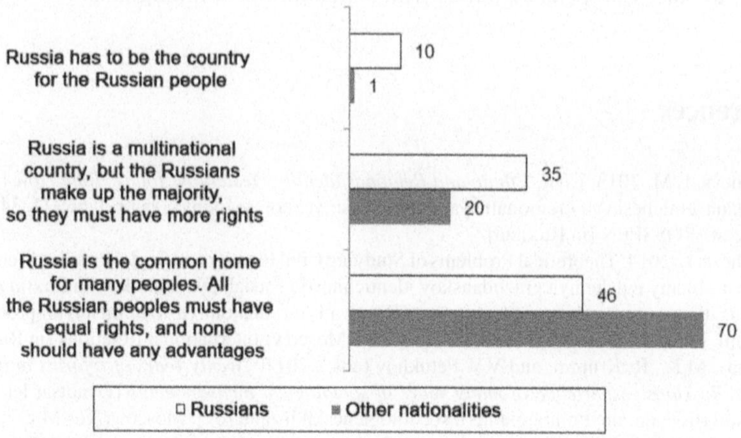

Fig. 11.4 The opinion of Russians and representatives of other nationalities about Russia as the Common Home for the Russian Peoples, 2014, %

The idea that Russia should give advantages to the ethnic majority is accepted by 37–38% of older age groups, and 46% of younger people.

The increasing identity of Russians may be aimed at positive goals, but risks acquiring a nationalist nature, both civil and ethnic. Thus, the Russian President considered it important to point out that "nationalists should recall that Russia was formed as a multi-national and multi-confessional state from the start… by challenging our multi-nationality, and seeking to develop Russian, Tatar, Caucasian, Siberian or some other nationalism and separatism, we are embarking on the destruction of our genetic code—in fact, we start destroying ourselves."[28]

Thus, the national identity has an evident basis in the identification and feeling of belonging as Russian citizens, brought together by main values and a shared sense of responsibility. Russian civil identity is strengthened at the expense of growing patriotism, stimulated by the speeches of leaders, the return of the Crimea, the activity of mass media and the support of all population groups. 65% of respondents expressed a feeling of love, pride and respect for today's Russia. 52% would like to see it become

[28] Speech by V.V. Putin at the Valday Forum. 19.09.2013.

"one of the economically developed and politically influential countries of the world" with a developed economy and high level of well-being of the citizens.

Russians and other nationalities in Russia identify with the common goals and dreams of equality of opportunity, justice and lawfulness in this difficult pluralist world. The majority of Russians, while identifying as citizens of the country, at the same time do not forget about their ethnicity and want the state to support their culture and religion. The level of tolerance in ethnic and social groups depends on the contacting groups, the nature of their interaction, and the situation of mass immigration. On the whole, the tolerance of Russians for a more pluralist society is similar to other European countries with a high inflow of immigrants.

References

Drobizheva, L.M. 2013. *Civil, Ethnic and Regional Identity: Yesterday, Today, Tomorrow* [Grazhdanskaia, etnicheskaya i regionalnaya identichnost: vchera, segodnya, zavtra], 66, 72, 343, 362. Moscow: ROSSPEN [in Russian].

Drobizheva, L. 2014. Theoretical Problems of Studying Civil Identity and Social Practice [Teoreticheskie problemy izucheniya grazhdanskoy identichnosti i sotsialnaya praktika]. In *Russia and the World: Anatomy of present-day processes* [Rossiya i mir: anatomiya sovremennykh protsessov. Sbornik statey]. Collection of Articles, 130–146. Moscow: International Relations [in Russian].

Gorshkov, M.K., R. Krumm, and V.V. Petukhov (eds.). 2011. *Twenty years of reforms in the eyes of the Russians: experience of many years of sociological measurements* [Dvadtsat let reform glazami rossiyan: opyt mnogoletnikh sotsiologicheskikh zamerov]. Moscow: Ves Mir.

Miller, A.I. 2008. Subject of the nation in the Russian policy of the past years // Two presidential terms of V. V. Putin: dynamics of changes. M., 2008. p. 320.

Putin, V.V. 2012. Russia: National Issue [Rossiya: natsionalnyy vopros]. *Nezavisimaya Gazeta*, January 23 [in Russian].

Shtompka, P. 2014. *Trust is the Basis of the Society* [Doverie – osnova obshchestva]. Moscow: Logos, p. 166.

Tishkov, V.A. 2013a. *Russian Nation: History and Sense of the National Identity* [Rossiiskiy narod: istoriya i smysl natsionalnogo samosoznaniya]. Moscow: Nauka [in Russian].

Tishkov, V.A. 2013b. *Russian Nation* [Rossiyskiy narod], 66. Moscow: Nauka.

Work and Employment in 2013. 2014. *Work and Employment in 2013* [Trud i zanyatost v 2013 g], 28. Moscow: Federal Service of State Statistics [in Russian].

Zorin, V. Yu, and M. A. Astvatsaturova. 2014. Strategy of the State National Policy of the Russian Federation [Strategiya gosudarstvennoy natsionalnoy politiki Rossiyskoy Federatsii]. In *Studies in Applied and Urgent Ethnology* [Issledovaniya po prikladnoy i neotlozhnoy' etnologii], Issue 236, p. 16. Moscow: IEA RAS [in Russian].

Chapter 12
Towards a More Diversified and Integrated Society: Insights from Social Psychology

Yiyin Yang and Wenjun Gao

As modern China evolves into a more diversified society, the moderate relationship of social differentiation and integration, social prosperity and cooperation have increasingly become an important issue.

From the perspective of social change, China's traditional social order and social cohesion mechanism (for instance, the design of China's social structure and order of differential pattern)—though impacted by the processes of industrialism and commercialism—has certain foundational value and vitality through which it can regenerate. From the perspective of individual basic social needs and adaptation towards change, adaptive strategies for constructively dealing with the relationship between society and the individual has emerged every so often. Per the *Theory of Transitional Society* and *Psychology of Transitional Society*, it is meaningful to explore the features of China's currently diversified society in order to reveal the interactive process between individual and social transition. In studying the experiences of individuals, this exploration will improve the association between theory and reality. This chapter focuses on describing the differentiation and integration features of China's currently diversified society from the perspective of social psychology as a discipline and based on data analysis of a large-sample questionnaire survey. The conclusion applies basic judgment and analysis of the data to describe the condition of Chinese national identity.

The trend toward social diversification, represented by increasing numbers of social groups, comes from the diversification of social character and life paths resulting from great changes in China's social structure and lifestyle. For example, vocation and leisure is completely different among people from different social classes; forms of leisure also vary to a great extent among people of the same class. Richness in the selection of social life has created many new categories. For instance, those who have no travel experience now form "Tour Pal" groups; young graduates

Y. Yang (✉) · W. Gao
CASS Institute of Sociology, Beijing, P.R. China

P. Li and M. K. Gorshkov (eds.), *Life Expectations of the People*,
Research Series on the Chinese Dream and China's Development Path,
https://doi.org/10.1007/978-981-16-2505-3_12

who stay in big cities waiting for development opportunities while living in small and cramped spaces between the urban-rural continuum are termed "Antizen"; and people obsessed with playing games on their mobile phone are called "Thumb Tribe" and/or "Phubbers." There are numerous fan groups with strong social cohesion that continuously verifies the sayings, "like attracts like, birds of a feather flock together" and "different people have different aspirations."

This kind of change comes with increasing social complexity (Triandis et al. 1988). Formerly, social identity was mainly ascribed to such factors as age, gender, dialect, residence, ethnicity, race, educational background, profession, industry and other similar social groupings. Within a diversified society, there are an increasing number of social group categories formed by acquired factors. These are termed "psychological groups" and are mainly divided by lifestyle, values, psychological characteristics and behavioral preferences. Psychological groups are one of the core concepts of social identity theory created by English social psychologist Tajfel, and refers to groups that form from a certain psychological connection between individual and group. This kind of group is not a statistical group that can be classified according to certain attribute(s) of the social population, for instance by income or age. Rather, they are a homogeneous group formed through individual selection and expression of an individual psychological state. Formed through initiative, selectivity, participation and constructivism, this is a new stratification of social identity into which people assign themselves through interactions formed by social economic behaviors in a pluralistic society. It transcends traditional social categories and social stratifications, and represents a greater degree of life vitality highlighted by will.

Groups that are formed by lifestyle, value choice, behavioral preference and social emotion reach social consensus through communication. Groups continually search for more suitable media communication platforms—through which they can articulate their own will more clearly—while recognizing their own organizing agent. This serves as a new perspective for analyzing the source of social psychological power which drives the differentiation and integration of a pluralistic society.

12.1 Analysis of the Diversification of Current Chinese Society

At present, Chinese society is already more or less diverse, as represented by different social strata, lifestyles and values. More specifically, China's social diversification is expressed by consumption levels and patterns, media usage, social values and experiences of social emotions.

12.1.1 Diversity of Consumption Groups

Consumption level, being an important indicator of living standard, is a basic differentiating social category. Our survey investigated the living consumption of families based on four aspects, with the purpose of analyzing the characteristics of different consumer groups. The four categories of consumer spending were divided as follows: (1) spending for daily consumption, including basic life necessities such as food, clothing, water & electricity, transportation, communication, medical care, house rent, mortgage or down payment; (2) consumer spending for performing family obligations, including support for the elderly and social spending; (3) consumer spending for improving the quality of life, including spending on culture, entertainment, tourism, household appliances, furniture and vehicles; and (4) consumer spending for promoting family development, including education investment. The ratio between consumption of each kind and total expenditures among respondents serves as the object of analysis to identify degrees of social differentiation.

According to an analysis of the survey results, the shares of overall consumer spending is as follows: 72.9% is on spending that's necessary for maintaining daily life, 13.5% is on performing family responsibility, 9.4% is spent on promotion of family development, and 7.8% is spent on improving the quality of life. This shows that, currently, consumption is concentrated on meeting basic life needs and maintaining social relations, whereas the percentage of spending on family development and improving the quality of life are relatively low (Table 12.1). Therefore, the degree of differentiation is not that high from this perspective.

Second, we've analyzed the demographic characteristics of groups with different consumption levels by identifying respondents with more typical consumption characteristics. Specifically, if a respondent whose proportion of consumption in one of the consumption categories is among the top 25% of all respondents, and that in the other three consumption categories is below the top 25%, we identify that respondent as a typical consumer of one kind of consumption, that is, he/she focuses more on one particular kind of consumer spending compared with other respondents. Among the

Table 12.1 Distribution of respondents with typical consumption characters

Type of Consumer Spending	Number	Percentage taken in all respondents (%)	Percentage taken in selected respondents (%)
Focus on maintaining daily life	2181	21.3	77.8
Focus on maintaining family responsibility	1469	14.3	21.6
Focus on improving the quality of life	1527	14.9	22.4
Focus on promoting family development	1630	15.9	23.9
In total	6807	66.3	100.0

10,260 respondents, 6807 representing different consumption characteristics were chosen through this approach. Table 12.1 provides a general picture of consumption differences, with differences based on age, level of education, residence, income, assets and other aspects shown in Tables 12.2, 12.3, 12.4, and 12.5.

The results show a distinct age stratification in the type of consumption spending. First, older respondents spend more on consumption for maintaining daily life and

Table 12.2 Interaction analysis of consumption spending type and age (unit: %)

	Proportion of consumption spending by type (%)			
	Focused on maintaining daily life	Focused on performing family responsibility	Focused on improving the quality of life	Focused on promoting family development
Generation born in 1950s or before	30.1	27.1	18.3	13.8
Generation born in 1960s	19.8	25.9	18.1	25.0
Generation born in 1970s	16.0	18.0	20.1	30.7
Generation born in 1980s	24.4	21.5	32.0	11.8
Generation born after 1990s	9.8	7.6	11.4	18.7
Total	100.0	100.0	100.0	100.0

Table 12.3 Interaction analysis of consumption spending type and degree of education (unit: %)

	Proportion of consumption spending type			
	Focused on maintaining daily life	Focused on performing family responsibility	Focused on improving the quality of life	Focused on promoting family development
Primary school and below	35.9	35.5	24.6	26.3
Middle school	35.3	35.6	32.1	30.9
High school, secondary specialized school and vocational high school	17.1	16.2	21.5	22.1
Junior college	5.9	6.1	9.3	8.2
Undergraduate and above	5.7	6.5	12.5	12.5
In total	100.0	100.0	100.0	100.0

Table 12.4 Interaction analysis of consumption spending type and residence (unit: %)

	Proportion of consumption spending type			
	Focused on maintaining daily life	Focused on performing family responsibility	Focused on improving the quality of life	Focused on promoting family development
Township	59.6	48.1	61.3	60.8
Countryside	40.4	51.9	38.7	39.2
In total	100.0	100.0	100.0	100.0

Table 12.5 Interaction analysis of consumption spending type and economic assets (unit: yuan)

	Proportion of consumption spending type			
	Focused on maintaining daily life	Focused on performing family responsibility	Focused on improving the quality of life	Focused on promoting family development
Annual total income of individual	21,227.6	28,888.0	40,369.0	17,381.5
Annual total income of family	56,123.5	61,344.1	95,540.6	53,717.0
Family net asset	46,695.1	48,588.5	180,423.0	51,155.1

performing family responsibility, among which, the generations born in the 50s and 60s comprise about a half. Second, the groups that focus the most on improving quality of life, at 50%, are the generations born in the 1970s and 1980s. People of this age group comprise the social backbone of the country. Born and raised in a time of general stability and abundance, this generation already has relatively stable work, a clear career trajectory, and stable path toward economic accumulation. Thus, they are more likely to focus consumption on improving their quality of life, including more spending on tourism, entertainment, and purchases of vehicles, household appliances and other supplies, as compared with their parents. The greatest proportion of consumption related to family development is found among the generations born in the 1960s and 1970s; people in these two groups generally have children who are mostly still in their school years, resulting in more money being spent on family education compared to other groups. Finally, the generation born after the 1990s does not represent a majority among any of the four types of consumption. This is likely due to the fact that they have not established a solid economic foundation, and some of them are still economically dependent, thus they do not have a fixed mode of family consumption. However, they do have a distinct consumption characteristic; a greater number of those born after the 1990s focus their consumption on promoting family development and improving quality of life, with less of a focus on consumption for maintaining daily life and performing family responsibilities.

Also, the type of consumption spending is to a certain extent correlated with degree of education. Respondents with lower levels of education spend more money on maintaining their daily life and performing family responsibilities, whereas those with a higher degree of education focus more on improving quality of life and promoting family development.

The consumption differences between urban and rural areas are also very distinct. For consumption in the categories of improving quality of life and promoting family development, the share of respondents from urban areas is 20% higher than from rural areas. A higher share of urban residents also had a greater focus on maintaining daily life than rural residents. Respondents from rural areas, being self-sufficient in certain food items and with lower housing expenses, likely spend less money on this. With respect to consumption for family responsibility, the proportion of respondents from rural areas is slightly higher than that from urban areas, which may be due to the fact that residents put more emphasis on human relationships and support in a rural environment.

There is also an interaction effect between consumption spending type and economic conditions statistically. Economic indicators of individual income, family income and net assets have consistently shown that people in better economic conditions—respondents with higher incomes and more family net assets—spend more money on improving quality of life, whereas respondents in relatively poor economic conditions, aside from maintaining necessities of daily life, spend more on education. A probable explanation is that lower income families hope to change their economic situation and improve family income through greater education of family members.

In summary, there exists a psychological pull to pursue a contented life, which unites people of different social groups. That is to say, a common aspiration of the people is to have a better life. The family is the basic unit in which people spend money on and focus on development. In addition to providing for the basic needs of daily family life, consumption is centered on relationships, including support for the elderly and raising children, particularly the education of children which is seen as a path towards a prosperous future. Consumption differences among age groups and between urban and rural residents reflect the condition and speed of change occurring in China's social and population structure.

12.1.2 Diversified Characteristics of Media Usage

In modern society, people can access information in increasingly diversified ways and through a growing number of channels, including through traditional media, such as TV, radio, newspapers, magazines and books, and non-traditional media like the internet. We first describe the characteristics of media usage from two specific aspects: the use of traditional media by all respondents; and two, engagement with the internet for those respondents who use the internet regularly (accounting for

40.6% of all respondents). As indicated in Tables 12.6 and 12.7, the results show that among traditional media, respondents read books and newspapers the most, and watch TV/listen to the radio much less frequently, although there is a greater number that watches TV occasionally. With regard to usage of the internet, respondents mostly use the internet for activities such as online shopping, receiving and sending email, occasional browsing of the news, looking up information, or chatting with friends.

Table 12.6 Overview of traditional media usage by all respondents (unit: %)

Usage of traditional media	Percent of people with different frequencies of usage					
	Almost every day	Multiple times per week	At least one time per week	At least one time per month	Several times per year	Never
Watch TV	3.2	2.8	7.4	13.9	69.0	3.6
Listen to the radio	4.7	1.8	2.1	3.1	5.2	83.0
Read newspapers and magazines	7.6	6.9	8.9	9.4	10.4	56.8
Read books	9.7	7.0	7.5	9.4	11.2	55.2

Table 12.7 Overview of relevant activities of respondents who use the internet normally and frequency of usage (unit: %)

Using Internet	Percent of people with different frequencies of usage					
	Almost every day	Multiple times per week	At least one time per week	At least one time per month	Multiple times per year	Never
Browsing news	2.9	4.5	9.9	18.9	56.8	6.9
Receiving and sending email	10.4	11.0	10.2	12.5	13.7	42.2
Looking up information	6.4	10.0	14.2	27.8	27.1	14.5
Chatting with friends	5.5	6.6	11.5	20.0	39.4	17.0
Using microblog/blog	4.9	7.1	7.9	10.9	19.8	49.5
Playing online games	7.4	7.8	10.8	12.2	13.5	48.3
Online shopping	22.2	21.2	9.0	6.4	3.5	37.8
Online investment and financing	4.3	3.3	1.3	1.2	1.9	88.0

To clearly compare the characteristics of traditional media and internet usage by people from different social classes, we average the frequency value of the use of different types of traditional media and different internet activities, with the minimum and maximum value being 0 and 5, respectively. A higher score indicates more frequent usage of the media or internet activity. The results are shown in Tables 12.8, 12.9, and 12.10.

Preference in media usage is very distinct across age groups: older people more frequently use traditional media, while younger people have a higher frequency of

Table 12.8 Interaction analysis of media preference and age

	Media preference	
	Frequency of traditional media usage	Frequency of internet media usage
Generation born after the 1950s and before	1.701	1.456
the Generation born after the 1960s	1.755	1.555
Generation born in the 1970s	1.907	1.908
Generation born in the 1980s	2.040	2.348
Generation born after the 1990s	2.306	2.543

Table 12.9 Interaction analysis between media preference and education level

	Media preference	
	Frequency of traditional media usage	Frequency of internet media usage
Primary school and below	1.330	1.270
Middle school	1.715	1.673
High school, secondary specialized school and vocational high school	2.361	2.100
Junior college	2.648	2.545
Undergraduate and above	2.906	2.854

Table 12.10 Interaction analysis between media preference and residence

	Media preference	
	Frequency of media traditional usage	Frequency of internet usage
Township	2.179	2.286
Countryside	1.539	1.832

internet use. Specifically, the generation born in the 50s and 60s use traditional media more frequently than the internet, while the generation born after the 80s and 90s use the internet more frequently than traditional media; the generation born in the 70s uses these two kinds of media with almost the same frequency.

Respondents with different levels of education do not show a distinct difference in media preference. Instead, the results show a basic trend of people with higher education levels using all sorts of media more frequently than those with lower education levels; the frequency of traditional media use is a bit higher than internet use regardless of education level.

Respondents from urban and rural areas also show differences in preference of media use. Compared to rural residents, urban residents more frequently use both traditional media and the internet. Both groups use the internet more than traditional media, with a larger gap found among respondents from rural areas.

Social categories defined by media preference and preferred method of information consumption, while seemingly nothing other than the free selection of an individual, in fact reflects differences in the style of social interaction in a true sense. How and why people use the internet—for communication (i.e. sending email and chatting with friends), for expression (microblogs and blogs), for information retrieval (browsing the news and looking up material), for economic reasons (managing money matters and shopping) and for leisure (playing games)—satisfy different emotional, social and economic needs, and thus constitutes an important factor in psychological groupings. These psychological grouping serve a secondary need (manufacturing and publishing information) on the basis of a preliminary need (acquiring information).

Groups with a higher media demand preferences more easily accept indirect and unfamiliar information, and in a public society, they are more likely to trust the system and experts, and more willing to use shared information. They thus become a group defined by information consumption, information dependence and information processing. They selectively arrange, assess and spread information from content and other published materials. They utilize market, social contact and entertainment information, and are more likely to have a multivariate and tolerant attitude, more free will, and are more likely to be influenced and mobilized. They are also more likely to get information through the internet and thus are connected to network structures. In short, they can easily be rallied or divided.

12.1.3 Diversity of Values

This study investigated the values of respondents by asking "what are the features of a good society?" The values listed in the questionnaire relate to 12 socialist core values published by the 18th National Congress of the CPC: prosperity, democracy, civilization and harmony at the state level; freedom, equality, justice and rule of law at the society level; and patriotism, dedication, integrity and kindness at the citizen level.

Table 12.11 Ranking of socialist core values selected by respondents

	Percent of respondents who selected the value in the sample (%)
Equality	47.2
Democracy	43.6
Justice	40.0
Prosperity	39.5
Civilization	39.4
Harmony	37.3
Integrity	22.3
Patriotism	22.1
Rule of law	20.2
Freedom	18.6
Kindness	9.0
Dedication	3.9

First, the core values were ranked by degree of attention, according to the number of respondents for each selection. Second, the most representative values, according to the ranking result, were selected in order to analyze the differences and similarities between different groups. The analysis results are listed as follows:

Table 12.11 shows the ranking of the 12 core values of a "good society" according to the number of respondents for each selection. The results show that the majority of people attach more importance to values at the society and state level, such as equality and justice at the society level, and democracy, prosperity, civilization and harmony at the state level. These are then followed by values at the citizen level, such as integrity and patriotism. Second, democracy is most valued at the state level; equality is most valued at the society level; and integrity is most valued at the citizen level. This study then compared the differences among groups according to respondents' selection of these three values.

43.6% of survey respondents consider democracy to be one of the key characteristics of a "good society." These respondents likely have a relatively stronger democratic value orientation, while the reverse case is likely true for the rest of the respondents who did not choose democracy as a key characteristic. By comparing their demographic characteristics, the results of which are shown in Table 12.12, it can be found out that these two groups vary in age, education degree and residence: compared with the rest of the respondents, those who attach importance to democracy and take it as a standard of a good society are relatively younger. Among the 43.6% that selected democracy, the generation born after the 1990s comprises the largest share of respondents. Those with higher levels of education, with a bachelor degree or above, comprise the largest proportion of respondents that value a democratic orientation, whereas the majority of respondents who have graduated from middle school, elementary school and below did not choose democracy; nearly half

Table 12.12 Interaction between democratic values and demographic characteristics (unit: %)

		Democratic value orientation	
		Relatively weak orientation of democracy	Relatively strong orientation of democracy
Age	Generation born after the 1950s and before the	57.2	42.8
	Generation born in the 1960s	58.7	41.3
	Generation born in the 1970s	55.8	44.2
	Generation born in the 1980s	57.5	42.5
	Generation born after the 1990s	51.6	48.4
Education Degree	Primary school and below	66.0	34.0
	Middle school	61.2	38.8
	High school, secondary specialized school and vocational high school	49.1	50.9
	Junior college	41.8	58.2
	Undergraduate and above	38.5	61.5
Residence	Township	52.4	47.6
	Countryside	62.4	37.6

of respondents living in urban areas hold democratic values, while the proportion among rural residents was less than 40%.

47.2% of respondents consider equality to be a characteristic of a "good society"; Respondent groups with a relatively stronger and weaker value orientation of equality are shown in Table 12.13. The differences in this value orientation are mostly associated with age, with younger groups generally attaching more importance to equality than older groups, among which a large number are from the generations born in the 70s, 80s and 90s. No distinct difference is shown among respondents with different education levels and place of residence.

22.3% of respondents consider integrity to be one of the main characteristics of a "good society." Respondents with a relatively stronger and weaker value orientation of integrity are shown in Table 12.14. The differences in this value orientation vary based on age, education level and residence. Those who attach importance to integrity are relatively younger, with a much larger proportion of those born after 1990s supporting this value than the generation born after the 1950s. A larger share of respondents with a higher education level -holding a bachelor degree or above—and a greater number of urban residents than rural residents attach importance to the value of integrity.

Table 12.13 Interaction between values of equality and demographic variables (unit: %)

		Value orientation of equality	
		Relatively weaker	Relatively stronger
Age	Generation born after 1950s and before the	55.8	44.2
	Generation born in the 1960s	54.1	45.9
	Generation born in the 1970s	52.4	47.6
	Generation born in the 1980s	50.3	49.7
	Generation born after the 1990s	51.5	48.5
Education degree	Primary school and below	53.5	46.5
	Middle school	52.9	47.1
	High school, secondary specialized school and vocational high school	50.7	49.3
	Junior college	53.9	46.1
	Undergraduate and above	55.0	45.0
Residence	Township	53.3	46.7
	Countryside	52.4	47.6

The economic asset situation of respondents was calculated in two ways, by family annual income and net assets. We divided family annual income reported by respondents into five levels: lower, low, middle, high and higher, taking 20% as the point for division. Family net assets were calculated by taking the difference between family property such as household savings, production & operation assets, valuables and vehicles, and family's aggregate debts. Family net assets were also divided into the same five levels: lower, low, middle, high and higher, taking 20% as the point for division.

Tables 12.15, 12.6, and 12.17 compare value orientation based on different income and asset levels. The results show that the proportion of respondents holding democratic values increases with higher family annual income and net assets. This is especially the case with respect to family net assets, where there is a 10% higher share of respondents that attach importance to democratic values in higher net asset brackets than those with lower net assets. While differences toward the value of integrity among different income and asset levels is not as large, there is a higher share of respondents that value integrity among those with higher family annual incomes compared with those who have lower annual incomes.

The results show that democracy, equality and integrity are considered the most important values worthy of pursuit for a good society. The focus on these values

Table 12.14 Interaction between values of integrity and demographic variables (unit: %)

		Value orientation of integrity	
		Relatively weaker	Relatively stronger
Age	Generation born after the 1950s and before the	81.1	18.9
	Generation born in the 1960s	79.0	21.0
	Generation born in the 1970s	77.7	22.3
	Generation born in the 1980s	75.2	24.8
	Generation born after the 1990s	74.6	25.4
Education degree	Primary school and below	80.5	19.5
	Middle school	78.9	21.1
	High school, secondary specialized school and vocational high school	77.3	22.7
	Junior college	74.7	25.3
	Undergraduate and above	68.1	31.9
Residence	Township	75.5	24.5
	Countryside	80.9	19.1

Table 12.15 Interaction between democratic values and income & asset level (unit: %)

		Democratic value orientation	
		Relatively weaker	Relatively stronger
Family annual income	Lower	61.8	38.2
	Low	60.4	39.6
	Middle	57.0	43.0
	High	52.9	47.1
	Higher	52.2	47.8
Family net assets	Lower	60.7	39.3
	Low	60.7	39.3
	Middle	59.5	40.5
	High	54.5	45.5
	Higher	50.7	49.3

Table 12.16 Interaction between values of equality and income & asset level (unit: %)

		Value orientation of equality	
		Relatively weaker	Relatively stronger
Family annual income	Lower	52.0	48.0
	Low	53.7	46.3
	Middle	52.8	47.2
	High	51.3	48.7
	Higher	54.4	45.6
Family net assets	Lower	54.3	45.7
	Low	52.5	47.5
	Middle	52.9	47.1
	High	53.4	46.6
	Higher	51.2	48.8

Table 12.17 Interaction between values of integrity and income and asset level (unit: %)

		Value orientation of integrity	
		Relatively weaker	Relatively stronger
Family annual income	Lower	81.1	18.9
	Low	78.9	21.1
	Middle	78.2	21.8
	High	77.6	22.4
	Higher	74.0	26.0
Family net asset	Lower	75.6	24.4
	Low	79.0	20.1
	Middle	80.7	19.3
	High	79.2	20.8
	Higher	78.7	21.3

reflects prominent problems with current society. In other words, the lack of democracy, equality and integrity rightly highlights the importance of these three values. The emphasis on these three values varies based on age, education level, and place of residence (urban vs. rural areas). This shows that the differentiation in social values among different population groups is relatively severe.

12.1.4 Diversity of Mood and Emotional Experience

Social diversity is reflected not only by different socio-economic classes and psychological groups, but also by emotional experience. People can be divided according to key moods and emotions, namely, "people with positive emotional experience" and "people with negative emotional experience." This differentiation provides a sense of the situation of social members' satisfaction with life.

In this analysis, we asked respondents to attach a value between 1 to 5 to several key emotional experiences, with a score of 1 representing no experience with that emotion, and a score of 5 representing significant experience with that emotion. The results show that, in daily life, respondents generally experience positive emotions such as pleasure and enjoyment, and only occasionally experience anger, worry, sadness, aversion and other negative emotions. Overall, the results show that current Chinese society is dominated by positive emotion, and the experience of negative emotion is occasional and infrequent (Table 12.18).

To more clearly compare the emotional characteristics of different groups, several emotions are simply divided into positive and negative emotions. Scores for pleasure and enjoyment are calculated as positive emotions, whereas the scores for anger, worry, fear, sadness and sorrow are calculated as negative emotions. We divided respondents into the positive or negative emotional groups as follows: if a respondent whose frequency of positive emotional experience is among the top 25% of all respondents and the frequency of negative emotional experience is among the bottom 25%, then that respondent will be classified into the positive emotional group; similarly, if the frequency of negative emotional experience is among the top 25% and that of positive emotional experience is among the bottom 25%, then that respondent is placed in the negative emotional group. Table 12.19 shows the overall results of

Table 12.18 Frequency of respondents' daily emotional experience

	Frequency of emotional experience
Pleasure, enjoyment	3.391
Anger,	2.317
Worry, fear	2.040
Sadness and sorrow	1.927
Aversion	1.873

Table 12.19 Distribution of respondents with typical emotional experience

Type of emotional experience	Number	Percentage of all respondents (%)	Percentage of selected respondents (%)
Typical positive emotion	1386	13.5	60.9
Typical negative emotion	891	8.7	39.1
In total	2277	22.2	100.0

the 2,277 respondents and their typical emotional experience. Tables 12.20, 12.21, 12.22, and 12.23 describe the differences among the two emotional groups based on age, education level, place of residence, income and assets, etc.

Different age groups show distinct emotional characteristics. The generation born after the 1950s has the highest share of respondents with typically positive emotional experiences. Compared to the other age groups, the share of respondents from the

Table 12.20 Interaction analysis between typical emotional experience and age (unit: %)

	Type of typical emotion	
	Typical positive emotion	Typical negative emotion
Generation born after the 1950s and before	35.4	21.5
Generation born in the 1960s	25.3	23.3
Generation born in the 1970s	16.5	25.7
Generation born in the 1980s	14.2	20.0
Generation born in the 1990s	8.6	9.5
In total	100.0	100.0

Table 12.21 Interaction analysis between type of typical emotional experience and education degree (unit: %)

	Type of typical emotion	
	Typical positive emotion	Typical negative emotion
Primary school and below	33.5	43.0
Middle school	34.1	32.7
High school, secondary specialized school and vocational high school	19.0	14.4
Junior college	6.2	6.4
Undergraduate and above	7.2	3.5
In total	100.0	100.0

Table 12.22 Interaction analysis between type of typical emotional experience and residence (unit: %)

	Type of typical emotion	
	Typical positive emotion	Typical negative emotion
Township	56.4	46.7
Countryside	43.6	53.3
In total	100.0	100.0

Table 12.23 Interaction analysis between typical emotional experience and economic income (unit: yuan)

	Type of typical emotion	
	Typical positive emotion	Typical negative emotion
Individual total annual income	22,994.440	15,829.853
Family total annual income	61,864.845	45,337.030
Family net asset	81,707.979	21,621.823

1950's generation that has a typically negative emotional experience is somewhere in the middle. People in this age group are generally in the period of retirement and old age, their children are mostly married and settled down, and thus they have relatively less life burden and experience pleasure and enjoyment most of the time. For the generation born in the 1960s, the percentage of people with positive and negative emotional experiences are almost the same. People in this age group still have certain pressures of life: their children are yet to get married, their parents are old, and they themselves are close to retirement, thus, their emotional experience is mixed, and typical positive and negative emotions might exist at the same time.

For the generation born in the 1970s, the percentage of respondents with typical negative emotional experience is the highest among all age groups. This might be indicative of the fact that people in this age group are gradually entering middle age, their careers are at a critical period, and with respect to family life, they have both the elderly to support and children to raise. They thus feel life pressures from multiple aspects, and therefore are more liable to experience negative emotions. For the generation born in the 1980s, theirs career are relatively on the rise, their parents are not that old, and their children are very young, without much educational pressures. Thus, they have less experience with extreme negative emotions, but as they must work hard to maintain both career and family, the positive experiences of pleasure and relaxation are also not as frequent. For the generation born after the 1990s, the percentage of respondents with both emotional experiences are the lowest. Most of the people in this age group are still in school and have not become independent, while those who have started to work do not experience much career pressure, but neither do they yet experience the joy of a successful career, the pleasure of family life and deep feelings toward a stable partner. As such, they rarely experience extreme positive and negative emotions.

Emotional experience varies with level of education as well; respondents with lower education levels are more likely to have typical and extreme emotions, among which, a large proportion of graduates from middle school and below have both typical negative and positive emotional experiences. In contrast, graduates of junior college and above have a low proportion of respondents that express typical negative emotions.

On the whole, urban residents have more typical positive emotions and less typical negative emotions as compared to rural residents.

Additionally, emotional experience is also connected with economic conditions. For those with higher individual/family annual income or family net assets, a greater share of respondents have typical positive emotional experiences than negative ones. In other words, respondents with good economic conditions are more likely to experience typical positive emotion.

On the whole, there is a greater number of people who experience positive emotions than negative ones. Groups at both ends of the life cycle, namely older and younger age groups, have greater levels of positive emotion than middle age groups. Good economic conditions directly contribute to more positive emotional experiences. Groups with high levels of education—especially in the middle-age groups, experience the most pressure in both work and life, have the highest life expectations, and are more likely to have contradictions and challenges in their social life. They thus have the largest share of negative emotional experiences.

12.2 Psychological Basis of Integration Between Groups

Differentiation among social groups also corresponds to their integration. The integration of various groups requires some basic boundary conditions. For instance, for there to be a group of beautiful people, it is necessary to make some members more beautiful to meet the standards of the group. In other words, class differences among society are not zero-sum, outsiders are to be treated with as little social prejudice as possible. Cooperation under a common target requires tolerance towards and inclusion of different groups under a shared concept of equality and social experience. This is the only way to achieve a win–win situation and construct a harmonious social environment.

12.2.1 Perceived Degree of Intergroup Conflict

Social differentiation can be reflected in people's perception of social categories. These perceptions impact people's behavioral decisions when they are together, and are important in achieving the goal of social harmony. Herein, we have investigated people's perceptions towards social conflicts between rich and poor, employer and employee, officials and the people, locals and outsiders, and different ethnic and religious groups. Respondents were asked to apply a 4-point scale indicating their perceptions of social conflict, with the severity of the perceived conflict increasing with a higher score. Analysis of the average value (Table 12.24), shows that on the whole, people do not consider there to be severe conflict between different social groups. The overall average conflict score was 2.131, which is less than the median of 2.5. The social groups in which respondents considered there to be relatively stronger social conflict included the "poor and rich," and "officials and the people."

Table 12.24 Overview of the perception of severity of social conflict

Type of group conflict	N	M	SD
Rich and poor	9722	2.425	0.859
Employer and employee	8920	2.215	0.715
Different races or ethnic groups	8204	1.850	0.696
Different religious groups	7940	1.828	0.703
Locals and outsiders	9558	1.912	0.726
Officials and the people	9345	2.449	0.882
Overall mean value	10,110	2.131	0.569

Table 12.25 Attitudes of urban people towards migrant workers (unit: %)

Attitude	Percent
Migrant workers can come as long as they are willing to and there should be no restrictions	50.6
Migrant workers should be allowed to work in the city if there are sufficient work opportunities	41.7
The number of migrant workers should be strictly restricted	7.2
Migrant workers should not be allowed to work in the city	0.5
Total	50.6

12.2.2 Degree of Urban People's Tolerance Towards Migrant Workers

Most respondents in urban households have tolerant attitudes towards migrant workers. Many of them (66.5%) hold the opinion that there should be no restrictions on migrant workers at all and they should be allowed to move to urban areas if they are willing; others (29.2%) agree that migrants should be allowed to worked in a city only if there are enough work opportunities. However, there are a few who think that it is necessary to control the number of migrant workers or prohibit them from working in the city (Table 12.25).

The vast majority of respondents (96.0%) are positively tolerant towards the issue of where children of migrant workers should go to school in the city. Among which, the majority (76.0%) believe that there should be no restrictions on their choice of public school, but some (20.1%) hold the opinion that they should be able to go to school in the city, but their family conditions need to be considered. Only very few people think that children of migrant workers should not be allowed to attend city schools, or that they should only go to schools specifically for children of migrant workers (Table 12.26).

Table 12.26 Attitudes of urban people towards the issue of whether children of migrant workers should go to public schools in the city

Attitude	Percent (%)
They can as long as they are willing to and there should be no restrictions	76.0
They can go to public schools in the city, but some restrictions need to be made with respect to family conditions	20.1
They should only be allowed to go to schools for children of migrant workers	3.3
Children of migrant workers should not be allowed to go to schools in the city	0.7
Total	100.0

12.2.3 General Characteristics of National Identity

National identity is a type of emotional experience that arises out of a certain psychological connection between the individual self and the state. It is a source of identity from which an individual derives dignity and love. As a social psychology associated with the idea of the modern nation-state, national identity leads people to be loyal to the state, recognize state boundaries and acquire equal state citizenship. Moreover, it differentiates citizens of one state from other countries with national uniqueness.

National identity is a mechanism for integration in a diversified society. It can unite different social groups, reducing differences and highlighting commonalities. However, there are diverse, deep, and complex sources of national identity as a psychological resource (Yang 2002). National identity can be derived from satisfaction towards the current situation of the state, understanding and love for the land within and history and culture of the state, or attachment towards language, religion and ethnicity, custom and faith, etc. National identity is strongly connected with language identity, religious identity, custom identity, values identity, race identity, political identity and so on. It also could connect with sentiment, one's feelings toward and appraisal of the current and future situation of the state. Accordingly, national identity may also form certain strained relationships with these other identities, causing competition and conflict between different identity sources and management strategies. For instance, there still exists certain conflict between the ethnic identity of certain ethnic minorities in China and national identity. In turn, the relationship to the state will have an impact on national identity (Gao et al. 2013).

We have created a national identity scale comprised of 5 subjects in order to measure respondents' attachment towards the state and individual investment. We adopted the Likert 4-point scoring scale, in which the median value is 2.5. The degree of conformity to national identity increases from 1 to 4, with a score of "1" representing "inconformity to a very large extent" and a score of "4" representing "fits quite well." The statistical results show that the mean value "M" equals 3.210, and "SD" equals 490. The results are shown in Fig. 12.1.

Analysis of the statistical data shows that there is a skewed distribution in feelings toward national identity, but overall there is a large concentration above the mean value. About 77.9% of respondents scored strong (score larger than 3) and very

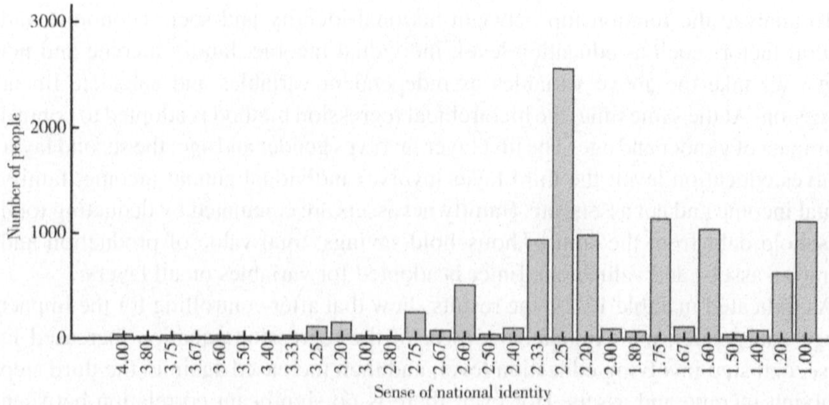

Fig. 12.1 Basic situation of national identity

Table 12.27 Result of national identity test of respondents of different genders

Gender	National Identity			
	N	Median value M	SD	
Female	5172	3.216	0.504	$t = 1.209$
Male	4965	3.204	0.476	$p = 0.227$

strong (score larger than 3.5) in feelings of national identity. The greatest number of respondents showed a strong (score of "3") level. The conclusion that can be drawn is that the national identity of the Chinese people is strong.

To interpret this conclusion in a more detailed way, we conducted a feature analysis based on demographic variables. Respondents in this investigation come from 30 different provinces, municipalities directly under the central government and autonomous regions in China—excluding Xinjiang Uygur Autonomous Region, Taiwan Province, Hong Kong Special Administrative Region and Macao Special Administrative Region. There were 10,260 respondents all together, with 5223 of them, or 50.9%, being male, and 5,037, or 49.1%, being female. Respondents ranged in age between 18 and 69, with the average age being 41. The specific demographic variables analyzed include age, gender, education level, urban-rural household registration and media preference.

As indicated in Table 12.27, the analysis shows that there is no significant difference in national identity between male and female respondents.

To analyze the impact of age upon national identity, age is adopted as an independent variable for linear regression. In order to control a variable impact that might be caused between age and gender, gender is also incorporated into the regression equation, and Enter is adopted for all variables. Table 12.28 shows that there is a significant positive correlation between age and national identity, with national identity increasing with the age of respondents.

To analyze the relationship between national identity and socio-economic and cultural factors such as education level, individual income, family income and net assets, we take the above variables as independent variables and calculate linear regression. At the same time, the hierarchical regression method is adopted to control the impact of gender and age. The first layer involves gender and age; the second layer involves education level; the third layer involves individual annual income, family annual income and net assets, etc. (family net assets are calculated by deducting total household debt from the sum of household savings, total value of production and operation assets, and valuables). Enter is adopted for variables on all layers.

As indicated in Table 12.29, the results show that after controlling for the impact of age and gender, the explanatory power of the regression equation increased in the second step involving education level, and then increased again in the third step involving income and assets. However, there is no significant correlation between each variable and national identity. This indicates that education level has an impact on national identity independent of other demographic variables, but this is not the case with income. In the final regression equation, education level is significantly

Table 12.28 Regression analysis results of national identity and age

Dependent variable	Independent variable	Standardized coefficient beta	*F value*	Adjusted coefficient of determination R^2
National identity	Gender	−0.012	29.435***	0.025
	Age	0.159***		

***Indicates that $p < 0.001$

Table 12.29 Regression of national identity towards education level and income

Variable	Standardized coefficient of the first layer	Standardized coefficient of the second layer	Standardized coefficient of the third layer
Gender	−0.029*	−0.035**	−0.035**
Age	0.148***	0.127***	0.126***
Education level		−0.051***	−0.046***
Individual Annual Income			0.032
Family annual income			−0.037
Family net assets			−0.025
R^2	0.023	0.025	0.026
ΔR^2	0.023	0.002	0.001
ΔF	82.457***	15.625***	2.639*

***Indicates that $p < 0.001$, **indicates that $p < 0.01$, *indicates that $p < 0.05$

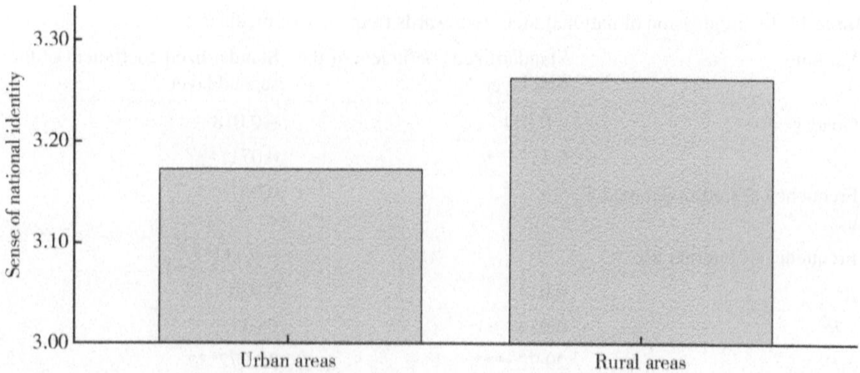

Fig. 12.2 Comparison of national identity between urban and rural residents

negatively correlated with national identity; respondents with a higher education degree have a lower degree of national identity.

The results shown in Fig. 12.2 show that there is a significant difference in feelings of national identity between respondents from townships and the countryside, with the national identity of rural residents ($M = 3.172$) being much stronger than urban residents ($M = 3.263$) ($t = 9.313, p < 0.001$).

This study also analyzed whether the usage of traditional media and the internet is connected with feelings of national identity or not. We first compared respondents who normally use and do not use the internet, and found that the degree of national identity in respondents who normally do not use the internet ($M = 3.267$) is substantially higher than those who regularly use the internet ($M = 3.131$) ($t = 13.861, p < 0.01$).

In our next stage of analysis, we compared the relationship between frequency of media usage and national identity. We conducted a regression analysis using the frequency of media use (both traditional media and the internet) and national identity as the independent variable and dependent variable. Using the hierarchical regression method, the first layer involves gender and age, and the second layer involves frequency of use of traditional media and the internet. Enter was adopted for variable(s) for all the layers, the results of which are shown in Table 12.30. After controlling for the impact of gender and age, we found that the frequency of media use increases the explanatory variation of the regression equation. In the final regression equation, the frequency of traditional media use and internet use are respectively positively and negatively correlated with national identity. That is, respondents who use traditional media more frequently have stronger national identity, and the reverse case is true for those who more frequently use the internet.

Analysis of the above data shows that though current Chinese society has a diversity of social groups, social differences are not that severe from the perspective of social mentality. Most people's consumption is centered on family livelihood, and the use of media and social groupings drive all individuals to a certain extent. What's worth noticing is that people of different age groups vary greatly in their responses to

Table 12.30 Regression of national identity towards frequency of media use

Variable	Standardized coefficient of the first layer	Standardized coefficient of the second layer
Gender	−0.011	−0.018
Age	0.117***	0.071***
Frequency of traditional media use		0.067***
Frequency of internet use		−0.111***
R^2	0.014	0.025
ΔR^2	0.014	0.011
ΔF	29.725***	22.972***

***Indicates that $p < 0.001$, **indicates that $p < 0.01$, *indicates that $p < 0.05$

values, lifestyles and patterns of consumption. A rapidly changing society has raised challenges relating to intergenerational communication, inheritance and continuation of social values, and the maintenance of cultural tradition.

Conflict between social groups is mainly experienced between the rich and poor, and officials and the people. The attitude towards foreigners is relatively tolerant.

From the preliminary anlaysis of the impact of demographic variables on national identity as shown above, national identity does not vary between different genders and economic levels. However, it does increase with age and decrease with education level and frequency of new media use. We can conclude from this that all people, regardless of economic status and gender, have and need national identity. Those who are highly educated, urbanized and use new media more frequently have a strong sense of pursuing individual uniqueness. Rural residents, elderly people and people using traditional media have a stronger desire to pursue a sense of belonging. Thus, it can be said that the degree to which one associates with national identity is negatively correlated with the degree of individualization to a significant extent.

12.3 Conclusion and Discussion

A pluralistic society, aside from featuring differentiation and diversification in social groups, has its mechanisms for integration which ensures coexistence, richness, vitality and cohesion. The development and advancement of society is realized through a constant process of balancing and re-balancing.

From our investigation, we can draw the following conclusions: First, the pursuit of well-being is the ultimate desire and action of most Chinese people. The definitive motive of pursuing happiness in terms of individual and family life serves as the driving force behind social development and serves as a psychological guarantee of a stable transformation for society.

Second, the use of new media has become very common. Mass media and personal media coexist and interact with each other. In addition to serving the purpose of acquiring information and guaranteeing interpersonal communication, new media has become a communication tool through which social attitudes and group opinions are formed, thus playing a dual role of social differentiation and integration.

Third, social equality, democracy and integrity are social values to which the public attaches the greatest importance. On one hand, different emphases on these values among different groups reflect social differentiation that could prove challenging during periods of social transition. On the other hand, these values reflect the eagerness of the public to have a reliable system of democracy and equality, so as to create an ideal society of prosperity. By getting involved with public affairs in a democratic way, the public can derive a sense of pride and agency, an important form of social integration. Formation of social consensus from the perspective of social values serves as the basis for creating a community with common destiny and values, and is also the most precious psychological resource for social integration.

Fourth, the overall social emotion in China is a positive one, although there is still a certain sense of social anxiety, particularly among young people. Social anxiety is a double-edged sword: moderate anxiety can be transformed into motivation to climb the socio-economic ladder, however, excessive anxiety might lead to anger, irrational expression, and a give-up mentality, which, once spread, will become a negative factor for social development.

Fifth, though people are discontent with the polarization between the rich and the poor and the relationship between officials and the people, there is no feeling of severe conflict. In general, there is tolerance towards and acceptance of foreigners, and the impact of prejudice and discrimination is not considered unsolvable. If methods are employed to strengthen the homogeneity and shared goals of groups with different interests, it is possible to limit the degree of social differentiation, and the resultant force of society shall be increased.

Sixth, national identity is the most powerful resource for social integration. People can be united together to the greatest extent at the state level. With a million people united as one, the wills united will be like a fortress. Nevertheless, this psychological resource should be treasured and protected, as once the emotional components of national identity are harmed, they are not easily recovered.

References

Gao, Wenjun, Yiyin Yang, Zhao Zhiyu and Jiangping Feng. 2013. Study on Social Identity of Nation-and-State and Intergroup Perception—Investigation of Residence of Han Nationality and Ethnic Minorities in Yunnan Province. *Journal of Yunnan Normal University* (5): 64–75.

Tajfel, H. 1982. Social Psychology of Intergroup Relations. *Annual Review of Psychology* 33 (1): 1–39.

Triandis, H.C., R. Bontempo, M.J. Villareal, M. Asai, and N. Lucca. 1988. Individualism and Collectivism: Cross-Cultural Perspectives on Self-Ingroup Relationships. *Journal of Personality and Social Psychology* 54 (2): 323–338.

Yang, Yiyin. 2002. Independence and Power of Cultural Identity: Evolution and innovation of Malaysia Chinese's Cultural identity. From volume 3 "Culture, Education and Identity" of "Symposium of Research on Overseas Chinese" compiled by Zhang Chunwu and Tang Xiyong, Taibei: published by Federation of Overseas Chinese Association, 407–420.

Chapter 13
Moving Towards a Greener and More Beautiful Society

Yan Cui

Building a beautiful China is one of the important components of the "China Dream." To realize the dream of the great rejuvenation of the Chinese nation, it is necessary to enter a new era of ecological social development, one that is characterized by respect for and protection of nature. This can be done by increasing the quality of development; implementing a basic state policy of saving resources and protecting the environment; voluntarily promoting green development; and incorporating the construction of an ecological civilization into all aspects of economic, political, cultural and social development. Only by doing so can we largely improve the ecological environment, build up a new industrial structure that saves resources and protects the environment, and realize the goal of creating a beautiful China.

In recent years, environmental problems have become increasingly prominent in China as the nation has undergone modernization. Balancing economic development and environmental protection has become one of the important premises of accomplishing sustained social development. However, given that economic structural transformation and the elimination of backward production facilities cannot be achieved overnight, the problems of environmental pollution that accompany extensive development will not be effectively solved in the short-term. As a first step, the public's awareness of environmental issues should be improved. The public currently has a weak recognition of the value of the environment and the significance of environmental protection. It is undeniable that the public's involvement in environmental protection, especially in terms of voluntary environmental organization, is still at a low level. There is a common mindset of a "free ride" and little voluntary action towards environmental protection. Yet it is worth noting that people's environmental awareness increases with strengthened propaganda and the improved modernity of the citizenry. Besides having more knowledge of the environment, the public does pay more attention to environmental protection and environmental quality. Currently, due

Y. Cui (✉)
CASS Institute of Sociology, Beijing, P.R. China

P. Li and M. K. Gorshkov (eds.), *Life Expectations of the People*,
Research Series on the Chinese Dream and China's Development Path,
https://doi.org/10.1007/978-981-16-2505-3_13

to limitations under the current system of environmental supervision and protection, the public does not have effective channels for participation in and formulation and implementation of environmental policies. In particular, involvement in institutional environmental organizations is at an extremely low level. By establishing a new system of social governance, exploring more effective systems for environmental management, and promoting public participation in environmental organizations, we can achieve an environmental governance structure based on public involvement, and thus get closer to the goal of achieving a beautiful China.

13.1 The Public's Environmental Assessment and Environmental Awareness

13.1.1 Environmental Assessment of the Public

Western scholars have found that the environmental awareness of the public is directly influenced by the quality of their surrounding environment. People's environmental awareness increases when environment pollution is severe (Bao and Wang 2003; Cao 2002; Chen 2003). In this chapter, we use survey data to analyze the environmental assessment and environmental awareness of the public. We used data from the China General Survey conducted by the Chinese Academy of Social Sciences Institute of Sociology in 2013 to measure the public's awareness of environmental problems. First, the data shows that the public's current satisfaction with the environment is at a low level. About 25% of respondents thought that noise, water and other pollution were very severe or relatively severe in their communities, and about 30% of respondents thought that air pollution in their communities was very severe or relatively severe. Furthermore, urban residents are significantly less satisfied with the environment than rural residents. For instance, 34.8% of urban residents thought noise pollution in their communities was very severe or relatively severe, while only 12.9% of rural residents thought so. For air pollution, 38.6% of urban residents thought it was very severe or relatively severe, among rural residents the proportion was only 14.8%. Similarly, 30.1% of urban residents thought water pollution was very severe or relatively severe, with only 19.5% of rural residents holding the same opinion. Therefore, from this rural-urban comparison, urban residents are considerably less satisfied with the environment than rural residents (Table 13.1 and Fig. 13.1).

13.1.2 Environmental Awareness of the Public

With the fast pace of economic development, environmental problems have increasingly become one of the most important factors affecting quality of life. As environmental problems become more prominent, there is stronger environmental awareness

Table 13.1 The public's assessment of environmental pollution (%)

	Rural residents				Urban residents			
	Noise	Air pollution	Water pollution	Environmental health	Noise	Air pollution	Water pollution	Environmental health
Very severe	4.5	5.1	6.9	4.1	13.6	13.0	10.2	8.5
Relatively severe	8.4	9.7	12.6	14.1	21.2	25.6	19.9	21.6
Not very severe	32.3	32.0	31.5	46.2	46.2	44.2	44.7	53.6
No pollution	54.0	52.6	48.0	34.2	18.7	16.7	23.2	15.8
Hard to tell	0.8	0.7	1.0	0.9	0.3	0.5	2.1	0.5
Total	100.0	100.0	100.0	100.0	100.0	100.0	100.0	100.0

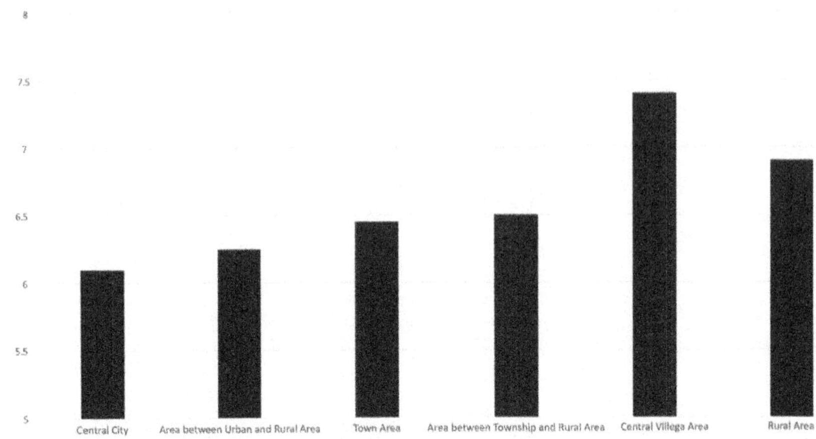

Fig. 13.1 Assessment of the public's satisfaction with the environment in different regions

and appeals for environmental protection from citizens. For instance, only 7.3% of urban and rural residents fully agree with the statement that "economic development is more important than environmental protection," and only 3.5% of urban and rural residents fully agree with the statement that "environmental protection is the responsibility of government, and has nothing to do with me." A full three-quarters of urban and rural residents were very willing to participate in non-governmental environmental organizations. However, a "free ride" mindset still exists: 16.1% of respondents agreed with the statement that "if no one else pays attention to environmental protection, why should I care?" Still, about 70% of respondents thought that it was necessary for the government to strengthen environmental protection work, but the cost should not be paid by the public.

The data also indicates significant differences in environmental awareness between urban and rural residents. For instance, only 29.1% of urban residents agreed with the statement that "economic development is more important than environmental protection," yet 43.7% of rural residents held this opinion. While only 13% of urban residents agreed with the statement, "as no one else pays attention to environmental protection, why should I care," this view was held by 21% of rural residents. In terms of environmental consciousness, only 14.9% of urban residents thought that "environmental protection is the responsibility of government, and has nothing to do with me," while 24.3% of rural residents agreed with this statement. Also, there is a difference in sense of efficacy between urban and rural residents. 50% of rural residents thought that "since they know nothing about environmental protection, it is of out their capacity to make any comment." Yet only 36% of urban residents held this view (Table 13.2).

There are also significant differences in environmental awareness between different social groups. Among the elite class, only 20.8% agreed with prioritizing economic development over environmental protection, yet the proportion was 37.4%

Table 13.2 Environmental awareness of the public (%)

	Rural areas				Urban Areas				Throughout the country			
	Fully agree	Relatively agree	Relatively disagree	Full disagree	Fully agree	Relatively agree	Relatively disagree	Full disagree	Fully agree	Relatively agree	Relatively disagree	Full disagree
Economic development is more important than environmental protection in China	9.5	34.2	46.1	10.2	6.4	22.7	54.3	16.6	7.3	25.2	48.1	12.9
I am too busy with work and study to care about the ecological environment	9.5	43.2	40.8	6.6	7.5	37.1	46.0	9.4	8.1	37.2	41.4	7.6
If no one else cares about environmental protection, why should I care	3.0	18.0	55.9	23.0	2.3	10.7	54.6	32.4	2.8	13.3	52.3	27.4
Environmental protection is the responsibility of government, and has nothing to do with me	4.5	19.8	51.9	23.8	2.6	12.3	51.5	33.7	3.5	15.2	49	28.5
I would be very willing to participate in a non-governmental organization if I have the time	24.6	55.5	16.5	3.4	25.4	55.2	15.0	4.3	23.8	50.8	14.8	3.6

(continued)

Table 13.2 (continued)

	Rural areas				Urban Areas				Throughout the country			
	Fully agree	Relatively agree	Relatively disagree	Full disagree	Fully agree	Relatively agree	Relatively disagree	Full disagree	Fully agree	Relatively agree	Relatively disagree	Full disagree
I know nothing about the problem of environmental protection, and it is out of my capacity to make any comment	8.5	41.5	41.4	8.6	6.6	29.4	49.5	14.6	7.1	32.2	43.1	11.4
I have my own thoughts about the problem of environmental protection, but the government will not take them	17.1	51.5	27.0	4.3	18.5	48.9	27.6	5.0	17	45.2	24.8	4.3
The government should put more effort into the work of environmental protection, yet the cost should not be paid by the public	25.1	47.7	23.7	3.6	25.5	45.8	25.7	3.0	24.7	44	23.2	3
I will definitely disagree with the building of a chemical plant in my community	44.1	32.9	16.2	6.8	61.6	27.3	8.7	2.4	51.8	28	10.7	4.2

among the lower class. In terms of awareness of environmental subjects, only 7.5% of the elite class thought that "environmental protection is the responsibility of government, and has nothing to do with me," while 14.6 and 19.3% of the middle and lower classes held this view respectively. With respect to efficacy, only 17% of respondents from the elite class had a relatively low internal sense of efficacy, yet the proportions jump to 35.0% and 44.2% among the middle class and lower class respectively (Tables 13.3, 13.4, 13.5, 13.6, and 13.7).

According to general western theories, environmental awareness is positively associated with education level. In other words, an increase in education level will affect an individual's choice between "naturalism" and "anthropocentrism," as higher education can make individuals realize the significance of a harmonious coexistence between human beings and nature. Therefore, people with higher education tend to pay more attention to the environment, have a higher sense of environmental efficacy, and have more voluntary environmental involvement. Data shows that this theory is well supported by current Chinese society; survey respondents with higher levels of education had higher scores for indicators of environmental priority, environmental concerns, environmental subjectivity, individual sense of environmental efficacy and environmental involvement than those with relatively lower levels of education.

As pointed out by western scholars, environmental awareness is more prevalent among the middle class. Individuals will have higher requirements for environmental quality only if their basic living conditions have been satisfied. During the early reform era in China, what the public most wanted was an increase in their level of material life. Only after solving the problem of food and clothing and reaching a fairly well-off situation will people gradually become aware of the significance of a good environment with respect to life quality and health. Data suggests that social status is positively associated with indicators of environmental awareness; groups whose subjective socio-economic status is that of upper class and middle-to-upper class scored an average of 4% higher in environmental awareness compared to those in middle-to-low and low classes. In terms of other environmental indicators, environmental subjectivity was about 5% higher, a sense of individual environmental efficacy about 15% higher, environmental concerns about 10% higher, and environmental involvement about 4% higher. From the perspective of professional classification, party staff and those employed by government bodies and state-owned enterprises scored about 7% higher on average in environmental prioritization, and about 5% higher on environmental subjectivity. In other words, employees of the above organizations fall into the elite class of society, as they have higher levels of access to information and social cognition, etc.

To sum up, the Chinese public currently has a relatively low assessment of environmental quality, especially in terms of air pollution and water pollution. Yet in general, the public's environmental awareness is relatively low. There are large differences between social groups. The elite social group already had a strong awareness of environmental priority and environmental concerns, and they also had higher individual and government environmental efficacy. In comparison, a large proportion of the lower social classes still agreed that economic development should take priority

Table 13.3 Comparison of environmental awareness among different social classes[1] (%)

	Elite class		Middle class		Workers and farmers	
	Disagree	Agree	Disagree	Agree	Disagree	Agree
Economic development is more important than environmental protection in China	79.2	20.8	71.1	28.9	62.6	37.4
I am too busy with work and study to care about the ecological environment	65.1	34.9	51.6	48.4	43.3	56.7
If no one else cares about environmental protection, why should I care	93.9	6.1	86.3	13.7	82.6	17.4
Environmental protection is the responsibility of government, and has nothing to do with me	92.5	7.5	85.4	14.6	80.7	19.3
I would be very willing to participate in a non-governmental organization if I have the time	14.6	85.4	18.3	81.7	18.4	81.6
I know nothing about the problem of environmental protection, and it is out of my capacity to make any comment	83.4	16.6	65.0	35.0	55.8	44.2
I have my own thoughts about the problem of environmental protection, but the government will not take them	37.7	62.3	33.2	66.8	30.3	69.7
The government should put more effort into the work of environmental protection, yet the cost should not be paid by the public	35.8	64.2	28.8	71.2	29.4	70.6
I will definitely disagree with the building of a chemical plant in my community	9.5	90.5	11.7	88.3	15.6	84.4

[1] The "elite class" includes respondents whose education level is above junior college, whose occupation is manager or professional, and who consider themselves in the middle-upper or upper class. The "middle class" includes respondents whose education level is above junior college, whose occupation is clerk, service worker or commercial staff, and who consider themselves in the middle or lower-middle class. The working and farming class includes respondents whose education level is below junior middle school, whose occupation is worker or farmer, and who consider themselves in the lower class.

Table 13.4 Comparison of environmental awareness among different educational groups

	Low-education group		Middle-education group		High-education group	
	Agree	Disagree	Agree	Disagree	Agree	Disagree
Economic development is more important than environmental protection in China	40.98	59.02	28.64	71.36	18.24	81.76
I am too busy with work and study to care about the ecological environment	52.96	47.04	42.03	57.97	32.15	67.85
If no one else cares about environmental protection, why should I care	20.23	79.77	10.45	89.55	6.18	93.82
Environmental protection is the responsibility of government, and has nothing to do with me	23.31	76.69	11.92	88.08	6.50	93.50
I would be very willing to participate in a non-governmental organization if I have the time	78.13	21.87	85.68	14.32	84.49	15.51

(continued)

Table 13.4 (continued)

	Low-education group		Middle-education group		High-education group	
	Agree	Disagree	Agree	Disagree	Agree	Disagree
I know nothing about the problem of environmental protection, and it is out of my capacity to make any comment	50.94	49.06	30.28	69.72	13.95	86.05
I have my own thoughts about the problem of environmental protection, but the government will not take them	70.18	29.82	64.74	35.26	61.07	38.93
The government should put more effort into the work of environmental protection, yet the cost should not be paid by the public	73.99	26.01	69.25	30.75	65.02	34.98
I will definitely disagree with the building of a chemical plant in my community	81.06	18.94	88.75	11.25	89.79	10.21

Table 13.5 Comparison of environmental awareness among respondents of different social classes (%)

	Upper class		Middle class		Lower class	
	Agree	Disagree	Agree	Disagree	Agree	Disagree
Economic development is more important than environmental protection in China	32.82	67.18	34.63	65.37	36.70	63.30
I am too busy with work and study to care about the ecological environment	38.24	61.76	45.88	54.12	51.35	48.65
If no one else cares about environmental protection, why should I care	12.76	87.24	15.07	84.93	18.18	81.82
Environmental protection is the responsibility of government, and has nothing to do with me	14.50	85.50	17.41	82.59	20.86	79.14
I would be very willing to participate in non-governmental organization if I have the time	83.36	16.64	81.47	18.53	79.06	20.94
I know nothing about the problem of environmental protection, and it is out of my capacity to make any comment	29.86	70.14	39.45	60.55	45.87	54.13
I have my own thoughts about the problem of environmental protection, but the government will not take them	60.66	39.34	67.17	32.83	69.68	30.32
The government should put more effort into the work of environmental protection, yet the cost should not be paid by the public	66.97	33.03	70.55	29.45	73.90	26.10
I will definitely disagree with the building of a chemical plant in my community	85.63	14.37	83.80	16.20	83.18	16.82

Table 13.6 The public's assessment of the issue of environmental pollution (%)

	High sense of individual efficacy	Low sense of individual efficacy
High sense of government efficacy	22.60%	9.80%
Low sense of government efficacy	35.70%	31.90%

Table 13.7 Social classes and sense of efficacy (%)

	High sense of self-efficacy (%)	Low sense of self-efficacy (%)	High sense of government efficacy (%)	Low sense of government efficacy (%)
Upper class	70.14	29.86	39.34	60.66
Middle class	60.55	39.45	32.83	67.17
Lower class	54.13	45.87	30.32	69.68

over environmental protection, and they were more inclined to think that individuals had no impact on environmental protection, nor had any impact on government departments. As a result, they had low enthusiasm for environmental involvement.

13.1.3 Sense of Individual and Government Environmental Efficacy

A sense of efficacy is one of the major issues of discussion in Western theories of social participation, especially in terms of political participation. Specifically, discussion on sense of efficacy focuses on two aspects: a sense of individual efficacy and a sense of government efficacy. A sense of individual efficacy mainly refers to whether the individual is internally motivated to take action, while the latter mainly refers to an individual's assessment of a government's responsiveness, that is, whether the government is able to provide timely and effective feedback and responsd to relevant appeals. Existing theories suggest that benign interaction between the public and government is determined by the following two conditions: first, that the public has relatively high self-efficacy, with the perception that they have the necessary knowledge and ability to take action; the other is that the government is capable of maximally satisfying the public's appeals in the current system, following which a positive interaction between the public and government will be achieved. On the contrary, if the public has a high sense of self-efficacy while the government has a low efficacy, there will be confrontation—or even conflict—between the public and government. We call this negative interaction. If the individual has low self-efficacy, they will always be indifferent and unwilling to interact regardless of the sense of government efficacy. Data suggests that, for the environmental problems in current Chinese society, the predominant situation is that both the individual and the government has a low sense of efficacy, with 30.9% of respondents belonging in this category. Consequently, the results also suggest that more respondents had a negative interaction relationship with the government (35.70%) than a positive one (23%).

In terms of the sense of self-efficacy among socio-economic classes, respondents from the upper class had a higher sense of efficacy than respondents from the middle and lower classes in general. The proportion of the upper class with a high sense of self-efficacy was 15% higher than that of the lower class, indicating that there are large differences in recognition and assessment of environmental problems and initiatives among different social classes. However, it is worth noting that differences related to the sense of government efficacy were not that large among different social classes. Over 60% of all social classes had a negative evaluation of the sense of government efficacy. Thus, respondents from different classes are mostly united in their low evaluation of the government's execution and feedback ability with respect to environmental protection and supervision.

13.2 The Public's Participation in Environmental Protection

Previous studies have shown that the existence of environmental problems will increase environmental awareness and the concern of the public, resulting in the promotion of environmental actions like voluntary participation in environmental protection activities. Among these actions, the most typical is participation in an environmental organization. As discussed above, according to western theories, several assumptions might be supported, including: an environmental organization's level of response will increase with the severity of environmental pollution in the individual's community and the individual's social status; and both age and educational level will be significantly associated with the level of an environmental organization's response (Taylor 1997; Rainey and Johnson 2009).

Based on these traditional western theoretical hypotheses, we analyzed the responses on environmental problems and awareness in the 2013 CSS. First, the results show that age was significantly associated with participation in environmental organizations. In particular, the generations born in the 1970s, 1980s and 1990s were most likely to actively participate in environmental protection. According to Table 13.8, for the generation born in the 1970s, the probability of a respondent being an active participant in an environmental organization was 2.5 times higher than not being an active participant. This suggests that the generation born in the 1970s is the most sensitive to environmental problems, and is the most enthusiastic in participating in environmental organizations. The generation born in the 1960s has the least probability of participating in environmental organizations. The results also

Table 13.8 Age and environmental organization participation (%)

	Active participant of an environmental organization	Normal participant of an environmental organization	Not a participant of an environmental organization
Generation born in the 1960s	20.7	56.0	23.3
Generation born in the 1970s	30.3	57.5	12.2
Generation born in the 1980s	26.7	56.9	16.4
Generation born in the 1990s	25.6	59.2	15.1

Table 13.9 Education level and environmental organization participation (%)

	Active participant of an environmental organization	Normal participant of an environmental organization	Not a participant of an environmental organization
Lower-educated group	23.3	54.8	21.9
Middle-educated group	29.7	56	14.3
Highly-educated group	30.6	56.9	12.5

indicate a positive correlation between education level and participation in environmental organizations; respondents with higher educational levels were more likely to participate in environmental organizations. Except for the group with only an elementary school education, the probability for all other educational groups of being an active participant in an environmental organization was over two times that of not being a participant, supporting the hypothesis that education can strengthen values of "naturalism." The results shed light on the importance of increasing civil quality in promoting participation in environmental efforts (Tables 13.9, 13.10 and 13.11).

Table 13.10 Environmental pollution and environmental organization participation (%)

Water pollution	Active participant of an environmental organization	Normal participant of an environmental organization	Not a participant of an environmental organization
Very severe	37.7	44.6	17.7
Relatively severe	25.6	55.4	19.0
Not that severe	21.2	59.6	19.2
Does not occur	26.2	53.0	20.8

Table 13.11 Social status and environmental organization participation (%)

	Active participant of an environmental organization	Normal participant of an environmental organization	Not a participant of an environmental organization
Upper class	30.0	53.3	16.6
Middle class	24.5	57.0	18.5
Lower class	24.7	54.3	20.9

Moreover, we find that respondents who considered environmental problems in their communities to be severe were more likely to participate in environmental protection organizations than those who considered them to be not severe. Taking the example of water pollution, respondents who considered this type of pollution to be very severe were two times more likely to be active participants in environmental organizations than not (cross-tabulation analysis passed the chi-square test). Thus, we know that environmental participation in China is still pollution-driven. In other words, the major driving factor of the public's participation in environmental organizations is to solve the environmental problems they confront themselves. This pattern in China is quite different from that found in western countries, where concern for the environment as a whole is more of a driving factor.

Finally, there was no significant difference among socio-economic classes in the likelihood of being a normal or active participant of an environmental organization. In contrast to the theories of western environmental sociology, it is possible for all social classes to be participants of environmental protection organizations in China. According to western theories, people with higher social status have stronger environmental awareness and concerns, and they also have certain social resources and the capacity for action. According to these theories, social status should be positively associated with participation in environmental organizations. However, in current Chinese society, most participation in environmental organizations is a "passive response." In other words, the participation behavior of Chinese citizens is not voluntary, but a passive response strategy when their environmental rights are violated (Hong 2008). So, unlike western countries, participation in environmental organizations in China is more about the protection of rights, and participation behavior usually occurs when environmental rights are violated. Due to the difference in their fundamental driving force, there was no significant difference among the different social groups in their participation in environmental organizations.

13.3 More Discussion of Data

In summary, the results show that respondents with higher levels of education were more likely to participate in environmental organizations. This is consistent with past studies that show that higher cultural levels help people to understand the significance of environmental protection and establish correct concepts about the environment, thus increasing the inclination to participate in environmental organizations. Thus, education level is positively associated with social economic status. Since the middle and upper classes have higher requirements for quality of life than the lower class, they typically hold a more active attitude towards environmental protection. Moreover, a greater degree of social resources and a larger social network of people with higher social status will increase the probability of participation in social groups. The data also shows that gender has no significant impact on participation in environmental organizations, and that the likelihood of participating in environmental organizations reduces with age.

According to an in-depth analysis of the data, we find that the Chinese response to problems in the environment is still geared at safeguarding individual environmental rights and interests. That is to say, the public is motivated to participate in environmental protection organizations only when the problem of environmental pollution is severe in their community.

The data also shows that environmental concerns and prioritizing the environment have become important psychological mechanisms for an environmental organization participant. This suggests that the public's concern and awareness of the quality of the environment will increase with economic development and modernization. At the same time, since environmental problems frequently occur during the transformation of the mode of development in China, it is natural that the public's environmental participation may become more common, and that environmental organizations will become more active.

13.4 Promoting Participation in Environment Protection

Environmental problems become increasingly severe with economic development and urbanization. As a result, social conflicts due to environmental pollution are occurring more frequently, leading to a negative impact on social stability. Therefore, to solve the environmental problems at present, it is necessary to promote participation in environmental protection. In addition, with the increase in awareness of rights and interests, people are more inclined to make claims through action when their environmental rights and interests are violated. As pointed out by Hong Dayong, "Chinese people are in a transformation from environmental concerns to environmental action, and this is reflected by the sharp increase in the number of environmental disputes" (Hong 2008). The government needs to adjust its thoughts on environmental monitoring, promote the building of civil society, and realize innovations in environmental management.

According to the results, the public's participation in environmental organizations in China has the following characteristics. First, the public's responsiveness to environmental organizations is not driven by environmental values but is more a reflection of passive environmental behavior influenced by psychological egoism. As a result, the public's environmental participation remains focused on solving daily environmental protection issues, and does not yet reach the level of involvement in environmental decision-making and cooperation in environmental supervision. Second, from the perspective of political participation, the current internal mechanism of the public's environmental response is more about the protection of rights. This reflects the fact that the government often does not make effective and timely responses to appeals made by citizens, and there is no interactive mechanism between officials and the public. Given the existing system of imperfect participation channels and the high cost for the expression of public opinion, some citizens tend to choose to engage in antagonistic behavior outside of the system rather than direct negotiation with the government when their legal rights are violated, in turn leading to mass disturbances.

For a long time, environmental protection and environmental supervision were dominated by the government in China. The public's influence was very limited due to the lack of institutional and systematic channels and opportunities for voluntary environmental participation. In addition, non-governmental environmental protection organizations did not have enough resources to mobilize the public. It is therefore necessary to further strengthen the ability of the public to participate in and construct the system and perfect channels for public participation in order to ensure the institutional effectiveness of public participation. The author proposes the following suggestions for promoting the constructive environmental participation of the public.

First, it is necessary to strengthen environmental awareness education, to go beyond the current low level of awareness that is limited in focus only to daily and localized environmental problems. Environmental awareness should encompass not just the utilitarian concerns of the surrounding environment, but also an understanding of the relationship between human beings and nature and an overall understanding of the value of the environment. However, analysis shows that in today's China, participation in environmental organizations is mainly the result of experience with local environmental pollution. To change this situation, it is necessary to cultivate long-term education for citizens in order to improve their overall understanding of environmental problems. Only through these initiatives can an environmentally friendly and economical society be established. In other words, correct values are an important premise to motivate voluntary social participation among citizens. Having correct values will make it possible for citizens to participate effectively in making, evaluating and supervising environmental policies in consideration of overall social interest, and reduce the utilitarian attitude towards environmental participation.

Second, we should construct and improve channels for public environmental participation. By promoting reforms of the political system and innovations in social management, we can create opportunities for the public's social participation, especially in terms of environmental participation. This will also broaden channels for the public to directly or indirectly participate in making and supervising environmental policies. As a consequence, the public's participation will then be institutionally guaranteed. The experiences of western countries suggest that the introduction of public participation can largely reduce the costs of environmental supervision and improve supervision efficacy. Therefore, consistent with the objective law of social development, we should construct a new mode of environmental management based on a new type of social administration system, rather than a bureaucratic system (Cobb and Elder 1983; Adler 2001a, b; Zheng 2004; Gong 2006). On one hand, this requires the full guarantee of citizens' legal rights to participate in social management and their freedom to exercise their rights of political participation. On the other hand, it is necessary to broaden channels of participation, establish and build a system of "environmental shareholders" and strengthen the management function of the public's social participation, so as to make civil organizations the guardians of the greatest public good. In addition, non-governmental environmental protection organizations should strengthen their organization and mobilization abilities on the basis of their non-profit nature, which will guarantee activity and longevity of civil environmental participation.

Moreover, environmental participation in China is currently limited by aspects of the political system. First, environmental management is bureaucratic with little positive interaction between officials and ordinary people. In addition, existing institutions, such as public hearings, do not satisfy the requirements necessary for the public's environmental participation. Due to a lack of institutional channels of participation, it is also quite difficult for non-governmental environmental organizations to organize and absorb the participation of citizens and social elites. In other words, the governmental monopoly on environmental governance at all levels has directly led to an estrangement between the public and government monitors. At present, fixation with GDP growth among some local governments has meant a lack of interest in environmental problems and lax enforcement of pertinent laws, which have had a negative impact on public environmental participation.

Lastly, China currently faces many of environmental problems. Individuals are not the only victims of environmental pollution, and safeguarding environmental rights often occurs in the form of group action. To properly deal with group action and avoid the evolution of environmental problems into social problems, we need to review the system of environmental participation. Only through perfecting institutional means for safeguarding environmental rights, building up formal mechanisms for orderly participation, and realizing the normalization of public affairs management can we effectively prevent the occurrence of mass disturbance and social conflict, and thus eliminate a major hidden peril to social stability. Only then can the problems stemming from asymmetric information between the government and citizens be avoided, and the trust between officials and ordinary people be strengthened. Under such conditions, citizens will turn from passively safeguarding their rights to voluntary participation and negotiation. In addition, the management abilities of civil organizations should be strengthened, and all social management activities should be regulated and institutionalized.

In conclusion, to maximize the public's environmental rights and interests, and inspire the public's environmental awareness and values through propaganda and education, the legitimate environmental rights and interests of the public should be effectively guaranteed. This can be accomplished by granting rights to civil environmental protection organizations, providing institutional guarantees for the public's participation in and supervision of environmental issues, and providing more channels for the public to realize environmental appeals. In keeping with the demands of social development, only through incorporating the power of civil society into the practice of environmental governance will environmental supervision institutions be able to fulfill their role, and the level of environmental governance in China be substantially improved.

References

Adler, Jonathan H. 2001a. Let 50 Flowers Bloom: Transforming the States into Laboratories of Environmental Policy. *Environmental Law Reporter* 31(11): 31 ELR 11284.

Adler, Jonathan H. 2001b. Free and Green: A New Approach to Environmental Protection. *Harvard Journal of Law & Public Policy* 24(2).

Bao, Qingde and Zhihong Wang. 2003. Between In and Out: A Review of Anthropocentrism Studies. *Science Technology and Dialectics* 20(2): 12–14. [in Chinese].

Cao, Mingde. 2002. Ethical Transition from Anthropocentrism to Eco-Centrism. *Journal of Renmin University of China* 16(2): 41–46. [in Chinese].

Chen, Jianlan. 2003. A Critique of Non-Anthropocentrism Environmental Ethics. *Beida Journal of Philosophy* 4(1): 178–179. [in Chinese].

Cobb, Roger W. and Charles D. Elder. 1983. *Participation in American Politics: The Dynamics of Agenda-building.* Baltimore: Johns Hopkins University Press.

Gong, Yingzhou. 2006. An Enlightenment from Foreign Non-government Organizations of Environmental Protection. *Social Sciences Review* 21 (6): 69–78.

Hong, Dayong. 2008. New Direction of Improving Environmental Governance in China. *Social Sciences in Hunan* 21 (3): 79–92.

Rainey, Shirley A., and Glenn S. Johnson. 2009. Grassroots Activism: An Exploration of Women of Color's Role in the Environmental Justice Movement. *Race, Gender & Class* 16 (3/4): 144–173.

Taylor, Dorceta E. 1997. American Environmentalism: The Role of Race, Class and Gender in Shaping Activism 1820–1995. *Race, Gender & Class* 5 (1): 16–62.

Zheng, Zhunhao. 2004. Policy Participation and Influential Model of NGOs. *Chinese Public Administration* 5: 32–35. [in Chinese].

Chapter 14
Towards an Environmentally Sustainable Society

I. A. Khaliy

Achieving the goal of a clean environment cannot happen spontaneously. A significant portion of environmental problems are not apparent from the start. Many important changes in the wildlife and urban environment are known only to specialists, and may remain invisible to the general population for a long time. Societal and individual attitudes toward wildlife and the immediate habitat also change repeatedly. For instance, during the period of industrialization in the West and Russia, the value of nature was denied, and environmental ideas were not supported by society. In the USSR in the 1930s, nature was only valued in a transformed form, and anthropocentric attitudes were promulgated by state ideology and promoted in the media, literature and films.[1] In other words, extensive efforts were needed not just to create a clean environment, but to raise environmental concerns in the individual and public consciousness. This is how the environmental movement started. Since the 1970s, the government, and more specifically, the environmental authorities, started to engage in environmental education and awareness-building. However, the state was not permanently involved. Social and economic problems quite easily moved environmental concerns to the periphery of public consciousness, even when high levels of pollution and adverse changes in the environment became evident.

Data from the 2012 nationwide survey on Russians' dreams completely confirmed this.[2] For instance, when asked which of twelve slogans best reflected the respondent's personal dream for Russia's future (choosing up to three answers), only 13%

---

[1] For more details see, for example, Winer (1991).

[2] All-Russian Study of RAS Institute of Sociology "What do the Russians dream about?" [O chem mechtayut rossiyane?] (2012).

The original version of this chapter was revised: Affiliation has been updated in this chapter. The correction to this chapter can be found at https://doi.org/10.1007/978-981-16-2505-3_19

I. A. Khaliy (✉)
Institute of Sociology of FCTAS RAS, Moscow, Russia
e-mail: lipl@cass.org.cn

P. Li and M. K. Gorshkov (eds.), *Life Expectations of the People*,
Research Series on the Chinese Dream and China's Development Path,
https://doi.org/10.1007/978-981-16-2505-3_14

selected the answer "addressing global challenges facing the world (environmental and others)." At the same time, 45% of Russians chose "social justice, equal rights for all citizens, and a strong state taking care of its citizens"; 28% selected human rights; 27% chose "ensuring stability without revolutions and upheavals;" and another 27% desired Russia to reclaim the status of a great power. Solving global environmental problems as a goal for Russia's future fell behind the nationalist idea of a "Russia for Russians (14%)," but was more popular than the ideas of rapprochement with the West (9%), and pursuing a liberal economy of market freedom and minimum state intervention (7%). In other words, even though an environmental component is present in the desire of some Russians as it relates to the country's future, it does not occupy a role of objective significance to Russian society.

This is not surprising, as formulation of environmental protection goals above all requires a degree of developed environmental awareness related to public understanding of environmental concerns and risks. Therefore, to understand what role environmental protection may play in the model of an ideal society, it is important to explore the current state of environmental awareness in Russia.[3] More specifically, we assessed a range of parameters, including:

1. The main environmental concerns of Russians.
2. The level of concern among Russians about the environmental conditions in their places of residence.
3. Changes in Russians' domestic behavior as a result of ecological consciousness.
4. Russians' attitudes to environmental NPOs and their willingness to participate in environmental protection activities.
5. Russians' assessment of environmental protection activities by government authorities.
6. The perception of Russians toward the country's ability to achieve sustainable development.

In this chapter, we focus only on the first three questions. With respect to the **main concerns of Russians**, the surveys in different years paint approximately the same picture: the state of the environment is not a main concern for Russian citizens. When presented with an open-ended question where environmental problems are not mentioned as a possible option, environmental concerns do not appear at all. For example, at the end of 2001, when responding to the open-ended question about what the main problems of the country were,[4] Russians mentioned economic problems and unemployment (24%), low living standards (20%), lack of an efficient

[3] The sociological data on which our analysis is based was collected in more than 30 regions of the country in the course of empirical surveys conducted in the past 30 years. Moreover, the data of mass nationwide representative surveys of several sociological organizations, conducted in different years, was used and their comparative analysis was carried out. For more detailed information on the results of these surveys, see: Khaliy (2007, 2010, 2012, 2014), Aksenova (2005). Levchenko (2011), Institutionalization of the Environmental Policy (2006).

[4] See: Field of opinions. Dominants [Pole mnenii. Dominanty] 2001. No. 042, November 9. Nationwide survey of the population dated November 3–4, 2001 (http://www.fom.ru/survey/dominant/310/760/2507.html).

mechanism of public administration (16%), crime and drug addiction (15%), the war in Chechnya, ethnic conflicts (14%), and even spiritual crisis (6%). However, environmental problems were never mentioned. When asked what the main problems were not just for the country, but for the respondents themselves and their families, Russians most frequently mentioned living problems (75%), namely—financial problems, salaries, and price of goods (53%), health problems and the quality of healthcare (13%), housing problems (10%) and problems with public utilities (4%). Russians also mentioned such concerns as studies and work (13%), family problems (2%), and fear about their future (2%).[5] Again, environmental problems were not mentioned at all; obviously this concern is not within the range of problems that worry them in everyday life.

Today this picture has changed very little. Russians hardly recall the environment when it comes to their main goals, and if they do mention the subject, it is usually exceptional and related to very specific situations in their place of residence. However, environmental concerns do come into play if this option is specifically included in a proposed list of possible responses to an appropriate question. This trend is evident not only in the 2012 RAS IS survey, "What do Russians dream about?" but also in the studies of the Levada Center devoted to the main problems and concerns of Russians in 2014 and previous years (Table 14.1).

As we see, environmental problems occupy a middle position in the rating of problems worrying Russians, changing position by +1 −2 points depending on the year of the survey.

We then assessed **the level of concern among Russians about the environmental conditions in their places of residence**. When asked questions about their daily environment, Russians appear much more concerned about environmental conditions than in the all-Russian rating of problems in Russian society. Obviously, this is due to higher awareness of these problems and their impact on everyone's daily life. It is no mere chance, as stated above, that Russians' main goals related to the environment are always connected with the situation in their place of residence.

In this context, we analyzed data from the Levada Center surveys from a retrospective view (Table 14.2).

As is clear, and quite symbolic, from Table 14.2, aside from a general improvement of assessments of the environmental situation in one's place of residence (vastly explaining the weak concern among Russians about environmental problems in general), there is a small but stable number of respondents who found it difficult to answer the question (2–7% across different years). At the same time, the number of respondents who considered their local environment to be "more bad than good" and "very bad" constantly exceeded half of all respondents. We may observe from this data that there is a building global awareness of the negative environmental situation, along with the feeling of its gradual improvement.

We then looked at the extent to which the country's citizens are worried about the negative state of the environment in their place of residence (Table 14.3).

[5] Survey of the population. 22.11.2001, Environmental problems. POF database (http://bd.fom.ru/report/map/dd014424).

Table 14.1 The most acute problems of present-day Russian society according to Russians, % (rated in accordance with the data of 2014)

Problems	2006	2008	2010	2012	2014
Price increases	71	81	71	72	69
Poverty and impoverishment of the population	55	50	51	53	51
Rise in unemployment	36	27	47	36	33
Corruption and bribery	23	23	28	37	32
Economic crisis, production slowdown in the sphere of industry and agriculture	31	31	36	33	29
Sharp stratification of the rich and poor, unfair distribution of income	32	34	29	36	27
Crisis of ethics, culture and morality	26	30	28	31	26
Inaccessibility of many types of medical care	30	33	27	27	25
Influx of migrants	11	8	10	15	23
Rising drug addiction	25	26	26	30	21
Increase in commercial educational institutions, inaccessibility of education	28	26	16	18	17
Deterioration of the state of the environment	20	23	21	20	16
Growing crime rate	29	23	20	17	14
Dominance and misbehavior of officials	10	9	14	15	12
Threat of explosions and other terrorist attacks in the place of residence	12	7	6	9	12
Rising nationalism and deterioration of inter-ethnic relations	8	6	7	9	10
Weakness of state power	14	8	11	11	8
Terrorist attacks in the North Caucasus	6	3	5	3	7
Brutality and cruelty of police officers	8	6	12	9	7
Absence of fair justice	5	5	6	7	7
Delays in payment of salaries, pensions, benefits, etc.	6	3	7	4	4
Restriction of civil rights and democratic freedoms (freedom of speech, press, movement and others)	2	1	3	5	4
Conflicts among different branches of power at different levels	4	2	2	3	3
Growing incidence of AIDS	7	7	5	5	3
Other	2	2	2	2	2

Source Levada Center studies [Digital resource] // Humanitarian Technologies Center (http://gtmarket.ru/news/2014/03/13/6627)

As we see from Table 14.3, Russians have an average degree of concern for the ecological situation in the country. Although the degree of concern decreased in the 2000s and reached its minimum in 2014, the majority of the population still expresses concern about the state of the environment in their place of residence—64% as of 2014. Almost nobody found it difficult to answer the question.

Table 14.2 Assessment of the environmental situation (air and water purity, noise level, the state of nature, etc.) in Place of Residence, 1991–2014, %

Assessments	1991	1998	2000	2011	2012	2013	2014
Very good	3	5	5	7	3	3	4
More good than bad	14	28	36	33	29	26	39
More bad than good	33	37	38	43	46	49	40
Very bad	46	28	15	16	19	16	10
Not sure	5	2	6	2	4	7	7

Source Environmental problems and safety [Ekologicheskie problemy i bezopasnost] Levada-Center. Press issue 10.07.2014 (http://www.levada.ru/10-07-2014/ekologicheskie-problemy-i-bez opasnost)

Table 14.3 The extent to which Russians are worried about the state of the environment in their place of residence, 1989–2014, %

Degree of concern	1989	1990	2011	2012	2013	2014
Worried to a large extent	53	58	24	25	21	14
Rather worried	27	34	49	49	52	50
Rather not worried	8	4	13	14	11	15
Not worried at all	7	1	12	10	11	18
Not sure	4	3	2	2	5	3

Source Environmental problems and safety [Ekologicheskie problemy i bezopasnost] Levada-Center. Press issue 10.07.2014 (http://www.levada.ru/10-07-2014/ekologicheskie-problemy-i-bez opasnost)

Next, we looked at what exactly worries Russian citizens about the state of the environment.

From the data provided in Table 14.4, a sense of pragmatism among citizens' perception of environmental problems emerges. The top two concerns are those considered vital to human life—the state of water bodies and the air. The next top three concerns in the ranking are those that worry Russians as "consumers," and depend on manufacturers rather than nature, such as the quality of drinking water, food and sanitary conditions of settlements.

Analysis of villagers' environmental consciousness is especially complex. In the 20 years that passed since the collapse of the USSR, traditional agriculture in Russia has all but been destroyed. The foremost concern relates to risk farming. Villages have been abandoned, and peasant houses are occupied by summer visitors. In black earth regions, the situation was slightly better between 1990 and 2000, and in recent years it has even started to recover. However, former collective farms have been replaced by agricultural holdings which use, first of all, technologies that do not require a significant number of employees, and second, use a rotational management schedule. As a result, they do not create jobs for former collective farmers. However, in the course of our studies in the Tambov, Orlov and Kursk regions, we managed

Table 14.4 The main environmental problems in Russians' place of residence, 2011–2014 (% of those who are worried by the state of environment; several variants could be selected)

Main problems	2011	2012	2013	2014
Pollution of water bodies (rivers, lakes and seas)	50	59	54	52
Air pollution	48	52	52	51
Bad, polluted drinking water	36	35	34	30
Unhygienic state of the territory	30	36	30	27
Harmful chemicals in food	28	22	29	26
Climate change	24	22	21	23
Increased level of radiation	13	16	17	17
Disappearance of forests	19	15	16	16
Increased level of noise pollution	10	13	14	12
Lack of green plantings	10	9	9	11
Acid rain	9	10	8	10
Shallowing of water bodies, emergence of deserts and water regime infringement	12	14	10	9
Disappearance of certain species of birds, fish, animals, plants, insects, or changes in the flora and fauna	10	11	9	8
Unsuitability of water for irrigation	3	3	4	3
Other	1	2	2	2
Not sure	2	3	5	3

Source Environmental problems and safety [Ekologicheskie problemy i bezopasnost] Levada-Center. Press issue 10.07.2014 (http://www.levada.ru/10-07-2014/ekologicheskie-problemy-i-bezopasnost)

to find districts where local authorities assign land plots exclusively to the locals, and in this case, the peasants have started keeping a farm. However, the farmers face problems when selling their products. They cannot compete with the cheaper -sometimes to the level of dumping- imports and production of agricultural holdings. In addition, there are very few distribution channels for local farmer products.

The environmental concerns of locals under these conditions are primarily associated with the implementation of Western technologies in agriculture, such as cattle-breeding and product processing, primarily by agricultural holdings. New grain crop varieties, feeds and technological processes seem dangerous for human and animal health. For example, local farmers are very suspicious about strains of wheat where, according to the observations of locals, weeds do not grow and birds do not nest. Almost complete lack of information greatly strengthens suspicions and intensifies rumors among the local population. Yet the main problem for the villages still includes elementary physical survival, and under these circumstances, economic considerations push environmental problems to second place.

Table 14.5 Particular manifestations of deterioration of the environment in place of residence, according to Russians (% of those who are worried about the state of environment; several variants could be selected)

Particular manifestations of deterioration of the environment	2011	2012	2013	2014
Human health deteriorates	59	59	62	56
Green areas disappear	34	42	35	33
Natural riches are wasted	33	28	31	30
The natural order is breached	29	28	32	28
There are fewer possibilities to have a rest in the open air	22	30	25	25
Other	7	7	5	3
Not sure	6	11	9	10

Source Environmental problems and safety [Ekologicheskie problemy i bezopasnost] Levada-Center. Press issue 10.07.2014 (http://www.levada.ru/10-07-2014/ekologicheskie-problemy-i-bez opasnost)

Where do Russians see deterioration of the environment in their settlements and their surroundings if we put aside the perception of these problems by villagers (Table 14.5)?

When assessing the consequences of environmental deterioration, the country's population has been steadily giving priority to the deterioration of human health. This is the most significant component of Russians' environmental concern. In this regard, we would like to note that health is a very important value for Russians in general and often appears in the set of their basic personal desires, no matter in what form the question about their desires is asked. This is not surprising, as the absence of health makes well-being and social justice pointless. The role of health in the idea of well-being is found not only in sociological research but also in the traditional wishes for good health in connection with any holiday. The connection to health problems is what allows most citizens to recognize the importance of the environment. This issue is the sort of channel that strengthens the pro-ecological orientation of the society.

Concern about the preservation of green areas is also very rational and for the most part directly relates to health. Russian citizens consistently associate air quality with the level of city greening. This is largely the result of many years of propaganda focused on the role of vegetation as an urban air filter. Furthermore, green areas traditionally play an important role in recreational behavior of the citizens who attach particular importance to going for walks with children. There is also a health element to this aspect.

Under these circumstances, one would typically expect that **greater environmental consciousness will affect the behavior of Russians in everyday life to** become more ecologically oriented or, at least, conform to the level of their concern about the state of environment. But is this true (Table 14.6)?

Table 14.6 clearly shows that the vast majority of Russians try to do something to preserve the environment. This willingness to comply with accessible environmental standards is evidence that Russians demonstrate behavior that reflects their level of

Table 14.6 Activities of an environmental nature actually oerformed by Russians, 2013–2014, %

Activity types	2013	2013
I only throw garbage away in specially designated places	85	92
I collect waste after outings	9	60
I participate in little picks and territory cleaning activities	32	39
I walk or cycle instead of using motor vehicles	7	7
I take dangerous waste (mercury lamps, batteries and old electronics, etc.) to special collection stations	6	6
I substitute plastic bags with environmentally bags/paper bags, or go to the shop with my own bags or a shopping bag	4	4
I sort garbage (separate paper, metal, glass, etc.)	3	4
I do nothing of the above	5	2
Not sure	1	<1

Source Ecology. Domestic habits. POF. 13.05.2012 [Ekologiya. Bytovye privychki. FOM. 13.05.2012] (http://fom.ru/obshchestvo/10878)

Table 14.7 Activities of Russians aimed at saving natural resources, 2013–2014, %

Activity types	2013	2013
I save water, gas and electricity in everyday life	73	82
I buy energy-saving consumer products and equipment	37	40
I use modern thermal insulation technologies for my house/flat	9	7
I knowingly buy products manufactured from secondary raw materials (special tissues, office supplies, etc.)	4	4
I use alternative heating (based on solar power, heat pumps, biomass or biogas)	1	1
I do none of the above	14	9
Not sure	1	2

Source Ecology. Domestic habits. POF. 13.05.2012 [Ekologiya. Bytovye privychki. FOM. 13.05.2012] (http://fom.ru/obshchestvo/10878)

concern with environmental problems. However, most usually do only what is easily accessible to them (the first three activities in Table 14.6). It may be supposed that if all the other forms of environmental activities were organized at a proper level, the other activities listed in Table 14.6 would be more popular with the majority of the population.

Table 14.7 shows the same tendency of Russians to do things related to the preservation of natural resources that are easily accessible to them. It can be presumed that further environmentalism in Russians' domestic behavior depends on the efficiency of environmental management.

Let us sum up the results of our research. Public awareness of present-day Russians may only be conditionally referred to as environmental. Environmental awareness is based on pragmatic attitudes of a people who want to live in a comfortable and healthy environment, rather than rooted in the idea of the preservation of nature. In this vein, it is not surprising that the surveys show that the protection of wildlife, conservation of rare species of animals and plants, etc. occupy the last place in the ranking of Russians' concerns about environmental problems. Anthropocentrism is still at the core of environmental awareness in Russia; in other words, the focus of Russians is on human interests, even in connection with environmental conditions. Russian goals for an eco-oriented society corresponds to this general tendency.

In addition, as the empirical data shows, pragmatism in the approach to environmental subjects is implemented in practice in the environmental behavior of the population; people are ready to carry out environmentally-oriented activities only if relevant conditions are created. However, they do not want to create such conditions by themselves, and in any case, they do not have the opportunities to do so. Moreover, the majority of the population does not plan to influence those who are obliged to engage in the creation of such conditions as part of their official activities, either, but understands that it is necessary. The whole process is labor-intensive and time-consuming, and people do not want to spend time and energy on environmental issues when their lives are, in most cases, still centered around problems of basic survival.

Finally, as in past years, the main engagement in environmentally-oriented activities are through environmental public organizations. These organizations alone bear the responsibility of raising environmental awareness and implementing activities in conjunction with authorities across all branches and levels in order to improve conservation of the environment and wildlife. Unfortunately, today environmental education depends on them alone, as ecology was eliminated as a subject in secondary schools (and higher institutions).

However, it should be understood that environmental awareness cannot be formed without knowledge, as environmental problems are often not visible, and therefore do not have a direct influence on the consciousness. As a result, there is a probability that mass surveys will show different results in the future (including the near future). At the same time, even an increase in environmental consciousness does not mean that environmental protection will become a national dream for most citizens. This will require a very serious deterioration of environmental conditions impacting quality of life, or active promotion and awareness-building organized by the state. The efforts of the environmental movement alone are insufficient. Russia will not be able to become an environmentally sustainable society without activation of environmental protection activities by the state and the state's active participation in raising the population's environmental awareness.

References

Aksenova, O.V. 2005. Social and Economic Consequences of Political Reforms: From Centralization to Localization of the Russian Environmental Policy [Sotcialno-ekologicheskie posledstviya politicheskogo reformirovaniya: ot tsentralizatsii k lokalizatsii ekologicheskoy politiki Rossii]. In *Russia under reforms: Yearbook 2005* [Rossiya reformiruiushchayasya: Ezhegodnik 2005], ed. L.M. Drobizheva, 296–317. Moscow: Institute of Sociology RAS. [in Russian].

Institutionalization of the Environmental Policy. 2006. Russia: Social Practices, the State Strategy and Managerial Decisions [Institutsionalizatsiya ekologicheskoy politiki v Rossii: sotsialnye praktiki, strategiya gosudarstva, upravlencheskie resheniya], ed. I.A. Khaliy, 272 p. Moscow: Institute of Sociology RAS. [in Russian].

Khaliy, I. A. 2007. *Present-Day Public Movements. Innovative Potential of Russian Transformations in the Traditionalist Environment* [Sovremennye obshchestvennye dvizheniya.Innovatsionnyy potentsial rossiyskikh preobrazovaniy v traditsionalistskoy srede]. Moscow: Institute of Sociology RAS. [in Russian].

Khaliy, I.A. 2010. The stages of Russian Environmental Movement Interaction with the Authorities [Etapy vzaimodeistviya rossiyskogo ekologicheskogo dvizheniya s vlastyami]. *Political Science* [Politicheskaya nauka]. Issue 2: 132–157. [in Russian].

Khaliy, I.A. 2012. Environmental Movement in the Soviet Union: Self-Organization of Environmental Professionals [Ekologicheskoe dvizhenie v Sovetskom Soyuze: samoorganizatsiya ekologov-professionalov]. *Bulletin of the Institute of Sociology* [Vestnik Instituta sotsiologii]. Issue 5: 61–69. www.vestnik.isras.ru. [in Russian].

Khaliy, I.A. 2014. Environment as a Factor of Activity for Political Parties at the Local Level [Okruzhayushchaya sreda kak faktor aktivnosti politicheskikh partiy na mestnom urovne]. *Vlast*. Issue 1: 27–31. [in Russian].

Levchenko, N.V. 2011. The Influence of Citizens on the Management System (Using the Example of Homeless Animals Problem) [Vliyanie grazhdan na sistemu upravleniya (na primere problemy bezdomnykh zhivotnykh)]. *Bulletin of the Institute of Sociology* [Vestnik Instituta Sotsiologii]. Issue 3: 254–267. www.vestnik.isras.ru. [in Russian].

Winer. D.R. 1991. *Ecology in Soviet Russia* [Ekologiya v Sovetskoy Rossii]. Translation from English. Moscow, Progress: 244–263.

Chapter 15
Moving Towards a More Corruption-Resistant Society

Lei Fan

Transparent politics is the basis for the healthy development of the economy, as well as social harmony and stability. Since China's reform and opening-up, the transition from a planned economic system to a market system led by the government has caused excessive administrative intervention and control of the market in some fields, which has not only resulted in a failure of resource allocation in the market, but has also created ample opportunity for corruption. Additionally, due to China's underdeveloped corruption-prevention system, the situation of corruption in some areas continues to deteriorate. The increasing severity of corruption has not only caused great economic loss to the state but has also resulted in a serious crisis in society, and even poses a direct threat to the power of the ruling party. Thus, the prevention and punishment of corruption has become a major concern for successive Chinese government administrations, and has also become a key benchmark in the public's evaluation of the government's achievements. Building a clean and effective government is not only a matter of social consensus, but also a foundational element of the "Chinese Dream" for the future.

15.1 Changes in the Severity of Corruption in China Since Reform and Opening Up

Corruption is a common problem in governments all over the world, as demonstrated by recent research into global corruption. The 2005 *Global Corruption Report* analyzed corruption in the field of construction and found: "Corruption in procurement plagues both developed and developing countries…When the size of a bribe takes precedence over value for money, the results are shoddy construction and poor

L. Fan (✉)
CASS Institute of Sociology, Beijing, China

P. Li and M. K. Gorshkov (eds.), *Life Expectations of the People*,
Research Series on the Chinese Dream and China's Development Path,
https://doi.org/10.1007/978-981-16-2505-3_15

infrastructure management. Corruption wastes money, bankrupts countries, and costs lives."[1]

Due to the universal problem of corruption, many in-depth studies on this issue have been conducted. The focus of corruption studies has gradually shifted from analysis of specific cases to analysis from political, sociological and economical perspectives. Starting in the 1990s, corruption became the subject of social science research, and an increasing amount of attention has been paid to it.

"Corruption" is normally defined as the abuse of power by government agencies and public servants for personal gain. This definition is the generally accepted definition of all international organizations, including the World Bank. Yet, in reality, corrupt behaviors take many forms.

Civil servants and government agencies are generally the agents of corrupt behavior. In defining "corrupt conduct," New South Wales of Australia specified in the *Independent Commission Against Corruption Act* that: "corrupt conduct includes: any conduct of any person (whether or not a public official) that adversely affects, or that could adversely affect, either directly or indirectly, the honest or impartial exercise of official functions by any public official, any group or body of public officials or any public authority; any conduct of a public official that constitutes or involves the dishonest or partial exercise of any of his or her official functions; any conduct of a public official or former public official that constitutes or involves a breach of public trust; any conduct of a public official or former public official that involves the misuse of information or material that he or she has acquired in the course of his or her official functions, whether or not for his or her benefit or for the benefit of any other person." This definition of corruption is deliberately broad in order to prevent legal loopholes, yet it still centers around civil servants. In recent years, entrepreneurs, employees and even foreign civil servants can be considered agents of corruption, and their behaviors can be included in the scope of corruption.

In terms of corrupt behavior, acceptance of money or property in violation of the law are considered "bribery" according to traditional definitions. Such definitions emphasize that money and property are what constitutes bribery. Recently however, the scope of bribery has expanded to encompass other material benefits beyond money or property -such as free tourism and sexual services- as well as non-material benefits such as job offers or protection from and avoidance of legal punishment or disciplinary action.

With China's reform and opening-up, corruption began to spread along with economic transition and social change. Despite great determination and effort on the part of the Chinese government, which resulted in important anti-corruption achievements, China still has a high-incidence rate of corruption due to limitations in its economic development. The problem of corruption has not been prevented on a large scale, and corruption is still very severe.

While accepting the definition or corruption generally adopted by international society (referring to the behavior of "abusing public rights for personal gain"), according to China's own unique characteristics, we can divide the phenomenon

---

[1] Transparency International: *Global Corruption Report of 2005*.

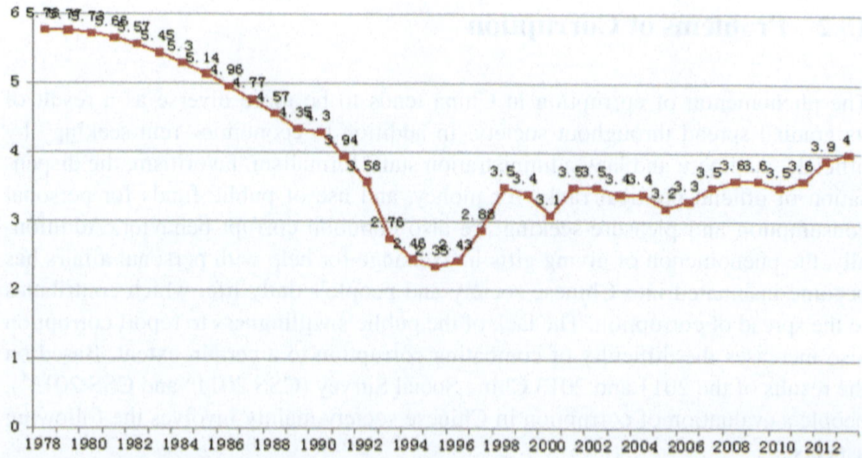

Fig. 15.1 China corruption perception index (CPI)

of corruption in China into four categories: (1) duty crime, particularly an economic crime, of a public servant; (2) abuse of power to seek personal gain in certain sectors and industries; (3) abuse of public funds to pursue luxury consumption and extravagance; and (4) corrupt, degenerate and immoral behavior of party members and cadre.[2] In this regard, the definition of corruption in China is broader compared with other countries; in addition to clearly defining corrupt behavior as abusing public power to seek personal gain, corruption also relates to party conduct, government conduct, industry conduct, and individual conduct of CCP members and cadres. This makes anti-corruption work more complex in China compared with other countries.

Since the 1990s, the severity of corruption has attracted the most attention from the general public among all social problems. Transparency International has released a Corruption Perception Index (CPI) every year since 1980. According to this Index, the CPI of China has decreased substantially since the middle of the 1990s, reaching as low as 2.4 at one time. Since the end of 1990s, China has been devoted to anti-corruption work and continuously allocates significant resources into anti-corruption, which has controlled the problem of corruption in Chinese society to a certain extent. China's CPI reached 3.5 in 1998, and thereafter hovered between 3.4 and 3.6, indicating a fierce battle between anti-corruption authorities and the forces of corruption. The CPI started to rise in 2012 and reached 4.0 in 2013, indicating a breakthrough in China's anti-corruption efforts (Fig. 15.1).

[2] He (2003).

15.2 Problems of Corruption

The phenomenon of corruption in China tends to be more diverse as a result of its gradual spread throughout society. In addition to economic "rent-seeking" by officials, mediocre and lazy administration staff, formalism, favoritism, the dispensation of official political ranks for money, and use of public funds for personal consumption and pleasure-seeking are also common corrupt behavior. Additionally, the phenomenon of giving gifts in exchange for help with personal affairs has become insinuated into Chinese society and people's daily life, which contributes to the spread of corruption. The lack of the public's willingness to report corruption also increases the difficulty of combating corruption to a certain extent. Based on the results of the 2011 and 2013 China Social Survey (CSS 2011[3] and CSS 2013[4]), people's evaluation of corruption in Chinese society mainly involves the following aspects:

1. Abuse of power among CCP members and cadres is still serious

First, formalism, bureaucratism and the abuse of power are still considered quite serious among CCP members and cadres. Results of the CSS (Table 8.1) show that the public thought the most prominent problematic behaviors of CCP members and cadres were: "formalism and lack of practical work" (63.9%), "bureaucratism or being careless with the public interest" (59.8%), "the abuse of power to seek personal gain" (58.7%), "consumption of and extravagance with public funds" (57.3%), dereliction of duty and lazy politics like "procrastination and a lack of conscientiousness" (54.2%) (Table 15.1).

Second, strengthening the work style of party and government cadres is an important component of anti-corruption work in China. While the work style of party and government cadres has become better, there still exists violations of what is termed the "Eight Rules." In December 2012, the Political Bureau of the Central Committee reviewed and passed eight rules for improving work style and maintaining close ties with the public. These include requirements that CCP members and cadres conduct grassroots outreach to make investigations, simplify reception, streamline meetings, improve the style of meetings, practice strict thriftiness, and perform all official duties honestly. The implementation of the "Eight Rules" became a major starting point for the party and government sectors across all levels to practice anti-corruption work, and was widely supported by the public. After half a year of implementation, the

---

[3] Data is from the third wave of the "China Social Survey" conducted by the Institute of Sociology in the Chinese Academy of Social Sciences from July to November 2011 (CSS 2011). Using a PPS sampling method, this survey covers 480 villages (or neighborhood committees) from 100 counties (cities, districts) and 5 large cities in 28 provinces, municipalities and autonomous regions in China. 7,036 rural and urban residents aged 18 or above were successfully interviewed.

[4] Data is from the fourth wave of the "China Social Survey" conducted by the Institute of Sociology in the Chinese Academy of Social Sciences from June to October 2013 (CSS 2011). Using a PPS sampling method, this survey covers 604 villages (or neighborhood committees) from 151 counties (cities, districts) in 31 provinces, municipalities and autonomous regions in China. 10,206 rural and urban residents aged between 18 and 69 were successfully interviewed.

Table 15.1 Which problems do you think are prominent among CCP members and cadres at present?

	2011		2013	
	Sample Size	Percentage	Sample Size	Percentage
Formalism and lack of practical work	3632	59.1	5753	63.9
Do not care about the public interest	3272	53.3	5387	59.8
Abuse of power to seek personal gain	3215	52.3	5283	58.7
Consumption of and extravagance with public funds	3351	54.5	5160	57.3
Procrastination and lack of conscientiousness	2594	42.2	4880	54.2
Practice of fraud for pursuing political performance	3052	49.7	4535	50.4
Buying and selling official positions	1362	22.2	2409	26.8
Failure to follow and execute decisions made by the central government	1392	22.7	1910	21.2
Others	87	1.4	131	1.5

results showed that over 50% of respondents thought that the relevant issues covered by the "Eight Rules" were improved, while about 20% of respondents thought there was no change and about 10% thought that violations of the "Eight Rules" had worsened (Table 15.2).

2. Holding banquets, sending gifts, and asking people to put in a nice word when dealing with family matters are pervasive in Chinese society

In a society built on personal relationships, the social factors that breed corruption exist not only among the cadre group. Requests for help with benefits (*qingtuo*), sending gifts, and other customs related to spending money to have things done for the public is common. From the perspective of getting things done, people consider the practice of banquets, sending gifts, and asking somebody to put in a nice word normal, and not associated with the problem of corruption. This suggests that the phenomenon of corruption in China not only includes "black corruption," which is generally condemned by society, but also "gray corruption," which is a matter of debate within Chinese society, and "white corruption," which is not thought of as punishable by most Chinese people.

From the CSS survey, we find that when dealing with such matters as seeing a doctor, entering a school, seeking a job or job transfer, and going to court, quite a number of people still tend to request help by holding banquets and sending gifts. The data suggests that, in addition to the above, people also tend to request help by holding banquets and sending gifts when trying to secure a social security subsidy or reimbursement for medical expenses, among other real life events. The highest rate of help-requests with benefits (those with high occurrence when confronted with such problems) relate to the following: going to court (49.0%); processing a business

Table 15.2 What changes have occurred for party and government cadres in terms of the following behavior since 2013 (%)

	Significantly worsened	Relatively worsened	Relatively improved	Significantly improved	No change	Do not know
Conducts grassroots surveys as a mere formality, does it for show	2.6	6.6	44.0	7.5	19.2	20.2
Conducts business in a pompous manner with large retinues, requires above-standard reception while conducting grassroots surveys	1.8	6.8	40.2	11.8	16.3	23.0
Frequently holds unnecessary meetings and celebrations in a frequent way	1.1	5.2	39.6	12.3	16.1	25.6
Eating and drinking using public funds	2.9	7.6	37.6	17.6	13.6	20.7
Spamming money, requiring pomp and ceremony, general lavishness, extravagance and waste	2.5	7.3	39.0	13.0	15.0	23.3

license (26.5%); work transfers, raises in salary, and job promotions (18.0%); looking for a job (16.3%); and entering a school (13.9%). In addition, as shown in Table 8.3, matters that are more likely to be successfully accomplished when accompanied by a request for help with benefits (based on the percentage of respondents who have had things successfully done by requesting help with benefits) include: seeing a doctor (91.4%); children's education (89.8%); processing a business license (87.4%); and receiving a social security subsidy or reimbursement for medical expenses (83.4%). This has made bribing doctors with money, arbitrary charges for education, and other forms of legal injustices a popular and implicit part of Chinese society (Table 15.3).

Table 15.3 Situation and rate of success when requesting help in dealing with family affairs by holding banquets and sending gifts (%)

	Rate of help-request with benefits		Rate of success	
	2011	2013	2011	2013
Seeing a doctor	9.9	11.5	93.3	91.4
Entering a kindergarten, school or higher education	11.4	13.9	91.1	89.8
Seeking a job	17.1	16.3	63.4	63.2
Work transfer, salary raise and job promotion	11.2	18.0	82.8	71.8
Going to court	35.5	49.0	56.3	51.9
Processing a business license	10.2	26.5	87.5	87.4
Receiving a social security subsidy or reimbursement for medical expenses	5.7	5.3	89.6	83.4

3. Corruption increases the public's judgment of the severity of conflict between officials and ordinary people

In the current stage of China's social development, social conflict is becoming more attention-grabbing. Data from the CSS 2013 shows that over 50% of urban and rural residents believe there is no or relatively little severe conflict among different social groups, indicating that people are satisfied with China's relatively stable and harmonious society. The social conflicts that were reflected in the survey mainly relate to conflicts between officials and the ordinary people, and between rich and poor people. 41.7% of respondents considered the conflict between officials and ordinary people to be relatively severe or very severe, and 42.9% of respondents considered the conflict between rich and poor people to be relatively severe or very severe (Table 15.4). Therefore, the major sources of current social conflict are the intensified conflicts between officials and the people, and between the rich and poor.

Table 15.5 shows a cross-tabulation of the severity of conflict between officials and ordinary people and the severity of corruption as assessed by the public. Among the respondents who considered the conflict between officials and ordinary people to be severe, 91.9% considered corruption to be severe in current society; among the respondents who thought that there was no or not severe conflict between officials and ordinary people, only 58% of them considered corruption to be severe in current society. Such results suggest that people's understanding of the severity of corruption in general impacts their assessment of the severity of the conflict between officials and ordinary people.

Table 15.4 The public's assessment of social conflict (%)

	No conflict	Not severe	Relatively severe	Very severe	Hard to tell	Total
Between rich and poor people	14.9	37.1	32.9	10	5	100
Between employers and employees	12	47.2	22.2	3.6	15	100
Between different races/ethnic groups	27	42.4	8.6	1.6	20.4	100
Between different religious groups	28	40.3	8.1	1.6	22	100
Between locals and migrants	29.6	48.7	13.2	2.1	6.4	100
Between officials and ordinary people	14.4	35.3	30.9	10.8	8.6	100

Table 15.5 Cross-tabulation of the severity of conflict between officials and ordinary people and the severity of corruption as assessed by the public (%)

		Conflict between officials and the public				
		No conflict	Not severe	Relatively severe	Very severe	Hard to tell
Do you consider corruption severe in China's current society?	Very severe	26.6	24.1	36.9	66.8	26.1
	Relatively severe	31.4	49.6	49.7	25.1	35.5
	Not severe	24.2	17.1	8.1	4.8	9.1
	No corruption	1.7	0.3	0.2	0.1	0.2
	Hard to tell	16.2	8.9	5.0	3.3	29.1
	Total	100.0	100.0	100.0	100.0	100.0

15.3 The Public's Evaluation of the Severity of Corruption and Anti-Corruption Work

At present, the anti-corruption struggle in China is at a stalemate, with the forces of corruption and anti-corruption competing with each other intensely. On one hand, there is highly unified consensus and support for anti-corruption efforts; the anti-corruption work of rooting out both "tigers and flies" has been comprehensively promoted, international cooperation on anti-corruption has continued, and the punishment of corruption is at an unprecedented level of severity. On the other hand, the proneness, frequency and popularity of corruption still exists in Chinese society, and new forms of corruption are occurring in some fields. At this stage of the stalemate, the public's overall evaluation of anti-corruption work is contradictory and complex, mainly reflected by the following three aspects:

1. The public thinks corruption is quite severe in current Chinese society

Results from the CSS survey show that urban and rural residents still consider corruption to be severe in current Chinese society. According to the 2013 CSS, 33.4% of respondents considered corruption quite severe at present and 43.3% of respondents considered corruption to be relatively severe, together accounting for 76.7% of all respondents; this proportion was 74.2% in the 2011 CSS survey. Although the proportion of urban and rural residents who considered corruption to be "very severe" reduced slightly from 2011 to 2013, corruption is still considered very severe in general (Table 15.6).

2. The public has a positive view of the current achievements of anti-corruption work conducted by the CCP and government

In recent years, the party and government have been devoted to improving the system of preventing corruption, and have continuously put more effort into their anti-corruption work. The CSS surveys show that the public has a positive evaluation of the efforts made by the party and government in anti-corruption work. The central government in particular has put more effort into anti-corruption work in the last two years, and correspondingly, the public's assessment of their achievements has

Table 15.6 The public's assessment of the severity of corruption

	2011		2013	
	Sample size	Percentage	Sample size	Percentage
Very severe	2622	37.3	3429	33.4
Relatively severe	2589	36.9	4441	43.3
Not severe	953	13.6	1341	13.1
No corruption	48	0.7	46	0.4
Hard to tell	811	11.5	1002	9.8
Total	7024	100.0	10,258	100.0

increased substantially. In the 2011 survey, only 29.5% of respondents considered the party and government to have significant achievements in anti-corruption work; in 2013, this percentage increased to 42.7% (Table 15.7).

3. The public's confidence in future anti-corruption work has increased

Up to present, there has been certain achievements in anti-corruption work in China, and the spread of corruption is basically under control. However, the phenomenon of corruption is still severe, and a culture of corruption still exists in society. The system and mechanisms for public supervision have not been effectively completed, increasing the difficulty of anti-corruption work to a large extent. Since the Eighteenth National Congress of the CPC, the central government has been determined to deal with corruption among leaders and cadres, regulate critical power sectors, and improve the practices of public officials in order to increase the people's confidence in future anti-corruption work. After more than a year of anti-corruption work, Chinese people have become more confidant in future anti-corruption efforts. In 2011, 57.6% of respondents expressed confidence that significant achievements in anti-corruption work would occur over the next 5–10 years; this percentage increased to 73.3% in 2013 (Table 15.8).

Table 15.7 Do you think the party and government have significant achievements in anti-corruption work at present?

	2011		2013	
	Sample size	Percentage	Sample size	Percentage
Significant	382	5.4	826	8.1
Relatively significant	1690	24.1	3546	34.6
Relatively insignificant	2822	40.2	3842	37.5
Not significant	1120	16.0	777	7.6
Hard to tell	1006	14.3	1265	12.3
In total	7020	100.0	10,256	100.0

Table 15.8 The public's confidence in prospect of substantial reduction in corruption in the next 5 to 10 years

	2011		2013	
	Sample size	Percentage	Sample size	Percentage
Very confident	1300	18.5	2438	23.8
Confident	2738	39.1	5073	49.5
Not very confident	1256	17.9	1297	12.7
Not confident	874	12.5	567	5.5
Hard to tell	841	12.0	868	8.5
Total	7009	100.0	10,243	100.0

Table 15.9 The public's general attitude towards anti-corruption work

	2011		2013	
	Sample size	Percentage	Sample size	Percentage
Severe corruption, low achievement and no confidence	1720	32.1	1669	20.2
Severe corruption, low achievement and high confidence	1835	34.3	2491	30.2
Severe corruption, high achievement and no confidence	248	4.6	-	-
Severe corruption, high achievement and high confidence	-	-	2951	35.8
No severe corruption, high achievement and high confidence	1553	29.0	1142	13.8
Total	5356	100.0	8254	100.0

4. The public tend to be to more rational, cautious and optimistic about anti-corruption work

From the public's assessment of the severity of corruption and the current achievements in anti-corruption work, as well as their confidence in future anti-corruption efforts, it can be concluded that the public has a rather rational, cautious and optimistic attitude toward anti-corruption work in general. By conducting a cluster analysis of these three questions in 2011 and 2013, we find that the proportion of respondents who hold the attitude of "severe corruption, low achievement and no confidence" fell by 15.2% from 2011 to 2013, and those who reported "severe corruption, high achievement and high confidence" accounted for 35.8% of total respondents. This suggests that structural changes have occurred in anti-corruption work in the intervening two years, as the proportion of respondents who held a negative attitude or who were blindly optimistic about anti-corruption work declined, and the proportion of respondents who expressed a rational, cautious and optimistic attitude toward anti-corruption work increased (Table 15.9).

15.4 Building a More Corruption-Resistant Society

1. The rule of law and building a more corruption-resistant government

At present, the fundamental factors in the spread of corruption in China include a weak understanding among the public, and especially some government officials, of the idea of the rule of law; low operationalization of anti-corruption efforts in the legal system; and undeveloped mechanisms for restricting the abuse of power. The overall goal of improving the rule of law in China was raised in the fourth plenary session of the Eighteenth National Congress of the CPC, and focused on bringing anti-corruption work into the legal system. China's leaders believe that anti-corruption work can be actively promoted, and an incorruptible government could gradually be built, by establishing the idea of the rule of law, improving the legal system with respect to anti-corruption, and upgrading mechanisms for restricting abuse of power.

According to the CSS surveys, building an incorruptible government is the general objective of the public at present. The public's assessment of the government's work is twofold: one, they appreciate the achievements made to improve people's livelihoods; and two, they have higher requirements for the openness, fairness and justice of government work. The results show that people had positive evaluations of government work in terms of meeting the basic demands of people's livelihoods, such as compulsory education, medical and health services, fighting crime, and maintaining social order and social security. The satisfaction rate in these respects was 60% (Table 15.10). Such results fully reflect the perception that all levels of government have made improvements in guaranteeing people's basic livelihoods.

However, the respondents were not quite satisfied with government work in the following aspects: being honest, fulfilling duties and fighting against corruption; the disclosure of information and improving government transparency; and the rule of

Table 15.10 The public's satisfaction with government work (%)

	CSS 2008[5]	CSS 2011	CSS 2013
Compulsory education	78.5	78.0	81.2
Medical and health services	71.2	67.4	69.9
Fighting crime and maintaining social order	70.1	64.6	63.3
Social security	62	60.9	62.2
Developing the economy and increasing people's income	61	56.4	51.7
Environmental protection and pollution control	56.5	55.6	49.5
Enlarging employment and increasing opportunities	54.1	48.1	43.6
Enforcing rule of law and the fair implementation of laws	56.6	42.3	42.8
Providing low rent housing and affordable housing for middle-and-low income people	43.3	39.6	34.4
Disclosure of government information and increasing the transparency of government work	57.2	37.1	37.1
Being honest, fulfilling duties and fighting against corruption	48.3	32.7	32.4

[5] The 2008 Chinese Social Survey (CSS 2008), whose sampling frame is designed on the basis of city and county statistics from the fifth population census, used a multi-stage, stratified sampling method. It covers 7200 families in 520 villages/committees in 260 townships (towns, streets) from 130 counties (cities, districts) and 28 provinces and municipalities. 7139 effective questionnaires were received through door to door sampling.

law and the fair implementation of laws. The satisfaction rates for these aspects were below 40%, and largely declined in comparison with the survey results of 2008.This suggests that there is still a long way to go in order to meet the public's requirement of building an incorruptible government.

The central government's streamlining and decentralization of administration has promoted the reform and transformation of government functions. This not only pays dividends in upgrading the Chinese economy, but is also a critical step in defining the boundaries of governmental power, releasing and delegating power to society, and further narrowing the space for corruption to occur. Through this streamlining and decentralization process, there are increased opportunities for market-oriented allocation of resources, and a shift from administration-oriented to service-oriented government functions. Consequently, by strengthening transparency, the opportunities for power rent-seeking can be fundamentally narrowed and the goal of a clean government can finally be achieved.

3. Strengthen social supervision and improve supervisory mechanisms

The critical factor for effectively preventing corruption is to create a social environment with supervision by institutions, supervision by public opinion and supervision by the public. Since China's reform and opening-up, certain achievements have been made in promoting anti-corruption and strengthening public supervision, yet many issues remain that must be dealt with seriously. Currently, the major problems of public supervision include a weak consciousness related to the supervision of corruption, low enthusiasm for anti-corruption efforts, unsophisticated channels of public supervision, a lack of feedback, and so on. In reality, the proportion of people that are willing to actively participate in anti-corruption efforts and report corruption using their real names is small. The results of the survey show that only 12.4% of respondents would report cases of corruption using their real names, 35.7% would report anonymously, and 38.7% would not report it at all (Table 15.11). In the 2013 CSS, 73.2% of respondents believed that at present, they would be attacked and retaliated against if they reported suspected corruption. Therefore, how to protect the safety of informants is a key point for anti-corruption work in the future.

Boosting the public's confidence in anti-corruption work is helpful in increasing their willingness to participate in the social supervision of corruption. Results from the 2013 CSS show that people's willingness to report cases of corruption increased

Table 15.11 Would you report case(s) of corruption?

	2011		2013	
	Sample size	Percentage	Sample size	Percentage
Report using one's real name	847	12.1	1272	12.4
Report anonymously	2313	32.9	3660	35.7
Wouldn't report	2864	40.8	3968	38.7
Hard to tell	996	14.2	1346	13.1
Total	7020	100.0	10,246	100.0

Table 15.12 Relationship between confidence in anti-corruption efforts and willingness to report corruption (%)

		Are you confident that our country will achieve obvious achievements in anti-corruption work in the next 5 to 20 years?				
		Very confident	Relatively confident	Lack of confidence	With only a bit of confidence	Hard to tell
Would you report cases of corruption?	Report with real name	23.3	9.8	8.1	7.4	7.0
	Report anonymously	37.5	39.8	34.1	26.6	14.9
	Wouldn't report	28.9	38.2	50.5	57.2	39.7
	Hard to tell	10.2	12.2	7.3	8.8	38.3
	Total	100.0	100.0	100.0	100.0	100.0

with their confidence in anti-corruption work. As shown in Table 8.12, among those who were confident in anti-corruption work, 60.8% were willing to report corruption using their real name or anonymously. Among those who were not confident, only 34% were willing to report either with their real name or anonymously. These results suggest that one of the main problems with social supervision of anti-corruption is that some respondents give up their supervisory rights because of a lack of confidence in preventing corruption. Therefore, boosting the public's confidence in anti-corruption work is helpful in strengthening the effectiveness of public supervision of corruption (Table 15.12).

4. Broaden the channels of political participation and increase political participation

Well-organized and effective political participation is an important bridge between the government and the public. Improving the political participation and willingness of the public to interact with governmental behavior is a necessary condition for winning extensive public support for anti-corruption work. At present, limited channels for political participation and a low willingness for participation among Chinese people are key chokepoints in anti-corruption work. The CSS surveys indicate that there are two features of current political participation by Chinese people.

First, a key feature of people's political participation is participation within institutions. Ranking first among all of the different types of political participation, 43.5% of respondents have participated in a neighborhood or village committee election. This suggests that under the arrangement of current institutions, expression of personal willingness is the major form of political participation. In addition, people have relatively few political activities outside of institutions. 39.3% of respondents would choose to discuss political issues with people around them. The rates of other forms of political participation, such as discussing political issues on the internet, expressing opinions to newspapers, radio and other media, and petitioning the government, were quite low.

Second, people's willingness to participate in politics is relatively low, and most would only choose moderate ways to participate. The 2013 CSS shows that over 50% of respondents were not willing to participate in politics, reflecting the relatively low willingness to participate in politics (Table 15.13).

We divided respondents into three groups based on their expressed willingness to participate in politics. Those who were not willing to take part in most forms of political participation are the group with "no willingness" for political participation; those willing to take part in one or two forms of political participation are the group with a "low willingness" for political participation; and those who were willing to take part in three or more forms of political participation are the group with a "high willingness" for political participation. Among the "no willingness" group, only 34.7% were willing to report corruption using their real name or anonymously. This share was much higher (63.4%) in the group with a high willingness for political participation (Table 15.14). It can be observed that broadening the channels of political participation and increasing people's willingness to participate in politics are both helpful in boosting enthusiasm for participation in anti-corruption work and consequently building up an environment for the effective social supervision of corruption.

5. Strengthening the establishment of an incorruptible culture

Compared with political, economic and other factors, social culture is a deeper component in the spread of corruption. The culture of corruption in Chinese society is influenced by traditional ideologies, including patriarchy, hierarchy and bureaucracy; it is also influenced by the culture of social relationships, including face-saving (*mianzi*) and requests for help with benefits. In terms of psychological factors, the culture of corruption is influenced by the psychological imbalance captured in the saying, "as everyone is corrupt, honest people will suffer a loss." There is also the assumption that in conformity to officialdom's unspoken rules, "uncorrupt persons will be kicked out," and a general belief in the notion that corruption provides "large returns with low risks." Compared with political, economic and other institutional factors, the culture of corruption in society plays a greater role in influencing the public's perception of corruption and what defines corrupt conduct.

The CSS data shows that respondents who engaged in help-requests with benefits thought corruption was more severe than those who had not; they were also less confident in the achievements of anti-corruption efforts. The data shows that over 85% of respondents who had requested help with benefits considered corruption to be quite severe or relatively severe, while the share of respondents who had not engaged in such behavior was about 10 percent lower at 75.3% (Table 15.15). In terms of confidence in anti-corruption work, 65.9% of respondents who had requested help with benefits were confident in the achievements of future anti-corruption work. The share was about 10 percent higher among those who had not requested help with benefits at 75.2% (Table 15.16). This implies that engaging in the behavior of requesting help with benefits in real life increased the assessment of the severity

Table 15.13 Have you taken part in the following events in the past three years? If not, are you willing to participate?

	Yes		If not, then are you willing to?					
			Willing to		Not willing to		Hard to tell	
	Sample size	Percentage	Sample size	Percentage	Sample size	Percentage	Sample size	Percentage
Discuss political issues with people around	2854	39.3	1598	35.6	2638	58.8	251	5.6
Discuss political issues on the internet	455	6.3	2021	29.7	4343	63.9	430	6.3
Express opinions to newspapers, radio and so on	116	1.6	2206	31.0	4564	64.1	346	4.9
Express opinions to governmental sections	529	7.3	2519	37.4	3910	58.0	309	4.6
Petition the government	255	3.5	1607	23.1	5003	71.9	350	5.0
Participate in a neighborhood/ village committee election	3157	43.5	1994	47.5	2037	48.5	168	4.0
Participate in a demonstration	64	0.9	710	9.9	6048	84.5	396	5.5
Participate in a worker strike, trader strike, student strike, etc	63	0.9	557	7.8	6206	86.8	388	5.4

Table 15.14 Relationship between willingness for political participation and reporting corruption (%)

		Willingness for political participation groups		
		Group with no willingness for political participation	Group with low willingness for political participation	Group with high willingness for political participation
Would you report suspected acts of corruption?	Report with real name	9.5	13.1	15.1
	Report anonymously	25.2	34.6	48.3
	Wouldn't report	47.5	39.9	28.1
	Hard to tell	17.8	12.4	8.6
	Total	100.0	100.0	100.0

Table 15.15 Assessment of the severity of corruption among respondents who had requested help with benefits and those who had not (%)

		Respondents who had not requested help with benefits	Respondents who had requested help with benefits
Do you consider the phenomenon of corruption in our society to be severe?	Quite severe	31.6	44.2
	Relatively severe	43.7	41.0
	Not severe	13.6	9.8
	No corruption	0.5	0.4
	Hard to tell	10.6	4.6
	Total	100.0	100.0

Table 15.16 Confidence in anti-corruption efforts among respondents who had requested help with benefits and those who had not (%)

		Respondents who had not requested help with benefits	Respondents who had requested help with benefits
On the whole, are you confident that our country will make significant achievements in anti-corruption work in the next 5 to 10 years?	Very confident	24.5	22.9
	Relatively confident	50.7	43.0
	Relatively unconfident	11.8	17.4
	Unconfident	4.7	8.4
	Hard to tell	8.3	8.2
	Total	100.0	100.0

of corruption, and reduced confidence in the current and future achievements of anti-corruption work.

In conclusion, corruption in current Chinese society is relatively severe, and the appeals of the Chinese people for anti-corruption work are consistent with efforts made by the Chinese government against corruption. Under the conditions of relatively little social conflict, a benign interaction between the government and the people can be achieved. Anti-corruption work will gradually step into the stage of building and improving the system in the future. However, the public's low willingness for political participation and limited channels for political participation constitute the main barriers to forming a benign relationship between the government and the public. In the future, with the improvement and modernization of the governance system and governance capability, Chinese people will become more willing to participate in politics. Developing honest and capable political administrations and government in China is both an important appeal of the public and an important ruling idea for the government.

Reference

He, Zengke. 2003. "Research in the Issues of Corruption and Combating Corruption During Chinese Transition (Part I)." Comparative Economic and Social Systems (105): 18–29. [in Chinese].

Chapter 16
Towards a Fairer and Less Corrupt Society

N. V. Latova and Yu. V. Latov

It has already been mentioned before that most Russians nowadays dream of social justice, equal rights and, at the same time, a strong state that takes care of its citizens. That is their notion of an ideal future society. Many Russians also emphasize such values as "human rights, democracy, freedom of expression" (28%), "stability and economic development without revolutions or turmoil" (27%), and "Russia becoming a great power again" (27%).[1] In essence, the core of this "macro-dream" is associated with state-society relations. In a way, we can even say that "the Russian dream" is that of a "good" state; even global geopolitical and economic problems fall by the wayside.

State-society relations constitute one of the key issues in social studies. It runs like a golden thread throughout the history of social thought, from Confucius and Aristotle in ancient times, to J. Locke and T. Hobbes in the early modern period, to our contemporaries J. Buchanan and F. Fukuyama. All the great thinkers considered state-society relations to be fundamental for public order and peace. They understood that, should those in power stop helping those they are ruling, and should the latter become completely alienated from the authorities, the state and society are doomed. They dreamed of a harmonious relationship between those in power and society and tried to develop new practical ways that would help bring utopia to life.

Yet, there are two fundamentally different approaches to dealing with the "key issue" of social studies. Western tradition emphasizes government responsibility

---

[1] Unless stated otherwise, in this chapter we will refer to the data derived from the IS RAS survey "What Russians Dream About" conducted in 2012.

[2] See http://en.wikiquote.org/wiki/Talk:Thomas_Paine.

The original version of this chapter was revised: Affiliation has been updated in this chapter. The correction to this chapter can be found at https://doi.org/10.1007/978-981-16-2505-3_19

N. V. Latova (✉) · Yu. V. Latov
Institute of Sociology of FCTAS RAS, Moscow, Russia

P. Li and M. K. Gorshkov (eds.), *Life Expectations of the People*,
Research Series on the Chinese Dream and China's Development Path,
https://doi.org/10.1007/978-981-16-2505-3_16

towards its people (Thomas Paine allegedly said, "It is the duty of the patriot to protect his country from its government"[2]). Oriental tradition, on the other hand, perceives the state as one big patriarchal family, with those in power compared to wise parents and their subjects to respectful children (Confucius). Both traditions condemn abuse of power and promote the ideal of an honest government. However, they have a different understanding of what abuse of power actually is and how to fight it ("bottom-up" or "top-down").

Nowadays the issue of state-society relations implies two core questions: how to develop democracy ("the rule of the people") and how to overcome corruption ("depravity" of those in power). The former is more instrumental: people have always showed tolerance towards rulers that were "not too democratic" (from Caesar to Lee Kuan Yew) if they were fair and diligent in their duties. However, the history of humankind proves that, "Indeed, it has been said that democracy is the worst form of Government except all those other forms that have been tried from time to time" (W. Churchill).[3] So, in the long term, the fight against corruption is inseparable from the fight for democracy, which is believed to be the "fairest" form of government achievable.

The minimization of corruption is one of the keys to progress and harmonious social development nowadays. Government corruption is detrimental for state-society relations, since it causes high transaction costs and social unrest. It results in an unfavorable investment climate, which, in its turn, slows down industrial development, and in a lack of political stability due to disrupted social ties.

Corruption exists more or less everywhere, both in developing countries with weak or non-existent democratic institutions and in developed democratic societies. But in some cases corruption is just a deviation, and in other cases it is one of the main "rules of the game." So, how can one marginalize corruption, thus reducing its negative effects?

There are several forms of administrative control. First, there are special internal governmental control systems where "the most honest" civil servants control other, "less honest" civil servants. Second, there are various civil initiatives, civil society organizations and dedicated individuals that take up control functions. Such external control systems are more effective because citizens, who make use of public services, are the least loyal towards corruption. In other words, the level of corruption is often inversely related to democratization levels: the higher the degree of external (independent) control over corruption practices is, the more difficult it becomes for politicians and civil servants to be opportunistic.

On average, it took developed countries two or three centuries to achieve a low-corruption society. Still, developing countries now have a chance to learn from others' experience and therefore reach their goals faster. South Korea is an example of a country that managed to work its way from being an authoritarian regime to a

[3] Parliament Bill HC Deb 11 November 1947. http://hansard.millbanksystems.com/commons/1947/nov/11/parliament-bill#column_206.

modern developed society in just half a century; nowadays it is absolutely comparable to Western European states in terms of key quality characteristics (living standards, democratic institutions, international competitive capacity, level of corruption, etc.). The Chinese "economic miracle" of the 1980s–2000s also resulted in lower corruption levels, though the country is still lagging in terms of democratic development.

However, it is much more common that rapid economic growth benefits the few elite, while large swathes of the population become more and more frustrated with corrupt politicians and civil servants, though they have little practical advocacy experience. This can cause a country to experience a chain of "revolutions" (such as in Egypt or Indonesia) that result in the succession of political and economic elites but doesn't really change "the rules of the game." In the end, corruption levels in such a situation decrease very slowly if at all.

It is still difficult to say which of the two paths (the "South-Korean" or "Indonesian" path) Russia has been following in the past two decades. In order to do so, one needs to closely monitor the population's dreams and perceptions regarding state-society relations.

This chapter seeks to assess the following:

1. The public perception of current social conflicts (and comparative acuteness of the relations between state and society);
2. The public perception of corruption (abuse of power by civil servants);
3. The general perception of the government (trust in the government), which is indicative of the intensity of conflict in state-society relations;
4. The level of people's social (and political) activity as evidence of the maturity level of civil society.

Our analysis is based primarily on the results of annual surveys conducted by the Institute of Sociology of the Russian Academy of Sciences using a nationally representative sample.[4] This data will help us understand what ideal state-society relations mean for Russians and to what extent reality matches their ideals.

In every society there are stress points that alarm people. Tension arises when people see discrepancies between what they want, or even what they dream of, and what they witness in real life. The way people perceive social conflicts allows us to understand their dreams and aspirations, and even forecast potential social developments. The number of social conflicts and their intensity define the level of social modernization and create a certain institutional environment that can either propel or hamper social progress and development.

---

[4] The following survey data was used: The Rich and the Poor in Modern Russia (2003); New Russians: Who Are They? What Is Their Life Like? What Are Their Aspirations? (2004); Property in the Life of Russians: Speculations and Reality (2005); The Low-Income in Modern Russia (2008); Is the Russian Society Ready for Modernisation? (2010); 20 Years of Reforms through the Eyes of Russians (2011); What Russians Dream About (2012); Poverty and Inequality in Modern Russia: 10 Years Later (2013); Middle Class in Modern Russia (February 2014); IS RAS monitoring conducted in October–November 2014.

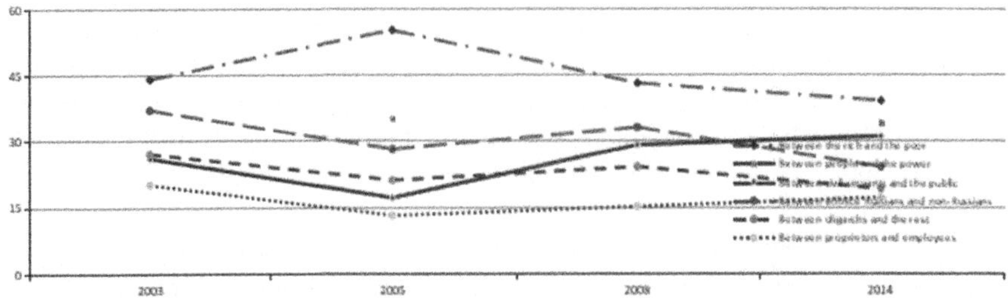

Fig. 16.1 Pressing social conflicts in post-Soviet Russia: perception dynamics, 2003–2014, %[5]

When asked what social conflicts are the most intense in modern Russia, the respondents tended to give the same five to six answers (depending on the options given). Moreover, the responses have been rather stable in the period between 2003 and 2014 (see Fig. 16.1).

As Fig. 16.1 shows, the most common answer (40–60% of all cases) given by the respondents of national surveys is the disparity between the rich and the poor. This is not unexpected, and indicates a pressing social problem rather than an actual conflict between different social groups. The rich versus poor problem shows that people see the issue of "wealth" distribution as a very contradictory one. However, people often have a very broad understanding of who "the rich" are. These can be civil servants, entrepreneurs or other groups of the population who just happen to be luckier or more talented. This problem can be referred to as "class divide" from a socio-economic point of view.

The conflict between ordinary people and those in power was the second most prominent issue in 2014. Such phrasing was only used in the 2005 and February 2015 surveys, but the respondents chose it equally often in both years.

The third most pressing conflict was that between civil servants and the public. It is interesting that there is little difference between this answer and the previous one: 34% of the respondents pointed out the conflict between "people and those in power," and 31% between "civil servants and the public". From an academic point of view, these are different things because "the power" includes both civil servants, who are appointed, and politicians, who are elected. Does an average Russian understand the difference? We can assume that in the eyes of the respondents, these two answers were maybe not synonymous but very similar.[6] Usually the same respondent doesn't choose both these answers at the same time. If we sum the number of those who

[5] Only the most common answers are shown in the figure; the respondents could choose up to 3 options.

[6] It is also possible that when talking about "civil servants," people usually imagine low-ranking civil servants that they actually have to interact with, while when talking about "those in power," they imagine high-ranking officials that do not communicate directly with the citizens but can cause all kinds of trouble. Such an interpretation can be drawn from the results of the 2005 bureaucracy survey. When asked, "What is the lowest level of civil servants that have real power over people?" most of the respondents (56%) said that "any civil servant, even the lowest-ranking one, has real power over people." Many also believed that "only civil servants who have a right to manage funds

chose at least one of the two, it turns out the conflict between people and the state is the most prominent one in Russia (55% in 2014). This conflict can be considered a class one from the point of view of the Asiatic mode of production theory (i.e., if Russia is understood as a neo-autocratic society with a state class and a subject class).[7]

24 to 37 percent of the respondents see the conflict between ethnic Russians and non-Russians as the most important one. Such phrasing, as given in the questionnaire, reflects two lingering problems: the problem of foreign migrant workers with a different ethnic background and the problem of Islamic/North-Caucasian terrorism. In February 2014 this answer came fourth, which is probably due to the fact that Islamic terrorism has become less of a danger in Russia recently. This is a non-class ethnic conflict. The situation in modern Russia is very similar to that of a century ago; class conflicts at that time were often "blurred" because of rising ethnic/cultural conflicts ("the Jewish question," "the Polish question," etc.).

Traditional class conflicts (as understood by Marx, which was primarily the struggle between the proletariat and bourgeoisie) were mentioned by Russian respondents surprisingly rarely. The closest option they could choose was the conflict between "proprietors and employees," yet on average it was only chosen by 20% of the respondents (17% in 2014). The conflict between "the oligarchs versus the rest of society" was named significantly more often (19–27% of the respondents). This might be due to the fact that oligarchs are usually close to those in power (they often have both property and power themselves), so they are also perceived negatively, just like other members of political establishment.

So, of the five or six most pressing social conflicts in Russia, class ones (from a Marxist point of view) are the most common; they are much more typical for "Asiatic" societies (state vs its subjects) than for capitalist societies (capitalists vs employees). In other words, the views of the Russians often coincide with the Asiatic mode of production theory ("politarism", "state mode of production") rather than with classical capitalism. The former implies a struggle between the main social classes, understood as bureaucracy ("those in power," "civil servants," "nomenklatura") versus the public ("the people," "citizens").

This can be considered proof of the fact that *in modern Russia, capitalist social struggle involving property relations is less relevant than social conflicts between "those in power" and the rest.* As a result, we can state that corruption (abuse of power) is one of the sides of the main class conflict in Russia; it is particularly important due to the fact that lasting class conflicts between stable social groups often

have power" (23%) or that "only the highest-ranking officials, such as ministers, governors, etc., have real power" (21%).

[7] The conflict between state and society doesn't necessarily have to be a class one (as is the case in contemporary developed countries). You can see whether social conflict is a class conflict or not judging by its intensity and stability. We know that class conflicts are usually more intense and more stable than non-class ones.

Table 16.1 Corruption perception dynamics in Russia, 2004–2013, %

Options the Respondents Could Choose From	2004	2005	2008	2011	2013
Have you ever had to pay a bribe?					
Often	-	2	2	4	-
Rarely	-	17	15	16	-
Never but I don't think it is something unacceptable	-	15	15	16	-
I am against bribery	-	58	64	59	-
Can bribery be justifiable in certain circumstances?					
It is not unacceptable (2004), one shouldn't be too judgmental (2013)	9	-	-	-	6
It is acceptable in certain circumstances	23	-	-	-	40
It is absolutely unacceptable	68	-	-	-	54

cause other social calamities.[8] According to representative survey data,[9] corruption is one of the main issues that bother people in Russia. Announcing a fight against corruption is more common during election campaigns than announcing a struggle for democracy; many parties feel that this is a burning matter that can make voters more critical of the government. Russian government nowadays devotes much more attention to the issue of corruption as well (especially since the adoption of the new anti-corruption law in 2008).

National survey data allows us to trace Russians' attitude toward corruption from the following points of view: their involvement in corrupt practices; and their level of tolerance towards corruption.

In order to evaluate people's involvement in corrupt practices in the period between 2004 and 2013, we either directly asked respondents how often they had to pay bribes (2005, 2008 and 2011 IS RAS surveys) or we asked whether they perceived bribery as something unacceptable or not (2004 and 2013 IS RAS surveys). If we compare the answers (see Table 16.1), we can see that *even though most Russians have a negative view towards bribery in general, they "get used" to it and even start seeing it as "normal" and justifiable in certain circumstances.*

When asked whether they have ever paid bribes, most of the respondents say of course that they are "against bribery." However, the percentage of those who chose this answer declined from 64 to 59% between 2008 and 2011, while the share of those who often paid bribes doubled. The share of those who rarely bribed or did not bribe at all but at the same time didn't find it unacceptable grew as well. Analysis of the respondents' employment structure provides us with a deeper understanding of corruption in Russia. In 2008–2011, the number of bribe-givers grew by approximately 3% across all occupational groups except for professionals and the

[8] The conflict actually began in 2013 as a struggle between corrupt politicians and civil society, later also developing an ethnic dimension to it.

[9] This is one of the five problems that alarm Russians most; other problems include housing sector crisis, low income, and low access to free education and healthcare.

self-employed. The entrepreneurs experienced the highest bribe-giving rate growth of nearly 10%. INDEM Foundation corruption research results are consistent with our data: according to INDEM, there was a huge leap in corruption "development" in the second half of the 2000s, particularly in the sphere of business corruption.[10] Most probably, such growth was possible due to the fact that people who had not bribed before but were not against the practice started paying bribes too. If the share of those who were against bribery hadn't changed, we could have claimed that there were no changes in the "status quo" in terms of corruption perception in Russia. However, we cannot afford to be so optimistic: the share of those who are against corruption declined significantly across nearly all occupations groups (except for the self-employed). Strangely enough, students exhibited the fastest corruption tolerance increase (the share of students who didn't accept bribery declined by 8%). Today's students are the citizens of tomorrow, so we might assume that most Russians are just "getting used" to corruption as something inevitable, as one of the "rules of the game."

Comparison of the 2004 and 2013 survey data provides us with additional information: in 2004, 68% of respondents stated they would never pay or receive a bribe, while in 2013, only 54% of respondents said that "bribery was unacceptable in any circumstances." Interestingly enough, the share of those who said that "one shouldn't be too judgmental" towards corruption declined from 9 to 6%, yet the share of those who believed that bribery "could be acceptable in certain circumstances" nearly doubled (from 23 to 40%). Probably, most Russians prefer to adapt to "dirty tricks" (as famous Russian satirist M. Saltykov-Shchedrin put it[11]) rather than to develop a counter-strategy against something they find intolerable.

Ironically, even stiffer national anti-corruption policy had no effect on the perception of corruption. In 2010, the president introduced the National Strategy for Countering Corruption, one of the goals of which was "the elimination of reasons and conditions that enable corruption in Russian society."[12] Had such declarations been accompanied by real actions, they could have contributed to reducing corruption in Russia. Unfortunately, that is not the case.

Is the Russian situation unique in the world? Transparency International has been publishing the Corruption Perceptions Index (CPI) for 20 years. The CPI is based on aggregate expert evaluations provided by various NGOs, and it can be used to

---

[10] See: Galitsky E., Levin M. Korruptsionnye vzaimootnosheniya biznesa i vlasti (opyt empiricheskogo analiza) // Voprosy Ekonomiki. 2007. № 1 (Галицкий Е., Левин М. Коррупционные взаимоотношения бизнеса и власти (опыт эмпирического анализа) // Вопросы экономики. 2007. № 1); Levin M., Satarov G. Korruptsiya v Rossii: klassifikatsiya i dinamika // Voprosy Ekonomiki. 2012. № 10 (Левин М., Сатаров Г. Коррупция в России: классификация и динамика // Вопросы экономики. 2012. № 10).

[11] Saltykov-Shchedrin M. The Liberal / Collected works.Volume 16. Moscow, Khudozhestvennaya Literatura. 1974.

[12] Presidential Decree № 460 of April 13, 2010, "On National Strategy for Countering Corruption and National Anti-Corruption Plan for 2010–2011" (Указ Президента Российской Федерации от 13.04.2010 № 460 «О Национальной стратегии противодействия коррупции и Национальном плане противодействия коррупции на 2010–2011 годы» // Российская газета. 2010. 15 апреля.).

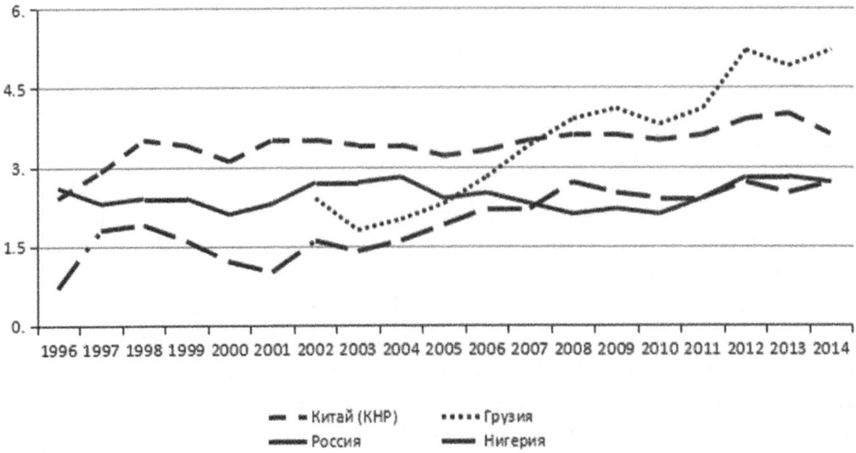

Fig. 16.2 CPI dynamics in China, Georgia, Russia, and Nigeria in 1996–2014[15] Based on Transparency International data (http://www.transparency.org)

consider the Russian situation from a comparative international perspective. The CPI ranges from 0 to 100, with 0 standing for the highest level of tolerance towards corruption (total corruptness) and 100 standing for the lowest (no corruption). Until 2013 however, the CPI only ranged from 0 to 10. Therefore, to compare the most recent data with earlier data, we divide the most recent (100-point scale) data by 10.[13]

Denmark, New Zealand and Finland scored highest in the CPI in 2014 (with a 92, 91 and 89 rating respectively). Russia scored only 27 (one point lower than in 2013), placing it in the 136th position together with Nigeria, Lebanon, Kyrgyzstan, Iran, and Cameroon.[14] In other words, Russia is currently in the lowest third of the CPI rating together with countries that haven't yet developed an efficient national market economy.

CPI dynamics shows that in the 1990s–2010s, the perception of corruption in Russia fluctuated by 2–3 points (on a 10-point scale) (see Fig. 16.2). This means that the country was highly corrupt overall, similar to Nigeria, which is often referred to as a "cleptocracy."[16] At the same time, some other countries with an originally high

[13] There are different views on how objective the CPI is and on data comparability across different years. However, most experts agree that CPI is the best available tool to compare corruption levels in different countries and time periods.

[14] See: http://www.transparency.org.

[15] New methodology introduced in 2012 made CPI a 100-point scale rather than a 10-point scale used previously. Still, 2012–2014 CPI data is comparable to earlier data if divided by 10.

[16] Geveling L.V. Kleptokratiya. Sotsial'no-politicheskoye izmereniye korruptsii i negativnoy ekonomiki. Bor'ba afrikanskogo gosudarstva s destruktivnymi formami organisatsii vlasti. Moscow, Izdatelstvo "Gumanitariy" Akademii gumanitarnykh issledovaniy. 2001. (ГевелингЛ.В.Клептократия. Социально-политическоеизмерениекоррупциииинегативнойэкономики. Борьбаафриканскогогосударствасдеструктивнымиформамиорганизациивласти. М.: Изд-во«Гуманитарий»Академиигуманитарныхисследований, 2001.).

Table 16.2 Dynamics in the level of trust towards state and public institutions among Russians, 2007–2014, %

Institutions	2007		2010		2014	
	Trust	Do not trust	Trust	Do not trust	Trust	Do not trust
The Government	51.2	47.4	57.1	21.3	55.5	24.4
Law enforcement agencies	28.7	70.1	21.4	57.8	28.1	48.6
Judicial system	29.2	69.4	19.1	53.0	24.3	48.7
Social and human rights organisations	53.3	45.1	34.5	25.1	36.9	26.8

level of corruption (such as Georgia or China) have managed to reduce corruption significantly—a trend reflected in the CPI over time. In Russia, such a trend might have begun in 2011, but it still too early to say whether that was the beginning of a long-term change or just another fluctuation (same as in the early 2000s).

It comes as no surprise that corruption is a big issue for Russians: nearly half of them believe it should be dealt with as soon as possible and they dream of a fairer and less corrupt society. It is therefore highly important to develop an efficient system of anti-corruption methods in Russia, both for the government and civil society.

In all countries, the struggle against corruption originally started from the top down, when the state would become too alarmed about the opportunistic behavior of civil servants who were accepting just too many bribes. Civil society only became part of the anti-corruption struggle much later because it usually takes longer to develop than the state. Just like many other developing countries, Russia is a country where "the state is stronger than the society"[17] (K.-A. Wittfogel), so in Russia anti-corruption is primarily perceived as a prerogative of the state.

What do the citizens think of this situation? How do they perceive the state on the whole and individual institutions?

In recent years, the IS RAS survey asked respondents to choose the statement they agreed with more: "Despite all shortcomings, our authorities do deserve support" or "People in power should be replaced, no matter what." On the whole, the responses didn't change much over time between 2012 and 2014 (from 70 and 30% to 75% and 25% respectively). Moreover, according to the results of the IS RAS survey conducted in October–November 2014, the recent event in Ukraine brought the Russian government even more supporters (84%). However, such an overall high level of support does not mean that the citizens trust specific institutions or organizations equally.

Since 2007, the IS RAS surveys asked respondents about their level of trust in state institutions three times, in the 2007, 2010 and fall 2014 national surveys (see Table 16.2). Empirical data shows that the level of trust towards state institutions has remained rather stable.

[17] Wittfogel K.-A. Oriental Despotism; a Comparative Study of Total Power. Yale University Press, 1957.

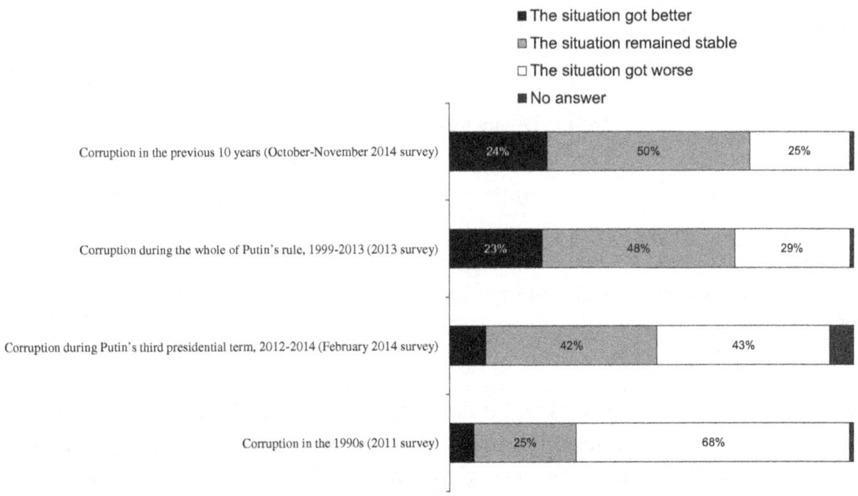

Fig. 16.3 Public perception of corruption in Russia from the 1990s to 2014, %

Table 16.2 shows that at least 50% of Russians tend to trust the government, though only one-third have trust in law enforcement agencies and the judicial system. The level of public trust in NGOs, which sometimes take up the work of the government, particularly in the sphere of anti-corruption, declined from 53% in 2007 to approximately 35% in 2010 and later years. This might be due to the fact that NGOs didn't live up to people's expectations and turned out to be too weak to really represent the citizens and fight for their rights. Therefore, the government and the state are perceived as the main anti-corruption policy actors in Russia.

How successful is Russian anti-corruption policy?

Comparison of data from multiple surveys yields a solid picture (Fig. 16.3). People firmly believe that Putin's rule (the 2000s–2010s) was by far more successful in terms of anti-corruption than Yeltsin's rule (the 1990s). Most Russians are very critical of the latter period: more than two-thirds of respondents agreed that the situation with corruption got worse during the 1990s. With respect to anti-corruption policy under Putin, most Russians agree that the situation deteriorated rather than improved. There is no survey where the majority of the respondents would state that the situation with corruption had improved. At the same time, many Russians are relatively optimistic: they believe that the level of corruption has become rather stable (nearly two-fifths of the respondents from the 2003, 2013, and 2014 surveys).

We have seen that Russians see the state as the main actor of anti-corruption policy. However, can it be successful if driven by the state alone? Maybe this is exactly the reason for the lack of dynamics in the anti-corruption sphere in the post-Soviet period?

On the one hand, some governments have been very effective in anti-corruption without the support of civil society. The most successful example is probably Singapore. Singapore's anti-corruption struggle is particularly impressive since it is a rather authoritarian state. In Singapore, there are anti-corruption bodies within the system of law enforcement which report directly to the prime minister. They act based on the presumption of guilt regarding well-paid public officials. As a result, it took Singapore only two decades to lose its image as another corrupt Asian country and become an "Asian tiger," one of the least corrupt states in the world.

On the other hand, Singapore is more of an exception due to a coincidence of several factors: it was a small high-income country, with well-paid civil servants, led by a smart and determined person. It is a rather rare combination because a weak civil society usually allows bureaucrats to become a class of "masters" fueled by their own interests rather than that of the nation. The cases of many countries show that anti-corruption policy driven by the state is only rarely effective. It is reasonable to assume that national anti-corruption policy in Russia won't be too successful as well unless supported by civil society.

So, anti-corruption policy brings little result if civil society is not involved in its implementation. The question is, is Russian civil society strong enough to provide necessary support? How does the state perceive civil initiatives?

If we turn to civil and political participation, we can see what Russians are really prepared to do to bring their goals and ideals to life. By analyzing their real-life behavior, we can learn about their life stance and capacity to translate "the mathematics of their dream" (J. London)[18] into reality.

The term "civil society" has become quite popular in modern Russia, both among academicians and journalists, though there is no consensus about what it actually means. It is often understood in a very trivial way, as "society of citizens;" in this sense, there is of course civil society in Russia. But the term is actually much deeper; it refers to the capacity of citizens to control the state and sometimes take over its functions (human rights work, social services, etc.). Non-governmental organizations don't necessarily have to be in opposition to the government, but they do form a kind of external force.

There is a number of ways how one can become a member of a civil society organization in Russia. Yet, according to 2014 data, 78% of Russians did not belong to any organization, association or community. 7% of the population were members of labor unions, 6% participated in various online-communities, and 2% were involved in charity. In other words, most of those engaged in some kind of social activity had nothing to do with politics.

There are two indicators that help evaluate the level of civil society development in Russia: (1) potential willingness to defend one's rights together with other people, not individually; and (2) real level of civil participation.

Survey respondents were asked (in 2003, 2008, 2013 and February 2014) how they would react in case of a dramatic drop in their living conditions. The answers to this question were used to evaluate their potential participation level. As anticipated, many said that they would "look for new sources of income" (29–45%) or "do something-I-don't-know-what-yet" (26–40%). It is quite interesting that in 2003, more people went with the former answer than the latter (45% vs 33%). By February

[18] London J. The Iron Heel.

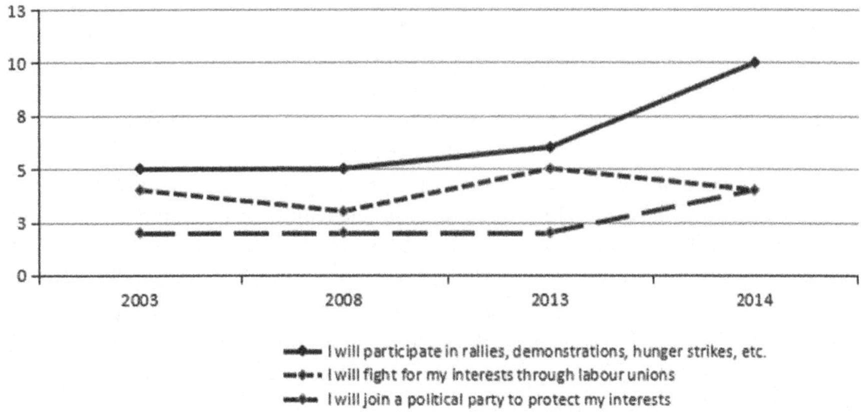

Fig. 16.4 Potential civil participation dynamics in Russia, 2003–2014, %

2014 their self-sufficiency had started to dissolve, and more people chose the latter answer (40%) rather than the former (36%).

However, some of the respondents said they would undertake certain steps typical for developed civil societies (Fig. 16.4).

Looking at the figures, we see three important things. First of all, the share of those ready to participate in some kind of civil activity is relatively low (10–15%).[19] Secondly, the share of those who say they could act more radically (even go on a hunger strike) is nearly equal or even higher than the share of those who prefer less noticeable but more institutionalized forms of action (parties, labor unions). This might be typical for developing countries: civil society in such countries often operates in "pulse mode;" celebrated protest activities yield one-time results but don't allow the society to really control the government (post-Soviet Ukraine is a good example). Third, in the 2010s, Russians seemed more willing to participate in institutionalized advocacy activities than in the 2000s. This shows that civil society in Russia is actually taking shape and playing a real policy role.

The question is, does reality match the declared intentions of the respondents? We now explore what Russians have been doing to protect their interests.

First, very few of the respondents answered positively when asked about their participation in politics (political parties, rallies, demonstrations, strikes) in the previous year: 2% in 2003, 1% in 2008, 2% in 2013, and 4% in February 2014. It could be that these figures are understated. On one hand, there are other, non-political forms of civil activity (such as volunteering); on the other hand, "politics" to most people is perceived as something completely unrelated to their everyday life ("high politics"), and actually ethically dubious ("dirty politics"). Therefore, it also

[19] Interestingly enough, the three potentially socially active groups have nearly no overlap. This might be due to the fact that respondents could only choose two options. Very few would rely on civil organizations to protect their interests. Most of them would choose one collective advocacy form and an individual one.

Table 16.3 Responses to the question: "What have you personally done in the past year to protect your interests?" 2003–2010, %

Options	2003	2008	2010
I have participated in rallies, demonstrations, hunger strikes	1	1	1
I have participated in events organized by political parties and movements	1	1	2
I have participated in events organized by labor unions	2	1	3

makes sense to analyze what type of activities respondents undertake in pursuit of their interests (Table 16.3).

In fact, the share of Russians who participate in certain types of political activities is very low (3–5%). Political participation is the exception rather than the rule; only 15% of respondents are ready to do something should their living standards fall dramatically, and only 5% actually take action. However, the share of those ready to do something and speak out increased in the 2010s. We can conclude that civil society is slowly growing in Russia, though it is still very weak.

Its weakness prevents us from talking of civil society as the state's real partner (or competition) in terms of anti-corruption policy implementation. What makes it even worse is that in the 2000s–2010s, the state repeatedly ignored civil initiatives aimed at gaining real control over public bodies. In 2012–2014, opposition leaders (such as Alexey Navalny, Boris Nemtsov and others) explicitly promoted anti-corruption ideas. However, the state did not show any support for them and only continued to press them. As of the mid-2010s, the strong Russian state and the weak civil society don't treat each other as partners in the struggle against corruption.

* * *

We can make several conclusions on whether existing state-society relations in Russia match people's ideals regarding a "normal," fair, and healthy society.

1. The conflict between the "people" and "those in power" is one of the most prominent in modern Russia; institutional corruption is still perceived negatively by the majority of the population, though people seem to be getting more used to it.
2. Russians are rather critical of the government's anti-corruption policy. Most believe that corruption levels may have stabilized but definitely did not go down. On average, the respondents' perceptions correspond with Transparency International monitoring results.
3. Civil society is weak in modern Russia. No more than 5% of the population participates in some kind of civil activities; only 10–15% say they could probably become more active if necessary. Nearly 80% of all Russians do not participate in any civil activities and aren't willing to do so. A weak civil society can neither help nor control the state, especially when the latter is actively against any attempts to increase civil control over public officials, even if that would

help fight corruption. The state and civil society haven't managed to form a tactical union in the field of anti-corruption.

4. On the whole, current state-society relations do not really match "the Russian dream." This is largely due to the fact that "the Russian dream" is inherently self-contradicting: on the one hand, Russians want to live in a "fair" society, devoid of corruption, with the state respecting public opinion; on the other hand, they are unable to build civil society institutions that would control the state and shape public opinion.

"The Russian dream" actually reflects the well-known Russian fairy-tale *Wish Upon A Pike*. Its protagonist, Emelya, wants to sleep all day long by the stove and get everything he wishes from the magical Pike without making any effort.[20] The image of an ideal leader in Russia ("a kind and wise ruler") is typical for many non-European civilizations—rom the Incan to the Chinese, from antiquity to modern times. N. Gogol put the idea very well in one of his letters to V. Belinsky: "Everyone takes the Tsar for a model. Should he start ruling well, without any distortions, everything goes well by itself."[21] Unfortunately, such a situation is not very common in real life. Moreover, nothing gets better "by itself" because even a good leader cannot replace "good" institutions. Typically for a non-European development model, a "kind and wise ruler" is very rare. Some rulers have managed to find good balance between extremes (like Khrushchev during the Thaw), thus cultivating the illusion that the goal of a good ruler can actually come true.

Apparently, post-Soviet Russia has achieved a balance somewhere in the "golden mean" throughout the 2000s–2010s. Most of the population is rather happy with the regime, even though it is a highly corrupt one. Those who are not particularly happy aren't frustrated enough to actually try and change it ("topple it"). In the past 15 years, we have witnessed a relatively stable (yet slightly fluctuating) system where people are not really satisfied with the state but also do not want to change it. They actually do not have much chance at change, despite the fact that the current situation doesn't match their idea of a fair society. It is difficult to say whether this period constitutes a kind of extended turning point or whether it is directional for Russia's development over the coming decades.

References

Galitsky, E., and M. Levin. 2007. Corruptin in Business and Government Relations. Voprosy Ekonomiki 1. [in Russian].

[20] In 2012, the respondents were asked which fairy-tale reflected their dreams best. 23% chose for *Wish Upon A Pike* (an ordinary guy accidentally gets lucky), which was the second most common answer. The first most common answer with 40% was *Cinderella* (in the end, virtue and diligence will be rewarded).

[21] Gogol N.V. Letter to V.G. Belinsky, end of July—early August 1847, Oostende. / Gogol N.V. Collected works. Moscow, Leningrad. Publishing house of the USSR Academy of Sciences, 1937–1952.Volume 13. Letters, 1846–1847. P. 444.

Geveling, L.V. 2001. Kleptocracy. The Socio-Political Measurement of Corruption and Negative Economic. Fighting of African State with Destructive Forms of Organization of Power. Moscow: Publishing house "Humanists" of the Academy of Humanitarian Research.

Levin, M., and G. Satarov. 2012. Corruption in Russia: Classification and Dynamics. Voprosy Ekonomiki 10. [in Russian].

Presidential Decree № 460 of April 13, 2010, "On National Strategy for Countering Corruption and National Anti-Corruption Plan for 2010–2011". Rossiiskaya gazeta 15.04. 2010. [in Russian].

Saltykov-Shchedrin, M. 1974. The Liberal. Collected Works 6. Moscow: Khudozhestvennaya Literatura. [in Russian].

Wittfogel, K.-A. 1957. Oriental Despotism: A Comparative Study of Total Power. Yale University Press.

Chapter 17
Moving Towards a Happier Society

Junxiu Wang

On March 23, 2013, Chinese President Xi Jinping delivered a speech at Moscow University of International Relations, in which he stated: "Since modern times, the greatest dream of the Chinese people has been to realize the great rejuvenation of the Chinese nation, which we call the 'Chinese Dream.' Its basic meaning lies in the realization of national prosperity, national rejuvenation and the well-being of the people." This expression has been summarized in the same way by the state, the nation, and the people. The emphasis of the "Chinese Dream" is on the happiness of the people. The idea of a "Chinese Dream" has become a symbol of China's new concept of development in recent years. After China's reform and opening-up, economic development gradually became the focus, with the GDP becoming an important indicator for measuring the economy at the state and local levels. It also became the most important indicator for assessing governmental performance at different levels. However, new social problems have occurred as China's GDP has increased, such as the polarization of the rich and the poor and the destruction of the ecological environment. People's happiness has not been increasing with general improvements in their living condition. Therefore, under the new concept of "people-centered sustainable development," the people's happiness has been defined as the target for governmental administration (Wang 2011). Like many other countries in the world, the concept of looking at happiness from the perspective of development has been gradually accepted by the Chinese government and the people.

J. Wang (✉)
CASS Institute of Sociology, Beijing, China

P. Li and M. K. Gorshkov (eds.), *Life Expectations of the People*,
Research Series on the Chinese Dream and China's Development Path,
https://doi.org/10.1007/978-981-16-2505-3_17

17.1 Chinese People's Sense of Happiness

1. Happiness Is the Most Important Indicator of Social Development

In the 1970s, the King of Bhutan raised the notion of replacing Gross National Product (GNP) with Gross National Happiness (GNH). He thought that the target of governmental administration should lie in realizing happiness, paying attention to the balanced development of materials and spirit, and putting the protection of the environment and traditional culture above economic development. Thereafter, France, America, England, the Netherlands, Japan and other advanced countries developed studies on the happiness index, with the purpose of incorporating their people's subjective well-being into the index for measuring social development.

Subjective well-being is an important comprehensive psychological index for measuring the quality of individual life. It is similar to many other concepts, including satisfaction, happiness, sense of well-being, subjective welfare and psychological well-being. Psychologists generally treat happiness as a kind of attitude that contains, at least, both cognition and emotion. In other words, people's sense of happiness includes both the judgment of reason and emotion (Robinson et al. 1997). Studies on this issue in the field of psychology date back to the 1950s, but these were mainly conducted from the perspective of mental health. By the 1970s and 1980s, studies were expanded to examine the quality of life, as appeared in the survey of the American social overview. Some relevant interdisciplinary studies—in addition to exploring the relationship between happiness and individual character, age, gender and other demographic variables—also explored the relationship between happiness and income, employment and inflation, as well as the relevant political system, economic policy, social policy and so on. There have also been many surveys on happiness in recent years, but there are several general problems with these studies that raise suspicion toward the validity of the results: First, the studies used unregulated measuring tools. In most cases, only one item was used for inquiring about the degree of respondents' happiness or degree of satisfaction with life. Second, the measurements often only include cognitive judgment, and lack the emotional aspect. Third, most of the surveys use non-random sampling. Last, some data that describe the character and variation of Chinese people's happiness are not from a national sample. In this sense, the results of this study are of significant importance.

2. Overview of Chinese Residents' Happiness

The method of measuring satisfaction with life, deemed subjective well-being, varied in different periods until measuring tools for the study of satisfaction were developed. One such measuring tool is the Satisfaction With Life Scale (SWLS), compiled by Diener et al. in 1985, which has only five questions for measuring the degree of satisfaction with life (Veenhoven 1996). For this survey, we adopted a six-point scale, and respondents were asked to choose from one of the following six answers for each of the five questions: strongly disagree, disagree, not quite agree, agree to a certain extent, agree, and quite agree.

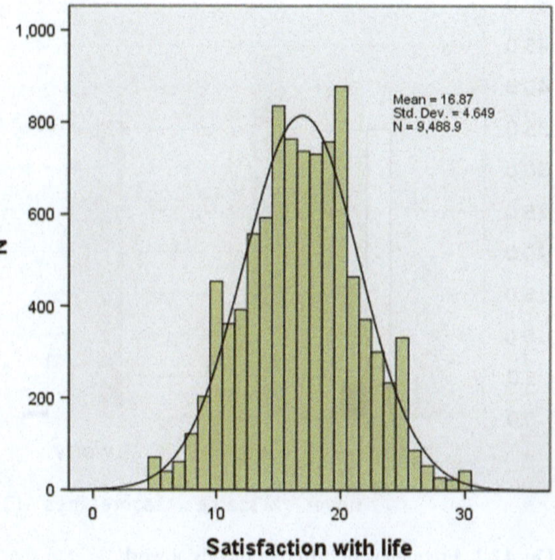

Fig. 17.1 Score distribution of degree of satisfaction with life

The total score for the five questions lies within a range of 5–30. Statistical results show that the average score of respondents' overall satisfaction with life is 16.87, which is equivalent to 3.37 on the six-point scale, somewhere between not quite agree and agree to a certain extent. As shown in Fig. 17.1, respondents' satisfaction with life is near to normal distribution, with an average score of 16.87 as the center point.

3. Emotion Experienced at Work and Home

Another assessment approach taken by psychologists and emotional sociologists is to divide feelings into primary, or basic, emotions and secondary emotions. Turner (2009, pp. 2–3) holds the opinion that primary emotions are the foundation of other emotions, which are consolidated in the autonomous nervous system of human beings and improve the adaptability of mammals, including primates. Some psychologists think that human beings experience six basic moods: happiness, surprise, fear, sadness, agony and disgust (Eysenck 2000, p. 743). Turner's approach concluded that there are representative opinions about basic emotion (Turner and Stets 2007, pp. 11–12). In this study, we selected five of Turner's representative opinions that are generally regarded as being basic emotions: "pleasure/enjoyment," "frustration/anger," "worry/fear," "disgust" and "sadness/sorrow" (emotions described with two words signify the degree from relatively weak to relatively strong emotion). To measure mood, survey respondents were asked: "Please think back on your life in previous years; on the whole, how often did you experience the following five moods in the daily life situations listed below? The situations were divided into two categories: work (including work, labor and school) and home.

The results of this measure of emotions (as shown in Fig. 17.2) show that residents tend to have relatively prominent positive emotions when they are at work, engaging in labor or studying at school. Respondents chose "always" (4.5%), "often" (34.9%), and "sometimes" (36.5%) under "pleasure" and "enjoyment." For negative

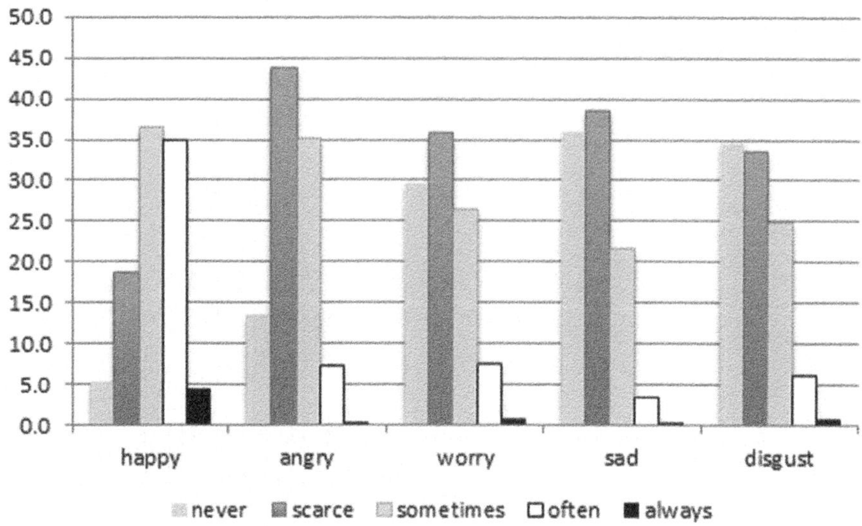

Fig. 17.2 Frequency of different moods at work

moods, the percentage of people who chose “always” was extremely low, between 0.3 and 0.8%. Those who chose “often” ranged within 3.5–7.4%, and those who chose “sometimes” ranged between 21.7 and 35.2%. When totaled, the percentages ranked as follows in descending order: “frustration/anger” (42.9%), “worry/fear” (34.6%), “disgust” (31.8%), and “sadness/sorrow” (25.5%). On the whole, Chinese residents tend to have the following negative emotions in their work situations: “frustration/anger” and “worry/fear.”

Similar to their work situation, respondents also tend to have relatively prominent positive emotions at home (as shown in Fig. 17.3). The percentages of people who chose “always,” “often,” and “sometimes” were 9.2, 53.7 and 25.9% respectively, adding up to 88.8% in all. This figure is even higher than the figure for work (75.9%). Among negative emotions, the proportion of people who chose “always” ranged between 0.3 and 0.8%, while the share for “often” fell between 2.6 and 5.3% and the share for “sometimes” ranged between 14.3 and 29.6%. When added together, these three percentages are ranked as follows in descending order: “frustration/anger” (35.1%) “worry/fear” (25.2%), “sorrow, sadness” (22.2%), and “disgust” (17.1%). These figures are all lower than the figures for work and study.

To understand the relationship between residents’ recognition of their sense of happiness and mood, their “satisfaction with life” scores are divided into three groups: those with an average score of 15 or less were the “not satisfied” group; the “satisfied” group had an average score of 20 or more; and the “normal” group had an average score in the middle of the two (between 15 and 20). The results of the analysis of the moods of “pleasure” and “enjoyment” when going to work and/or school are shown in Table 17.1 and Fig. 17.4. The proportion of people who chose “always” or “often” for pleasure and enjoyment increased with higher satisfaction with life. Among the

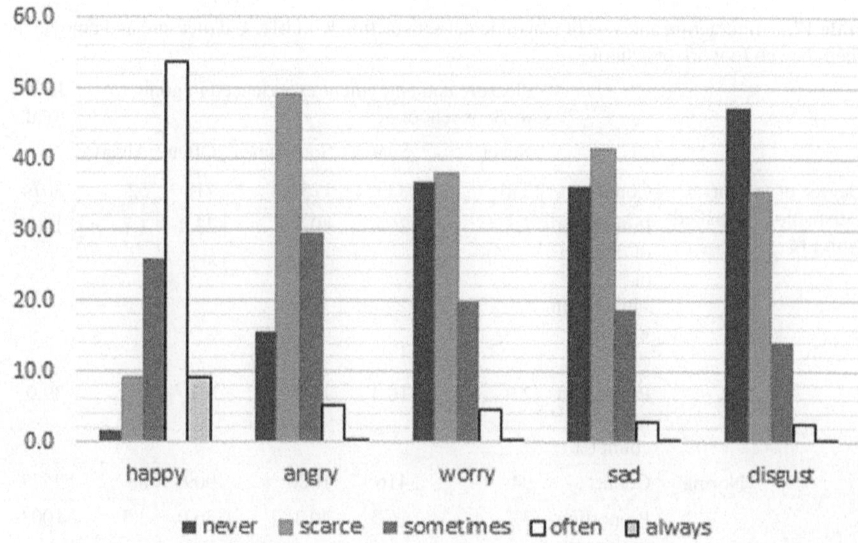

Fig. 17.3 Frequency of different moods at home

"satisfied with life" group, 9.2% chose "always" for these positive emotions, while 3.5% of the "normal" group and 1.7% of the "not satisfied" group chose this option. The shares of those who chose "often," was 48.8% in the "satisfied" group, 36% in the "normal" group and 13.4% in the "not satisfied" group. In contrast, the proportion of those who chose "never" and "rarely" for pleasure and enjoyment increases with a higher degree of satisfaction; the proportion of those who chose "never" for pleasure and enjoyment were respectively 3.6, 3.7 and 7.5%, while the figures for "rarely" for pleasure and enjoyment are 10.6, 16.5 and 26.8%.

As Table 17.2 and Fig. 17.5 show, the proportion of people who chose "always" and "often" for pleasure and enjoyment increased with a higher degree of satisfaction with life. 16.5% of those in the "satisfied" group chose "always," while 7.7% of the "normal" group and 5.3% of the "not satisfied" group chose this option. The shares of those that chose "often" in the "satisfied," "normal," and "not satisfied" groups were 60.2, 58.1 and 45.5% respectively. In contrast, the proportion of people who chose "never" and "rarely" for pleasure and enjoyment decreased with higher satisfaction with life; the proportion of those who chose "never" for "pleasure" and "enjoyment" were respectively 1.4, 1.1 and 2.5%, while the figures for "rarely" were 5.4, 7.2 and 14%.

Further analysis of the correlation degree between recognition of one's sense of happiness and emotion shows that the degree of satisfaction with life recognized as a sense of happiness correlates in varying degrees with different moods (see Table 17.3). The correlation coefficient between the total scores for degree of satisfaction with life and feelings of pleasure and enjoyment while working and/or studying is 0.303, and the figure for staying at home is 0.263. The degree of satisfaction with

Table 17.1 Interaction analysis of respondents' satisfaction with life, and pleasure and enjoyment when they go to work or school

			Pleasure and enjoyment experienced in going to work or school					In total
			Never	Scarce	Sometimes	Often	Always	
Degree of satisfaction with life	Not satisfied	Count	230	823	1251	718	52	3074
		Proportion of degree of satisfaction with life (%)	7.5	26.8	40.7	23.4	1.7	100.0
		Proportion of total count (%)	2.9	10.4	15.9	9.1	0.7	39.0
	Normal	Count	94	416	1020	909	88	2527
		Proportion of degree of satisfaction with life (%)	3.7	16.5	40.4	36.0	3.5	100.0
		Proportion of total count (%)	1.2	5.3	12.9	11.5	1.1	32.1
	Satisfied	Count	82	241	637	1112	209	2281
		Proportion of degree of satisfaction with life (%)	3.6	10.6	27.9	48.8	9.2	100.0
		Proportion of total count (%)	1.0	3.1	8.1	14.1	2.7	28.9
In total		Count	406	1480	2908	2739	349	7882
		Proportion of degree of satisfaction with life (%)	5.2	18.8	36.9	34.8	4.4	100.0
		Proportion of total count (%)	5.2	18.8	36.9	34.8	4.4	100.0

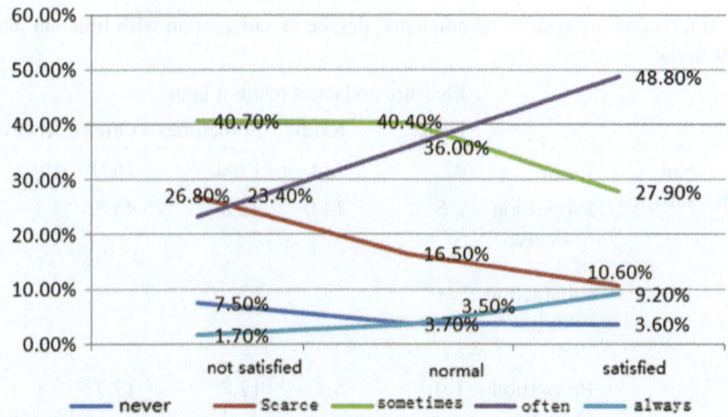

Fig. 17.4 Frequency and degree of pleasure and enjoyment when going to work or school

life is negatively and significantly correlated with different negative moods, with a coefficient of about 0.20. Respondents' experiences of different moods when they are at work and home are correlated to a varying extent. The correlation coefficient between the feelings of pleasure and enjoyment experienced at work and that experienced at home is 0.456, while the correlation coefficient between the moods of frustration/anger, worry/fear, sadness/sorrow, and different levels of disgust are respectively 0.431, 0.504, 0.587 and 0.478. This indicates that the same moods under different situations are highly correlated. Positive moods and negative moods for the same situation have a significant negative correlation, different negative moods are positively correlated, and the coefficients of correlations between negative moods in the same situation are larger than that for different situations.

17.2 Degree of Satisfaction with Life for Different Groups

1. Degree of Satisfaction with Life for Males and Females

Scores for the degree of satisfaction with life for females and males are 17.15 and 16.61 respectively, a significant difference (Fig. 17.6).

2. Degree of Satisfaction with Life for People of Different Age Groups

Scores for degree of satisfaction with life was 16.09 for those under 35, 16.85 for those aged between 36 and 50, and 18.13 for those aged 51 and above. This indicates that there are significant differences in life satisfaction among different age groups, with the degree of satisfaction with life increasing with age (Fig. 17.7).

3. Degree of Satisfaction with Life for People with Different Marital Status

As shown in Fig. 17.8, the degree of satisfaction with life for people of different marital status varies. The respondents in a first marriage have the highest degree

Table 17.2 Interaction analysis of respondents' degree of satisfaction with life, and pleasure and enjoyment at home

			Pleasure and enjoyment at home					In total
			Never	Rarely	Sometimes	Often	Always	
Degree of Satisfaction with Life	Not satisfied	Count	92	514	1204	1671	195	3676
		Proportion of degree of satisfaction with life (%)	2.5	14.0	32.8	45.5	5.3	100.0
		Proportion of total count (%)	1.0	5.4	12.7	17.7	2.1	38.9
	Normal	Count	32	214	772	1728	229	2975
		Proportion of degree of satisfaction with life (%)	1.1	7.2	25.9	58.1	7.7	100.0
		Proportion of total count (%)	0.3	2.3	8.2	18.3	2.4	31.5
	Satisfied	Count	38	151	464	1689	462	2804
		Proportion of degree of satisfaction with life (%)	1.4	5.4	16.5	60.2	16.5	100.0
		Proportion of total count (%)	0.4	1.6	4.9	17.9	4.9	29.7
In total		Count	162	879	2440	5088	886	9455
		Proportion of degree of satisfaction with life (%)	1.7	9.3	25.8	53.8	9.4	100.0
		Proportion of total count (%)	1.7	9.3	25.8	53.8	9.4	100.0

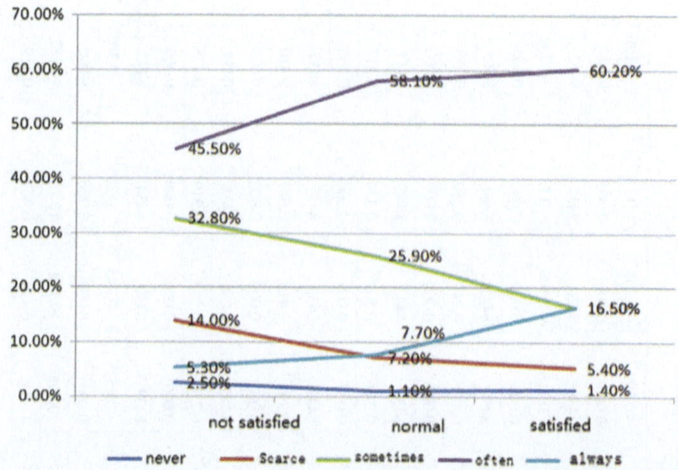

Fig. 17.5 Frequency and degree of experiencing pleasure and enjoyment at home

of satisfaction with life, followed by remarried respondents, and then widowed respondents. Cohabited, unmarried and divorced respondents' degrees of satisfaction with life are lower than the average level, among which, divorced and unmarried respondents have the least satisfaction with life.

4. Degree of Satisfaction with Life of People with Different Education Levels

The scores for degree of satisfaction with life for low, middle, and high education groups was 17.08, 16.52 and 16.54 respectively, reflecting significant differences between three groups. The scores for respondents with middle and high education levels were nearly the same, with the figure for those with higher education a bit higher. The score for respondents who graduated from middle school or lower is the highest (Fig. 17.9).

5. Satisfaction with Life of Respondents with Different Social Class Identity

There is a significant difference between the satisfaction with life scores for different socio-economic groups. The scores for respondents with the socio-economic status identity of "low," "mediocre," "middle," "above average" and "high" were 14.45, 16.18, 18.09, 19.36 and 22.12 respectively. The sense of happiness decreases with lower self-identified socio-economic status (Fig. 17.10).

6. Degree of Satisfaction with Life of Residents Living in Different Regions

There is a significant difference between the degree of satisfaction with life for urban and rural residents (Table 17.4). Rural residents are more satisfied with their lives than urban residents. We further analyzed the degree of satisfaction with life of urban and rural residents living in different types of communities, the results of which are shown in Fig. 17.11. Residents living in the countryside or center of

Table 17.3 Analysis of correlation between degree of satisfaction with life and moods experienced at work/school or at home

				Go to work or school					Stay at home				
			Degree of satisfaction with life	Pleasure/enjoyment	Frustration/Anger	Worry/Fear	Sadness/Sorrow	Disgust	Pleasure/Enjoyment	Frustration/Anger	Worry/Fear	Sadness/Sorrow	Disgust
	Degree of satisfaction with life	Correlation	1	0.303**	−0.229**	−0.199**	−0.217**	−0.222**	0.263**	−0.199**	−0.208**	−0.242**	−0.199**
		Significance		0.000	0.000	0.000	0.000	0.000	0.000	0.000	0.000	0.000	0.000
		N	9489	7885	7883	7877	7878	7871	9454	9438	9429	9432	9432
Gat to work or school	Pleasure/Enjoyment	Correlation	0.303**	1	−0.220**	−0.165**	−0.182**	−0.249**	0.456**	−0.118**	−0.109**	−0.136**	−0.132**
		Significance	0.000		0.000	0.000	0.000	0.000	0.000	0.000	0.000	0.000	0.000
		N	7885	8493	8486	8474	8471	8470	8465	8452	8441	8444	8446
	Frustration/Anger	Correlation	−0.229**	−0.220**	1	0.384**	0.419**	0.399**	−0.128**	0.431**	0.243**	0.289**	0.253**
		Significance	0.000	0.000		0.000	0.000	0.000	0.000	0.000	0.000	0.000	0.000
		N	7883	8486	8493	8474	8472	8471	8464	8453	8442	8445	8447
	Worry/Fear	Correlation	−0.199**	−0.165**	0.384**	1	0.524**	0.394**	−0.136**	0.249**	0.504**	0.374**	0.317**
		Significance	0.000	0.000	0.000		0.000	0.000	0.000	0.000	0.000	0.000	0.000
		N	7877	8474	8474	8481	8469	8463	8453	8442	8438	8437	8439
	Sadnes/Sorrow	Correlation	−0.217**	−0.182**	0.419**	0.524**	1	0.447**	−0.195**	0.290**	0.418**	0.587**	0.410**
		Significance	0.000	0.000	0.000	0.000		0.000	0.000	0.000	0.000	0.000	0.000
		N	7878	8471	8472	8469	8478	8462	8451	8440	8434	8438	8439
	Disgust	Correlation	−0.222**	−0.249**	0.399**	0.394**	0.447**	1	−0.159**	0.253**	0.263**	0.319**	0.478**
		Significance	0.000	0.000	0.000	0.000	0.000		0.000	0.000	0.000	0.000	0.000
		N	7871	8470	8471	8463	8462	8477	8449	8438	8430	8434	8442
Aat home	Pleasure/Enjoyment	Correlation	0.263**	0.456**	−0.128**	−0.136**	−0.195**	−0.159**	1	−0.255**	−0.245**	−0.285**	−0.302**
		Significance	0.000	0.000	0.000	0.000	0.000	0.000		0.000	0.000	0.000	0.000
		N	9454	8465	8464	8453	8451	8449	10,215	10,195	10,179	10,183	10,182
	Frustration/Anger	Correlation	−0.199**	−0.118**	0.431**	0.249**	0.290**	0.253**	−0.255**	1	0.414**	0.467**	0.419**

(continued)

Table 17.3 (continued)

				Go to work or school					Stay at home				
			Degree of satisfaction with life	Pleasure/ enjoyment	Frustration/ Anger	Worry/ Fear	Sadness/ Sorrow	Disgust	Pleasure/ Enjoyment	Frustration/ Anger	Worry/Fear	Sadness/Sorrow	Disgust
		Significance	0.000	0.000	0.000	0.000	0.000	0.000	0.000		0.000	0.000	0.000
		N	9438	8452	8453	8442	8440	8438	10,195	10,202	10,175	10,180	10,177
	Worry/Fear	Correlation	−0.208**	−0.109**	0.243**	0.504**	0.418**	0.263**	−0.245**	0.414**	1	0.585**	0.487**
		Significance	0.000	0.000	0.000	0.000	0.000	0.000	0.000	0.000		0.000	0.000
		N	9429	8441	8442	8438	8434	8430	10,179	10,175	10,189	10,176	10,170
	Sadness/Sorrow	Correlation	−0.242**	−0.136**	0.289**	0.374**	0.587**	0.319**	−0.285**	0.467**	0.585**	1	0.586**
		Significance	0.000	0.000	0.000	0.000	0.000	0.000	0.000	0.000	0.000		0.000
		N	9432	8444	8445	8437	8438	8434	10,183	10,180	10,176	10,194	10,177
	Disgust	Correlation	−0.199**	−0.132**	0.253**	0.317**	0.410**	0.478**	−0.302**	0.419**	0.487**	0.586**	1
		Significance	0.000	0.000	0.000	0.000	0.000	0.000	0.000	0.000	0.000	0.000	
		N	9432	8446	8447	8439	8439	8442	10,182	10,177	10,170	10,177	10,191

**In significant correlation at the level of 0.01 (two sides)

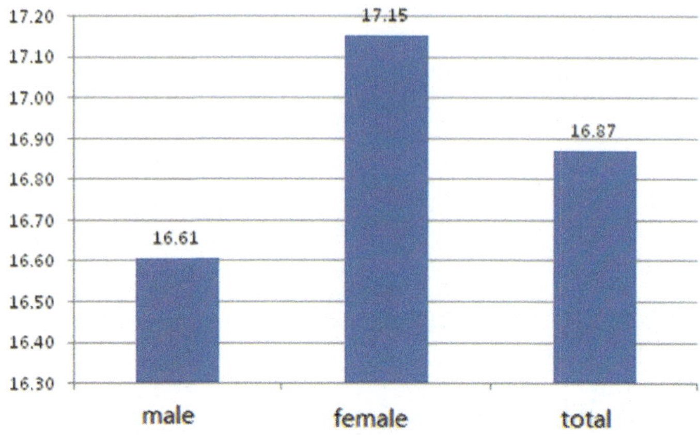

Fig. 17.6 Score for degree of satisfaction with life for male and female groups

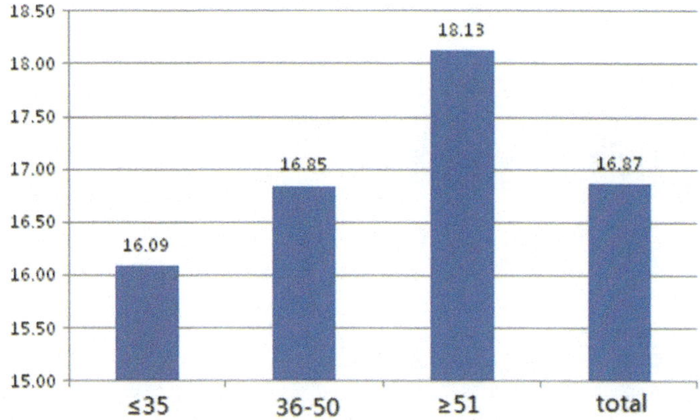

Fig. 17.7 Score for degree of satisfaction with life for people of different age groups

a township are the most satisfied with life, followed by those living in the urban-township fringe zone. The figure for residents living downtown, in urban townships, and rural–urban fringe zone are lower than the average level, among which those living in the rural–urban fringe zone and downtown ranked the least satisfied.

17.3 Residents' Sense of Happiness and Relevant Factors

To understand the relevant factors that have an impact on respondents' sense of happiness, this study investigated various variables such as a sense of security, the degree of satisfaction with work, social security, individual situations, family life and medical treatment, individual income, family consumption, family income, changes

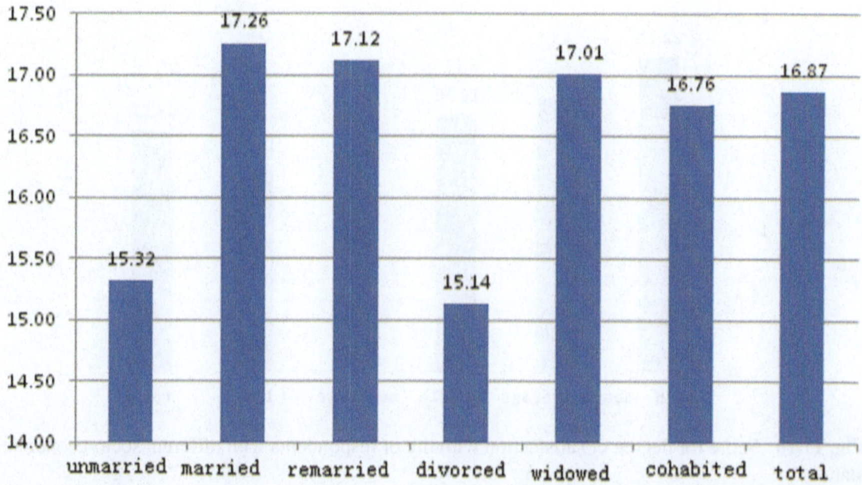

Fig. 17.8 Score for degree of satisfaction with life for different marital status

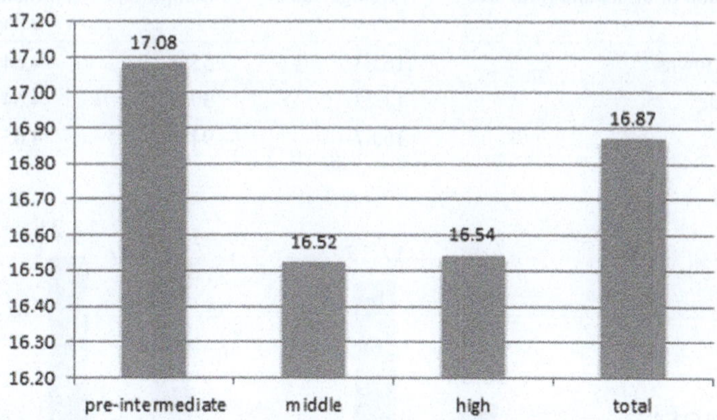

Fig. 17.9 Scores for satisfaction with life of respondents with different education levels

in the past, expectations of the future, social fairness, social trust, social status and social support, among other factors. We investigated the correlations between these factors and the degree of satisfaction with life, the results of which are shown in Table 17.5.

Residents' sense of security refers to the safety of individual and family property, personal safety, transportation safety, medical safety, food safety, labor safety, privacy safety of individual information and the safety of the ecological environment. We analyzed respondents' ratings of these aspects. The degree of satisfaction with work is based on a sum of ratings of work environment, easiness, safety, income, and welfare and benefits, as well as relationships with leaders and colleagues, opportunities for promotion and exertion of personal ability. The degree of satisfaction

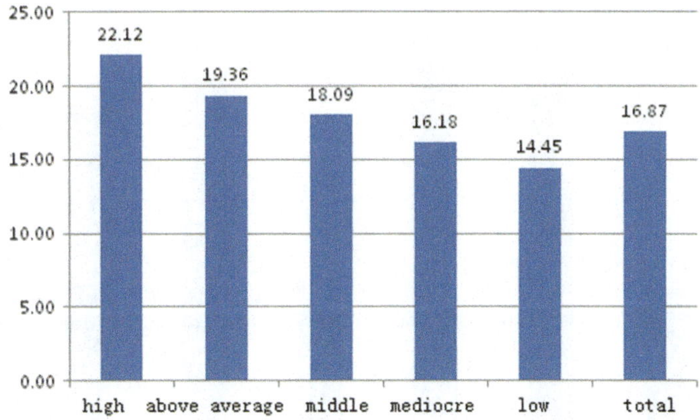

Fig. 17.10 Score for degree of satisfaction with life of respondents with different socio-economic status

Table 17.4 Comparison of degree of satisfaction with life between urban and rural residents

Classification of urban and rural area marker	Average value	Sample size	Standard deviation
Cities and towns	16.63	5568	4.64
Countryside	17.22	3921	4.64
In total	16.87	9489	4.65

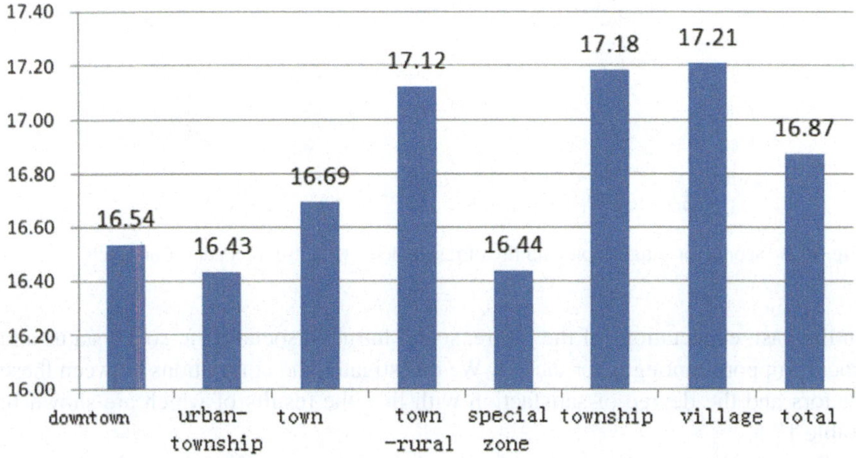

Fig. 17.11 Score for satisfaction with life of residents living in different areas

Table 17.5 Correlation analysis between degree of satisfaction with life and various life-specific aspects

		Satisfaction with life	Security	Satisfaction with work	Satisfaction with social security	Satisfaction with individual situation	Satisfaction with family life	Satisfaction with medical treatment	Satisfaction with environment
Satisfaction with life	Relevance	1	0.239**	0.277**	0.282**	0.360**	0.435**	0.242**	0.248**
	Significance		0.000	0.000	0.000	0.000	0.000	0.000	0.000
	N	9449	8187	2628	8449	9373	9416	7648	9448
Security	Relevance	0.239**	1	0.077**	0.280**	0.107**	0.090**	0.252**	0.319**
	Significance	0.000		0.000	0.000	0.000	0.000	0.000	0.000
	N	8187	8676	2570	7827	8609	8643	7026	8675
Satisfaction with work	Relevance	0.277**	0.077**	1	0.333**	0.494**	0.489**	0.327**	0.260**
	Significance	0.000	0.000		0.000	0.000	0.000	0.000	0.000
	N	2628	2570	2774	2532	2753	2768	2204	2774
Satisfaction with social security	Relevance	0.282**	0.280**	0.333**	1	0.269**	0.247**	0.346**	0.298**
	Significance	0.000	0.000	0.000		0.000	0.000	0.000	0.000
	N	8449	7827	2532	9054	8973	9018	7368	9053
Satisfaction with individual situation	Relevance	0.360**	0.107**	0.494**	0.269**	1	0.619**	0.275**	0.273**
	Significance	0.000	0.000	0.000	0.000		0.000	0.000	0.000
	N	9373	8609	2753	8973	10,166	10,142	8208	10,165
Satisfaction with family life	Relevance	0.435**	0.090**	0.489**	0.247**	0.619**	1	0.261**	0.249**
	Significance	0.000	0.000	0.000	0.000	0.000		0.000	0.000
	N	9416	8643	2768	9018	10,142	10,217	8244	10,216
Satisfaction with medical treatment	Relevance	0.242**	0.252**	0.327**	0.346**	0.275**	0.261**	1	0.298**

(continued)

Table 17.5 (continued)

		Satisfaction with life	Security	Satisfaction with work	Satisfaction with social security	Satisfaction with individual situation	Satisfaction with family life	Satisfaction with medical treatment	Satisfaction with environment
	Significance	0.000	0.000	0.000	0.000	0.000	0.000		0.000
	N	7648	7026	2204	7368	8208	8244	8276	8276
Satisfaction with environment	Relevance	0.248**	0.319**	0.260**	0.298**	0.273**	0.249**	0.298**	1
	Significance	0.000	0.000	0.000	0.000	0.000	0.000	0.000	
	N	9448	8675	2774	9053	10,165	10,216	8276	10,259

**In significant correlation at the level of 0.01 (both sides)

with social security is based on satisfaction with pensions and guaranteed medical care. The degree of satisfaction with one's individual situation is based on satisfaction with individual education level, health situation, and social life. The degree of satisfaction with family life is based on ratings of family relationships, the economic situation of the family, and the degree of satisfaction with leisure and entertainment. The degree of satisfaction with the environment is based on ratings of noise, air and water pollution of the community, and the severity of the health environment in daily life, which is negatively correlated with the total score. The degree of satisfaction with medical treatment is based on ratings of the attitudes of medical staff, the abilities and ethics of physicians, the environment and facilities of hospitals and the degree of satisfaction with the medical treatment itself. To evaluate changes from the past, we asked the question: "Compared with five years ago, what changes have occurred in respect to your living standards?" To study expectations for the future, we asked: "What changes will occur to your life in the coming five years?" We evaluated the perception of "social fairness" by adding up the ratings of fairness for the college entrance examination system, compulsory education, political rights enjoyed by citizens in practice, the administration of justice and law enforcement, public medical care, opportunities for work and employment, allocation of property and income, pensions, differences in benefits among different industries and regions, the selection of party and government cadres, and the rights and benefits in urban and rural areas. The social trust scale is adopted for social trust. Socio-economic status is divided into five grades, and is based on respondents' self-identified status. Social support is based on ratings for party and government support, different levels of support from worker, youth and women organizations, and support from neighborhood and/or village committees, work units, religious organizations, the private network of family members, families, patriarchal clans, friends, fellows, and business partners, as well as charity organizations, news media, and social support from netizens. Other variables include persȯnal income, family consumption and family income.

Results of this study show that the degree of satisfaction with life is significantly and positively correlated to a sense of security, with a correlation coefficient of 0.241. Among all specific life-related aspects, the correlation between the degree of life satisfaction and the degree of satisfaction with family life and one's individual situation are the most correlated, with correlation coefficients of 0.408 and 0.341 respectively. The correlation coefficients for satisfaction with work, social security, the environment and medical treatment are 0.268, 0.280, 0.241 and 0.237 respectively.

Social factors including social fairness, social trust and social support are significantly correlated with the degree of satisfaction with life, with the correlation coefficients of 0.337, 0.260 and 0.42 respectively, with social support being the least correlated. Among household factors such as personal income, family consumption, family income, social status and other factors, only family consumption is not significantly correlated with the degree of satisfaction with life. Personal income and family income have a low correlation, whereas social status has a significant negative correlation with the degree of satisfaction with life, with a correlation coefficient of

0.341. In other words, respondents who consider themselves to have a higher social economic status are less satisfied with life. Changes from the past and expectations for the future are also significantly correlated with the degree of satisfaction with life, with correlation coefficients of 0.328 and 0.228 respectively (Table 17.6).

17.4 Conclusion and Discussion

In this study—using a national random sample—the average score for overall degree of satisfaction with life was 16.87, or at a middle level. The score of the same national sample is near to the normal distribution, which indicates that the scale for the degree of satisfaction with life is positive overall.

Using five basic moods—"pleasure/enjoyment," "frustration/anger," "worry/fear," "disgust" and "sadness/sorrow"—to measure the degree of happiness, we found that positive moods occur more often than negative ones both at work (including study) and at home, though the positive moods are more frequently felt in home environments.

A cross-analysis of the basic moods—i.e. cognitive components, or the degree of satisfaction with life and emotional components—contributing to the sense of happiness show that no matter whether at work (or school) or at home, respondents with higher degrees of satisfaction with life tend to have more positive moods such as pleasure and enjoyment.

The degree of satisfaction with life between different groups can be summarized as follows: females are more satisfied with life than males; young adults are less satisfied with life than middle-aged adults, who are in turn less satisfied than older people; those who are unmarried and divorced are the least satisfied; those who are less educated have a higher degree of satisfaction with life; those who consider themselves to have higher socio-economic status are less satisfied with life; urban residents are less satisfied with life compared to rural residents; and urban residents living in the urban–rural fringe area are the least satisfied with life.

Correlation analysis of the degree of satisfaction with life also shows that the degree of satisfaction with life is significantly positively correlated with a sense of security. For specific aspects of life, a sense of satisfaction with family life and individual situations are the most correlated with the degree of overall satisfaction with life. The sense of satisfaction with life is also significantly correlated with a sense of satisfaction with work, social security, the environment and medical treatment. Social factors—such as social fairness, social trust and social support—all have significant correlations with the sense of satisfaction with life, among which social support is the least correlated. There is no significant correlation between family consumption and degree of satisfaction with life. Personal income and family income are less correlated with satisfaction with life, while self-identified socio-economic status is significantly negatively correlated with the sense of satisfaction with life. The degree of satisfaction with life increases with both appraisal of changes from the past and expectations for the future.

Table 17.6 Correlation analysis between degree of satisfaction with life and social factors

		Satisfaction with life	Personal Income	Family consumption	Family income	Changes from the past	Expectation for the future	Social fairness	Social trust	Social status	Social support
Satisfaction with life	Relevance	1	0.036**	−0.018	0.058**	0.337**	0.243**	0.337**	0.264**	−0.346**	0.048**
	Significance		0.001	0.074	0.000	0.000	0.000	0.000	0.000	0.000	0.000
	N	9449	9078	9438	8831	9396	8187	5773	8721	9313	9380
Personal income	Relevance	0.036**	1	−0.005	0.905**	0.018	0.008	−0.011	−0.010	−0.070**	−0.013
	Significance	0.001		0.634	0.000	0.076	0.437	0.422	0.348	0.000	0.205
	N	9078	9834	9823	9308	9776	8420	5776	8915	9674	9761
Family consumption	Relevance	−0.018	−0.005	1	0.009	−0.037**	0.005	−0.010	−0.021*	0.005	−0.015
	Significance	0.074	0.634		0.370	0.000	0.648	0.459	0.042	0.616	0.136
	N	9438	9823	10,247	9539	10,185	8748	5943	9254	10,075	10,171
Family income	Relevance	0.058**	0.905**	0.009	1	0.041**	0.027*	−0.019	−0.018	−0.127**	−0.014
	Significance	0.000	0.000	0.370		0.000	0.013	0.156	0.088	0.000	0.182
	N	8831	9308	9539	9543	9502	8237	5660	8692	9413	9470
Changes in the past	Relevance	0.337**	0.018	−0.037**	0.041**	1	0.441**	0.213**	0.129**	−0.269**	0.067**
	Significance	0.000	0.076	0.000	0.000		0.000	0.000	0.000	0.000	0.000
	N	9396	9776	10,185	9502	10,197	8720	5924	9218	10,030	10,122
Expectation of future	Relevance	0.243**	0.008	0.005	0.027*	0.441**	1	0.183**	0.116**	−0.237**	0.052**
	Significance	0.000	0.437	0.648	0.013	0.000		0.000	0.000	0.000	0.000
	N	8187	8420	8748	8237	8720	8755	5393	8042	8644	8696
Social fairness	Relevance	0.337**	−0.011	−0.010	−0.019	0.213**	0.183**	1	0.324**	−0.118**	0.034**
	Significance	0.000	0.422	0.459	0.156	0.000	0.000		0.000	0.000	0.008

(continued)

Table 17.6 (continued)

		Satisfaction with life	Personal Income	Family consumption	Family income	Changes from the past	Expectation for the future	Social fairness	Social trust	Social status	Social support
	N	5773	5776	5943	5660	5924	5393	5949	5725	5890	5925
Social fairness	Relevance	0.264**	−0.010	−0.021*	−0.018	0.129**	0.116**	0.324**	1	−0.087**	0.051**
	Significance	0.000	0.348	0.042	0.088	0.000	0.000	0.000		0.000	0.000
	N	8721	8915	9254	8692	9218	8042	5725	9265	9142	9197
Social Status	Relevance	−0.346**	−0.070**	0.005	−0.127**	−0.269**	−0.237**	−0.118**	−0.087**	1	−0.035**
	Significance	0.000	0.000	0.616	0.000	0.000	0.000	0.000	0.000		0.000
	N	9313	9674	10,075	9413	10,030	8644	5890	9142	10,086	10,011
Social support	Relevance	0.048**	−0.013	−0.015	−0.014	0.067**	0.052**	0.034**	0.051**	−0.035**	1
	Significance	0.000	0.205	0.136	0.182	0.000	0.000	0.008	0.000	0.000	
	N	9380	9761	10,171	9470	10,122	8696	5925	9197	10,011	10,184

** Significant correlation at the level of 0.01 (both sides)
* Significant correlation at the level of 0.05 (both sides)

The above findings provide a relatively sound basis for understanding Chinese residents' sense of happiness, which features a lower degree of satisfaction with life with respect to cognitive aspects, even as positive emotions are prominent in daily life. To a certain extent, this is due to the fact that Chinese residents with high expectations are not satisfied with reality—this should remind the government to consider residents' attitudes when making social policies in order to continuously satisfy residents' life necessities. The differences in the degree of satisfaction with life between different groups is very similar to those found in many previous studies, and the differences thereof are basically expected. The results of relevant factors that have an impact on the degree of satisfaction with life show that it is necessary to pay attention to any impact on the sense of satisfaction with family life and the individual life. Self-identified social economic status, social fairness and social trust have more impact on the degree of happiness when compared with income, and these should be the focus of social governance for the future. Besides providing concrete, positive life changes, it is also necessary for governmental work to give residents confidence in social development and improvement.

References

Eysenck, M.W. 2000. *Psychology*, trans. Yan Gonggu. Shanghai: East China Normal University Press.

Robinson, J.P., P.R. Shaver, and L.S. Wrightsman. 1997. Overview of Character and Social-psychology Measurement" (Volume I) , (Taiwan) Yuan-Liou Publishing Co., Ltd., Page 92–103.

Turner, Jonathan. 2009. *Human Emotion: Theory of Sociology*, trans. Sun Juncai and Wen Jun. Beijing: Oriental Press.

Turner, Jonathan, and Jan E. Stets. 2007. *Sociology of Emotions*, trans. Sun Juncai and Wen Jun. Shanghai: Shanghai People's Publishing House.

Veenhoven, R. 1996. Developments in Satisfaction Research. *Social Indicators Research* 37: 1–46.

Wang, Junxiu. 2011. *Focus on the Honor and Happiness of the People, Promotion of Social Fairness and Harmony—"General Report of Study on Chinese Social Psychology in 2010 and 2011"*. "Report of Study on Chinese Social Psychology in 2011", compiled by Wang Junxiu and Yang Yiyin. Beijing: Social Science Documentation Publishing House.

Chapter 18
Towards a Happier Society in Russia

P. M. Kozyreva, A. E. Nizamova, and A. I. Smirnov

Russia is currently undergoing a process of deep and rapid modernization in multiple aspects, including economic, political, social, and spiritual life. These changes contribute to a major shift towards a more advanced, economically developed, and fair society. Such a society would enable the citizens to use their innovative potential in an efficient way, offer them more opportunities for development, and cater to their material and spiritual needs. As the challenges of the transformation period fade away, the socio-economic situation in the country is getting better; there are fewer people who struggle to survive and more who care about the quality of life and a higher level of well-being for their households. Contemporary social engineering is more concerned about making life safer and happier.

Russians ceaselessly dream of happiness—both for themselves and for their friends and relatives. Every time they see new transformation coming, they try to bridge a connection to their personal dream of happiness and well-being related to the present moment or at least the foreseeable future. This dream, the quest for happiness, is so wide-spread in Russia that it makes one wonder: how happy are Russians? What do their feelings of happiness depend on? Does happiness have an impact on their present life and their plans for the future?

---

[1] Averintsev et al. (1989, p. 640).

[2] Ozhegov (1990, p. 782).

The original version of this chapter was revised: Affiliations have been updated in this chapter. The correction to this book can be found at https://doi.org/10.1007/978-981-16-2505-3_19

P. M. Kozyreva (✉) · A. E. Nizamova
HSE University, Moscow, Russia

P. M. Kozyreva · A. E. Nizamova · A. I. Smirnov
Institute of Sociology of FCTAS RAS, Moscow, Russia

P. Li and M. K. Gorshkov (eds.), *Life Expectations of the People*,
Research Series on the Chinese Dream and China's Development Path,
https://doi.org/10.1007/978-981-16-2505-3_18

Happiness is a very comprehensive and vague term that is often only understood intuitively, i.e. it's a multidimensional, poly-semantic concept. Broadly speaking, it's a feeling of ultimate satisfaction with one's living conditions, a feeling of having a meaningful life when one has succeeded in fulfilling their mission as a human.[1] It's a feeling of utmost satisfaction,[2] a positive emotional state stimulated by one's positive evaluation of their own destiny.[3] Every individual has their own distinct understanding of what happiness is. And yet, though the color of happiness has many shades for different people, most of them, according to M. Argyle, perceive it either as a feeling of satisfaction with their own life or as a state of joy or other positive emotions.[4]

The feeling of well-being is one of the fundamental components of happiness. Well-being can be measured through an evaluation of one's current level of life plus an evaluation of one's current living standards against past values. Well-being is about the dynamics of various human needs and to what extent they are satisfied in different spheres of life. When talking about what "the good life" means, people usually have several things in mind, including financial well-being, an interesting and well-paid job, good family relations, health, quality education, enough free time and ample opportunities for interpersonal communication, self-actualization, self-affirmation, and self-respect. T. Rath and J. Harter, the leaders of a large research project on well-being conducted by Gallup across more than 150 countries, have concluded that well-being consists of enjoying one's day-to-day life, having good relations with other people, enjoying a stable financial situation, being in good health, and feeling proud of one's contribution to society.[5] The desire for a better life is one of the basic motivators for people no matter at what stage in the life they are. The perception of well-being depends on two factors: satisfaction of one's daily needs and one's personal fulfilment.

Despite all the inconsistencies and incoherence of Russia's socio-economic and socio-political development, along with all the difficulties and ambiguities of a transitional society, Russians in the twenty-first century seem to be less troubled and more confident about building their own lives and developing their own strategies due to increased living standards across the country. Many individuals and households have entered a new level of well-being and are now acquiring new, more advanced models of consumption. Positive social changes have extended more opportunities for people and provided them with more adaptational resources, allowing for more dynamic mechanisms of social accommodation, increased self-confidence, and better ability to withstand unfavorable trends.

According to a 2012 survey conducted by the RAS (Russian Academy of Sciences) Institute of Sociology, only 6.3% of respondents said their families had benefited from the radical economic and democratic changes of the 1990s, while 52.9% claimed they had suffered losses. Yet when speaking of the reforms in the early 2000s, 36.7% of respondents said they had benefited, while only 12% were not happy with the

[3] Vorkachyov (2001, pp. 47–58).

[4] Argyle (1987, pp. 9–10).

[5] Rath (2010, p. 146).

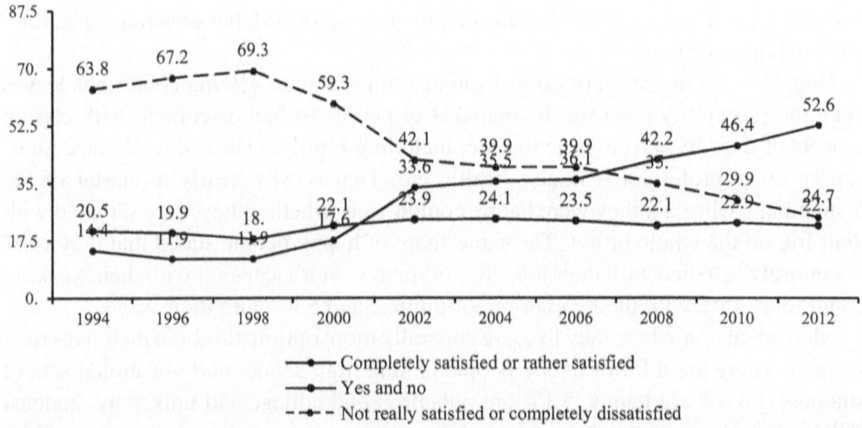

Fig. 18.1 The extent to which Russians are satisfied with life on the whole (%)

results. The share of optimistically inclined people has risen; respondents mention positive changes that have been happening in the country in general and in the living standards of the population in particular. This shows that Russians are now more upbeat about their social well-being. Even the 2008–2009 financial crisis didn't really affect public sentiment. According to the Russian Longitudinal Monitoring Survey of the Higher School of Economics (RLMS-HSE),[6] the share of people who are 'completely satisfied' or 'rather satisfied' with their life on the whole grew nearly 4.5 times between 1998 and 2012—from 11.9 to 52.6%—while the share of those more or less dissatisfied shrunk by nearly three times—from 69.3 to 24.7% (Fig. 18.1). These trends are the same across all socio-professional groups and are equally true for both rural and urban populations.

When evaluating one's personal well-being in light of specific circumstances and reflecting on whether one has had a fulfilled, successful life, nearly half of the respondents, 44.5%, said they were happy or fairly happy in 2012. 31.6% said they were rather happy than unhappy, and only 16.2% of Russians referred to themselves as not very happy or very unhappy. The data by WCIOM—The Russian Public Opinion Research Centre—seems even more optimistic: apparently over 75% of Russians felt happy in 2012–2014. 45% of the WCIOM respondents also believed they were surrounded by happy and joyful people who were living a fulfilled life. In 2014, the happiness index in Russia hit 64 (the index reflects the difference between all positive ('Certainly yes,' 'Rather yes') and all negative ('Rather not,' 'Certainly

[6] The Russian Longitudinal Monitoring Survey of the Higher School of Economics (RLMS-HSE) is run jointly by the National Research University 'Higher School of Economics' in Moscow and the Demoscope Centre together with the Carolina Population Center at the University of North Carolina at Chapel Hill and the Institute of Sociology by the Russian Academy of Sciences (More about the project at: http://www.hse.ru/org/hse/rlms, http://www.cpc.unc.edu/projects/rlms).

not') answers to the question: "Things happen, good or bad, but generally speaking, are you happy or not?").[7]

Happiness as the sense of utmost satisfaction with one's living conditions leaves open the possibility even for the happiest of people to feel discontent with certain aspects of their lives from time to time, including family relations, workplace interaction, other professional issues, health, etc. That is why nearly a quarter of the respondents who said they were happy couldn't say whether they were satisfied with their life on the whole or not. The same share of happy people stated that they were not entirely satisfied with their job. 28% of them weren't satisfied with their working conditions, 45% with their career opportunities, and 53% with their wages.

Men, no matter where they live, are generally more optimistic about their lives than women. There are a lot of happy people among high school and vocational school students (68.6% are happy, 5.1% are unhappy) and college and university students (67.4 and 4.1% respectively), and much fewer among unemployed pensioners (32.1 and 25.9% respectively), the jobless (30.4 and 26.1%), and the handicapped (24.4 and 38.1% respectively).

The feeling of happiness, which is basically a general evaluation of one's life and whether it is successful or not, is equally common for both urban and rural dwellers, though there a slightly more 'happy' people among the former. For most of them, happiness is strongly related to material well-being. The Laboratory for Comparative Social Studies, located at the Saint Petersburg campus of Higher School of Economics, has recently conducted a survey on happiness.[8] The survey was led by R. Inglehart, a prominent American sociologist and specialist in political science, who asserts that many Russians still haven't got over the deep crisis of the 1990s. That's why, argues Inglehart, for them there's still a strong association between happiness, financial well-being and adequate living standards. This is especially true for older generations of Russians, who are still struggling to accept the ongoing changes. Young people, however, grew up during the post-Soviet period and do not really remember the dramatic, even traumatic transformations of the 1990s.[9]

What determines Russians' social well-being and perception of life, including their own personal situation, is financial status. According to the RLMS-HSE data, happy people are better at overcoming troubles and are less preoccupied with financial problems than unhappy people. This is evident from the fact that happy respondents are nearly 2.5 times less likely to worry about maintaining their present level of well-being (26.4% among happy individuals versus 60.7% among those who said they

[7] WCIOM: Indeks Schastya v Rossii dostig 25-letnego Maksimuma [WCIOM: Happiness Index in Russia Hits 25 Years Maximum]. http://itar-tass.com/obschestvo/1158256. Accessed 7 July 2014.

[8] Proceedings of the 3rd International Sociological Conference 'Carrying On Grushin's Work'. Moscow, February 28–March 1, 2013. Panel verbatim. Section 6: Common and Unique. What Is Similar and What Is Different in Terms of Social Climate in Post-socialist Countries? http://wciom.ru/fileadmin/nayka/gr2013/transcripts/Section6_General%20and_special_session.pdf. Accessed 7 July 2014.

[9] V Sisteme Tsennostey Na Pervom Meste Dlya Zhiteley Rossii Stoyat 'Tsennosti Vyzhivaniya' [For Russians, 'Survival Values' Are on Top of the Values System]. http://zpsy.ru/public/35155.htm. Accessed 7 July 2014.

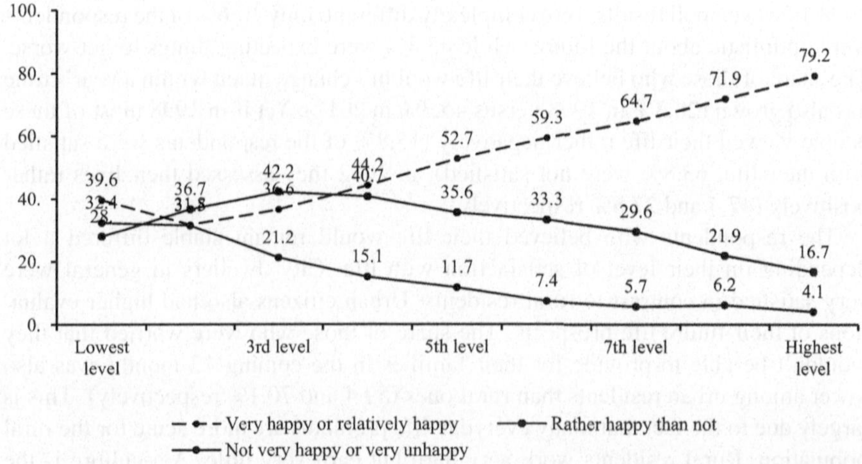

Fig. 18.2 How the feeling of happiness depends on one's self-positioning on the scale of financial well-being (%)

were not happy). The gap between those most satisfied and least satisfied with their financial well-being is even bigger between happy and unhappy people (42.8 and 10.6% respectively). Therefore, there are more unhappy than happy people among the poorest and most disadvantaged.

The share of those who identify as happy people rises together with the subjective evaluation of one's financial well-being. In other words, the better one perceives their life, the less probable it is that they will feel unhappy (Fig. 18.2). However, one should bear in mind that people tend to evaluate their own level of income and expenditures in comparison to that of family members, friends or other people. Therefore, people often underestimate or overestimate their financial status.

Our analysis shows that getting richer doesn't necessarily make people happier or more satisfied with their life. At the same time, over a third of the poorest respondents said they were happy. This can be due to low aspirations, an overall positive attitude to life, or the fact that they simply try not to get worried about things they can't change. Many of those who said they were happy don't envy others, expressing satisfaction with what they already have and don't want to have more. In other words, the main gap lies between hedonistic and eudemonic perceptions of life, i.e. different value systems. The way people evaluate their level of life determines their motivation in professional and everyday life.

Positive trends in the new century in terms of Russians' social well-being and social optimism are a result of general socio-economic stabilization, which is associated with higher living standards, less unemployment, broader professional opportunities, and more security. In other words, Russians can now fulfil the needs and desires that make their lives happier.

28.4% of the Russians surveyed in 2012 said they believed their life would get a little or much better within a year; only 9.7% expected their life to get worse. In

1998, however, poll results were completely different: only 10.6% of the respondents were optimistic about the future, while 43.4% were expecting things to get worse. The share of those who believe their life wouldn't change much within a year's time has also grown (28.3% in 1998 versus 45.3% in 2012). Yet if in 1998 most of these people viewed their life rather negatively (13.8% of the respondents were satisfied with their life, 63.8% were not satisfied), in 2012 they assessed their lives rather positively (47.4 and 27.8% respectively).

The respondents who believed their life would remain stable differed a lot depending on their level of satisfaction with life. City dwellers in general were very satisfied in contrast to rural residents. Urban citizens also had higher evaluations of their future life prospects. The share of those who were worried that they wouldn't be able to provide for their families in the coming 12 months was also lower among urban residents than rural ones (59.4 and 70.1% respectively). This is largely due to the fact that many everyday life problems are more acute for the rural population. Rural residents work very hard but earn very little. Agriculture is the sector with the lowest wages in Russia. In 2014, for example, the average salary in the countryside was only 14,000 rubles per month. People employed by medium- or large-scale agricultural enterprises earned a little more at 17,500 rubles per month, which is still slightly more than a half (52%) of the average salary in the countryside. Socio-economic equality is equally bad in both cities and rural areas. Income differentiation within the agricultural sector is so big that it is only surpassed by the banking sector. People employed in agriculture have fewer benefits than those who work in cities. They value social goods differently and, most importantly, people in the countryside simply have less access to various extra social benefits and services. The average household income per capita in urban areas is 1.8 higher than in rural areas. Pensions in rural areas are also lower, amounting, on average, to no more than 85% of that in urban areas. People in villages are also less educated, which puts them in a disadvantaged position in terms of social development.

The level of life and living conditions differ greatly between cities and villages. There's also significant variation between and within regions, creating a mosaic-like situation. Some regions are already moving towards a modernized society, others are still lagging behind, while a number of regions are even drifting towards social and cultural marginalization. In some regions, villages are getting bigger and the level of life there is getting higher, while in other regions, rural areas are degrading to the degree of total extinction.

As mentioned above, financial well-being is definitely important, but it is not the main reason behind the feeling of happiness for Russians. As living standards increase and poverty starts to disappear, people more often tend to feel happy not just because they are moderately well-off. Their understanding of happiness still very much depends on their yearning for freedom, which is one of the main values in Russia. A survey conducted by the RAS Institute of Sociology shows that two-thirds of Russians believe life is meaningless if there is no freedom. However, the Russian definition of freedom is very different from what Westerners are used to. Russians see freedom as an opportunity to exercise certain rights, while many Westerners strive to be independent.[10] What is also interesting in this regard is that, according to K.A. Abulkhanova, the Russian mentality is dominated by morality rather than political or legal awareness.[11]

Russians usually dream not just about having wealth, but also about living in a rational and fair society full of virtue, where incomes are determined by one's skill and qualifications, and everyone has equal opportunities for self-actualization. People are very much preoccupied with the lack of social justice (primarily with the nation's inability to manage its natural resources), huge socio-economic inequality, and unequal access to high-quality education and healthcare. For many people, happiness is associated with leading an interesting, active, and full life, as well as having an exciting and creative job, stable family and well-educated children.

Health is another highly important component of happiness. The share of happy people among healthy respondents was 82.2% in contrast to only 17.5% among those in bad health. Deteriorating health is exactly why many people feel less happy as they get older. Of course, the connection between health and happiness is bilateral: those who feel happy actually tend to have higher life expectancy. However, it's difficult to say which factor has the bigger influence on the other.

Happy people tend to be sick less often; they are more stable & resilient psychologically, have higher levels of self-command, are better at avoiding conflict situations, live longer and are more successful in life. Happiness is a good anti-depressant. Those who said they were 'very happy' were three times less likely to suffer from nervousness, irritation, or aggression than those who said they were 'very unhappy.' They were also 3.5–4.5 times less likely to experience anxiety, panic attacks, insomnia, and problems with memory or depression (Table 18.1). This is true for all the respondents, including the handicapped and the retired, who obviously have more health issues than others.

It is also well-known that positive people spread their optimism and good mood to others around them, while unhappy people create a negative socio-psychological environment that also affects others. In other words, both happiness and depression (or other negative psychological phenomena) can be passed from one person to another. The closer people are, the more likely they are to 'contract' others' moods and either improve or worsen their own emotional state.

Compared to cities, rural areas suffer from higher unemployment, worse living conditions and healthcare services, and lower social and cultural standards. This leads to shorter life expectancy; on average, people in the countryside live 2.5 years less than their compatriots in big cities. Even though it is widely believed that living in a village is healthy, rural dwellers start having health problems much earlier. On the other hand, they have lower demands, so their self-evaluation in terms of health is generally similar to that of urban dwellers. Health factors are much more important

[10] O Chyom Mechtayut Rossiyane: Ideal i Realnost. / Pod. red. M.K. Gorshkova, R. Krumma, N.E. Tikhonovoy. Moskva: Ves Mir. 2013. S. 324 [*What Russians Dream About: Ideals and Reality*, ed. M.K. Gorshkov, R. Krumm, and N.E. Tikhonova. Moscow: Ves Mir. 2013, p. 324].

[11] Abulkhanova (1997, pp. 7–37).

Table 18.1 Occurrence of various negative psychological issues by different categories of respondents among those who stated they were either 'very happy' or 'very unhappy' (%)

Psychological issues	All respondents		Respondents by category							
			Employed with an organization or plant		Employed elsewhere		All pensioners		Unemployed pensioners	
	Very happy	Very unhappy	Very happy	Very unhappy	Very happy	Very unhappy	Very happy	Very unhappy	Very happy	Very unhappy
Nervousness	20.9	67.3	21.0	57.9	16.2	66.7	22.7	63.2	25.9	66.2
Anxiety, regular panic attacks	14.9	60.7	12.8	45.6	13.1	41.7	22.9	61.5	26.6	64.0
Irritation, aggression	17.7	50.2	18.6	42.1	16.2	51.0	15.6	48.9	16.3	50.0
Insomnia	11.4	46.9	8.0	21.1	7.1	25.0	26.6	55.7	32.6	59.6
Problems with memory	15.9	54.5	11.6	31.6	13.1	33.8	36.9	68.4	45.0	73.5
Depression	12.0	53.8	12.4	45.6	10.1	52.0	11.5	55.2	12.8	56.6

for those living in villages; good health makes them much happier, while having health problems makes them much more unhappy than the urban population.

Another problem that affects one's physical and psychological well-being and intensifies with age, especially among the rural population, is the lack of friends or loneliness. Unsociable people obviously have fewer reasons to feel happy, especially in modern society. The situation is particularly bad in the countryside as young and middle-aged people more often leave the countryside for jobs in cities, sometimes forever. Loneliness, referring to virtually no communication and no opportunities for self-actualization, is very common for pensioners, widows/widowers, or just old people who have lost all their friends and relatives. Most of these people have a very stable and very limited number of contacts, and the situation barely changes as years go by. Losing touch with other people can be very frustrating, and can also lead to apathy, passiveness, anxiety, hesitation, and feelings of insecurity. Lonely people become outsiders, both internally and externally. Instead of being part of society, they become mere observers.

The table shows the correlations between happiness and a number of social well-being factors in Russia, providing more details about the trends and interdependencies mentioned above (Table 18.2).

Family life can be very different, so even though many people are happily married, they don't contribute to a higher number of happy people on the whole. The older they get, the fewer couples stay happy. According to Table 18.3, the share of happy people among those currently married and never married is more or less the same. Moreover, women who have been married more than once tend to get less happy about their life. Unmarried, co-habitating couples feel even less comfortable. This is particularly true for women who live together with their partners but don't consider themselves to be married. Those separated, widowed or divorced are even less happy. They lack support from a partner, and they are more likely to feel lonely or experience other negative psychological states. Speaking of gender differences, one can notice that men who are officially married but don't live with their families are much happier than women in the same position.

It is also interesting that respondents with children are in general less happy than those without any children (Table 18.4). Men and women who have children evaluate happiness differently. On the whole, fathers tend to be happier than mothers. People who still have underage children are happier than those whose children have already grown up and left their parents' home. The more children, the happier parents feel.

Further analysis shows that childless women are the least happy compared with those currently on maternity leave (62.6% of whom are happy while only 5.1% unhappy), those who are on leave to care for a child of less than 3 years old and have the right to come back to the same job (74.8 and 5.2% respectively), and housewives caring for their underage children or other family members (57.6 and 11.9%).

Among the positive recent social trends that are contributing to a happier life are weakening hostility, growing tolerance, and improved interpersonal trust. Russians have come to understand the importance of social consolidation and have started to better understand each other. People increasingly view truthfulness as better than lies, compromise and cooperation as better than conflict, and trust as key to mutual

Table 18.2 Level of correlation between happiness and certain social factors depending on the respondents' place of residence (Kendall τ**)

Factors	Average	Respondents by place of residence			
		Regional centers	Other cities	Small towns	Villages
Feeling satisfied with one's life on the whole	0.442	0.419	0.472	0.377	0.471
Feeling satisfied with one's work on the whole	0.192	0.179	0.194	0.238	0.208
Feeling satisfied with one's working conditions	0.180	0.167	0.192	0.312	0.173
Feeling satisfied with one's level of remuneration	0.163	0.146	0.199	0.141	0.162
Feeling satisfied with one's career opportunities	0.157	0.142	0.170	0.138	0.178
Feeling satisfied with one's financial status	0.224	0.227	0.244	0.088	0.244
Feeling sure that one would be able to find another job if necessary	0.141	0.139	0.189	0.080	0.192
One's opinion of how their financial status would change in the coming 12 month	0.153	0.135	0.150	0.125	0.150
One's opinion of how their life would change in the coming 12 month	0.183	0.175	0.191	0.146	0.190
Evaluations of one's health	0.279	0.277	0.270	0.237	0.312

**Correlation significance 0.05 (2-tailed)

understanding. These are the conclusions that can be made when analyzing responses to the question: "According to you, are most people trustworthy?" The responses demonstrate the level of general trust as opposed to personal trust (i.e. trust towards particular individuals such as friends, acquaintances, neighbors, etc., or groups of people).

A comparison of monitoring data from 2006 and 2012 shows that the share of those who believe one should always be cautious with other people has decreased from 56 to 46%, while the share of those who say they can only decide whether to trust an individual depending on their personal qualities or other important circumstances has increased from 26.8 to 37% (Table 18.5). These changes show that Russians are

Table 18.3 Correlation between happiness and marital status (%)

Marital status	Total		By gender			
			Men		Women	
	Happy	Unhappy	Happy	Unhappy	Happy	Unhappy
Never married	50.7	13.1	49.8	13.2	51.4	13.0
Officially married for the first time	50.1	10.7	50.4	10.2	49.7	11.1
Officially married for the second (third. etc.) time	48.6	11.9	50.4	10.0	46.9	13.7
Divorced	30.7	26.7	31.3	27.8	30.5	26.1
Widowed	27.6	30.6	25.9	31.9	27.9	30.5
Officially married but living separately from the partner	33.7	24.3	41.3	21.7	27.9	26.0
Co-habitating partners that are not officially married but consider themselves husband and wife	46.4	15.3	47.7	14.6	45.1	16.0
Co-habitating partners that are not officially married and do not consider themselves husband and wife	40.1	22.3	45.1	22.6	36.7	22.2

Table 18.4 Correlation between happiness and having children (%)

			Men		Women	
	Happy	Unhappy	Happy	Unhappy	Happy	Unhappy
No children	51.6	12.0	50.8	14.0	52.2	14.0
Have children	42.0	17.0	45.9	13.5	39.6	19.2
By number of children						
1 child	41.9	17.7	47.8	13.5	38.5	20.0
2 children	42.6	15.9	45.6	12.9	40.7	17.9
3 children	40.4	18.1	41.2	16.0	39.9	18.5
4 children or more	40.9	9.9	43.1	12.0	39.6	22.7
By number of underage children						
1 child	49.6	11.7	52.4	9.3	47.5	13.5
2 children	55.9	9.3	57.5	8.1	54.6	10.4
3 children or more	56.6	9.9	54.3	8.6	58.4	11.0

becoming more rational when it comes to interpersonal relations. In other words, their behavior is more sensible and based on their experience. This might be due to the fact that "there's always more about a person than we can actually learn or say about them."[12] That is why building a relationship based on trust is always risky. The risk can be bigger or smaller, but it is basically unavoidable.

[12] Belyanin and Zinchenko (2010, p. 14).

Table 18.5 Responses to the question: "According to you, are most of the people trustworthy?" based on the respondents' place of residence (%)

	Average		Respondents by place of residence							
			Regional centers		Other cities		Small towns		Villages	
	2006	2012	2006	2012	2006	2012	2006	2012	2006	2012
Most people are trustworthy	15.3	15.7	14.8	12.5	13.7	14.9	12.5	17.7	18.3	21.1
One should always be cautious with people	56.0	46.0	57.6	45.9	58.3	48.7	51.9	52.8	52.3	42.0
Depends on the person and situation	26.8	37.0	26.8	40.9	26.8	35.1	33.3	26.7	25.5	35.0
No answer	1.9	1.3	0.8	0.7	1.2	1.3	2.3	2.8	3.9	1.9

Positive dynamics in terms of general trust can be seen across different social groups, however the biggest changes occurred among the youngest respondents (the under-25 age cohort). Most of the respondents were high school or vocational school students. In 2012, 28.6% of young people said that most people are trustworthy, while 31.7% reported the opposite opinion. Retirees tend to trust others more, whether they are still working or not. Entrepreneurs and the unemployed are generally more suspicious than others. This is likely because both of these two specific groups are very different from the rest of the society.

Even though there have been no dramatic changes, what is happening is still highly important in terms of social consolidation in Russia. More trust and cooperation and more intertwined social networks lead to a more stable and efficient society and strengthens democratic values. General trust is one of the basic components of social capital. As the level of general trust grows, it intensifies spiritual cohesion, brings people together (because they share common values and goals), helps them coordinate their interests, and motivates them to work together. There is also a correlation between trust and patriotism in society, particularly when it comes to one's personal, intimate love for the motherland and for one's family and friends.

And yet, the level of trust in modern Russian society is still lower than that of the Soviet period. Modern Russians are thus less happy in terms of social communications, and believe that social life is dominated by cautiousness and suspicion. Lack of interpersonal trust, understanding, and mutual respect generates a lack of trust at the institutional level as well. Russians today are very cautious in their relations with others and are often intolerant; they also tend to distrust most public institutions, political parties, civil organizations, businesses, and members of the political and economic elites.

According to recent comparative international studies, Russia is somewhere between industrialized and developing countries in terms of general trust. Scandinavian and Northern European countries score the highest with respect to level of trust; these are also regions with very high living standards and social stability. These are the conclusions that can be drawn from several data sources, including the European Values Study (EVS)[13] and World Values Survey (WVS) conducted in 1990–2000 across dozens of countries.[14]

The 2006–2012 period brought another positive trend: the share of respondents who trust their colleagues has grown from 80.7 to 82%, and the share of those who trust their management has grown from 63.2 to 68.3%. Nearly 70% of Russians believe that they can more or less trust most of the people in their closest circle. The closest and most intimate relations people can have are those with their relatives and friends, which are, according to the absolute majority of the population, incredibly important.

Sensing the support of one's friends and colleagues is the only wide-spread positive feeling in Russia, shared by nearly half (48%) of the population. Strangely enough, it is less common among rural dwellers (39%) than those who live in big

[13] http://www.europeanvalues.nl.

[14] http://www.worldvaluessurvey.org.

cities (65%) or regional centers (52%). This is probably indicative of the transformations in traditional rural cooperation culture.[15] It is also important to mention that over two-thirds of all households receive some kind of help from their families and friends. As some people don't get any support—they are the ones helping others instead—the total number of those involved in close cooperation with friends and family members is 80%.

Still, in general, rural dwellers are more trusting. They are more likely to trust colleagues and management at their workplace. Rural life provides perfect conditions for interpersonal trust with its intense professional, family, neighborhood and other trust-based ties that contribute to stronger social capital. People know each other well and build close relations with each other, no matter what their age or social status. It is also important that rural life is more static, i.e. norms and values are less likely to change.

Members of the urban population are, on the other hand, more pragmatic; they often say that one should be cautious with others, especially if they live in big cities, where people are even suspicious of their neighbors. They tend to see more bad things in others, while those who live in small cities are generally more gracious towards others. When talking about people from other cities, Muscovites, for example, point out such traits as envy, egoism, hypocrisy, and laziness. Those living in other areas first remark on the open, easygoing, and hard-working nature of people. Respondents residing in different areas also have different views on what makes a successful businessman. Those in big cities say, for example, that it's important for a businessman to have good connections with other entrepreneurs and powerful politicians, while rural dwellers stress talent, good education, and the ability to work hard.

Higher levels of interpersonal trust and better social relations make people happier and more satisfied with their lives. Happy and trusting people are also friendlier than others. They try to maintain peace with the world, find ways to cooperate with others, and maintain good relations with relatives, neighbors, colleagues, employees, friends and other people. Professional teams that mostly consist of happy people are generally more satisfied with their work and performance. People working in such groups are friendly with one another, which ultimately makes the group stronger and more efficient. They have fewer communication problems, and misunderstandings, tension, hostility or distrust between them is very unlikely. People working in such teams treat each other with care and respect.

Employers also prefer happy employees. According to a recent study conducted at Warwick University, happy people are on average 12% more efficient than those who aren't happy. It therefore makes sense for companies to keep their employees happy. The same study confirmed that happy people are more hard-working and get sick less often.[16] People who are satisfied with their life mention hard, dedicated

---

[15] Dvadtsat Let Reform Glazami Rossiyan: Opyt Mnogoletnikh Sotsiologicheskikh Zamerov. / Pod red. M.K. Gorshkova, R. Krumma, V.V. Petukhova. Moskva: Ves Mir. 2011. S. 60–62 [The 20 Years of Reforms Through the Eyes of the Russians: The Results of Longitudinal Sociological Studies, ed. M.K. Gorshkov, R. Krumm, and V.V. Petukhov. Moscow: Ves Mir. 2011, pp. 60–62].

[16] Branson (2014).

work and leadership skills among the most important factors of well-being. They are more motivated to perform better.

Our analysis has shown that the Russians' quest for happiness isn't meaningless at all, and their perceived level of happiness reflects the dynamics of their well-being at a personal and family level. However, we should remember that the start of the twenty-first century has brought a number of complex problems upon Russia, hitting rural areas particularly hard. The situation can be improved through modernization aimed at enabling significant changes across all social groups. The difficult and ambitious task of making life better and happier depends on the process of stabilization and integration, on the application of new approaches towards social capital, and wider use of the principles of social justice, trust and mutual help.

References

Abulkhanova, K.A. 1997. Russian Mentality: Cross-Cultural and Typological Approaches. In *Russian Mentality: Issues of Fundamental and Applied Psychology*, ed. K.A. Abulkhanova, A.V. Brushlinsky, M.I. Volovikova, 7–37. Moscow: IP RAN. [K.A. Abulkhanova. Rossijsky Mentalitet: Krosskulturny i Tipologichesky Podkhody. // Rossijsky Mentalitet: Voprosy Psikhologicheskoy Teorii i Praktiki. / Pod red. K.A. Abulkhanovoy, A.V. Brushlinskogo, M.I. Volovikovoy. Moskva: IP RAN. 1997. S. 7–37] [in Russian].

Argyle. M. 1987. *The Psychology of Happiness*. London: Methuen. [Cited by the 2003 Russian translation. St Petersburg: Piter. 2003, pp. 9–10].

Averintsev, S.S., E.A. Arab-Ogly, L.F. Ilyichyov, et al. (eds.). 1989. *Philosophic Encyclopedia*, 2nd ed., 640. Moscow: Sovietskaya Entsiklopediya. [Filosofsky Entsiklopedichesky Slovar. Pod red.: S.S. Averintsev, E.A. Arab-Ogly, L.F. Ilyichyov i dr. 2-e izdanie. Moskva: Sovietskaya Entsiklopediya. 1989. S. 640.] [in Russian].

Belyanin, A.V, and V.P. Zinchenko. 2010. *Trust in Economics and in Social Life*, 14. Moscow: Liberal Mission Foundation. [A.V. Belyanin, V.P. Zinchenko. Doverie v Ekonomike Obshchestvennoy Zhizni. Moskva: Fond 'Liberalnaya Missiya'. 2010. S. 14] [in Russian].

Branson, R. 2014. Strive to Pursue Happiness. www.virgin.com/entrepreneur/richard-branson-strive-to-pursue-happiness [Cited by the Russian translation: R. Branson. O Vazhnosti Schastya. Nezavisimaya Gazeta. April 2, 2014.].

For Russians, 'Survival Values' Are on Top of the Values System. http://zpsy.ru/public/35155.htm. Accessed 7 July 2014.

Ozhegov, S.I. 1990. *Thesaurus of the Russian Language*, ed. I.Y. Shvedova, 782. Moscow: Russky Yazyk. [S.I. Ozhegov. Slovar Russkogo Yazyka. Pod. red.: I.Y. Shvedova. Moskva: Russky Yazyk. 1990. S. 782.] [in Russian].

Proceedings of the III International Sociological Conference 'Carrying On Grushin's Work'. Moscow, February 28–March 1, 2013. Panel verbatim. Section 6: Common an Unique. What Is Similar and What Is Different in Terms of Social Climate in Post-socialist Countries? http://wciom.ru/fileadmin/nayka/gr2013/transcripts/Section6_General%20and_special_session.pdf. Accessed 7 July 2014.

Rath, T.J. Harter. 2010. *Wellbeing: The Five Essential Elements*. New York: Gallup Press. [Cited by the 2011 Russian translation. Moscow: Alpina. 2011.].

Twenty Years of Reforms Through the Eyes of Russians: The Experience of Long-Term Sociological Measurement, ed. M.K. Gorshkov, R. Krumm, V.V. Petukhov, 60–62. Moscow: Ves Mir. [Dvadtsat Let Reform Glazami Rossiyan: Opyt Mnogoletnikh Sotsiologicheskikh Zamerov. / Pod red. M.K. Gorshkova, R. Krumma, V.V. Petukhova. Moskva: Ves Mir. 2011. S. 60–62] [in Russian].

Vorkachyov, S.G. 2001. *The Idea of Happiness: Concept and Image* / Izvestiya of the Russian Academy of Sciences. *Literature and Language Series* 60 (6): 47–58. [S.G. Vorkachyov. Kontsept Schastya: Ponyatijny i Obrazny Komponenty / Izvestiya RAN. *Seriya Literatury i Yazyka*. 2001. Tom 60. № 6. S. 47–58] [in Russian].

WCIOM: Happiness Index in Russia Hits 25 Years Maximum. http://itar-tass.com/obschestvo/1158256. Accessed 7 July 2014.

Correction to: Life Expectations of the People

Peilin Li and M. K. Gorshkov

Correction to:
P. Li and M. K. Gorshkov (eds.), *Life Expectations of the People*, Research Series on the Chinese Dream and China's Development Path, https://doi.org/10.1007/978-981-16-2505-3

The original version of this book was published with incorrect affiliation details for some of the chapter authors which have now been updated. The book has been updated with the changes.

The updated version of the book can be found at
https://doi.org/10.1007/978-981-16-2505-3

P. Li and M. K. Gorshkov (eds.), *Life Expectations of the People*,
Research Series on the Chinese Dream and China's Development Path,
https://doi.org/10.1007/978-981-16-2505-3_19

Index

P. Li and M. K. Gorshkov (eds.), *Life Expectations of the People*, Research Series on the Chinese Dream and China's Development Path, https://doi.org/10.1007/978-981-16-2505-3

The manufacturer's authorised representative in the EU is Springer Nature Customer Service Centre GmbH, Europaplatz 3, 69115 Heidelberg, Germany. If you have any concerns regarding our products, please contact ProductSafety@springernature.com

Printed and bound by CPI Group (UK) Ltd, Croydon, CR0 4YY
30/09/2026
02225288-0007